SECOND EDITION

PSYCHOLOGY
AND THE
REAL WORLD

Essays Illustrating Fundamental
Contributions to Society

EDITED BY

Morton Ann Gernsbacher
University of Wisconsin-Madison

James R. Pomerantz
Rice University

WORTH PUBLISHERS
A Macmillan Education Company

Publisher: Rachel Losh
Associate Publisher: Jessica Bayne
Senior Acquisitions Editor: Christine Cardone
Senior Developmental Editor: Mimi Melek
Assistant Editor: Catherine Michaelsen
Executive Marketing Manager: Katherine Nurre
Director of Editing, Design, and Media Production: Tracey Kuehn
Managing Editor: Lisa Kinne
Associate Media Editor: Anthony Casciano
Photo Editor: Christine Buese
Cover Design: Blake Logan
Interior Design: Lissi Sigillo
Illustration Services: Casey Sussman, Perfect Pix Studios
Project Editor: Jodi Isman
Production Manager: Sarah Segal
Composition: Northeastern Graphic, Inc.
Printing and Binding: RR Donnelley
Cover Art: Gary Ruddell

Library of Congress Control Number: 2014947197

ISBN-13: 978-1-4641-7395-0
ISBN-10: 1-4641-7395-8

Printed in the United States of America

Second printing

Worth Publishers
41 Madison Avenue
New York, NY 10010
www.worthpublishers.com

About the Federation of Associations in Behavioral & Brain Sciences (FABBS) Foundation

The FABBS Foundation is an educational, nonprofit organization established to enhance understanding of the sciences of mind, brain, and behavior. Its efforts are focused on educating the public about the contributions of these sciences to the well-being of individuals and society, recognizing scholars who have made significant contributions to these sciences, and facilitating productive dialogue between scientists and relevant stakeholders to inform policies and improve lives.

What We Do

FABBS represents the interests of its scientific societies by:

- Educating federal representatives and Congress about the importance of research in the sciences of mind, brain, and behavior
- Advocating for legislation and policy that enhance training and research
- Providing sources of expertise and knowledge to federal agencies, Congress, and the media
- Encouraging the sound use of science in the creation of public policy
- Fostering effective interaction between agencies and organizations that fund research and the community of scientists and scientific societies
- Facilitating information exchange among constituent societies as well as other scientific organizations

For additional information about FABBS, visit www.fabbs.org

CONTENTS

MALCOLM GLADWELL

Malcolm Gladwell is a staff writer at the *New Yorker* magazine and the author of *The Tipping Point* (2000), *Blink* (2005), *Outliers* (2008), *What the Dog Saw* (2010), and *David and Goliath* (2013).

When I was a cub reporter at the *Washington Post*, too many years ago now to mention, I was assigned to the Business desk. Business was not what you wanted to cover at the *Washington Post*. The glamorous desk was National, and three years after I started, a position finally opened on the National desk. It was to be a science writer. I jumped at it.

At the time, I knew nothing at all about science. I did not take a single science course in college. (If memory serves, I took virtually nothing except courses in eighteenth- and nineteenth-century English history.) For that matter—due to an administrative loophole too tedious to go into here—I barely took any science courses in high school. I didn't like science. It seemed arid and technical. But better to be arid and technical on the National staff, I reasoned, than to spend my days in the Siberia that was Business. So I became a science reporter. On the day I started, I went to the mailroom and informed the news clerks that I was now to receive all the mail that had previously gone to my predecessor. They immediately presented me with an enormous box, at the top of which was that month's issue of the *Journal of Personality and Social Psychology*.

I have often wondered how my life might have been different if the magazine at the top had been, say, *Physics Today* or, God forbid, the *Journal of Waste Management*. But fate was shining on me. I sat down at my desk and started reading, and before long I got the prickly sensation that reporters get when they stumble upon a story. This was a different kind of story from the traditional newspaper kind, of course. It didn't involve scandal or outrage or leaked documents. But it was still a story: What psychology was all about, I realized, was an attempt to construct some kind of coherent narrative out of the chaos and jumble of everyday experience. I believe that to this day. And that is the spirit with which to read the essays that follow.

One of things that is so fascinating about academic research is how personal it is. By that I mean, academicians have the freedom to pursue things that interest them, and as a result their career arcs become fundamentally revelatory. You can't look at the cases handled by a corporate lawyer and get a clear sense of what the corporation is like, or what seizes that lawyer's imagination. He or she is required to handle what comes in the door. But the careers of academic scientists very quickly become particularized and idiosyncratic; it is hard not to look at the careers of psychologists psychologically.

One of the essays in this volume, for instance, is by Paul Ekman. Ekman is the father of the idea that expressions of emotion are both meaningful and universal: A smile of embarrassment is the same in Toronto as it is Timbuktu. We did not always think that. An earlier generation of psychologists and anthropologists thought that emotions were culturally specific, and to make his claim Ekman had to confront some of the most deeply held orthodoxies of his era. If you meet Ekman—as I have had the pleasure of doing—you'll understand why. He came to intellectual maturity in the rebellious 1960s in the Bay Area. He is by nature a persistent man, with a stubborn streak a mile wide. What you see in this volume is an essay written toward the end of a lifetime of accomplishment. But behind that essay are dozens of dogged steps of discovery: papers that no one believed at first, and long years spent painstakingly mastering the subtleties of facial expression of emotion.

There is also an essay by Robert Sternberg on his attempt to construct a college admissions process that more closely reflects the true range of human abilities. That's a very specific and socially useful exercise. But as you read it keep in mind that there's a reason why Sternberg took up this question: He himself was someone who, as a student, did poorly on so-called "predictors" of achievement. The question he's trying to answer is the question at the center of his own career.

This is part of what I mean when I say that I think of academic psychology as telling a story. Stories are narratives about people and their choices, and the kinds of questions that psychologists ask are invariably personal. That's also why we refer to the social sciences as "soft sciences." That word—soft—was originally intended, I imagine, in a condescending way. (The physicists decided that what they did was "hard," which meant that what the psychologists were doing across campus must be "soft.") But I see no reason for psychologists to take offense at "soft." It's actually right on the money. If Ekman was not a stubborn child of the 1960s, it is quite possible that his work might not have turned out exactly the way it did. If society had not told Sternberg that he had no intellectual future, it is quite possible his work might not have turned out the way it did either. "Soft" means a field that is shaped by the experiences and perspectives and idiosyncrasies of its researchers. "Soft" means something that can absorb more than a few blows. "Soft" means something that each new generation can reshape for its own purposes. This is not a volume of scientific commandments, written in stone. Stone is for Moses (and the physicists).

The organizing theme of this volume is "Psychology and the Real World," and as you read through the essays you will, I imagine, be struck by the sheer breadth of topics to which modern psychology has applied itself—from human perception to the use of memory in the courtroom, to teaching children how not to hate, and on and on.

There are many fields in the academy that, as they have gained in sophistication and knowledge, have left the rest of us behind. Just try and read any contemporary literary criticism if you're not a literary critic, or read some political theory if you don't yourself have a doctorate in the subject. Most of the social and institutional pressures inside the modern university are toward specialization—and that fact is probably inevitable. Academicians are supposed to explore the frontiers of knowledge, and intellectual life on the frontier is never going to be as easy or accessible as life in the ordered settlements of the coastal plain.

One of the great joys of psychology, though, is that you can be on the frontier and speak to the middle at the same time. The essay "When You Put Things Out of Mind, Where Do They Go?" is by Daniel Wegner, who is one of the heaviest of the heavyweights in the psychology business. (I read Wegner's book, *The Illusion of Conscious Will*, a few years ago, and I'm still recovering.) But think of where all that intellect has been focused: not on some hopelessly arcane question of interest only to a few, but on something that, I imagine, all of us have asked ourselves from time to time: Where did that thought go? Of course, we couldn't come up with an answer. But Daniel Wegner can. Psychology is the art of giving the most unexpected and thoughtful of answers to the most ordinary of questions. Read on—and enjoy.

I n 2004, a new nonprofit organization was born in Washington, D.C., called the FABBS Foundation. Its parent organization is FABBS (the Federation of Associations in Behavioral & Brain Sciences), a long-standing advocacy group that represents the combined forces of over 20 scholarly groups focused on the behavioral, psychological, cognitive, and brain sciences. The FABBS Foundation's mission is to enhance the public's understanding of the brain and behavioral sciences.

We created the first edition of *Psychology and the Real World* to help spread the good word about the contributions of psychology to the larger community and to society in general. This book joined the FABBS Foundation's other efforts, such as the Science Café series that we hold periodically in Washington, D.C., and elsewhere, featuring top behavioral and brain scientists speaking about their current findings. Videos of these events, along with other materials you may find interesting and useful, are available on the FABBS Foundation's Web site at www.fabbsfoundation.org.

Psychology and the Real World is distinguished from other books that seek to disseminate the interesting and useful research findings in the brain and behavioral sciences in two ways. First, our book puts front and center the relevance and applicability of psychological science. To create both the first and second editions, we approached leading scientists in our disciplines—those whose work best exemplifies the potential for a positive impact on society—and asked them to write short, personal essays saying plainly what they believe their life work has accomplished and what ramifications it has had, or may have, on society. For these leading scientists, the chance to speak simply and directly to a broad audience was a rare opportunity. A wide range of readers, from students in introductory psychology courses to members of the general public with interests in human behavior, now have the opportunity for intimate, personal encounters with some of the most imaginative psychological scientists currently at work. These essays put a human face on brain-behavior research and offer a personal glimpse into the thinking of the research scientists who have made these fields what they are today.

Second, this book represents an enthusiastic collaboration between the FABBS Foundation and Worth Publishers. Worth is the premier publisher of introductory psychology texts, and we are delighted that they have taken an active role in helping bring this book to life. Not only has Worth been generous with their time and energy in helping to edit and produce this book, they have provided significant funding to the FABBS Foundation to help support our other activities, including our Science Café series. Worth will make this book available at an affordable price to students whose instructors adopt one of Worth's introductory texts and will return all of the revenues so earned directly to the FABBS Foundation. Instructors who adopt a Worth introductory text along with this volume of essays are not only providing their students an important extra at a better-than-modest price, they are also helping provide financial support to the FABBS Foundation and thus to their sciences. Of course, this book is also available to instructors adopting texts from other publishers, just as it is available as a stand-alone volume to the general public; in those cases, Worth also returns a significant portion of the revenues to the FABBS Foundation.

We at the FABBS Foundation have been thrilled with the success of the first edition of *Psychology and the Real World,* and so we are doubly delighted to bring you the second edition you are holding in your hands. Some hard decisions went into the first edition. Choosing what to include in a volume of 34 essays about psychology was like being a kid in a candy store, or being in what psychologists call an "approach-approach" conflict where there are many good possibilities but you still have to make your selections. Based on the success of our first edition, we seem to have chosen well.

For the second edition, we looked closely at detailed feedback we received and at changes that have taken place in the field. Psychology, like all academic disciplines, is an evolving field, with old questions being solved but new ones arising in their place; with technology giving us new tools with which to examine our subject matter; and with theories being put to empirical test and then being revised.

We have added several new essays to the second edition of *Psychology and the Real World.* For example, Chapter 17 on Psychology at Work has been completely revised to include essays by Adam Grant and Ruth Kanfer on work motivation, and Mark Costanzo on the accuracy of lie detection in interrogation. In Chapter 3, Emanuel Donchin discusses cognitive psychophysiology and reading the mind; in Chapter 12, H. Hill Goldsmith discusses temperament. In Chapter 14, Alan Kazdin describes his research on treatments for children with severe aggressive and antisocial behavior, and Barbara Fredrickson introduces us to positive psychology in Chapter 15.

Of course, the authors of the essays retained from the first edition have updated and revised their essays to reflect changes and new developments in their respective fields. We hope these changes are received well by students and others reading this edition, as well as by instructors who assign this book for their classes.

Sadly, we mourn the passing of Susan Nolen-Hoeksema of Yale University, Daniel Wegner of Harvard University, and Carolyn Rovee-Collier of Rutgers University. Each of these psychological scientists contributed to the first edition, and their contributions are reprinted in this edition. Susan's seminal work on unhealthy mental rumination, Dan's provocative work on suppressing unwanted thoughts, and Carolyn's ground-breaking work on early developmental memories contributed greatly to the real world. We miss these three colleagues deeply.

We have plenty of people to thank for helping make the second edition possible. We are grateful to Zick Rubin, who has advised the FABBS Foundation on all of its publishing ventures. At Worth we are indebted to Christine Cardone who has championed this project with enthusiasm and Mimi Melek who transformed sticky prose into fluidity. We also thank Kevin Feyen, the editor at Worth with whom we started on this book in 2007 and who has been a believer and steadfast supporter from the beginning.

We are also grateful to Malcolm Gladwell for his thoughtful Foreword and Steven Pinker for his provocative Afterword. Gladwell's writings, in the *New Yorker* magazine and in books such as *David and Goliath, The Tipping Point, Blink,* and *Outliers,* communicate brilliantly the fascinating findings of psychological research as they play out in everyday life. Pinker, who as a practicing psychological scientist, has investigated many aspects of the mind, is also a talented writer. His recent book, *The Better Angels of Our Nature,* follows on the heels of his previously successful books, *The Blank Slate* and *The Language Instinct.*

We are grateful to our essay authors, those who revised and updated their essays from the first edition and those who appear for the first time in this volume. Their revisions help keep this new volume completely up to date. The enthusiasm they have shown for this book from the outset has been remarkable and inspiring. As was the case last time, these authors have believed in our cause and have all done their writing pro bono, allowing all the proceeds from book sales to flow to the FABBS Foundation, where they will make possible other projects like this one. On that score we thank Worth Publishers once again, for making a very generous financial contribution to the FABBS Foundation in advance to help get this second edition started, and also on an ongoing basis with a significant royalty payment with each volume sold.

Lastly, we thank the many instructors around the world who have adopted this book as a text, often as an accompaniment to a conventional textbook, to allow their students to read about the very best work of the very best psychologists working today, writing about their own work in the first person and explaining how they believe it has had a direct, positive influence on society. We thank those readers who liked the first edition well enough to share their thoughts with us to help guide us to this second edition. We look forward to hearing from you again with your reactions to the changes we have made.

Morton Ann Gernsbacher

James R. Pomerantz

July 2014

Introduction

Psychology and the Real World: An Introduction

James R. Pomerantz
and Morton Ann Gernsbacher

Psychology and the Real World: An Introduction

JAMES R. POMERANTZ Rice University
MORTON ANN GERNSBACHER University of Wisconsin-Madison

☐ **Please describe your current positions and research interests.**

JAMES POMERANTZ: I am a professor in the Department of Psychology at Rice University as well as an adjunct professor in the Department of Neuroscience at Baylor College of Medicine and in the Department of Neurobiology and Anatomy of the University of Texas Medical School at Houston. My research centers on visual perception and perceptual organization in humans. My greatest interest is in how we put together the bits and pieces of information our senses detect and organize them quickly and accurately into meaningful and unitary wholes.

MORTON ANN GERNSBACHER: I am Vilas Professor and Sir Frederic Bartlett Professor at the University of Wisconsin-Madison. I am fascinated by human communication. My initial research interests were focused on adult language comprehension. After a decade of purely behavioral research, I expanded my interests to the neural bases of communication. Then I became curious about atypical language processing, and more recently, I've been studying Internet-based communication. The common goal is to understand how we, as humans, communicate with each other.

Think back to the last time you took a multiple-choice test and were considering changing an answer because you feared it was wrong. Did you make that change, or did you stick with your initial choice? Most of us face that dilemma periodically, and we sometimes agonize over it because we simply don't know the right thing to do. Some of us believe our initial hunches are usually correct and so opt to stay put; others believe the opposite. Does anyone actually know the correct strategy? Why yes, psychologists know! Instead of armchair speculating or merely asking people's opinions, psychologists have studied actual test-takers and calculated how often changing answers helps or hurts their scores. Stay tuned for their answer.

Certain readers of this book—the great majority we hope—are convinced of the importance of psychological research and its contributions to society. We welcome you and anticipate your finding this book filled with fascinating, even delightful, examples of how psychology improves our lives. Other readers may be less sure about psychology and will take some convincing. We welcome you, too, and suggest that if you've been waiting to be persuaded, this book may alter your view of how thought and behavior can be analyzed and understood.

Go to your favorite news source and scan the headlines. On a typical day, you'll find a story or two on politics (sometimes defined wittily as what happens whenever two or more people enter a room) and articles on war and crime, people with influence and power, tragic accidents, the ups and downs in the economy, the state of education, and more. These events and their antecedents and consequences are all the purview of psychology, because what people (and other animals) do and why they do it is the domain of psychology, the science of mind and behavior. It is hard to think of any significant area of human activity that is not intertwined with psychology. Psychologists study the underlying causes and cures for human violence, the elements that combine to create leaders and heroes, the human errors that cause accidents and the consequences of such mistakes, the forces that make people more effective in their work, the best ways to foster learning, to name a few.

Psychology is all around us; psychologists work to understand what makes people tick. Of course, nonpsychologists are also curious about the people around them, and over the years most of us learn a lot about how others' minds work and how they are likely to behave. We spend time reflecting on our own minds and behaviors as well. In our "studies" of ourselves and of others, we come to know people as individuals, and we also learn about human behavior in general. For example, when we meet someone new, we can anticipate his or her response to a smile or scowl.

Because daily life makes us modestly expert in understanding the human mind and in predicting and explaining human behavior, what can we truly learn from a course in psychology? The one-word answer is: Plenty! As the essays in this volume demonstrate, vast areas of behavior are hidden from the casual observer. More importantly, some of what we think we know is just plain wrong.

Students of psychology are not alone in this regard. Most people have serious misconceptions about basic aspects of the world around them. Consider, for example, the laws of motion. When students who have taken physics courses are asked to predict, say, the path that a ball will follow when it rolls off a desk, most of their estimates won't even be close to correct. Merely living in the world and observing it for years does not necessarily lead to understanding it or even making reasonable predictions.

Psychology and Common Sense

If you think understanding and predicting human behavior consists mainly of using common sense, think again. Folk wisdom—manifested in the wise sayings that you have heard all your life from your elders—is supposed to reflect universal truths. Take the adage "birds of a feather flock together," which is intended to remind us that people prefer to spend their time with others who are similar to them. This seems to be such a universal law of human behavior that you might wonder why anyone would bother doing research to confirm the obvious. Why would we need to conduct research in the laboratory, or even in the field, to verify what we already know? The adage is based on years of intuition, and isn't that all that psychology is—well-known intuition?

Well, consider another bit of folk wisdom: "Opposites attract." This saying reminds us that we are attracted to, and so spend our time with, people quite different from ourselves. This saying, too, is based on years of thoughtful intuition; it, too, is considered a universal law. But these two wise sayings contradict one another and so cannot both be true. Which intuition correctly represents the way people actually behave: Do birds of a feather flock together, or do opposites attract?

The most direct way—perhaps the only way—to learn which pearl of wisdom is correct is through close, objective observation or through carefully controlled experiments. That is what psychologists do to learn the answers to questions that casual observation does not supply accurately. If we were to tell you that research has shown that opposites attract, would you be surprised? You should be because research has shown just the reverse: Birds of a feather do indeed flock together!

If belief in the supposed truth of "opposites attract" in the face of the supposed truth of "birds of a feather flock together" were an isolated example, we might have little reason to believe psychological research was needed. But belief in scientifically unsupported truisms is anything but isolated. Moreover, as you can see in Table 1, for many deeply held truisms, there is a conflicting truism, a full 180 degrees opposite in meaning. You can probably think of other examples of strongly held beliefs, assumed to be universal and intuitive, that stand in stark opposition to other strongly held beliefs, also assumed to be universal and intuitive. As satisfying and comforting as folk wisdom may seem, in the end it is research—properly designed and executed—that will give us the valid and reliable answers we seek about human behavior.

Psychology and Subjective Experience

Students new to psychology sometimes wonder how anything as subjective and unobservable as the mind can be studied scientifically. After all, can anyone ever truly know what is going on in someone else's head? This excellent question has good—and often clever—answers. Take, for example, a question many people thought unanswerable not long ago: Do infants see color the same way adults do? You cannot simply ask infants about this—any more than you could ask your family dog or cat whether it sees color.

The solution to this problem illuminates a key point: Psychology combines the study of the mind (not only perceptions but also sensations, memories, thoughts, feelings, and so forth) with the study of behavior (observable actions). Behavior, therefore, serves as a window, sometimes the only window, into the mind.

If you show infants a clear, bright patch of color, they will usually look directly at it (that is, they will fixate the patch of color, and their pupils will dilate perceptibly). Then they will look away—perhaps they get bored—at least until a new and distinct color pops up. Knowing this fact allows researchers to tell what colors (wavelengths) infants can see and which colors they perceive as different from other colors. Armed with this tool, psychologists have learned a lot about babies' vision, including that they appear to see the rainbow similarly to adults, with about the same bands of color. (Note that

TABLE 1

Contradictory Aphorisms

1. Absence makes the heart grow fonder, but out of sight is out of mind.
2. Look before you leap, but he who hesitates is lost (or, strike while the iron is hot).
3. A penny saved is a penny earned, but don't be penny-wise and pound-foolish.
4. Haste makes waste, but a stitch in time saves nine.
5. Turn the other cheek, but an eye for an eye.
6. Charity begins at home, but love thy neighbor.
7. Better safe than sorry, but nothing ventured, nothing gained.
8. All things come to those who wait, but the squeaky wheel gets the grease.
9. The grass is always greener on the other side of the fence, but there's no place like home.
10. Too many chefs spoil the broth, but many hands make light work.
11. Once burned, twice shy, but if at first you don't succeed, then try, try, try again (or, hope springs eternal).
12. Birds of a feather flock together, but opposites attract.
13. United we stand, divided we fall, but it's a dog-eat-dog world.
14. Good fences make good neighbors, but no man is an island.
15. Never put off until tomorrow what you can do today, but let's cross the bridge when we come to it.
16. Seek and ye shall find, but curiosity killed the cat.
17. A rolling stone gathers no moss, but stop and smell the roses.
18. The pen is mightier than the sword, but actions speak louder than words.
19. Don't judge a book by its cover, but the clothes make the man.
20. Half a loaf is better than none, but a miss is as good as a mile.
21. All that glitters is not gold, but where there's smoke there's fire.
22. What's good for the goose is good for the gander, but one man's meat is another man's poison.
23. The best things in life are free, but there's no such thing as a free lunch.
24. You are never too old to learn, but you can't teach an old dog new tricks.
25. Never look a gift horse in the mouth, but beware of Greeks bearing gifts.
26. Slow and steady wins the race, but time waits for no man.
27. Hitch your wagon to a star, but don't bite off more than you can chew.
28. The early bird gets the worm, but better late than never.
29. Variety is the spice of life, but never change a horse midstream.
30. Two heads are better than one, but paddle your own canoe.
31. A word to the wise is sufficient, but talk is cheap.
32. Do unto others as you would have others do unto you, but nice guys finish last.
33. Winners never quit, but quit while you're ahead.
34. The bigger the better, but the best things come in small packages.
35. What will be will be, but life is what you make it.
36. Cross your bridges when you come to them, but forewarned is forearmed.
37. With age comes wisdom, but out of the mouths of babes . . .
38. Two's company but three's a crowd, but the more the merrier.
39. Money is the root of all evil, but money makes the world go round.
40. The truth will set you free, but ignorance is bliss.

those bands are illusory; the rainbow simply consists of a smooth continuum of wavelengths. We learn a lot about the mind by studying such illusions.)

Consider another example. Can you recall the number of windows in the house in which you grew up? Many people report that in answering this question they "mentally walk" through that house, taking a tour in their mind's eye, counting windows as they go. In other words, they use mental imagery to answer a factual question. Is it possible to study such a subjective process objectively when it seems so inherently private? The answer is "yes" because mental imagery can be measured in terms of outward (publicly observable) behavior: We can measure the time it takes people to count the windows. It turns out that the larger the house you grew up in, the longer it takes you to finish counting. Thus, by timing a behavior associated with the mind's eye, its operation is revealed. You can demonstrate this yourself: Ask some friends to remain silent until they can name either the twentieth or the fortieth word in the Pledge of Allegiance, and time their responses. You'll see that it takes them longer, almost twice as long, to get to 40.

People also wonder whether psychologists can measure the properties of the mind, brain, and behavior with a degree of numerical precision sufficient to allow mathematical analysis. Most of us are familiar with intelligence tests that measure IQ on a scale centered on 100. We know that the higher one's IQ score, the more likely the person is to perform well in school, but we probably don't think that the quantification of IQ is so precise that we can perform basic math on it. For example, we wouldn't necessarily expect a person with an IQ of 160 to solve a problem twice as quickly or accurately as a person with an IQ of 80. Although that certainly is true, psychologists have become quite skilled at accurate measurement of many other aspects of mental life. We know quite well, for example, how much more physically intense we must make a sound for it to seem twice as loud to the human ear (hint: far more than simple doubling is required). We now know with some precision the rate at which people forget information they learn and how people's problem-solving abilities change as they age.

Predictability of Human Behavior

Looking at baby pictures, it's hard to tell who is going to turn out to be a Nobel Prize laureate or a selfless hero and who is going to turn toward a life of crime or experience debilitating depression. As random as these outcomes might appear, however, psychological and biological studies (including genetic studies of identical versus nonidentical twins) have revealed a lot about such matters. Consider this question: Who among us is most likely to die in a roadway accident? Traffic deaths often appear so open to chance, so dependent on coincidence and bad luck, that none of us seems safe on the road. Statistics provide a clearer picture of risk. For example, men between the ages of 21 and 24 who drive motorcycles between midnight and 4 A.M. face a road fatality risk that is 45,000 times higher than the norm. So, who dies on the road is far from random, as anyone working in a hospital emergency room can verify. In fact, human behavior is so nonrandom that people cannot behave randomly even when asked. For example, if people are asked to call out random numbers, the sequences they produce turn out to be highly systematic. Alas, we cannot be truly random even when we try.

Who Are Psychologists and What Do They Do?

Who are the people who study the mind, the brain, and behavior for a living? If asked to name a psychologist, many people think first of Sigmund Freud, although in truth he was instead a neurologist and psychoanalyst. However, his reputation does accurately convey the notion that the most populous group of psychologists, namely, clinical psychologists, treat people who are experiencing psychological difficulties or who wish to understand themselves better. But psychology is also a scientific discipline: Many psychologists work in laboratories—in colleges and universities, in hospitals and medical centers, and in private industry—trying to understand the workings of the mind and brain and to predict everyday behavior.

Some research psychologists focus on health, even though they themselves are not treating patients. The reason for their interest is clear: The U.S. Centers for Disease Control estimates that 50 percent of the variance in U.S. health outcomes—who is healthy and well versus who is sick and dies—is attributable to human behaviors such as smoking, failure to wear seatbelts, alcohol consumption, and other risky but voluntary behaviors. In contrast, only 20 percent of the variance in health outcomes stems from our environment, and only 20 percent arises from our genes. Determining the causes and best preventive measures for these behaviors is obviously of paramount importance to us all, and psychologists lead that effort.

Other researchers seeking to discover the best ways for people to learn and remember new information have encountered some critical and surprising results. For example, giving people hints often hurts their recall performance (for example, supplying people with the names of 25 U.S. states actually hurts their ability to recall the remaining 25); repeated studying and rereading is a poor way to learn new information—testing yourself rather than further studying is far superior; and making learning conditions easy and comfortable rather than difficult and unpleasant can be the best way to lock in new memories. Psychologists studying different cognitive functions—such as language, perception, thinking, and decision making—often supplement their behavioral experiments with neuroimaging techniques such as fMRI, which tracks brain activity by monitoring blood flow. These scientists argue that a combination of psychological and biological measures will converge to create a clear picture of the mind at work.

Social psychologists look at the behavior of people in groups, showing that, for example, individuals perform better in the presence of others than when they are alone, but that people also try less hard when they are on a team than when they are performing solo (the more people pulling on the rope in a tug-of-war game, the less hard each one pulls). Developmental psychologists look at how all kinds of mental activities and behaviors change as we age. Eleanor Gibson (1910–2002), a leading researcher in perceptual development, discovered in the 1950s that babies have visual (3-D) depth perception, and recently other researchers have determined that even 3-month-old infants can mentally rotate objects in their minds. Other psychologists study how people behave in the workplace—a topic that has significant implications for improving human efficiency and productivity—and how people work with artificial devices such as airplanes, where the consequences of human error can be severe.

Returning to our earlier question, is it a wise idea to change your answers to test questions if you fear your original answer may be wrong? Psychological research provides a clear response: Yes, change that answer! Decades of data demonstrate that about 50% of changes correct initially wrong answers, while 25% change from one wrong answer to another wrong answer, and only the remaining 25% change a correct answer to a wrong one.

So please join us in the coming pages of this book as many of today's foremost psychologists discuss personally and directly their life's work and its contribution to society. We find their stories fascinating and illuminating, and we hope you will too.

☐ Thinking Critically

1. The editors chose the contributors to this volume because the contributors' work demonstrates that critical thinking and a scientific approach can solve real-world problems. What other qualities of mind are important in an effective researcher?
2. What drew you to psychology, and how do you expect what you learn to influence your personal goals, skills, values, and development?

Methods of Psychology

Can the World Wide Web Be Used for Research?

John H. Krantz

**Integrity Testing for Personnel Selection:
The Role of Research Methods**

Paul R. Sackett

Can the World Wide Web Be Used for Research?

JOHN H. KRANTZ Hanover College

☐ **Please describe your current position and research interests.**

I am a professor of Psychology at Hanover College. One of my research interests is using the Web for psychological research, in particular, about how images and media can be used as psychological stimuli over the Internet. In addition, I have developed a set of online experiments to assist the teaching of cognitive psychology called Cognitive Toolkit. Finally, I am a co-author of both a forthcoming text on sensation and perception and the next edition of PsychSim, a set of introductory psychology Web activities.

☐ **How did you become interested in the Web as a possible source for research participants?**

My location at Hanover College inspired the idea. The Web was still quite new and mostly an academic tool at the time I first became involved. I could see its potential to reach much larger and more diverse participant populations than were available at Hanover, a school with a fairly homogenous population of only about 1,000 students. The Web has opened up many new possibilities not only for my colleagues and me but also for many of our students.

☐ **What has been the real-world impact of this work?**

The Internet allows us to ask new questions and reexamine old questions in new ways. The real-world impact is two-fold: First, many more people have the opportunity to participate in and access psychological research. Before the Web, most research was done with college students. Using the Web, researchers have access to a much wider population, which can make their samples more representative of the population as a whole. Building off this point, more people now have access to the research that psychologists use to learn about human nature. Second, with new tools come new understandings. Exactly what will be learned is very hard to predict, but the way we ask questions impacts what we can know.

Many introductory science texts make the scientific method sound like a fixed set of steps directly leading to discovery. Science sounds mechanical, automatic, and even rather boring. In the real practice of science, deciding on how to do a study is complex, calling on a range of decisions, all of which can impact the quality of the data. To use the common euphemism, doing science is also an art. In addition, scientists are always developing new ways to collect data in order to learn better about nature. But with each innovation, the scientist must know that good data have been collected. The method itself must be tested. In this essay, I will describe efforts to analyze the validity and usability of this increasingly popular method of collecting data for psychological research: the Internet.

The Web attracted research psychologists' attention because it offered a solution to one of the great problems they face: the availability of appropriate participants (Birnbaum, 1999). At many colleges and universities, researchers have long recruited experimental participants from among their students, most often from introductory psychology classes—a practice that has led to quips about psychology being "largely the science of the behavior of sophomores" (McNemar, 1942, p. 333). Typically, researchers don't want to know about the students' behavior; they are using them as stand-ins for people in general. However, if their student-participants are in any way different from the general population, for example, more educated, more affluent, and younger, their findings can be misleading. Given this limitation, research psychologists are always trying to find better ways to gather a more representative sample of the general population. Toward that end, the Web presents a new means of accessing a pool of potential research participants that make up a more representative sample than college students (Reips, 2000).

First Thoughts About the Web as a Source of Data

The Web became accessible to the general population in 1993, but it was a very different place: It had no images, movies, or sounds, or any of the other kinds of media that we expect to see on a webpage today. Web documents only had links that allowed movement within and between documents. One of the most important innovations for psychological researchers was the development of forms in which a person would enter information and send that information to another computer for storage (Musch & Reips, 2000). These forms are similar to the type that you fill out to make an online purchase or sign up for a course or an online group. Users input their names and other requested information, and those data are sent to the recipients' computer, where they are stored.

With the introduction of these forms, psychological researchers realized that the Web could be used to access participants who were *not* college students (Musch & Reips, 2000). But before they could undertake such studies, they needed to assess the quality of the data that would be obtained—information of paramount importance, given that collecting low-quality data would simply be a waste of time.

At that time, my colleagues and I and a number of other researchers discussed reasons why the Web might *not* be a good way to collect psychological data (Birnbaum, 1999; Krantz, Ballard, & Scher, 1997; Reips, 2000). This essay highlights one particularly important possibility that concerned us: lack of control over the environment.

For findings from a psychological experiment to be useful, the environment must be controlled very carefully—that is, all features of the environment must be the same for all people participating in the experiment. In setting up studies, researchers make predictions about cause-and-effect relationships among variables. (A variable is anything that can vary.) The only feature of the experiment that can change is the variable being studied (the independent variable), which the researcher systematically varies from condition to condition. This requirement that the environment remain constant is essential if researchers are to understand why participants respond the way they do. If the person's behavior differs in different conditions, and the only difference between conditions is the independent variable, then the researcher can conclude that the independent variable caused the change in behavior.

When using the Web, such environmental control is not possible. One participant might be working in a quiet room with few distractions on a laptop, while on a slow network connection. Another person might be using a mobile phone app, simultaneously checking for text messages in a crowded, noisy university laboratory. Of course, leaving the study online for a long time can attract a large population of participants, and if the group is large enough, variations between the environments might just average out. That is, among the varied conditions in which a cause-and-effect relationship is being tested, no differences might exist *on average* other than the independent variable. To test this notion, my colleagues and I used the Web to gather—and then evaluate—psychological data.

Our Early Study Using the Web

In one of the very first, if not the first, true experimental studies conducted on the Web, we repeated two earlier psychological studies of determinants of female attractiveness (Krantz, Ballard, & Scher, 1997). (For simplicity's sake, I will discuss only the first study.) To begin, we asked ourselves: What method is appropriate to determine if the data from a Web study are of high enough quality for scientific research? The solution, we decided, was to collect data from both the laboratory and the Web. If the data from the laboratory version of the experiment and the Web version of the experiment gave similar results, then the Web would likely be a valid source of data for this type of experiment.

In the original experiment, the researchers presented participants with nine outlines of female figures, varying in body type from very thin to obese. The participants were asked several questions about the outlined figures, including one that asked them to choose the figure that represents the ideal weight for females. An interesting finding was that the female participants chose a thinner ideal than did the males (Fallon & Rozin, 1985).

In our experiment, we modified the outlined figures to change the ratio of bust to hips, although the same nine weight levels were used. In some outlines, the bust-to-hip ratio was larger, in others it was the same, and in others it was smaller. Two examples are shown in Figure 1.

In both the laboratory and Web versions of our experiment, the outlined figures were presented one at a time and each participant saw all 27 variations (9 weight values by 3 hip-to-bust proportions). Instead of picking their ideal, our participants rated the attractiveness of each figure. A standard

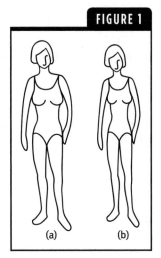

FIGURE 1

(a)   (b)

Sample figure outlines from the study. Note that (a) is also the standard. (From Fallon & Rozin, 1985. Copyright © 1985 by the American Psychological Association. Reproduced with permission. The use of APA information does not imply endorsement by APA.)

figure, shown in Figure 1a, was given an attractiveness rating of 200, and participants were asked to compare each of the other outlines (for example, Figure 1b) to this standard. For example, if Figure 1b was rated half as attractive as Figure 1a, the person was instructed to give Figure 1b a score of 100; a score of 400 would mean that Figure 1b was twice as attractive as Figure 1a. This traditional way of collecting data is called *magnitude estimation.* In the early study, participants were asked only to pick the ideal-weight figure.

Figure 2a shows how female participants rated the three outlines that show equal-size bust and hips, and Figure 2b presents men's ratings of the

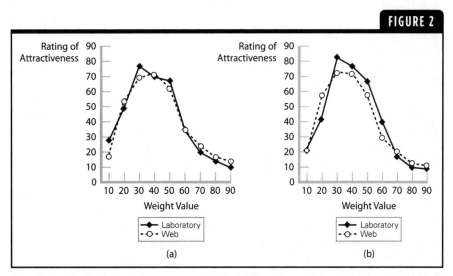

FIGURE 2

Sample results from the laboratory and Web. (a) Female participants' data and (b) male participants' data. (Data from Krantz, Ballard, & Scher, 1997)

same outlines. The horizontal axis of the graph shows the weight-value of the figures, with 10 being the thinnest and 90 being the heaviest. The vertical axis is scaled so that 100 represents the most attractive figure that each participant chose: The higher the number, the more attractive the figure.

Notice that the data from the laboratory and the Web versions of our study are nearly identical despite differences in environmental conditions, computers, and characteristics of the two groups of participants. One hundred percent of the laboratory participants were between the ages of 18 and 22, whereas only 24 percent of the Web participants were in this age range. All of the lab participants were from the United States, most from three states. Web responses came from six continents, although the majority of participants lived in the United States. Statistical analyses confirmed conclusions based on visual inspection of the data. In fact, one type of analysis, linear regression, indicated that the data from one version of the experiment can be substituted for the other version (Krantz, Ballard, & Scher, 1997). The data shown in Figure 2 are consistent with the rest of our findings.

One conclusion from the original study differed from ours. In the first study, which took place in the early 1980s, women chose a thinner ideal than did males. Although we did not ask which outline was ideal, analysis of ratings of the most attractive weight-value did not show a gender difference. Our male respondents chose a mid-range weight value of 30 as most attractive; most women picked either 30 or 40; and the difference between the genders was not statistically significant. We were unable to determine whether the inconsistency in results between our research and the earlier study is due to methodology or changes over time in perceptions of ideal weight.

Where Do We Go from Here?

No matter how provocative the findings, one study that uses Web-obtained data to produce conclusions similar to those of an earlier laboratory study does not demonstrate that the Web can be used for all types of psychological research. Nonetheless, we were encouraged—especially because in the years that followed our findings were replicated in many other studies. However, exceptions have been reported, generally with differences being smaller in Web studies than in laboratory studies, and some of the differences between data gathered via the Web and that collected in the laboratory are very interesting. In fact, the differences between Web and laboratory findings have sometimes revealed features of people's behavior that would be missed by either kind of study alone as will be discussed in the next paragraph (see Krantz & Dalal, 2000, for an early review of Web studies).

In one interesting study, researchers adapted to the Internet the *lost-letter technique* of social psychologist Stanley Milgram (1933–1984). In the original study, Milgram and his students "lost" a lot of stamped, addressed, return-addressed envelopes and counted the rate of returns. The few that got back to him were sent to the originally intended address instead of to the sender, suggesting an altruistic impulse on the part of the finders. In the Internet version, e-mail appeared to have been misdirected. The person getting the e-mail could send it to the originally intended recipient by forwarding or returning it to the sender. (Both addresses went to the researchers.) Those few e-mails that made their way back to the researchers came by way of the return-to-sender route. In snail mail, the easiest way to send on a letter is to drop it into a box and let it go to the originally intended recipient. In e-mail, returning it to the original sender is easier because the address is entered automatically; forwarding requires typing or cutting and pasting the address. So in both situations, altruists made the low-effort choice—a finding that recast the results of the original study (Stern & Faber, 1997).

The use of the Web for psychological research has grown tremendously. In fact, textbooks are now available that teach methods for collecting data over the Web (see, for example, Birnbaum, 2001; Fraley, 2004; Gosling & Johnson, 2010). In the mid-1990s, only a handful of Web-based studies had been published. Two decades later, several hundred if not thousands of Web-based psychological studies are being conducted at any one time on a wide range of topics. In fact, researchers link to sites that match potential participants with their studies. The Department of Psychology at Hanover College sponsors one such list, started in 1996—the *Psychological Research on the Net* list at http://psych .hanover.edu/research/exponnet.html (Krantz, 2013), which as of June 2014, links to more than 400 different psychology studies and adds over 400 new studies each year. As of June 2014, over 175,000 people visited the site looking for experiments in which to participate.

Despite the large number of links, many topics in psychology are not suitable for Web research. An examination of the *Psychological Research on the Net* page shows that topics in social psychology and related areas seem to be most appropriate. Web-based research exploring emotions and sensation and perception are much less common because they usually require complicated stimuli. Studies that require the use of images of faces and even video seem to be least commonly attempted. However, as the Web matures and it is easier to stream video, we might see more video studies coming forward (Krantz & Williams, 2010).

With the advent of new Web technologies, such as touch screens and mobile apps, research methods are changing again. Touch screens offer the ability to create response methods that are not limited by the way we collected responses with paper and pencil methods. For example, most surveys online still use the old fashion Likert scale where you are asked how much you agree with a statement on a 1 to 7 scale. On a computer screen, you can easily convert that to a line to press or with a touch screen have the person move their finger or even use more than one finger. Think of making an image bigger on your phone. It is possible that same movement could be used to collect data from participants. Mobile devices allow participants to respond right in the middle of ongoing behavior, for example, data can be collected throughout the day so a researcher might track a participant's mood throughout the day and ask questions as to what happened right before that time to get a clearer picture of how mood changes through the day (Plowman & Stevenson, 2012). In addition, we are not anonymous on the Web; we leave behind a lot of information about where we have been and what we have done. This data, gathered from millions of people, can be accessed by researchers at services such as Google. Collectively this data is called *Big Data* and may be useful to a broad range of social sciences. For example, by tracking how people move from site to site, it might be possible to track in a very detailed way how we follow our preferences. Another possibility might be able to identify general locations of all people that go to a particular website to see better what sorts of interests appeal to people from different regions.

The Web has enhanced psychological research in many ways. It allows greater access than was possible previously to a wider range of participants (Krantz & Dalal, 2000) and to groups of people who have been hard to study in the past (Mangan & Reips, 2006). It saves time and money for the research team (Reips, 2000). It can allow researchers to collect easily data from a far larger number of participants, permitting researchers to do more subtle data analyses than would be possible in lab-based experiments (Birnbaum, 1999; Reips, 2000). Most importantly, the proliferation of Web studies demonstrates the constant effort in the research community to improve methods of data collection. But as our experiment illustrates, researchers using new tools must examine the quality of their data. The basics of research, good design, careful data collection, and the analysis of data still hold. Research is subtle and interesting, and discovery is exciting.

☐ Thinking Critically

1. Apart from environmental control, what other problems might using the Web introduce into psychological research?
2. Why must doing research on the Web have to demonstrate that it is a good research method?
3. How is research on the Web continuing to evolve?

☐ Suggested Further Reading

Birnbaum, M. H. (2001). *Introduction to behavioral research on the Internet*. Upper Saddle River, NJ: Prentice Hall.

Krantz, J. H., & Dalal, R. (2000). Validity of Web-based psychological research. In M. H. Birnbaum (Ed.), *Psychological experiments on the Internet* (pp. 35–60). San Diego, CA: Academic Press.

Snijders, C., Matzat, U., & Reips, U.-D. (2012). "Big data": Big gaps of knowledge in the field of Internet science. *International Journal of Internet Science, 7*(1), 1–5.

☐ References

Birnbaum, M. H. (1999). Testing critical properties of decision making on the Internet. *Psychological Science, 10*, 399–407.

Birnbaum, M. H. (2001). *Introduction to behavioral research on the Internet*. Upper Saddle River, NJ: Prentice Hall.

Fallon, A., & Rozin, P. (1985). Sex difference in perceptions of desirable body shape. *Journal of Abnormal Psychology, 94*, 102–105.

Fraley, C. (2004). *How to conduct behavioral research over the Internet: A beginner's guide to HTML and CGI/Perl*. New York: The Guilford Press.

Gosling, S., & Johnson, J. A. (Eds.). (2010). *Advanced methods for behavior research on the Internet.* Washington, DC: American Psychological Association.

Krantz, J. H. (2013). *Psychological research on the Net* [Online]. Retrieved September 25, 2013, from http://psych.hanover.edu/research/exponnet.html.

Krantz, J. H., Ballard, J., & Scher, J. (1997). Comparing the results of laboratory and World Wide Web samples on the determinants of female attractiveness. *Behavior Research Methods, Instruments, & Computers, 29,* 264–269.

Krantz, J. H., & Dalal, R. (2000). Validity of Web-based psychological research. In M. H. Birnbaum (Ed.), *Psychological experiments on the Internet* (pp. 35–60). San Diego, CA: Academic Press.

Krantz, J. H., & Williams, J. (2010). Using graphics, photographs, and dynamic media. In S. D. Gosling & J. A. Johnson (Eds.), *Advanced methods for conducting online behavioral research* (pp. 45–61). Washington, DC: American Psychological Association.

Mangan, M., & Reips, U.-D. (2006). *Sleep, sex, and the strengths and weaknesses of the Web in surveying a difficult-to-reach clinical population.* Paper presented at the 2006 Society for Computer in Psychology conference, Houston, TX.

McNemar, Q. (1942). Opinion-attitude methodology. *Psychological Bulletin, 43,* 289–374.

Musch, J., & Reips, U.-D. (2000). A brief history of Web experimenting. In M. H. Birnbaum (Ed.), *Psychological experiments on the Internet* (pp. 61–88). San Diego, CA: Academic Press.

Plowman, L., & Stevenson, O. (2012). Using mobile phone diaries to explore children's everyday lives. *Childhood, 19*(4), 539–553.

Reips, U.-D. (2000). The Web experiment method: Advantages, disadvantages, and solutions. In M. H. Birnbaum (Ed.), *Psychological experiments on the Internet* (pp. 89–117). San Diego, CA: Academic Press.

Stern, S. E., & Faber, J. E. (1997). The lost e-mail method: Milgram's lost-letter technique in the age of the Internet. *Behavior Research Methods, Instruments, & Computers, 29,* 260–263.

Integrity Testing for Personnel Selection: The Role of Research Methods

PAUL R. SACKETT University of Minnesota

☐ **Please describe your current position and research interests.**

I am a professor of Psychology at the University of Minnesota, where my research focuses on the use of psychological testing for employment decisions and for academic admission decisions.

☐ **What got you interested in studying the quality of tests of employee honesty and integrity?**

My interest in the topic of integrity testing arose out of an inquiry from an employer wondering whether integrity tests were useful. There was little research on the topic at the time, and I began studying the topic.

☐ **What has been the real-world impact of this work?**

Integrity testing is widely used, having grown from a new and little-understood form of testing to a relatively mature field with an extensive body of supporting research.

Employers often face a complex problem when trying to choose among many applicants for a limited number of jobs. Under such circumstances, some employers turn to psychologists for help, asking whether psychological tests are available that will help them identify those applicants most likely to be effective employees. Psychologists typically respond with a wide range of possible employee-selection tests, including measures of ability, personality, interests, values, knowledge, integrity, and skill.

The goal of most testing in employment settings is the identification of applicants most likely to perform well on particular jobs. However, in some settings, employers have a different goal: They want to *avoid* hiring employees who might engage in various forms of counterproductive work behavior (for example, theft). In settings where employees have access to money or merchandise and work with limited monitoring or supervision, employers are highly motivated to avoid hiring anyone likely to steal. Several decades ago, employers with such concerns commonly administered polygraph examinations in an attempt to learn about applicants' possible past history of wrongdoing.

As the polygraph came under scrutiny and was made illegal eventually for most employers, paper-and-pencil tests of "honesty" or "integrity" emerged as alternatives. One test type is commonly called an overt, or clear-purpose test. This type of test focuses on respondents' beliefs about theft: how often it occurs and how widely; how it should be punished; how easy theft is;

what respondents' thoughts are about theft and whether they agree or disagree with common rationalizations for theft; and how they assess their own honesty. A second type of test is commonly called a personality-oriented, or disguised-purpose test. This type of test is closely linked to normal-range personality assessment measures, is not explicitly aimed at theft, and includes items dealing with dependability, conscientiousness, social conformity, thrill seeking, trouble with authority, and hostility.

The market for these tests is huge: Several million applicants are tested each year. Many test vendors have entered the market; at one point, they were offering over 40 tests. Mainstream psychological test publishers developed a few of these tests; many others had little to no research backing. Given the extensive interest in and use of the tests, the obvious question is whether they work: Do the tests, in fact, predict behavior on the job?

My involvement in this area began with such a question. In 1977, I received a phone call from an organization asking whether a particular test was valid. Knowing nothing about the test in question, I set out to research the topic. A colleague and I gathered up all the research studies we could find and published an article summarizing what was known about integrity tests (Sackett & Decker, 1979). Little did I know that more than 30 years later I'd still be interested in the topic of employee honesty and integrity. Over the years, I've published four more reviews of the state of our knowledge about integrity tests (Berry, Sackett, & Wiemann, 2007; Sackett, Burris, & Callahan, 1989; Sackett & Harris, 1984; Sackett & Wanek, 1996;). In 1979, I could locate only a handful of research studies; by the time I wrote the later reviews, I was able to examine and critique hundreds of studies.

Research Strategies for Evaluating the Effectiveness of Integrity Tests

To gain an understanding of integrity tests and how well they work, researchers have employed a wide variety of research methods. Among the most widely used are criterion-related validity studies in which tests are administered to a sample of job applicants or current employees and measures of on-the-job behavior (or whatever criterion you are attempting to predict) are obtained. Various statistical measures are used to index the degree to which test scores are related to job behavior. In other words, data are examined to determine whether individuals with high test scores do better on the job than those with low test scores.

Early studies of integrity testing used scores on a polygraph examination as the criterion. The question in this research was whether individuals with low integrity test scores were more likely than those with high scores to fail a polygraph exam, and research found this to be the case. However, critics were skeptical of these findings, questioning the accuracy of the polygraph method. If the polygraph is not a credible measure, showing that integrity test scores correlate with polygraph scores is not persuasive.

In response to this criticism, researchers conducted studies that did not use the polygraph as the criterion. Instead, test-takers underwent questioning directed at getting them to admit to prior theft from employers. Researchers using this strategy found that test scores are correlated with admissions of theft (that is, those with high integrity test scores admit less prior theft). Again, this evidence was met with skepticism. Among the complaints was the suggestion that test scores don't really predict theft but merely predict willingness to admit to theft. In other words, high and low test scorers may be just as likely to steal; they may merely differ in their willingness to admit to wrongdoing.

So, researchers tried yet another approach. Because self-reported theft was not seen as a credible measure, the focus shifted to measures of theft detected on the job. In these studies, firms would keep track of all employees caught stealing over the course of a year and then the test scores of employees who were caught stealing would be compared with those of employees who were not caught stealing. These studies showed that those caught stealing were very likely to have low test scores. At the same time, though, only a very small number of employees were caught in a given year, thus raising questions about how to interpret the test scores of those not caught. Skeptics could point out that many people with low integrity test scores were not caught stealing, and thus assert that the test mislabeled innocent people. Most importantly from the employer's point of view, those caught stealing may represent only a fraction of those actually stealing. And it's even possible that those caught stealing are not a random sampling of those who steal, but instead represent those who simply aren't very good at it. So, if we use theft detection as the criterion measure, we're left with the interesting finding that those caught stealing do tend to have low test scores, a finding consistent with what we'd expect if the tests worked as intended, but also with uncertainty about the issue of undetected theft.

Researchers continued exploring alternative research strategies. The idea of an objective measure of wrongdoing was attractive, but difficulties in detecting theft led to the use of indirect measures. In one creative study, researchers looked at the behavior of a sample of Salvation Army bell-ringers at Christmas time (Jones & Terris, 1981). The researchers gave an integrity test to all bell-ringers at the start of the holiday season, but they did not score the test or use it in the hiring decisions. They then measured the average amount of money collected each day for each bell-ringer. They had historical data for each location, and so each bell-ringer's dollar intake could be compared with the historical average for that location.

At the end of the holiday season, those with low integrity test scores turned in less money than those with high integrity test scores, a finding that they interpreted as evidence that dishonest bell-ringers were pocketing some of the money collected. However, low integrity bell-ringers could have been taking longer breaks, working fewer hours, and thus soliciting less money. Of course, taking extended breaks can be seen as a form of counterproductive behavior, and thus the integrity test is effective in identifying those prone to taking in less money, regardless of whether it is due to extended breaks or to theft. Nonetheless, we are left unsure of exactly why those with low integrity test scores turn in less money.

These methodological difficulties led to yet another approach, namely to move from on-the-job field settings to research carried out in the psychologist's laboratory. The appeal of laboratory research is the degree of control available to the researcher. Here researchers can design settings where opportunities for forms of wrongdoing or misbehavior are arranged and where settings are designed in such a way that the researcher knows with certainty how each participant behaves. In one study, participants took an integrity test and then engaged in a number of experimental tasks for which they were to be paid a certain amount (for example, $5). When they were finished, they were told, "Here's your $5," and they were handed an envelope containing two $5 bills. Not unexpectedly, those with high integrity test scores were more likely than those with low scores to report the extra money. Findings from these kinds of studies are consistent—for example, those with low integrity test scores are more likely to cheat on an experimental task or to give themselves more points than deserved when self-scoring a test they've taken (cf. Berry, Sackett, & Wiemann, 2007).

I find this approach an interesting inversion of the typical research strategy as advocated in textbooks. The common sequence is for research to begin in a laboratory and later to move into field settings to examine whether lab findings generalize to real-world settings. In the area of integrity testing, the question of interest is inherently an applied one (Do these tests predict wrongdoing on the job?), and thus most research has been done in applied settings. The use of a lab setting, with its accompanying degree of control over the situation, proves a useful supplement in response to questions about possible flaws in the measures obtained in field settings.

Debate continues as to how to interpret the research findings. While scholars generally agree that integrity tests are predictive of important workplace behavior, there is dispute about the merits of different research designs, leading to disputes about the strength of the predictive relationship between tests and outcomes (Ones, Viswesvaran, & Schmidt, 1993; Ones, Viswesvaran, & Schmidt, 2012; Sackett & Schmitt, 2012; Van Iddekinge, Roth, Raymark, & Odle-Dusseau, 2012). Research will continue to help resolve these disputes.

Lessons Learned

This story illustrates several important issues regarding psychological research methods. One is that in settings where research outcomes have significant real-life consequences (for example, the investigation of a type of test affecting the job opportunities of millions of people), research will be scrutinized very closely. Critics will examine the work carefully to determine whether possible alternative explanations for the results can be identified. This kind of analysis can be frustrating to the individual researcher whose work is being critiqued, but it is clearly good for the advancement of knowledge: Criticism prompts additional research to address the concerns raised by critics.

Second, evidence from a single study is rarely seen as fully persuasive. As developments in the investigation of integrity testing illustrate, triangulation across multiple research methods is crucial. Each method has strengths and weaknesses, and convergence of findings across methods plays a large role in the eventual acceptance of research findings. Note that the research on integrity testing has found that integrity tests are predictive of (a) polygraph exam performance, (b) self-reports of theft, (c) detected theft in organizational settings, (d) objective measures of various forms of wrongdoing in organizational settings, and (e) objective measures of various forms of wrongdoing in carefully controlled laboratory settings. This consistency in findings is quite convincing. It would have been quite a different matter had the results been different (for example, had the tests proven to predict polygraph exams but nothing else). A body of work showing that a research finding is *not* specific to one research setting or to one way of measuring the variables of interest is far more persuasive.

Other Research Issues in Integrity Testing

When psychologists assess the quality of integrity tests, a wide range of other important research questions arise: Do integrity scores vary by features such as race or gender? Can applicants raise their scores by giving distorted responses (that is, by faking)? Are the test scores reliable (that is, would a test-taker get the same or nearly the same score if he or she retook the test after a short interval)? For what range of jobs are the tests effective (that is, is predictive power limited to entry-level jobs, or are these tests also useful for higher-level jobs)? How do integrity test scores relate to other psychological measures (that is, are they correlated with measures of central personality traits)? The answer to the last question is yes; they correlate with three measures: conscientiousness, agreeableness, and emotional stability.

Important practical issues also influence employers' decisions as to whether or not to use an integrity test. One key notion is that the opportunity to be selective is a scarce resource. Consider an employer with, say, two applicants for each opening. The employer could choose to use an integrity test and screen out the lowest 50 percent of the applicant pool. But the employer may also want employees who learn quickly and solve problems effectively, and so another option would be to use a cognitive ability test and screen out the lowest 50 percent of the applicant pool on that measure. "Spending" your opportunity to be selective on screening for integrity prevents screening on cognitive ability, and vice versa. Alternately, the employer could use both tests but be less selective on each (that is, screen out the bottom 25 percent on both cognitive ability and integrity). A further research question is whether it is more useful to screen for one characteristic than for another.

Conclusion

In sum, psychologists have made great progress in understanding how well integrity tests perform as predictors of counterproductive work behavior. Over several decades, our knowledge base has moved from a handful of studies to hundreds. And, as is typical with research evidence, no single grand study answers all questions; rather, each smaller study serves as a piece in a larger puzzle. Researchers identify potential weaknesses in existing studies and work to design additional studies to remedy these weaknesses. For this to occur, they must not only be highly knowledgeable about their specialty area but also well-versed in research methodology. Thus informed, they can effectively evaluate the strengths and weaknesses of existing research studies and design and conduct studies that further understanding of issues that affect the lives of all of us.

☐ Thinking Critically

1. The research that Paul Sackett describes took place in the field and in researchers' laboratories. What are the advantages and disadvantages of each type of setting?

2. A premise underlying pre-employment integrity testing is that paper-and-pencil test results can predict real-world behavior. What are some arguments that support and contradict that notion?

☐ Suggested Further Reading

Berry, C. M., Sackett, P. R., & Wiemann, S. (2007). A review of recent developments in integrity test research. *Personnel Psychology, 60,* 271–301. doi:10.1111/j.1744-6570.2007.00074.x

Sackett, P. R. (1994). Integrity testing for personnel selection. *Current Directions in Psychological Science, 3,* 73–76.

☐ References

Berry, C. M., Sackett, P. R., & Wiemann, S. (2007). A review of recent developments in integrity test research. *Personnel Psychology, 60,* 271–301. doi:10.1111/j.1744-6570.2007.00074.x

Jones, J., & Terris, W. (1981). *Predictive validation of a dishonesty test that measures theft proneness.* Paper presented at the XVIII Inter-American Congress of Psychology, Santo Domingo, Dominican Republic, June, 1981.

Ones, D. S., Viswesvaran, C., & Schmidt, F. L. (1993). Comprehensive meta-analysis of integrity test validities: Findings and implications for personnel selection and theories of job performance. *Journal of Applied Psychology, 78,* 679–703. doi:10.1037/0021-9010.78.4.679

Ones, D. S., Viswesvaran, C., & Schmidt, F. L. (2012). Integrity tests predict counterproductive work behaviors and job performance well: Comment on Van Iddekinge, Roth, Raymark, and Odle-Dusseau (2012). *Journal of Applied Psychology, 97,* 537–542. doi:10.1037/a0024825

Sackett, P. R., Burris, L. R., & Callahan, C. (1989). Integrity testing for personnel selection: An update. *Personnel Psychology, 42,* 491–529. doi:10.1111/j.1744-6570.1989.tb00666.x

Sackett, P. R., & Decker, P. J. (1979). The detection of deception in the employment context: A review and critical analysis. *Personnel Psychology, 32,* 487–506. doi:10.1111/j.1744-6570.1979.tb02147.x

Sackett, P. R., & Harris, M. M. (1984). Honesty testing for personnel selection: A review and critique. *Personnel Psychology, 37,* 221–245. doi:10.111/j.1744-6570.1984.tb01447.x

Sackett, P. R., & Wanek, J. E. (1996). New developments in the use of measures of honesty, integrity, conscientiousness, dependability, trustworthiness, and reliability for personnel selection. *Personnel Psychology, 49,* 787–829. doi: 10.1111/j.1744-6570.1996.tb02450.x

Sackett, P. R., & Schmitt, N. (2012). On reconciling conflicting meta-analytic findings regarding integrity test validity. *Journal of Applied Psychology, 97,* 550–556. doi: 10.1037/a0028167

Van Iddekinge, C. H., Roth, P. L., Raymark, P. H., & Odle-Dusseau, H. N. (2012). The criterion-related validity of integrity tests: An updated meta-analysis. *Journal of Applied Psychology, 97,* 499–530. doi:10.1037/a0021196

Neuroscience

Neurobiology of Stress and Adaptation: Implications for Health Psychology, Behavioral Medicine, and Beyond

Bruce S. McEwen

Can the Mind Be Read in the Brain Waves?

Emanuel Donchin

Neurobiology of Stress and Adaptation: Implications for Health Psychology, Behavioral Medicine, and Beyond

BRUCE S. McEWEN The Rockefeller University

☐ **Please describe your current position and research interests.**

I am Alfred E. Mirsky Professor and Head, Harold and Margaret Milliken Hatch Laboratory of Neuroendocrinology at The Rockefeller University. My research interests are as follows: (1) stress effects on the brain and its relationship to adaptation and maladaptation—for example, depression, anxiety disorders, unsuccessful aging; (2) sex differences in the brain and actions of sex hormones on higher brain centers and cognitive function, as well as mood and other aspects of behavior not directly related to reproduction, including how gender and sex hormones affect the response to stress; and (3) effects of the social environment on brain and body function, especially socioeconomic status and health in adults and also during development, related to the allostatic load concept that I helped to introduce.

☐ **How did you become interested in brain-body interactions?**

This is explained in my essay: It was a combination of having Neal Miller as a mentor in my early faculty days at Rockefeller and having Alfred Mirsky and Vincent Allfrey, mentors during my graduate student years, helping to focus me on hormone action and regulation of gene expression in the brain, now called "epigenetics," which was a new area of neuroscience when I began.

☐ **What has been the real-world impact of this work?**

Our studies on stress and sex hormone action on the hippocampus have helped focus human-oriented studies on the central role of the brain as a target of stress and also on the nonreproductive actions of sex hormones that are relevant to age-related changes—for example, hormone therapy for cognitive and motor functional decline. The allostatic load model is having increasing influence in health psychology, epidemiology, psychiatry, and medicine, and it is helping social scientists better understand the biology of stress and the enormous influence of the social environment on the health of people with different income and education levels.

S tress, one of the most common words in many languages, has both positive and negative connotations. "Good stress" generally refers to situations where the successful response to a challenge is at least somewhat rewarding. In contrast, "being stressed-out" means that hard-to-handle experiences are producing distress—a sense that we lack control over the circumstances of our lives and are under great time pressure. The brain is central to stress both as interpreter of events and as regulator of behavioral and physiological responses to those events. Although adaptive in the short run, responses to stress can be damaging when they become chronic or dysregulated. For example, grabbing a cigarette or a drink or a donut may be soothing initially, but too much of that kind of comfort can have serious negative consequences.

Physiologically, a sudden, sharp rise in a person's level of cortisol, a glucocorticoid that is one of the primary stress mediators, has immediate beneficial effects, such as activation of an adaptive immune response and fear memories. By contrast, chronically high levels of the hormone are implicated in such potentially damaging health consequences as suppression of the immune system and metabolic syndrome (a group of indicators of increased risk for heart disease and diabetes). Thus, many of the same mediators are involved in both acute adaptation and chronic pathophysiology. Of course, individuals differ in the qualitative nature of their response to stress, which is influenced by their genetic constitutions, early experiences, and adult life history. Furthermore, the brain is itself a target of stress. Structural and functional changes brought about by acute and chronic stressors can alter how the brain processes information and responds to potential stressors.

My own research on stress began in the laboratory of Neal E. Miller at The Rockefeller University in 1966 and was shaped by his integrative view of brain-body interactions, which inspired our serendipitous discovery in 1968 that glucocorticoids are taken up and bind to receptors in the brain's hippocampal formation, where they influence a wide variety of both cognitive functions and generative, energy-conserving bodily processes. Since then, numerous studies with animals have produced findings relevant to such human stress-related disorders as depression and cognitive decline due to aging.

Moreover, through my involvement in the activity of the MacArthur Research Network on Socioeconomic Status and Health, the concept of stress has been reworked through the introduction of the terms *allostasis* and *allostatic load*, which emphasize that the same mediators that protect the body and brain and help it adapt to acute stressors also participate in wear and tear that contributes to diseases of modern life. The allostatic load concept is helping bridge the gap between biological knowledge and investigations of health-related topics in epidemiology and health psychology, among other disciplines, with the expectation that findings will influence public- and private-sector policies that can improve health and well-being (see Figure 1).

Hormone Access to the Brain

Our work on stress began with simple questions about whether the adrenocortical stress hormone in the rat, corticosterone, gains access to the brain and whether there are receptors in the brain for this hormone. Indeed, first with rats and later in the rhesus monkey, we demonstrated that steroid hormones— no doubt because of their greater lipid solubility—gain ready access to the

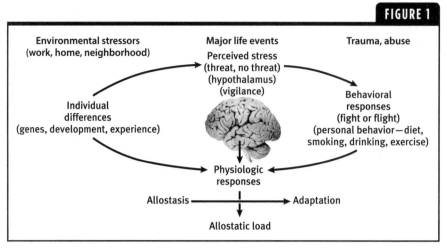

The allostatic load concept. Central role of the brain in allostasis and the behavioral and physi-ological response to stressors. (From *New England Journal of Medicine*, McEwen, B. S., Protec-tive and damaging effects of stress mediators, *338*, 171–179. Copyright © 1998 Massachusetts Medical Society. Reprinted with permission from Massachusetts Medical Society.)

brain, where receptors that have a high affinity for them retain them beyond the time that free steroid is cleared from the brain and body. Hormones active upon the brain include not only glucocorticoids, like cortisol, and mineralo-corticoids, like aldosterone, but also reproductive hormones, like estradiol, testosterone, and progesterone, as well as vitamin D. The finding of glucocor-ticoid and mineralocorticoid receptors in the hippocampus triggered the even-tual broadening of our concept of how even higher cognitive brain regions respond to external influences via hormones and other mediators.

The long-held belief that peptide and protein hormones cannot reach the brain has been revised on the basis of growing contrary evidence. We now know that the hippocampus has receptors for insulin-like growth factors (IGF-1) and insulin, and that it responds to circulating insulin to translocate glucose transporters to cell membranes. Circulating IGF-1 is a key mediator of the ability of physical activity to increase neurogenesis in the hippocampal formation. IGF-1 is taken up into the brain via a transport system different from that which transports insulin. IGF-1 is a member of the growth hormone family, and growth hormone is implicated in cognitive function and mood regulation.

Another peptide hormone, ghrelin, one of the proappetitive hormones (those that keep us eating and performing other functions necessary to life), has been shown to increase synapse formation in hippocampal neurons and to improve hippocampal-dependent memory. Another metabolic hormone, leptin, has been found to exert antidepressant effects when infused directly into the hippocampus. Leptin is transported into the brain, and both glucose and insulin mediate the ability of fasting to increase leptin transport into the brain. Leptin receptors are found in the hippocampus, among other brain re-gions, and leptin has actions in the hippocampus that reduce the probability of seizures, enhance aspects of cognitive function, and improve mood.

Furthermore, metabolic factors involving glucose regulation play a role in mild cognitive impairment with aging and in shrinkage of the hippocampus. Obese Zucker rats (a widely studied strain prone to obesity and insulin resistance) have poorer hippocampal-dependent memory than do lean Zucker rats, as well as impaired translocation of an insulin-dependent glucose transporter to hippocampal membranes. Moreover, a diet rich in fat has been shown to impair hippocampal-dependent memory, and a combination of a high-fat diet and a three-week predator exposure (a high-stress situation) causes dendrites and axons in the hippocampus to retract, even though neither treatment alone has this effect. This topic will be revisited shortly.

Stress Throughout the Life Course

Stressful experiences and stress hormones have effects throughout life. The "weathering hypothesis" recognizes the common observation that a hard life accelerates the aging process. Research on "weathering" effects indicates that increased anxiety and decreased exploration in a novel environment are associated with decreased lifespan of male and female rats compared with animals that show lesser anxiety and greater exploration. The hippocampus is vulnerable to "weathering" with age, and older individuals whose cortisol levels increase over time show more rapid decrements of cognitive function, as well as actual shrinkage in size of that portion of the brain as compared with people of the same age whose cortisol levels are not elevated. Besides cortisol, poor glucose control and factors related to diabetes are also involved in loss of cognitive abilities and shrinkage of the hippocampus and abnormal brain white matter.

One very productive direction of this research has been the investigation of the role of maternal care and early life stress. For example, "handling" studies of newborn rats have revealed that maternal caretaking can change the way genetic information is expressed, and the effect can persist across generations. One of the mechanisms involves DNA methylation, in which a group of carbon and hydrogen atoms attaches to regions of DNA that influence gene activity. This finding and other advances in developmental neuroscience provide the beginnings of a biological understanding of the effects of abuse, neglect, and trauma in childhood on the development of depression and antisocial behavior. A chaotic home life and lack of verbal stimulation have been shown to impair later self-regulating behaviors and cognitive function.

Protective and Damaging Effects of Stress Mediators: Allostasis and Allostatic Load

Contrary to popular belief, stress and stress hormones are not all bad. Mediators of the biological and behavioral stress response exert adaptive effects in the aftermath of acute stress; their negative effects occur when over- or underproduction of these chemicals impairs mechanisms chronically that govern metabolism, immune response, or organ function. For example, cortisol elevation in times of acute stress promotes certain forms of memory and enhances immune responses to injury and infection, but chronic exposure to even moderate levels of cortisol impairs memory, suppresses immune responses, and contributes to the metabolic syndrome.

The concepts allostasis and allostatic load incorporate this paradox and draw attention to the protective, as well as the damaging, effects of these mediators, which act in a nonlinear manner and influence simultaneously the brain and multiple body systems. By nonlinearity, I mean that the mediators of allostasis (such as cortisol, sympathetic and parasympathetic nervous systems, and cytokines—the substances that activate the white blood cells of the immune system) each regulate the output of the other mediators, which often results in U-shaped or otherwise nonlinear dose-response relationships. In addition, because the mediators of allostasis act simultaneously on many tissues and organs in the body, disorders such as depression, diabetes, and mild cognitive impairment in aging often occur together.

The allostasis and allostatic load framework has been helpful in integrating the biology of stress with the psychosocial factors that promote stress-related disorders and pathophysiology. Tests have been developed that permit prediction of stress effects in aging and health effects of socioeconomic status and social support. Findings from studies of the relationship of allostatic load to a positive life outlook have moved us closer to establishing a biology of resilience and positive health and expanding the concept of allostasis to include the biology of resilience.

The collaboration among neuroscience, biomedicine, and psychology made possible by this new conceptual framework has led to enormous progress in understanding brain-body relationships. For example, cumulative stress among caregivers of autistic children and in conditions such as obesity and diabetes has been shown to affect DNA, reducing the length and activity of a structure at the end of chromosomes. In one provocative observation, hippocampal volume was found to be related to low self-esteem and also to a failure to shut off cortisol secretion efficiently after a public speaking challenge. Low self-esteem is also a possible contributing factor in explaining how subjective ratings of socioeconomic status are frequently powerful predictors of health as are objective socioeconomic rankings. Research into positive factors in health has identified factors such as positive affect and positive social relationships along with quality sleep as factors that reduce allostatic load.

The Brain as the Central Organ of Stress and Adaptation

The line of research that began with the discovery of adrenal steroid receptors in the hippocampus has reinforced the notion that the brain is the key organ of the stress response for three principal reasons: (1) The brain interprets what is threatening and, therefore, stressful; (2) It regulates behavioral and physiological stress responses, the latter through the autonomic, immune, and neuroendocrine systems; and (3) It is a target of stress and of hormones related to stress and metabolic control (as summarized earlier) and undergoes structural and functional remodeling that affects its function. Thus, the amygdala and prefrontal cortex are now known to be vulnerable to stress, and stressful experiences are recognized as having an impact on the formation and extinction of fear-related memories, the ability to focus attention, and the cognitive functions that are necessary for goal-directed behavior. Stress-induced brain changes are reversible and are amenable to alteration by pharmaceutical agents and also by lifestyle factors such as exercise, diet, and social support, and healthy brain function will certainly be promoted by policies that encourage individuals to adopt healthier lifestyles and reduce stress.

Implications for Interventions and Policy

As the general public and policymakers in the public and private sectors learn more about the science of stress and adaptation, researchers in the field are hoping to see the adoption of rational policies that help people of all income and education levels move toward healthier and more satisfying lives—lives enhanced by programs that promote education, recreation and social support, and preventative health care. One recent example, the Experience Corps, trains elderly volunteers as teachers' assistants for neighborhood elementary schools. This program benefits the children and also the elderly volunteers by enhancing their physical and mental health and slowing age-related decline of cognitive function. Moreover, there is evidence that the eudamonic as opposed to a hedonic approach to well-being is beneficial to reduced allostatic load. Given the central importance of the brain in "stress," it will be interesting to determine how programs like this reduce measures of allostatic overload, as well as alter the function of the brain circuits that are responsive to chronic stress and allostatic load.

Acknowledgments I am indebted to the late Neal E. Miller because my own research on stress began in the Miller laboratory at The Rockefeller University in 1966 and was shaped by his integrative view of brain-body interactions. My thinking about brain-body interactions was further shaped by Eliot Stellar of the University of Pennsylvania, first through his textbook *Physiological Psychology* with Clifford Morgan, which I used as a student at Oberlin College under the tutelage of psychologist Celeste McCollough, and later by Stellar recruiting me into the MacArthur Health and Behavior Network, where I began to broaden my thinking about how the social environment shapes what is stressful.

☐ Thinking Critically

1. Explain the paradox implicit in Bruce McEwen's "allostatic load" concept. How is the concept useful in understanding certain health outcomes?

2. Compared with friends and family, how intense is your response to stress? What factors in your life trigger stress?

☐ Suggested Further Reading

Acheson, S. D. (1998). *Independent inquiry into inequalities in health report.* London: The Stationery Office.

Blackburn E. H., & Epel, E. S. (2012). Telomeres and adversity: Too toxic to ignore. *Nature, 490,* 169–171.

Caspi, A., McClay, J., Moffitt, T. E., Mill, J., Martin, J., Craig, I. W., et al. (2002). Role of genotype in the cycle of violence in maltreated children. *Science, 297,* 851–854.

Davidson, R. J., & McEwen, B. S. (2012). Social influences on neuroplasticity: Stress and interventions to promote well-being. *Natural Neuroscience, 15,* 689–695.

Dhabhar, F. S., Malarkey, W. B., Neri, E., & McEwen, B. S. (2012). Stress-induced redistribution of immune cells–from barracks to boulevards to battlefields: A tale of three hormones—Curt Richter Award winner. *Psychoneuroendocrinology, 37,* 1345–1368.

Erickson, K. I., Voss, M. W., Prakash, R. S., Basak, C., Szabo, A., et al. (2011). Exercise training increases size of hippocampus and improves memory. *Proceedings of the National Academy of Science USA, 108,* 3017–3022.

Evans, G. W., Gonnella, C., Marcynyszyn, L. A., Gentile, L., & Salpekar, N. (2004). The role of chaos in poverty and children's socioemotional adjustment. *Psychological Science, 16,* 560–565.

Fredrickson, B. L., Grewen, K. M., Coffey, K. A., Algoe, S. B., Firestine, A. M., et al. (2013). A functional genomic perspective on human well-being. *Proceedings of the National Academy of Science USA, 110,* 13684–13689.

Fried, L. P., Carlson, M. C., Freedman, M., Frick, K. D., Glass, T. A., Hill, J., et al. (2004). A social model for health promotion for an aging population: Initial evidence on the Experience Corps model. *Journal of Urban Health: Bulletin of the New York Academy of Medicine, 81,* 64–78.

Geronimus, A. T., Hicken, M., Keene, D., & Bound, J. (2006). "Weathering" and age patterns of allostatic load scores among blacks and whites in the United States. *American Journal of Public Health, 96,* 826–833.

Gianaros, P. J., Marsland, A. L., Sheu, L. K., Erickson, K. I., & Verstynen, T. D. (2013). Inflammatory pathways link socioeconomic inequalities to white matter architecture. *Cerebral Cortex, 23,* 2058–2071.

McEwen, B. S. (2007). The physiology and neurobiology of stress and adaptation: Central role of the brain. *Physiological Review, 87,* 873–904.

McEwen, B. S., & Alves, S. H. (1999). Estrogen actions in the central nervous system. *Endocrine Review, 20,* 279–307.

McEwen, B. S., & Gianaros, P. J. (2011). Stress- and allostasis-induced brain plasticity. *Annual Review of Medicine, 62,* 431–445.

McEwen, B., with Lasley, E. N. (2002). *The end of stress as we know it.* Washington, DC: Joseph Henry Press and Dana Press.

McEwen, B. S., & Milner, T. A. (2007). Hippocampal formation: Shedding light on the influence of sex and stress on the brain. *Brain Research Review 55,* 343–355.

McEwen, B. S., & Morrison, J. H. (2013). The brain on stress: Vulnerability and plasticity of the prefrontal cortex over the life course. *Neuron, 79,* 16–29.

Pruessner, J. C., Baldwin, M. W., Dedovic, K., Renwick, R. M. N. K., Lord, C., Meaney, M., et al. (2005). Self-esteem, locus of control, hippocampal volume, and cortisol regulation in young and old adulthood. *NeuroImage, 28,* 815–826.

Sapolsky, R. (1992). *Stress, the aging brain, and the mechanisms of neuron death.* Cambridge, MA: MIT Press.

Sapolsky, R. N. (2004). *Why zebras don't get ulcers.* New York: Owl Press.

Seeman, T., Epel, E., Gruenewald, T., Karlamangla, A., & McEwen, B. S. (2010). Socio-economic differentials in peripheral biology: Cumulative allostatic load. *Annals of the New York Academy of Sciences, 1186,* 223–239.

Yau, P. L., Castro, M. G., Tagani, A., Tsui, W. H., & Convit, A. (2012). Obesity and metabolic syndrome and functional and structural brain impairments in adolescence. *Pediatrics, 130,* e856–e864.

Zhang, T. Y., & Meaney, M. J. (2010). Epigenetics and the environmental regulation of the genome and its function. *Annual Review of Psychology, 61,* 439–466.

☐ References

McEwen, B. S. (1998). Protective and damaging effects of stress mediators. *New England Journal of Medicine, 338,* 171–179.

Can the Mind Be Read in the Brain Waves?

EMANUEL DONCHIN University of South Florida

☐ **Please describe your current position and research interests.**

I am Professor Emeritus at the University of Illinois-Urbana-Champaign and a Professor at the University of South Florida's Department of Psychology, serving as Chair from July 2001 to August 2008. I received my Ph.D. from the University of California, Los Angeles and was a research associate at Stanford's Department of Neurology and at the Neurobiology Branch at NASA-Ames Research Center. In 1968, I joined the Department of Psychology at the University of Illinois in Urbana-Champaign as an Associate Professor and remained there until 2001. My field of professional interest is cognitive psychophysiology. I use electrophysiological neuroimaging as a tool for developing an understanding of the manner in which the mind is implemented by the brain.

☐ **How did you become interested in studying cognitive psychophysiology and event-related potentials in the brain?**

I became particularly interested in event-related potentials (ERP) when using EEGs in my lab at the University of Illinois. I found that the brain responds differently to a surprising event, triggering an emotional response or peak response (P300) in our subjects. I became interested in the extent to which this emotional response changes brain activity and cognitive processes. By looking at the changes in the brain's activity in relation to psychological processes, we can better understand the relationship between the mind and the brain.

☐ **What has been the real-world impact of this work?**

My laboratory continues to develop a Brain Computer Interface, an ERP-based tool that makes it possible for severely disabled individuals to communicate with computers using the P300 as a channel of communication. In the last few years, using a portable system developed at the Wadsworth Center in Albany, NY, we tested this BCI with numerous individuals who suffer from ALS and are, therefore, completely paralyzed, yet with intact cognitive and affective systems. Additionally, we've been adapting the P300-based BCI to the control of robotics systems.

In the spring of 1985, I was visited by a local physician who had a rather sad tale. A young patient of his, whom I will call Robert, was severely injured in a motorcycle accident and sustained severe damage to his spinal cord. The patient was about 25 years old and prior to his injury, he was a vigorous, healthy young man. Since the accident, Robert had been entirely paralyzed from the neck down. He breathed through a tube, was fed intravenously, and could not speak.

There were indications that Robert's mind was still active. His mother, a well-educated school teacher and very sensible woman, claimed that she could communicate with him by asking him questions. If he wanted to say yes in response to questions, he kept his eyes open for a minute. When he meant no, he kept them closed for a minute. The attendants also reported that, on occasion, Robert could track moving objects across the room with his eyes. However, it was extremely difficult to interpret these signs of communication.

If Robert did have an alert mind, it was worth attempting to find some means of communicating with him. Robert's physician contacted me after reading in the popular press about research on the use of brain waves as a novel medium to allow communication between people and computers. Could Robert communicate by controlling his brain waves through whatever mental capacity had survived the ravages of his body? Would he be able to communicate with a computer that would translate his wishes into actions or words?

The Case of Mental Prosthesis

The questions that Robert's physician asked me are similar to the challenge of biocybernetics, which is the science of communication and control of living organisms. In both Robert's case and in biocybernetics in general, we are seeking mental prostheses. To meet this challenge, my research program adopted an approach that, in its basic theoretical assumptions and in its empirical base, was quite similar to the logic that supports the use of the interrogatory polygraphy (commonly known as using a lie detector to assess a suspect's guilt or innocence of a crime). There is nothing particularly mysterious about interrogative polygraphy. It is akin to how you infer from a companion blushing that a question you asked may have been embarrassing. Of course, while the blush tells you that an emotion was triggered in your companion, you do not really know if it was shame, excitement, anticipation, or anger. The polygraph is deciphered in the same way. The nature of the emotion is not directly derivable from the recordings. Indeed, the mind, when approached psychophysiologically, is not any more an open book than it is when approached in any other way. It is complex, multilayered, and often deceptive. It is, in fact, frequently self-deceptive. Answers are useful only to the extent that the proper questions are asked in the proper form.

Using Brain Waves to Read the Mind

Christopher Wickens, Earle Heffley, and I conducted research that studied how brain waves can be used to "read the mind" many years ago (Wickens, Heffley, Kramer, & Donchin, 1980). Participants were seated in front of a screen on which different shaped icons were moving. The participants had been told they would be playing the role of air traffic controllers. At any time, there could be as many as five triangles and five squares on the screen. Each icon would appear on one side of the screen and move at a randomly selected pathway toward the other side. We told the participants that the displayed symbols represented the movement of two fleets of planes—one fleet represented by triangles and the other by squares. Furthermore, they were told that only one type of icon, for instance, the triangles, represented planes in their domain of responsibility and the participants were instructed to ignore the other icons (planes).

To complete the story, we also told participants that all planes would emit signals. When a signal was emitted, the brightness of the icon associated with the plane would be increased briefly. The participants' task was merely to count the number of signals emitted by planes in their fleet and ignore the signals from all other planes. (In practical terms, this means that the participants must count all flashes that occur in triangles and ignore all flashes that occur in squares.) Note that both the triangles and squares appeared in just about the same part of the visual field, and there was no difference in the brightness of the flashes. Indeed, the only difference between the two flashes was that one was a signal in a relevant channel and the other had no relevance to the participants.

Now I can introduce the practical question addressed by this study. Assume you are told that a person may be paying attention to only one of two aspects of a display, and you would like to know with some certainty to which aspect the person is actually attending. For example, during the long shift that an air traffic controller is sitting in front of the screen, is he or she paying attention and, if so, is it attention to the proper signals? You know to what the controller is supposed to be paying attention; so do the computer and the controller. What no one knows, however, is whether the controller is actually directing attention in the correct direction. Can a procedure be devised for monitoring the degree to which attention is paid where it should be? How would you go about finding out?

Well, you might say, you can just ask the person, but this has two drawbacks. First, you cannot be sure you are getting a truthful response. Certainly you can imagine a situation in which you say, "Stop daydreaming and attend to your work," and the person responds, "I am!" regardless of what is actually happening. Moreover, even if people wish to be truthful, they may simply not be in control of their attention or know to what they have been paying attention.

Alternately, you might suggest that it is a simple matter to tell from the actual performance of the task to which of its aspects the operator has been paying attention. All we have to do, you may think, is observe what people do. Presumably, that to which the person responds is that to which attention is being paid. Unfortunately, often the need to respond to such queries interferes with the very task that the person is performing. So, asking an operator continually to report the direction of attention is a sure way of interfering with performance. It would be useful to find an observable measure that would reveal to which of two channels of input a person was paying attention.

The Event-Related Brain Potential

The measure we adopted for this purpose is a brain response called event-related potential (ERP). These are activities triggered in the brain by specific internal or external events. An "event" in our research study is a signal from a plane. We wanted to determine if there is a difference between a person's response to the counted planes and the response to the ignored planes.

We placed electrodes on the participant's head. When used for research, the placement must be very accurate, and an extra effort is made to clean the skin. However, for monitoring purposes, in what passes for the "real" world, it is actually easy to embed the electrodes in a helmet or in the headband of earphones. We then connected the electrodes to amplifiers that accept the very tiny voltages that accompany brain activity and pass these, highly amplified, to data processing and data recording devices. The signals obtained in this manner are, of course, the brain waves that are recorded routinely in clinical electroencephalography (EEG) labs. For all practical purposes, the signals appear as a randomly varying wave whose general properties are related to the participant's state of alertness, but from which very little, if any, information can be gleaned regarding specific cognitive activities.

However, through the sophistication of computing, it is possible to extract from the EEG an even fainter signal—the ERP. This ERP is the activity that can be recorded between a pair of electrodes, which is directly related to the triggering event or stimulus. So, we can obtain records of the brain's response to the signals sent by the planes as monitored by the participant.

We set up this experiment as a demonstration during a review visit by one of our granting agencies. As I waxed enthusiastically about our ability to detect the participant's direction of attention, the agency personnel asked if I was willing to submit our claim to a real test. He suggested that he enter the room with the participant, who would be told without my knowledge when to switch attention from one class of icons to the other. I should, he said, be able to tell when the participant did so by just looking at the screen. I agreed, with some concern. The next few minutes were tense, but it quickly turned out that all one had to do is look at the screen where the individual traces of the ERP were shown. The difference between responses to attended and unattended stimuli was surprisingly clear.

These data and this study, which are but a miniscule segment of a rather large body of work (e.g., Donchin, Spencer, & Wijesinghe, 2000; Spencer, Dien, & Donchin, 1999; 2001), permit a clear and affirmative response to our experimental question. It is indeed possible to "read the mind" in the traces of the ERP. In this case, we can—without asking a direct question and without requiring any overt activity by the participant—monitor shifts in the participant's attention. Indeed, this very design gives us a clue of how to approach cases like Robert. We can have him attend to triangles and squares, comparing the amplitude of the ERP to determine his response. Although there are still many steps that need to be implemented before we are able to create a communication system for patients like Robert, it is clear to us that we have a proper prosthetic approach.

☐ Thinking Critically

1. Emanuel Donchin's quest for a mental prosthesis has applications for persons like Robert who have "locked in" syndrome. Can you think of any other applications?

2. Have you ever been in a study or a clinic in which your brain waves were measured (through EEG or ERP)? What about a brain imaging study? If so, what was it like? If not, would you like to be in such a study?

☐ Suggested Further Reading

Farwell, L. A., & Donchin, E. (1988). Talking off the top of your head: Toward a mental prosthesis utilizing event-related brain potentials. *Electroencephalography and Clinical Neurophysiology, 70,* 510–523.

Kutas, M., McCarthy, G., & Donchin, E. (1977). Augmenting mental chronometry: The P300 as a measure of stimulus evaluation time. *Science, 197,* 792–795.

☐ References

Donchin, E., Spencer, K. M., & Wijesinghe, R. (2000). The mental prosthesis: Assessing the speed of a p300-based brain–computer interface. *IEEE Transactions on Rehabilitation Engineering, 8,* 174–179.

Spencer, K. M., Dien, J., & Donchin, E. (1999). A componential analysis of the ERP elicited by novel events using a dense electrode array. *Psychophysiology, 36,* 409–414.

Spencer, K. M., Dien, J., & Donchin, E. (2001). Spatiotemporal analysis of the late ERP responses to deviant stimuli. *Psychophysiology, 38,* 343–358.

Wickens, C.D., Heffley, E., Kramer, A., & Donchin, E. (1980). The event-related brain potential as an index of attention allocation in complex displays. *Proceedings of the 24th Annual Meeting of the Human Factors Society.* Santa Monica, CA.

Sensation and Perception

Human Vision as a Reality Engine

Donald D. Hoffman

Visual Search: Is It a Matter of Life and Death?

Jeremy M. Wolfe

Human Vision as a Reality Engine

DONALD D. HOFFMAN University of California, Irvine

☐ **Please describe your current position and research interests.**

I am a professor of cognitive science at the University of California, Irvine. In addition, I have appointments in the Departments of Philosophy and Computer Science. This might sound like an odd combination, but there is a simple reason: I want to understand how human vision works, hence the cognitive science. I am also interested in how our subjective perceptions are related to objective reality, hence the philosophy. Finally, I am interested in creating models of perception and reality that are precise enough to build working robotic-vision systems, hence the computer science.

☐ **How did you become interested in studying vision?**

My first interest is to understand conscious experiences, such as the experience of pain, the taste of mint, or the blue color of a clear sky. Do our conscious experiences arise from brain activities? If so, precisely how? If not, what is the relationship between conscious experiences and brain activities? Vision provides a concrete and fascinating arena in which to study these questions.

☐ **What has been the real-world impact of this work?**

It is natural for us to wonder what kind of creatures we are and what, if anything, makes us special in the universe. For me, the most exciting possible impact of the work on conscious visual experiences is that it might illuminate these perennial questions and help us better understand ourselves. As an added benefit, however, vision research can lead to practical applications that support automatic vision systems for driving, manufacturing, homeland security, medical image processing, and the visually impaired.

Vision feels easy. We simply open our eyes and look. Without apparent effort, we see a three-dimensional world packed with objects, colors, textures, and motions. This apparent ease leads naturally to the assumption that vision is a simple process, no more complex than taking pictures with a camera. But research in cognitive neuroscience reveals that roughly one third of the brain's neocortex—billions of neurons and trillions of synapses—are engaged when we simply open our eyes and look. Why should much of our most sophisticated computational power be engaged in vision? This is overkill if vision is, like a camera, just taking pictures. A digital camera needs nowhere near that much circuitry.

Why does vision engage all this computing power? Research in psychophysics and computational vision provides a remarkable answer. Your visual system is a reality engine: It creates all the depths, shapes, objects, colors, textures, and motions that you see. The term *reality engine* is borrowed from the field of virtual reality, where it refers to the powerful computers and sophisticated software used to generate the impression of immersion in a virtual world. In the case of human vision, enormous computing power is needed to create the visual worlds in which we find ourselves constantly immersed. That's why roughly half of your most sophisticated computing power is recruited for the job.

Admittedly, we don't feel as if we're constructing the visual world; it seems to always be there with us. We feel this way because our reality engine is so fast and effective that it creates what we see as fast as the eye can move. Thus, the very power and efficiency of the reality engine blocks our awareness of its existence. We can, however, find telltale signs of its operation if we know where to look.

For example, observe the two boxes in Figure 1. Are their gray tops the same shape, or are they different? They certainly look different. The one on the left looks long and narrow, the one on the right short and fat. Nevertheless, they are identical. You can verify this with a ruler, or by using tracing paper to copy the top of one box, and then placing it on the top of the other. You'll see that it fits perfectly. So why does it look to us like the tops have different shapes? The reality engine of vision is at work, creating impressions of shape and depth, using rules that normally work well. But in this figure, the normal operation of the reality engine constructs a visual reality that contradicts what we can measure.

Another illustration of your reality engine at work is shown in Figure 2. When you view this figure, you see a ghostly cube floating in front of black disks. The white lines of the cube are sharp and brighter than the background.

FIGURE 1

Identical box tops. The gray top of the box on the left has the same length and width as the gray top of the box on the right. Yet they look different. This unmasks an operation of our visual reality engine and shows that it can construct realities that contradict what we measure with a ruler. This figure was inspired by a similar demonstration with tables created by Roger Shepard (1990), which first appeared in Kubovy and Pomerantz (1981). Republished with permission of Taylor and Francis Group LLC books. Permission conveyed through Copyright Clearance Center, Inc.

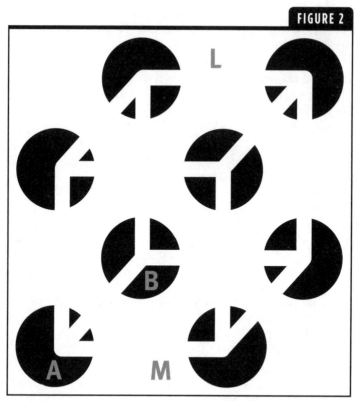

FIGURE 2

The subjective Necker cube. The white edges of the cube are entirely constructed by your visual reality engine. So also are the cubes that you see. Drake Bradley and Heywood Petry (1977) created the first subjective Necker cube figure. (From Bradley & Petry, 1977)

But if you cover two adjacent black disks, you will see that no line extends between them. If you then uncover those two disks, you will again see a line between them. That line is entirely the creation of your reality engine.

To understand what is happening, think of the reality engine as trying to create the most probable interpretation of the image. It notices the precise alignments of the white cutouts on adjacent black disks and decides that this alignment is probably not accidental but is due instead to white lines that occlude the disks. So it hallucinates these lines, making them a bit brighter than the background.

When your reality engine has constructed the illusory lines between the black disks, it notices that these lines have a regular pattern, consistent with being the projection of a cube. It decides that this is probably no accident, concluding instead that a cube probably occludes the black disks. So it hallucinates the cube and makes it float in front of the disks.

If you watch the cube for a while, you might see it suddenly flip. Sometimes you see a cube with corner *A* in front and sometimes a cube with corner *B* in front. Call these *cube A* and *cube B*. Your reality engine decides that cube A and cube B are both likely interpretations of this image, and so it first constructs one, then the other, repeatedly in an infinite loop. But there are more cubes here. Think of the black disks as holes in a white sheet of paper. You look through these holes, and behind them see a white cube (it might take a little time to see it). Again, you sometimes see a cube with corner A in front and sometimes with corner B in front. So here are two more cubes that your reality engine constructs. Call them *cube A'* and *cube B'*.

Now comes a strange question: Which of the four cubes is there when you don't look? Cube A or A'? Cube B or B'? The answer must be that no cube is there when you don't look. After all, each cube you see looks three-dimensional, but the page on which Figure 2 appears is flat. Therefore, a three-dimensional cube is only there when you look; its existence depends on your reality engine (Hoffman, 2000).

One last observation: Notice that when you see the cubes in front of the disks, the edges have a ghostly quality, but when you see the cubes behind, the edges are no longer ghostly, but instead have a paradoxical quality of being invisible and yet substantial or solid. This quality of ghostliness versus solidity is also the creation of your reality engine.

Evolution and User Interfaces

Our reality engine constructs everything we see. So the question naturally arises: What is the relationship between our visual constructions and the world that we don't construct, the world that exists whether or not we exist?

This question has a clear answer in evolutionary theory: Our sensory systems are shaped by natural selection to allow *Homo sapiens* to survive long enough to reproduce within its niche. *Homo sapiens,* like, say, the cockroach, is a species whose sensory systems guide adaptive behavior within a particular niche. We don't expect the sensory systems of a cockroach, or a maggot, or a nematode to give detailed insight into the true nature of reality. Instead, we expect those systems to give simple signals, suited for a particular ecological niche, that help avoid predators and find mates, similarly for *Homo sapiens* (Pinker, 1999).

Evolutionary theory leads us to think of our sensory systems as constituting a species-specific user interface. A user interface, like the Windows interface on your laptop, is useful because it does *not* resemble what it represents. For instance, a file icon on your computer screen might be red, rectangular, and in the upper-left corner of the screen, but this doesn't mean that the file itself is red, rectangular, or in the upper-left corner of the screen. The icon is there to guide behavior, not to resemble the file. The icon *hides* the complexity of the computer, all of its diodes and resistors and megabytes of software. That's what makes the user interface useful. And that's what makes the sensory systems of *Homo sapiens* useful. Our sensory systems don't resemble the complex reality that they represent, but instead present a greatly simplified set of icons that let us behave adaptively in our niche (Hoffman, 2000; Hoffman & Singh, 2012).

Medical Implications

If our visual system is a species-specific reality engine, then damage to the visual system should impair our ability to construct visual realities. The neurological literature provides many fascinating case histories of people struggling to live with such conditions.

For instance, activity in an area of cerebral cortex called the lateral fusiform gyrus is correlated with the perception of faces. If the fusiform face area, or FFA, is damaged, for example, by a stroke, the patient may be normal in every respect except one: He or she may be unable to recognize faces by looking at them—even the faces of family members, old friends, or the patient's own face seen in a mirror (Bruce & Young, 2012). Patients can still recognize people by voice, indicating that the specifically visual ability to recognize faces is the impaired function. Many people with FFA damage can still recognize facial expressions. Activity in a different area of cerebral cortex in the posterior superior temporal sulcus (PSTS) is correlated with the perception of facial expression. A patient with damage to the PSTS but not the FFA can usually recognize facial identity but not facial expression. This condition leads to serious social difficulties because we are so dependent on the ability to read facial expressions quickly in our daily social interactions.

Damage to other visual areas of cerebral cortex is correlated with other visual deficits (Behrmann, 2001). Bilateral damage to visual area V8 is correlated with achromotopsia, an inability to see color, in which the world appears only in shades of gray. Some people with achromatopsia can no longer dream in color or imagine colors. Similarly, damage to visual area V5 is correlated with an inability to see motion, while area V1 damage is correlated with scotomas, regions of the visual field in which the patient is blind.

Because damage to specific areas of the visual cortex and particular behavioral deficits are so closely correlated, visual deficits can be invaluable in diagnosing neurological disorders. For instance, some people with undiagnosed Alzheimer disease (AD) first complain that they cannot see. Ophthalmological examination reveals that their eyes are fine, but further examination reveals that regions of visual cortex are probably damaged with the plaques and tangles of AD. Research is in progress to use visual deficits, and concomitant changes in brain activity as measured by electroencephalograms (EEGs) to diagnose AD before clinical symptoms appear, so that medical interventions can be introduced as early as possible (Sneddon et al., 2005).

Technological Implications

If the visual system is a sophisticated reality engine that constructs our visual worlds, then we should be able to study its operation, reverse engineer it, and build computer systems that mimic it. To reverse engineer a complex system means to study its structure and function to try to understand how it works, often with the goal of trying to build a new system that has the same capabilities. To reverse engineer human vision means to study it through psychophysical, neurophysiological, and brain imaging experiments to learn the secrets of its operation.

Indeed, this is proving possible. We now have computer vision systems, inspired by insights from biological visual systems that take images streaming in from video cameras and construct depth, shapes, colors, motions, and objects (Shapiro & Stockman, 2001). These systems are advanced enough to autonomously drive cars on highways, using only computer vision to "see" the road.

Currently, the big open problem in computer vision is object recognition. It has proved remarkably difficult to recognize three-dimensional objects from arbitrary viewpoints, under arbitrary lighting, and with other objects obscuring them. The reason is that a single object can lead to dramatically different images as it is rotated, occluded, or presented under different lighting. A computer vision system must recognize that these widely different images are, in fact, images of precisely the same object. These technical difficulties make neuroscientists admire the speed and accuracy with which human vision solves this problem.

Efforts to reverse engineer visual object recognition, both in humans and other primates, has led to the surprising discovery that biological visual systems can recognize a three-dimensional object by using neural representations of just a few of its two-dimensional views. This insight has led to the discovery of theorems and algorithms for recognizing three-dimensional objects given only a few two-dimensional views. In this way, reverse engineering biological vision has provided key insights for solving a difficult technological challenge.

Computer vision systems are already in use in industry, the military, homeland security, and medical image processing. Once the problem of object recognition has been sufficiently resolved, we can expect computer vision systems to serve as prosthetic devices for the visually impaired, to be used widely in industry for flexible automated assembly, and, inevitably, to be used for smart bombs and other military applications.

Philosophical Implications

What is the relation between our perceptions and the world that exists independent of us? This question has puzzled philosophers at least since Plato and remains puzzling to this day. Advances in understanding human visual perception and the human visual system have helped to sharpen this question and to provide the basis for rigorous experiments that constrain our ideas. The question can now be posed as follows: What is the relationship between brain activity and conscious experience?

Vision researchers currently are studying many neural correlates of consciousness. Detailed information about conscious visual experiences and their neural correlates may enable neuroscientists to fashion a scientifically rigorous theory (Blackmore, 2012). I have already mentioned the correlations between neural activity in V8 and conscious color experiences, neural activity in V5 and conscious motion experiences, and neural activity in the FFA and conscious recognition of faces. These and other similar correlations are now being studied in great detail using brain-imaging techniques such as EEG, functional magnetic resonance imaging, positron emission tomography, and magnetoencephalography.

This problem is fascinating, in part, because we do not yet have a single scientific theory that can explain how neural activity could cause, or be, conscious experiences. If you find this surprising, just consider what neural activity is: It is primarily various ions, such as sodium and potassium ions, passing through holes in neural membranes; it is various neurotransmitters, such as serotonin and dopamine, diffusing across synaptic clefts and binding to receptors. How can ions running through holes or neurotransmitters diffusing through clefts cause, or be, my conscious experience of the smell of garlic or the sound of a flute? Why shouldn't such neural activity, whether of single neurons or interacting systems of neurons, go on without any conscious experiences at all? These difficult and open questions currently engage many vision researchers and neuroscientists (Koch, 2012).

SETI Implications

Are we alone in the universe or might there be other intelligent beings on other planets? The Search for Extraterrestrial Intelligence (SETI) program has, for decades, been looking for evidence of extraterrestrial intelligence. Suppose that SETI succeeds. How will we communicate with the extraterrestrials? Should we use Greek? English? French? Given that humans have enough trouble understanding foreign human languages, extraterrestrials aren't likely to do any better. Perhaps, then, we can use the same strategy that many traffic signs use: Instead of presenting the information in a specific language, present it by means of images. Most humans, despite their linguistic differences, understand such images; perhaps they will also be understood universally by sufficiently intelligent extraterrestrials. With this hope in mind, the *Pioneer 10* and *Voyager 1* and *2* spacecrafts were sent into space with many images of life on Earth (Drake & Sobel, 1992).

But if vision is a species-specific user interface, shaped by the selection pressures of a particular ecological niche, it is unlikely that images will have the same interpretation for a civilization near the star Alpha Centauri as they have on Earth. Instead, our interfaces will probably differ, and considerable effort will be required to translate between them. The difficulty we have communicating with, for example, dolphins, suggests how complicated such translation can be. If SETI does make contact, vision researchers may be at the forefront of efforts to establish reliable means of interstellar communication.

Conclusion

Vision is full of surprises. Its apparent ease hides its astonishing complexity and computational power. As we better understand vision, we will better understand ourselves, our evolutionary history, and the nature of our conscious experiences. We will create automatic vision systems for driving, manufacturing, homeland security, medical image processing, and the visually impaired. Perhaps, too, we will learn to succeed at interstellar communication.

☐ Thinking Critically

1. Donald Hoffman uses illusions to illustrate his argument that vision is a species-specific survival tool. Look back at Figures 1 and 2; think of other familiar illusions our reality engine creates. How do they contribute to human survival?
2. People in virtual-reality environments begin to act as if they are experiencing the real world. To what kinds of therapeutic and educational interventions might this tendency lend itself?

☐ Suggested Further Reading

Hoffman, D. D. (2000). *Visual intelligence: How we create what we see.* New York: W. W. Norton.

Hoffman, D. D. (2009). The interface theory of perception. In S. Dickinson, M. Tarr, A. Leonardis, & B. Schiele (Eds.), *Object categorization: Computer and human vision perspectives* (pp. 148–265). New York: Cambridge University Press.

Pinker, S. (1999). *How the mind works.* New York: W. W. Norton.

☐ References

Behrmann, M. (2001). Disorders of visual behavior. In F. Boller & J. Grafman (Eds.), *Handbook of neuropsychology* (2nd ed.). Amsterdam: Elsevier Science.

Blackmore, S. (2012). *Consciousness: An introduction* (2nd ed.). Oxford: Oxford University Press.

Bradley, D. R., & Petry, H. M. (1977). Organizational determinants of subjective contour: The subjective Necker cube. *American Journal of Psychology, 90,* 253–262.

Bruce, V., & Young, A. (2012). *Face perception.* New York: Psychology Press.

Drake, F., & Sobel, D. (1992). *Is anyone out there? The scientific search for extraterrestrial intelligence.* New York: Delacorte Press.

Hoffman, D. D. (2000). *Visual intelligence: How we create what we see.* New York: W. W. Norton.

Hoffman, D. D., & Singh, M. (2012). Computational evolutionary perception. *Perception, 41,* 1073–1091.

Koch, C. (2012). *Consciousness: Confesssion of a romantic reductionist.* Cambridge, MA: MIT Press.

Kubovy, M., & Pomerantz, J. (1981). *Perceptual organization.* Hillsdale, NJ: Erlbaum.

Pinker, S. (1999). *How the mind works.* New York: W. W. Norton.

Shapiro, L. G., & Stockman, G. C. (2001). *Computer vision.* New York: Prentice Hall.

Shepard, R.N. (1990). *Mind sights.* San Francisco: W. H. Freeman.

Sneddon, R., Shankle, W. R., Hara, J., Rodriquez, A., Hoffman, D. D., & Saha, U. (2005). EEG detection of early Alzheimer's disease using psychophysical tasks. *Clinical EEG Neuroscience, 36,* 141–150.

Visual Search: Is It a Matter of Life and Death?

JEREMY M. WOLFE Brigham and Women's Hospital and Harvard Medical School

☐ **Please describe your current position and research interests.**

For a psychologist, I have a somewhat unusual position. I am a professor in the Departments of Ophthalmology and Radiology at Harvard Medical School, and I run a lab that is part of the Department of Surgery at Brigham and Women's Hospital. For 25+ years, I taught Psychology at Massachusetts Institute of Technology and Harvard University. At my lab we study problems in vision and visual attention; specifically, the problem of how you find what you are looking for.

☐ **What drew you to study how the human brain copes with visual information, particularly with the overload of information with which we're constantly confronted?**

I became interested in vision when I got a summer job in a vision lab at Bell Telephone Laboratories when I was in high school. I became interested in visual attention and visual search when I tried and failed to replicate a basic finding in the search literature. That was about 25 years ago, and stimulating questions keep presenting themselves and we keep trying to answer them.

☐ **What has been the real-world impact of this work?**

As I hope my essay makes clear, our lives involve hundreds of search tasks each day, and our civilization asks us to perform some very difficult artificial visual search tasks like finding signs of cancer in a mammogram or a threat in a piece of luggage going through airport security. In my lab, our goal is to understand the basic mechanisms of search and the specific problems raised by artificial search tasks. We want to use that knowledge to improve performance on those search tasks that actually can be a matter of life and death.

How do you find what you are looking for in a visual world crowded with things that you are *not* looking for? This is the problem of visual search. Most of the time, it does not seem like much of a problem. I am sitting in my visually cluttered study. I look for my coffee mug and there it is to my right. I look for my cell phone and find it on my left. Of course, some searches are more difficult. If I want to locate my cat, I will need to get up and wander around the house, checking warm spots and assorted hiding places, but that isn't quite the problem of interest here because my cat starts from a position outside my field of view. We are interested in searches for stimuli that are, literally, right in front of your eyes.

Why do we need to search at all? The answer is obvious enough in the case of the cat who is outside the field of view, but why do I need to search for that piece of paper that is just lying there, clearly visible in front of me? The answer is that the eye provides us with too much input for the brain to process. The brain has attentional mechanisms that allow it to restrict processing to some subset of the input. As one quick illustration of this point, try reading two texts at the same time. Even if the letters are big enough that you can resolve both at the same time, you can't read them both. You can let your attention jump back and forth between them but you are limited to one at a time.

My lab is devoted to understanding how humans search. Most of the time, we pursue this interest in experiments that use simple stimuli presented on the computer screen. Figure 1 is an example. We collect behavioral responses and use the patterns in the data to deduce the underlying processes. Our hope and assumption is that studies with simple stimuli tell us something about how human observers search in the real world of cats and coffee mugs. On a practical front, results from basic research can be used to improve performance on some of the critical artificial search tasks that our civilization has invented. The security guard checking your bag for weapons and the radiologist scanning a mammogram for cancer are performing very demanding visual search tasks. We would like to make their jobs a bit easier.

How Do We Search for a Target in an Array of Distracters?

Look at Figure 1. It's designed to illustrate the fact that a search through the current contents of the visual field can be a problem.

Your task is to find the item illustrated at the top of the figure: a black disk inside a white disk inside a gray disk. If you found it quickly, look for the other one—there are two. After completing the task, two facts should be introspectively obvious: All of the items are clearly visible, and you still need to search through them before you can find what you are looking for.

If we were to measure the time you needed to find the target item and if we made you search through hundreds of displays that have different numbers of items like this, we would discover that your reaction time would increase by something like 30 to 60 milliseconds (30–60 thousandths of a second) for each additional item in the display. Depending on how we model the search process, we could estimate the number of these items that you processed each second to be somewhere in the vicinity of 15 to 30. That is quite fast. But look at the world around you. How many "items" are there in your current field of view? Actually, that seemingly obvious question turns out to be surprisingly hard to answer, but the number must be pretty large under most circumstances. Suppose the number was just 100. Finding something would take you several seconds. Imagine trying to do this while driving down the interstate at 65 miles an hour; this could be a disaster.

FIGURE 1

Find

It is hard to find the target item even though it must be visible when you first look at the image.

You must be doing something a bit cleverer than just searching at random through the set of all visible items. Figure 2 gives some insight into part of that cleverness.

The task is to find the big, black, vertical items. Why is this visual search so much easier than the first? The answer begins with Anne Treisman's influential feature-integration theory (Treisman & Gelade, 1980). She noted that search tasks in which the target is defined by a single basic feature like color, size, or orientation are trivially easy. If you are looking for a green item in a field of red items, you don't need to search, it pops out at you. Treisman argued that for anything more complicated than a basic feature search, you would need to attend to the item in order to "bind" its features into a coherent object. Thus, in Figure 2, where items are defined by various conjunctions of color, size, and orientation, you would need to attend to an item in order to determine if it has the right combination of black, vertical, and big.

Treisman distinguished between "preattentive" searches like green among red, in which all items could be processed at once, and "attentive" searches for targets that required binding. In these, attention would have to be directed to one item at a time. In our Guided Search model, we elaborated on Treisman's theory, adding the idea of "guidance" to explain why tasks like the one illustrated in Figure 2 are so easy (Wolfe, 1994, 2006; Wolfe, Cave, & Franzel, 1989). We agreed that you need to direct attention in order to bind big, black, and vertical features into a big, black, vertical object, but we added the notion that preattentive features could be used to guide attention toward the items that might possibly be the target. In the Figure 2 example, guiding attention

FIGURE 2

Find

Finding the big, black, vertical targets is easy because you can use the basic features to guide attention toward likely target items.

to items that are black would immediately eliminate most of the items. If you can guide to bigness, blackness, and verticalness, most of your work is done. Figure 1 is hard because guiding isn't possible. All the Figure 1 items have the same shape and the same colors, so you need to attend to one item after another until you stumble on the target.

In the real world, virtually all searches can be guided in some manner. If I am looking for that coffee mug, I can use color, size, and a few other basic attributes to eliminate most of the objects in my field of view as candidate mugs before directing my attention to the remaining mug-like blobs. The set of guiding attributes seems to be limited to between one and two dozen (Wolfe & Horowitz, 2004). These include properties like color, size, and orientation as illustrated in Figure 2, and a number of less obvious properties like a variety of depth cues. The field continues to debate some candidates for the status of guiding attribute. Faces are a good example. Some people think that you can guide attention to faces (Hershler & Hochstein, 2005), while others disagree (Vanrullen, 2006).

These guiding features are properties of the target and distractor objects, themselves, but those features are not the only factors guiding the deployment of your attention. The structure of real scenes provides additional guidance not available in the random collections of items in Figures 1 and 2 (Castelhano & Heaven, 2010). Thus, in Figure 3, if asked to find a boat, you will guide your attention to the river because that is where boats are likely to be (Wolfe, Vo, Evans, & Greene, 2011). This scene-based guidance can be sub-divided. For instance, you would look for boats on horizontal surfaces

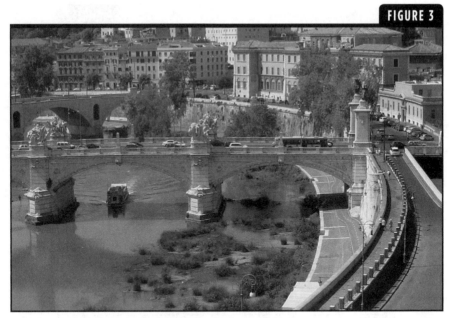

FIGURE 3

Look for a boat. Here you are guided by the structure of the scene as much as by any features of a boat. (Photo by Jeremy M. Wolfe)

because boats require physical support. They don't float in mid-air. Beyond that, once you had established the presence of water, that *semantic* information would further constrain the likely location of boats. Boats belong under bridges, not on them, even if it would be physically possible to put a boat on the bridge in Figure 3 (Biederman, Mezzanotte, & Rabinowitz, 1982).

Bottom-Up and Top-Down Guidance

We distinguish between two types of guidance: bottom-up and top-down. The differences can be illustrated with the help of Figure 4.

If you look at Figure 4, the white horizontal bar in the upper left will quickly attract your attention. The differences between it and its neighbors make it salient in a *bottom-up*, stimulus-driven manner. It catches your eye, no matter what you thought you were looking for. On the other hand, if you are asked to look for gray horizontal items, you will rapidly guide your attention to the item in the lower right. *Top-down*, user-driven guidance allows you to reconfigure your visual system so that you can look at the same display and yet direct your attention away from the most salient item and toward a new goal. You may even find that the gray horizontal item seems to gain in perceptual salience. This is a bit like entering new terms into your Internet search engine.

To summarize the basic guided search story: Faced with a stimulus and a desire to find something in that stimulus, a set of bottom-up processes direct your attention toward salient items in the scene, while a set of top-down processes guide your attention toward items possessing the attributes of the

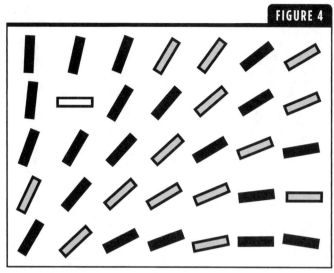

FIGURE 4

The white horizontal item attracts attention in a bottom-up manner. Other possible targets await top-down guidance.

target. In addition, the structure of the world, if meaningful, will also guide your attention. You don't want your search in a real scene to be governed in a bottom-up manner or you might spend all of your time staring at bright reflections, black shadows, or other eye-catching features of the scene (Tatler, Hayhoe, Land, & Ballard, 2011). These various sources of information are summed together to form an overall guiding representation that we call the priority map. The contributions of each guiding factor are weighted depending on the task. So, in Figure 4, when you are looking for gray horizontals, the bottom-up weights would be set as close to zero as possible because the bottom-up guidance is actually misleadingly pointing you toward the white horizontal item. Every few milliseconds, attention is redirected to the currently most active spot in this priority map and the search proceeds until the target is found or the search is abandoned.

From the Lab to the Real World

Even if visual search is a vital part of normal visual function, how could study of this topic ever be considered a matter of life and death? Of course, the title of this essay is deliberately melodramatic. Nevertheless, many search tasks—from finding your child on the playground to finding your dinner—really are quite important. Moreover, our civilization has created a number of artificial search tasks that are, at once, very hard and very important. Figure 5 illustrates one of these tasks.

Figure 5 shows a small part of the collection of cells that a technician trained in cytotechnology would examine in a Pap test for cervical cancer. In this case, the target is the black item that is bigger than the other black spots, on the left near the horizontal midline. This artificial search task is difficult (Evans, Tambouret, Wilbur, Evered, & Wolfe, 2011; Evered, 2005), and errors are serious

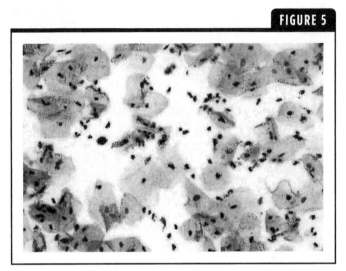

FIGURE 5

A small part of a cervical cancer screening specimen. Where is the target? (From Evans et al., 2011)

potentially—quite literally a matter of life and death. Other tasks fall into this category as well: cancer screening tests like mammograms; X-ray scans of carry-on bags for threats like guns, bombs, or knives; aerial surveillance for survivors when a fishing boat sinks in thousands of square miles of ocean. These tasks are difficult on purely visual grounds. Cancerous cells do not pop out of displays the way that a green dot pops out of a field of red dots.

Bringing the Real World Back to the Lab

In our lab, we have become interested in another common feature of all of these tasks—the search for rare items. In most real-world searches, the target is frequently present. If my coffee cup or my cat were present in only a small fraction of the instances when I looked for them, I might learn not to bother to look. However, in screening for cancer or searching for threats to air safety, we want the searchers to keep searching in spite of the odds, and we don't want them to miss the rare targets that do appear.

To study the effect of rarity on performance in visual search, we performed a simple experiment. Using a rough approximation of a baggage-search task, we asked observers to find tools in a display of other objects placed on a visually noisy background. Like the contents of an X-rayed carry-on, the display objects could overlap transparently, making the task a bit harder than the usual search task, although not as hard as the real baggage-screening task. Our observers were untrained, not professional screeners. We simply manipulated target prevalence. The target could appear on 50 percent or 1 percent of the trials.

This conceptually simple experiment poses a methodological challenge: If you want to know the percentage of targets that an observer misses, you need a reasonable number of target-present trials. Unfortunately, a reasonable number of target-present trials requires quite an unreasonable number of target-absent trials. At 1 percent target prevalence, to get a mere 20 target-present trials, we needed to mix those with 1,980 target-absent trials. This was a pretty boring experience for our observers.

The results are not boring. In this experiment, the 50 percent target-prevalence condition produced a rather standard 7 percent rate of misses. When prevalence was reduced to 1 percent, the miss error rate shot up to over 30 percent (Wolfe, Horowitz, & Kenner, 2005). To get a sense of this striking finding, imagine 20 images with targets present. If you embed those in a stack with 20 images that have no target, an observer in this experiment will miss one or two of the 20 targets. If you take the same 20 images and embed them in a series of 2,000 images, observers will now miss six or seven of those 20. We were doing this experiment in the lab with untrained observers, but we have since gone on to show that these "prevalence effects" happen, even when experts like radiologists are looking for breast cancer (Evans, Birdwell, & Wolfe, 2013).

Are observers just being careless? Probably not. Using images of luggage like those that you would see at an airport checkpoint, we had two observers independently look at the same series of 1,000 bags, using 2 percent prevalence and stimuli that looked like real X-rays of real luggage. If the two observers were just making careless errors, they'd be unlikely to make the *same* careless errors. In fact, if you have observers making careless errors, having two observers is a good way to improve overall performance. If each observer misses 30 percent of the targets, then the probability of both observers missing a target should be only 30 percent times 30 percent, or 9 percent. When we ran this experiment, however, we found that the combined error rate was only a little better than the individual error rates. You could predict the combined error rate quite well by looking at the error rate for the better of the two observers. If the better observer missed a target, the other observer probably missed it, too. Remember, it is likely that the same observers would have found that same target if it were part of a 50 percent prevalence condition (Wolfe et al., 2007).

What is going on here? In the language of signal detection theory, this is a *criterion effect*. As used here, the term *criterion* refers to an internal cut-off value above which you will say, "Yes, it is there," and below which you will say, "No, it isn't." When you aren't sure what you are seeing, your criterion depends on the specifics of the situation. For example, you catch a quick glance of someone in the supermarket. Was that the president of the United States? Was that your next-door neighbor? The visual stimulus would be the same in both cases, but you should set a very "conservative" criterion for the president decision. That is, you should require more evidence for the unlikely event that the president is in aisle 4 than for the more likely possibility that it is your neighbor.

We see this in the lab. When you are doing a hard task, there are several kinds of mistakes you can make. Sometimes you will say "no" when the target is present (a miss error). Sometimes you will say "yes," mistakenly reporting a target when none is present (a false alarm). The specifics of your task will cause you to choose (quite unconsciously, perhaps) what kind of errors to favor. Our data show that when targets are very rare, people tend to move their criterion toward "no" responses. This is reasonable. If the target is very rare, you should demand a lot of evidence before you say that you see it. That is the president-in-aisle-4 case. The problem is that this "rational" approach is maladaptive if it is important to avoid miss errors.

As mentioned earlier, these prevalence effects are not just laboratory phenomena. As experts search through the stimuli that they know so well, they too will miss more targets when those targets are rare. Experts can perform tasks that we, as untrained observers, cannot perform. However, they are still searching using the human "search engine." That search engine is very powerful but it has limits that do not go away, even with the extensive training required to become a radiologist or an airport screener. As experimental psychologists, our role is to identify the limits on human performance and to work with our colleagues from many fields to find ways to transcend those limits.

Acknowledgments This work was supported by the National Eye Institute, the National Institute of Mental Health, the Air Force Office of Scientific Research, and the Department of Homeland Security.

☐ Thinking Critically

1. How does Jeremy Wolfe's notion of a "prevalence effect" explain errors made by people trained to be accurate screeners?
2. You're searching for a lost possession, something unusual—for example, a bottle of hot sauce in a crowded refrigerator or a volume of poetry among a pile of books. Unlike an airport baggage screener, your search will be made *easier* by the item's low prevalence. Why?

☐ Suggested Further Reading

Wolfe, J. M., & Horowitz, T. S. (2004). What attributes guide the deployment of visual attention and how do they do it? *Nature Reviews Neuroscience, 5*(6), 495–501.
Wolfe, J. M., & Horowitz, T. S. (2007). Visual search. *Scholarpedia, 3*(7), 3325.
Wolfe, J. M., Vo, M. L.-H., Evans, K. K., & Greene, M. R. (2011). Visual search in scenes involves selective and non-selective pathways. *Trends in Cognitive Science, 15*(2), 77–84. doi:10.1016/j.tics.2010.12.001

☐ References

Biederman, I., Mezzanotte, R. J., & Rabinowitz, J. C. (1982). Scene perception: Detecting and judging objects undergoing relational violations. *Cognitive Psychology, 14,* 143–177.
Castelhano, M. S., & Heaven, C. (2010). The relative contribution of scene context and target features to visual search in scenes. *Attention, Perception, & Psychophysics, 72*(5), 1283–1297.
Evans, K. K., Birdwell, R. L., & Wolfe, J. M. (2013). If you don't find it often, you often don't find it: Why some cancers are missed in breast cancer screening. *PLoS ONE 8*(5): e64366. doi:10.1371/journal.pone.0064366
Evans, K. K., Tambouret, R., Wilbur, D. C., Evered, A., & Wolfe, J. M. (2011). Prevalence of abnormalities influences cytologists' error rates in screening for cervical cancer. *Archives of Pathology & Laboratory Medicine, 135*(12), 1557–1560. doi: 10.5858/arpa.2010-0739-OA

Evered, A. (2005). What can cytologists learn from 25 years of investigations in visual search? *British Journal of Medical Science, 62*(4), 182–192.

Hershler, O., & Hochstein, S. (2005). At first sight: A high-level pop out effect for faces. *Vision Research, 45*(13), 1707–1724.

Tatler, B. W., Hayhoe, M. M., Land, M. F., & Ballard, D. H. (2011). Eye guidance in natural vision: Reinterpreting salience. *Journal of Vision, 11.*

Treisman, A., & Gelade, G. (1980). A feature-integration theory of attention. *Cognitive Psychology, 12,* 97–136.

Vanrullen, R. (2006). On second glance: Still no high-level pop-out effect for faces. *Vision Research, 46*(18), 3017–3027.

Wolfe, J. M. (1994). Guided Search 2.0: A revised model of visual search. *Psychonomic Bulletin and Review, 1*(2), 202–238.

Wolfe, J. M. (2006). Guided Search 4.0: Current progress with a model of visual search. In W. Gray (Ed.), *Integrated models of cognitive systems.* New York: Oxford University Press.

Wolfe, J. M., & Bennett, S. C. (1997). Preattentive object files: Shapeless bundles of basic features. *Vision Research, 37*(1), 25–43.

Wolfe, J. M., Cave, K. R., & Franzel, S. L. (1989). Guided search: An alternative to the feature integration model for visual search. *Journal of Experimental Psychology: Human Perception and Performance, 15,* 419–433.

Wolfe, J. M., & Horowitz, T. S. (2004). What attributes guide the deployment of visual attention and how do they do it? *Nature Reviews Neuroscience, 5*(6), 495–501.

Wolfe, J. M., Horowitz, T. S., & Kenner, N. M. (2005). Rare items often missed in visual searches. *Nature, 435,* 439–440.

Wolfe, J. M., Horowitz, T. S., VanWert, M. J., Kenner, N. M., Place, S. S., & Kibbi, N. (2007). Low target prevalence is a stubborn source of errors in visual search tasks. *Journal of Experimental Psychology: General, 136*(4), 623–638.

Wolfe, J. M., Vo, M. L.-H., Evans, K. K., & Greene, M. R. (2011). Visual search in scenes involves selective and non-selective pathways. *Trends in Cognitive Science, 15*(2), 77–84. doi:10.1016/j.tics.2010.12.001

Learning

Making Things Hard on Yourself, But in a Good Way: Creating Desirable Difficulties to Enhance Learning

Elizabeth Ligon Bjork and Robert A. Bjork

Using Testing to Improve Learning and Memory

Henry L. Roediger, III, Kathleen B. McDermott, and Mark A. McDaniel

Making Things Hard on Yourself, But in a Good Way: Creating Desirable Difficulties to Enhance Learning

ELIZABETH LIGON BJORK and ROBERT A. BJORK
University of California, Los Angeles

□ **Please describe your current position and research interests.**

ELIZABETH LIGON BJORK: I am Professor and Senior Vice Chair of Psychology at the University of California, Los Angeles. My research interests have included visual attention and developmental processes but now focus on practical and theoretical issues in human memory and learning, particularly the role that inhibitory processes play in an efficient memory system.

ROBERT A. BJORK: I am Distinguished Research Professor of Psychology at the University of California, Los Angeles. My research focuses on human learning and memory and on the implications of the science of learning for instruction and training.

□ **How did you become interested in studying the facilitating effect of apparent impediments to learning?**

ELIZABETH LIGON BJORK: My interests in optimizing learning were triggered by interactions with students lamenting during office hours how hard they had studied, only then to perform poorly on a just-given exam. This motivated me to examine why students' study activities were sometimes so ineffective.

ROBERT A. BJORK: My interests go back to my efforts—as a graduate student—to understand the relationship of forgetting and learning, especially why inducing forgetting often enhances subsequent learning. My interests in the application of "desirable difficulties" were fanned by my experiences teaching and coaching and from what I learned as Chair of the National Research Council Committee on Techniques for the Enhancement of Human Performance (1988–1994).

□ **What has been the real-world impact of this work?**

Overall, the impact has been modest, but there are multiple indications that the impact of basic research findings on educational practices is increasing. It is a slow process, in part, because optimizing instruction requires some unintuitive innovations in how the conditions of instruction are structured.

A s teachers—and learners—the two of us have had both a professional and personal interest in identifying the activities that make learning most effective and efficient. What we have discovered, broadly, across our careers in research, is that optimizing learning and instruction often requires going against one's intuitions, deviating from standard instructional practices, and managing one's own learning activities in new ways. Somewhat surprisingly, the trials and errors of everyday living and learning do not seem to result in the development of an accurate mental model of the self as learner or an appreciation of the activities that do and do not foster learning.

The basic problem learners confront is that we can easily be misled as to whether we are learning effectively and have or have not achieved a level of learning and comprehension that will support our subsequent access to information or skills we are trying to learn. We can be misled by our subjective impressions. Rereading a chapter a second time, for example, can provide a sense of familiarity or perceptual fluency that we interpret as understanding or comprehension, but may actually be a product of low-level perceptual priming. Similarly, information coming readily to mind can be interpreted as evidence of learning, but could instead be a product of cues that are present in the study situation, but that are unlikely to be present at a later time. We can also be misled by our current performance. Conditions of learning that make performance improve rapidly often fail to support long-term retention and transfer, whereas conditions that create challenges and slow the rate of apparent learning often optimize long-term retention and transfer.

Learning versus Performance

This apparent paradox is a new twist on an old and time-honored distinction in psychology—namely, the distinction between learning and performance. Performance is what we can observe and measure during instruction or training. Learning—that is, the more or less permanent change in knowledge or understanding that is the target of instruction—is something we must try to infer, and current performance can be a highly unreliable index of whether learning has occurred. For a review of the history and current status of the learning versus performance distinction, see Soderstrom and Bjork (2013).

Learning Without Performance and Performance Without Learning

Decades ago, learning theorists were forced to distinguish between learning and performance because experiments revealed that considerable learning could happen across a period when no change was apparent in performance. In latent-learning experiments with animals, for example, periods of free exploration of a maze, during which the animal's behavior seemed aimless, were shown—once reward was introduced—to have produced considerable learning. Similarly, in research on motor skills, investigators found that learning continued across trials during which the build-up of fatigue suppressed performance.

More recently, a variety of experiments—some of which we summarize shortly—have demonstrated that the converse is true as well: Namely, substantial improvements in performance across practice or training sessions can occur without significant learning (as revealed after a delay or in another context). To the extent, therefore, that people interpret current performance as a valid measure of learning, they become susceptible to misassessing whether learning has or has not occurred.

Storage Strength versus Retrieval Strength

At a theoretical level, we (Bjork & Bjork, 1992) distinguish between the storage strength and the retrieval strength of information or skills stored in memory. Storage strength reflects how entrenched or interassociated a memory representation is with related knowledge and skills, whereas retrieval strength reflects the current activation or accessibility of that representation and is heavily influenced by factors such as situational cues and recency of study or exposure. Importantly, we assume that current performance is entirely a function of current retrieval strength, but that storage strength acts to retard the loss (forgetting) and enhance the gain (relearning) of retrieval strength. The key idea for present purposes is that conditions that most rapidly increase retrieval strength differ from the conditions that maximize the gain of storage strength. In other words, if learners interpret current retrieval strength as storage strength, they become susceptible to preferring *poorer* conditions of learning to *better* conditions of learning.

Introducing Desirable Difficulties to Enhance Learning and Instruction

So what are these better conditions of learning that, while apparently creating difficulty, actually lead to more durable and flexible learning? Such desirable difficulties (Bjork, 1994; 2013) include varying the conditions of learning, rather than keeping them constant and predictable; interleaving instruction on separate topics, rather than grouping instruction by topic (called blocking); spacing, rather than massing, study sessions on a given topic; and using tests, rather than presentations, as study events.

Before proceeding further, we need to emphasize the importance of the word *desirable*. Many difficulties are undesirable during instruction and forever after. Desirable difficulties, versus the array of undesirable difficulties, are desirable because they trigger encoding and retrieval processes that support learning, comprehension, and remembering. If, however, the learner does not have the background knowledge or skills to respond to them successfully, they become undesirable difficulties.

Varying the Conditions of Practice

When instruction occurs under conditions that are constrained and predictable, learning tends to become contextualized. Material is easily retrieved in that context, but the learning does not support later performance if tested at a delay, in a different context, or both. In contrast, varying conditions of practice—even varying the environmental setting in which study sessions take place—can enhance recall on a later test. For example, studying the same material in two different rooms rather than twice in the same room leads to increased recall of that material (Smith, Glenberg, & Bjork, 1978)—an empirical result that flies in the face of the common how-to-study suggestion to find a quiet, convenient place and do all your studying there.

A study of children's learning provides a striking illustration of the benefits of varying conditions of practice. Eight-year-olds and 12-year-olds practiced throwing beanbags at a target on the floor with their vision occluded at the time of each throw. For each age group, half of the children did all their practicing throwing to a target at a fixed distance (for example, 3 feet for the 8-year-olds), while the other half threw to targets that were closer or farther away. After the learning sessions and a delay, all children were tested at the distance used in the fixed-practice condition for their age group (Kerr & Booth, 1978).

Common sense would suggest that the children who practiced at the tested distance would perform better than those who had never practiced at that distance, but the opposite was true for both age groups. The benefits of variation—perhaps learning something about adjusting the parameters of the motor program that corresponded to the throwing motion—outweighed any benefits of being tested at the practiced distance. Many other studies have shown that when testing after training takes place under novel conditions, the benefits of variation during learning are even larger.

Spacing Study or Practice Sessions

The effects of distributed practice on learning are complex. Although massing practice (for example, cramming for exams) supports short-term performance, spacing practice (for example, distributing presentations, study attempts, or training trials) supports long-term retention. The benefits of spacing on long-term retention, called the spacing effect, have been demonstrated for all manner of materials and tasks, all types of learners (human and animal), and time scales. It is one of the most general and robust effects from across the entire history of experimental research on learning and memory.

Rather than describing any of the myriad studies that have demonstrated the benefits of spacing, we will simply stress the importance of incorporating spacing and avoiding massing in managing learning. Massing repeated-study activities is often not only convenient, but it can also seem logical from the standpoint of organizing one's learning of different topics, and it results frequently in rapid gains in apparent learning. Good test performance following an all-night cramming session is certainly rewarding, but little of what was recallable on the test will remain recallable over time. In contrast, a study schedule that spaces study sessions on a particular topic can produce *both* good exam performance *and* good long-term retention. Furthermore, because new learning depends on prior learning, spacing study sessions optimally can also enhance transfer of knowledge and provide a foundation for subsequent new learning.

Whether students so frequently mass their study activities because they believe that massing is good, or simply because they get behind and are forced into massed study sessions before exams, is not clear. There is recent evidence, though, that students believe that information that is more important or valuable should be studied again sooner, rather than later, perhaps owing to the intuition that restudying should happen before too much forgetting has occurred (Cohen, Yan, Halamish, & Bjork, 2013). Such an intuition, however, leads students to avoid spacing repeated study sessions—and, of course, also to avoid the benefits of spacing.

Interleaving versus Blocking Instruction on Separate To-Be-Learned Tasks

Interleaving the practice of separate topics or tasks is an excellent way to introduce spacing and other learning dynamics. In a classic comparison of interleaving and blocking (Shea & Morgan, 1979), participants practiced three different movement patterns, each requiring the participants to knock down three of six hinged barriers rapidly on a pinball-like apparatus in a prescribed order. All participants received 18 trials on each pattern, but in the interleaved condition, practice on a given trial was randomly determined, whereas in the blocked condition, one pattern at a time was practiced.

As you probably suspect, participants given blocked practice improved more rapidly than those given interleaved/random practice. Thus, if the researchers had stopped their study at the end of training, blocking of practice would have seemed the superior learning procedure. But, instead, participants returned 10 days later and were retested under either blocked- or interleaved-random conditions. Under interleaved-random-testing conditions, participants who had practiced under interleaved conditions performed far better than did the blocked-practice participants, who appeared, when tested under a random schedule, to have learned virtually nothing. Under blocked-testing conditions, performance was essentially the same for both groups, but the small difference still favored the interleaved group.

The skills literature includes many replications of the pattern that blocked practice *appears* optimal for learning, but interleaved practice actually results in superior long-term retention and transfer of skills (for a review, see Lee, 2012), and research illustrates that learners—as well as instructors—are at risk of being fooled by that pattern. For example, when participants who had learned three different keystroke patterns were asked to predict their performance on a test the next day, those given interleaved practice predicted their performance quite closely, whereas those given blocked practice were markedly overconfident (Simon & Bjork, 2001). In effect, the blocked-practice group misinterpreted their good performance during practice as evidence of long-term learning, rather than a product of the local (that is, blocked) conditions. Said differently, they misinterpreted the retrieval strength of a given keystroke pattern as an index of its storage strength.

Other results illustrate that the benefits of interleaved practice extend beyond the learning of motor skills. For example, when participants were asked to learn formulas for calculating the volumes of different solids, such as a truncated cone, in either a blocked or interleaved manner, interleaved instruction enhanced performance on a delayed test. The size of the long-term advantage of interleaved practice was striking: 63 percent versus 20 percent of new problems worked correctly a week later (Rohrer & Taylor, 2007).

More recently and surprisingly, we have found that interleaving even enhances inductive learning (Kornell & Bjork, 2008). When participants were asked to learn the styles of each of 12 artists based on a sample of six paintings by each artist, interleaving a given artist's paintings among the paintings by other artists—versus presenting that artist's paintings one after another (blocking)—enhanced participants' later ability to identify the artist responsible for each of a series of new paintings. This result is surprising because blocking would seem to make it easier to note the commonalities that characterize a particular artist's style. Indeed, as illustrated in Figure 1, the majority of participants—when asked after the test whether interleaving or blocking had helped them learn an artist's style better—definitely had the impression that blocking had been more effective than interleaving, the opposite of their actual learning. Blocking may indeed have facilitated noticing commonalities, but the final test required distinguishing among the artists, and interleaving may have fostered learning the differences as well as similarities among the styles of different artists.

FIGURE 1

The left panel shows the proportion of participants who selected "blocked," "interleaved," or "the same" in response to the question: "Under which condition do you believe you learned better?" The right panel indicates the proportion of participants who actually performed better in the blocked or interleaved conditions or performed the same in the two conditions. (Kornell & Bjork, 2008. Copyright © 2008 by SAGE Publications. Reprinted by permission of SAGE publications.)

Why might interleaving enhance long-term retention and transfer? One theory suggests that having to resolve the interference among the different things under study forces learners to notice similarities and differences among them, resulting in the encoding of higher-order representations, which then foster both retention and transfer. Another explanation suggests that interleaving forces learners to reload memories: If required to do A, then B, then C, and then A again, for example, the memory for how to do A must be reloaded a second time, whereas doing A and then A again does not involve the same kind of reloading. Such repeated reloadings are presumed to foster learning and transfer to the reloading that will be required when that knowledge or skill is needed at a later time.

From the standpoint of our theoretical framework (Bjork & Bjork, 1992), learning from reloading is an instance of a broader dynamic in human memory: Namely, that forgetting (losing retrieval strength) creates the opportunity for increasing the storage strength of to-be-learned information or skills. Said differently, when some skill or knowledge is maximally accessible from memory, little or no learning results from additional instruction or practice.

Generation Effects and Using Tests (Rather than Presentations) as Learning Events

An effect that rivals the spacing effect for its generality and its significance for instruction and learning is the generation effect, which refers to the long-term benefit of generating an answer, solution, or procedure versus being presented that answer, solution, or procedure. Basically, any time that you, as a learner, look up an answer or have somebody tell or show you something that you could, drawing on current cues and your past knowledge, generate instead, you rob yourself of a powerful learning opportunity. Retrieval, in effect, is a powerful "memory modifier" (Bjork, 1975).

Closely related to the generation effect are the benefits that accompany re-trieving information studied earlier. Much laboratory research (for example, Landauer & Bjork, 1978; Carrier & Pashler, 1992) has demonstrated the power of tests as learning events, and, in fact, a test or retrieval attempt, even when no corrective feedback is given, can be considerably more effective in the long term than reading material over and over. The reason why rereading is such a typical mode of studying derives, we believe, from a faulty model of how we learn and remember: We tend to think of our memories as working much like an audio/video recorder, so if we read and reread or take verbatim notes, the information will eventually write itself on our memories. Nothing, however, could be further from the way we actually learn and remember.

Unfortunately, the effectiveness of tests as learning events remains largely underappreciated, in part because testing is typically viewed as a vehicle of assessment, not a vehicle of learning. As Henry L. Roediger, Kathleen B. McDermott, and Mark A. McDaniel describe in their essay in this chapter, however, recent research using more educationally realistic materials and retention intervals has clearly demonstrated the pedagogical benefits of tests (for example, Roediger & Karpicke, 2006). Similar to the pattern with varia-tion, spacing, and interleaving, repeated study opportunities appear, in the short term, to be more effective than repeated testing, but testing produces better recall in the long term.

Two other pedagogical benefits of tests must be mentioned: First, tests have metacognitive benefits in terms of identifying whether information has been understood and/or learned. A student's ability, for example, when going back over a chapter in a textbook to judge whether information will be recallable on an upcoming examination is severely limited, whereas attempt-ing to answer a fellow student's questions on the chapter can identify what has and has not been learned.

The second, related benefit is that tests can increase the effectiveness of subsequent study opportunities even under conditions that insure learners will be incorrect on the test (Kornell, Hays, & Bjork, 2009). Even taking a test before a first reading of to-be-learned material can potentiate one's learn-ing of it, and not only for the specifically pretested information but also for related information (e.g., Little & Bjork, 2011). Thus, when needing to read a new chapter in your textbook that is followed by test questions, you may want to try answering those questions first and then read the chapter. Again, the basic message is that we need to spend less time restudying and more time testing ourselves.

Concluding Comments

For those of you who are students, we hope we have convinced you to take a more active role in your learning by introducing desirable difficulties into your own study activities. Above all, try to rid yourself of the idea that memory works like a tape or video recorder and that re-exposing yourself to the same material over and over again will somehow write it onto your memory. Rather, assume that learning requires an active process of interpretation—that is, mapping new things we are trying to learn onto what we already know. (There's a lesson here for those of you who are teachers—or parents—as well: Consider how you might introduce desirable difficulties into the teaching of your students or children.)

Be aware, too, when rereading a chapter or your notes, that prior exposures create a sense of familiarity that can easily be confused with understanding. And perhaps most importantly, keep in mind that retrieval—much more than restudying—acts to modify your memory by making the information you practice retrieving more likely to be recallable again in the future and in different contexts. In short, try to spend less time on the input side and more time on the output side, such as summarizing what you have read from memory or getting together with friends and asking each other questions. Any activities that involve testing yourself—that is, activities that require you to retrieve or generate information, rather than just representing information to yourself—will make your learning both more durable and flexible.

Finally, we cannot overstate the importance of learning how to manage your own learning activities. In a world that is ever more complex and rapidly changing, and in which learning on one's own is becoming ever more important, learning how to learn is the ultimate survival tool.

☐ Thinking Critically

1. What is the difference between a "desirable difficulty" and an "undesirable difficulty," and how do Elizabeth Bjork and Robert Bjork demonstrate that the former aids learning?
2. Reflect on undesirable difficulties typical of your own study habits. What kinds of learning do they impede? What might you substitute?

☐ Suggested Further Reading

Bjork, R. A. (2011). On the symbiosis of learning, remembering, and forgetting. In A. S. Benjamin (Ed.), *Successful remembering and successful forgetting: A festschrift in honor of Robert A. Bjork* (pp. 1–22). London: Psychology Press.
Bjork, R. A., Dunlosky, J., & Kornell, N. (2013). Self-regulated learning: Beliefs, techniques, and illusions. *Annual Review of Psychology, 64,* 417–444.

☐ References

Bjork, R. A. (1975). Retrieval as a memory modifier. In R. Solso (Ed.), *Information processing and cognition: The Loyola Symposium* (pp. 123–144). Hillsdale, NJ: Erlbaum.

Bjork, R. A. (1994). Memory and metamemory considerations in the training of human beings. In J. Metcalfe & A. Shimamura (Eds.), *Metacognition: Knowing about knowing* (pp. 185–205). Cambridge, MA: MIT Press.

Bjork, R. A. (2013). Desirable difficulties perspective on learning. In H. Pashler (Ed.), *Encyclopedia of the mind* (pp. 55–64). Thousand Oaks, CA: Sage Reference.

Bjork, R. A., & Bjork, E. L. (1992). A new theory of disuse and an old theory of stimulus fluctuation. In A. Healy, S. Kosslyn, & R. Shiffrin (Eds.), *From learning processes to cognitive processes: Essays in honor of William K. Estes, Vol. 2* (pp. 35–67). Hillsdale, NJ: Erlbaum.

Carrier, M., & Pashler, H. (1992). The influence of retrieval on retention. *Memory & Cognition, 20*, 633–642.

Cohen, M. S., Yan, V. X., Halamish, V., & Bjork, R. A. (2013). Do students think that difficult or valuable material should be studied sooner, rather than later? *Journal of Experimental Psychology: Learning, Memory, & Cognition, 39*, 1682–1696.

Kerr, R., & Booth, B. (1978). Specific and varied practice of a motor skill. *Perceptual and Motor Skills, 46*, 395–401.

Kornell, N., & Bjork, R. A. (2008). Learning concepts and categories: Is spacing the "enemy of induction"? *Psychological Science, 19*, 585–592.

Kornell, N., Hays, M. J., & Bjork, R. A. (2009). Unsuccessful retrieval attempts enhance subsequent learning. *Journal of Experimental Psychology: Learning, Memory, and Cognition, 35*, 989–998.

Landauer, T. K., & Bjork, R. A. (1978). Optimum rehearsal patterns and name learning. In M. M. Gruneberg, P. E. Morris, & R. N. Sykes (Eds.), *Practical aspects of memory* (pp. 625–632). London: Academic Press.

Lee, T. D. (2012). Contextual interference: Generalizability and limitations. In N. J. Hodges & A. M. Williams (Eds.), *Skill acquisition in sport: Research, theory, and practice* (2nd ed., pp. 79–93). London: Routledge.

Little, J. L., & Bjork, E. L. (2011). Pretesting with multiple-choice questions facilitates learning. In L. Carlson, C. Hölscher, & T. Shipley (Eds.), *Proceedings of the 33rd annual conference of the Cognitive Science Society* (pp. 294–299). Austin, TX: Cognitive Science Society.

Roediger, H. L., & Karpicke, J. D. (2006). Test-enhanced learning: Taking memory tests improves long-term retention. *Psychological Science, 17*, 249–255.

Rohrer, D., & Taylor, K. (2007). The shuffling of mathematics practice problems improves learning. *Instructional Science, 35*, 481–498.

Shea, J. B., & Morgan, R. L. (1979). Contextual interference effects on the acquisition, retention, and transfer of a motor skill. *Journal of Experimental Psychology: Human Learning and Memory, 5*, 179–187.

Simon, D., & Bjork, R. A. (2001). Metacognition in motor learning. *Journal of Experimental Psychology: Learning, Memory, and Cognition, 27*, 907–912.

Smith, S. M., Glenberg, A. M., & Bjork, R. A. (1978). Environmental context and human memory. *Memory & Cognition, 6*, 342–353.

Soderstrom, N. C., & Bjork, R. A. (2013). Learning versus performance. In D. S. Dunn (Ed.), *Oxford bibliographies online: Psychology*. New York: Oxford University Press. doi 10.1093/obo/9780199828340-0081

Using Testing to Improve Learning and Memory

HENRY L. ROEDIGER, III, KATHLEEN B. McDERMOTT, and MARK A. McDANIEL Washington University in St. Louis

☐ **Please describe your current position and research interests.**

HENRY L. ROEDIGER, III: I am the James S. McDonnell Distinguished University Professor in the Department of Psychology, Washington University in St. Louis. All three of us are interested in educational applications of memory research. In addition, I study issues related to creation of illusory or false memories, the relation of confidence to accuracy in reports from memory, and the study of collective memory.

KATHLEEN B. McDERMOTT: I am Professor of Psychology, Washington University in St. Louis. In addition to our educational applications work, I study illusory memories, the neuroimaging of memory using functional magnetic resonance imaging (fMRI), and episodic future thought (how people use memory to think about possible future events).

MARK A. McDANIEL: I am Professor of Psychology and Co-Director of the Center for Integrative Research on Cognition, Learning, and Education, Washington University in St. Louis. In addition to my work on educational applications of memory research, my research focuses on prospective memory (remembering to do things in the future) as well as aging and memory.

☐ **How did you become interested in how testing could be used to enhance learning?**

All three of us had been involved in basic laboratory research on the effects of testing memory. These effects are often powerful and many studies showed that successful retrieval during testing has a greater impact on long-term retention than does repeated studying. A natural next step was to ask if we could improve students' performance in the classroom from our program of test-enhanced learning. Of course, we also encourage students to use self-testing as a study strategy to promote good retention.

☐ **What has been the real-world impact of this work?**

Our work has encouraged teachers at every level, from elementary school to college and medical school, to begin using more frequent testing in their courses and to tell their students about self-testing as a study strategy. Two of us, in collaboration with Peter Brown, have recently published a book, *Make It Stick: The Science of Successful Learning,* written for anyone interested in understanding the topic (Brown, Roediger, & McDaniel, 2014).

How do you prepare for a test? If you are like most students, rereading your textbook—accompanied by underlining or highlighting—is your preferred study strategy. Perhaps you underline or highlight important points the first time you read a chapter, and maybe you reread critical parts that you marked earlier. Likely you reread your class notes, too. If these study strategies seem familiar, they are not unreasonable. Repetition often aids memory. But, unfortunately, the strategies are not particularly effective in creating durable learning. In fact, research shows that rereading has less influence on later memory than you might expect. In some studies, rereading was *no more effective* in improving learning than a single, initial reading (Callender & McDaniel, 2009).

Research by cognitive and educational psychologists has identified effective study strategies; most require more effort than simple rereading. Relating new information to what we already know, a strategy called elaboration, can make the material meaningful and, therefore, memorable. Similarly, when we outline or take notes, we recode the information—putting it in our own words—and much research shows that such active generation improves retention. Converting verbal information into vivid mental images can also improve learning. Spacing study sessions apart in time rather than massing them together also aids long-term retention. Research evidence strongly supports the effectiveness of these and many other active inquiry strategies in mastering information (Brown et al., 2014).

Research in our laboratories at Washington University in St. Louis has led us to advocate an additional strategy, which we call test-enhanced learning or retrieval-enhanced learning. As you read text material, try constructing a set of test questions (or use the ones supplied at the end of the chapter) and then later test yourself. If you can retrieve the information from memory, great; having retrieved it once, you will remember it even better. If you can't retrieve the answer, study the material again and retest yourself until you're sure you know it. But even if you are able to retrieve the answer once, don't stop. Test yourself repeatedly and keep retrieving answers. Repeated retrieval practice is the key to long-term retention (Karpicke & Roediger, 2007).

Our advice regarding test-enhanced learning represents the bottom line of this essay. In the next few pages, we'll describe some evidence that supports our advice (McDaniel, Wildman, & Anderson, 2012; McDermott, Agarwal, D'Antonio, Roediger, & McDaniel, 2014; Roediger, Agarwal, McDaniel, & McDermott, 2011).

Test-Enhanced Learning

Most students and teachers think of tests as assessment devices, designed to measure what students have learned and to provide a basis for assigning grades. In many college courses, especially large introductory courses, tests are infrequent, occurring perhaps two or three times a semester. Assessment is a perfectly valid reason for testing, but, as we have said, it can also improve learning.

Consider the powerful testing effect we demonstrated in an experiment comparing three groups who were asked to use different methods to study brief prose passages such as those you might encounter in a textbook. All participants read the passage once. Then one group (SSSS) studied the passage three more times; a second group (SSST) studied the passage two more times and then took one test; a third group (STTT) took tests on the passage three successive times after reading it once. When tested, participants simply recalled as much as they could, but because the tests were relatively immediate and the passages were reasonably short, they were able to recall about 70 percent of the information. Importantly, no feedback was given on test results (Roediger & Karpicke, 2006).

Then participants took a break. For some participants, the break lasted only 5 minutes; others were asked to come back to the laboratory after 1 week. How did the different study conditions affect later recall? As you can see in Figure 1, when tested after 5 minutes, the more students had studied, the better they did—evidence that cramming just before the exam can actually work! However, after 1 week, the outcome was completely reversed. Now students who had studied only once but recalled the material three times did best; those who had studied it three times and were tested once were next best; and those who studied material the most but were never tested performed worst. The clear implication is that for long-term retention—the kind educators hope to foster and students seek—repeated retrieval of material is better than reading it over and over.

The finding that the act of taking a test can enhance learning may seem surprising, but convincing supporting evidence has been reported in many different experiments over the years (see McDermott, Arnold, & Nelson, 2014, for a recent review of the literature). In fact, you can probably find

FIGURE 1

Proportion of ideas recalled after 5 minutes and after 1 week as a function of three experimental conditions. The data on the left side show recall on the final test given after 5 minutes; the data on the right, results after 1 week. (Roediger & Karpicke, 2006)

confirmation in your own elementary school experience. Think back: What strategies were suggested for learning multiplication tables, foreign language vocabulary, or other systems of material? You probably used some type of flash card with the problem or word visible and the answer hidden. Did you practice over and over until the information was so well learned that answers would immediately spring to mind? Such self-testing can be adopted for almost any type of material and can create effective means for learning large amounts of information and retaining it for long periods of time.

The Importance of Feedback

Participants in the test-enhanced learning experiment did not receive feedback after taking the test. As we noted, however, the first tests were given under conditions in which memory performance was reasonably good. Thus, we wondered whether the testing effect would occur under conditions where memory performance is mediocre or poor. Interestingly, the answer is *no*, or at least *not always*. If students are given a test on a large amount of material or if they are given a test long after the material has been studied, the testing effect disappears (Kang, McDermott, & Roediger, 2007). In fact, if performance on the test is very poor, the test offers no benefit at all.

Suppose a test, given under conditions of poor recall, is followed by feedback (that is, correct answers). How will performance on a retest compare with a condition in which untested participants simply read correct answers in advance? To answer that question, we asked students to read four brief articles about topics in psychology (Kang et al., 2007, Experiment 2). Each article had a different follow-up: a multiple-choice test, a short-answer test, a reading task involving the material that was tested in other conditions, or no activity (the control condition). The design of the study is shown in Figure 2. Because they were unaware there would be follow-up, all participants were presumed to have studied the articles in the same way. Moreover, information in the questions was carefully controlled. For example, one short-answer

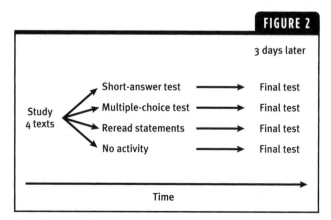

FIGURE 2

3 days later

Study 4 texts → Short-answer test ⟶ Final test
→ Multiple-choice test ⟶ Final test
→ Reread statements ⟶ Final test
→ No activity ⟶ Final test

Time

The design of the Kang, McDermott, and Roediger (2007) experiment. Students studied a passage and then either took a short-answer test, took a multiple-choice test, reread certain facts, or had no activity related to the passage. They took a final test 3 days later.

question was, "What is hostile media bias?" The multiple-choice question was the same, but four possible answers were provided. The reread-condition statement was, "Hostile media bias refers to the phenomenon in which people on both sides of a controversy perceive the media as being hostile to their group." Students who took the short-answer or multiple-choice test received feedback that consisted of statements like those presented in the reread condition. Students in the reread condition read statements for a third time to equalize exposure to the material. All participants took a final short-answer test (similar to a final exam) 3 days later.

As you can see in Figure 3, a short-answer test resulted in the best performance on the final test, with the multiple-choice test next best, although the difference between simply reading statements and taking a multiple-choice test was not very great. Not surprisingly, the no-review condition resulted in the worst performance. However, the relatively good performance in the rereading condition may reflect a flaw in the comparison condition: Participants read only statements that would later appear on the test—as if, for example, they had obtained a copy of the final exam. Nevertheless, after a delay, testing still led to better performance than rereading, just as it had before. Performance on the final test was better in the short-answer test with feedback condition and multiple-choice test with feedback condition, perhaps because of the extra effort involved in generating answers.

You may be thinking, "But wait! Maybe if a multiple-choice test had been the final test, then taking a prior multiple-choice test would have produced better performance than taking a short-answer test." We thought of that too, and we included it in our experiment conditions in which multiple-choice items made up the final test. We found that an intervening short-answer test still produced the best performance (Kang et al., 2007). The greater retrieval effort required to produce information on a short-answer test (relative to

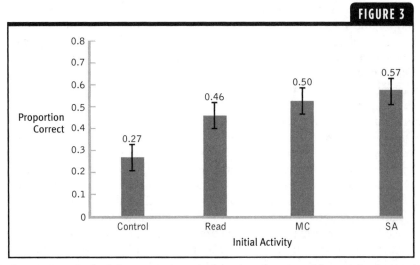

FIGURE 3

Performance on the final short-answer test is shown as a function of the activity that participants performed after reading. The immediate short-answer test with feedback produced the best performance on the final test. Data are from Kang, McDermott, and Roediger (2007).

recognizing it on a multiple-choice test) probably confers the greater benefit. Work in middle-school and college classrooms has confirmed that the match in test format from the quiz to the final test is not all that important; the most important thing is to take a quiz (and obtain feedback) in the process of preparing for the final test (McDaniel et al., 2012; McDermott, Agarwal, et al., 2014).

In other studies, we showed that delaying feedback a bit after a question is more effective than giving it immediately (Butler, Karpicke, & Roediger, 2008). Most teachers who provide feedback probably do this anyway. Quizzing can also improve retention of related but untested information (Chan, McDermott, & Roediger, 2006). This last finding has important implications for learning: Because only a small amount of material can be quizzed, a large part of the content of college courses is not tested. The possibility that self-testing might aid in the retention of material that instructors don't get around to quizzing is a comforting notion, although further research will determine whether this outcome occurs with a wide set of material.

Does Testing Work in the Classroom?

You may be wondering whether our laboratory research evidence has real-world relevance. After all, college students study for varying amounts of time and in different ways, and the time between classroom quizzes and a final test are much longer than they are in typical lab studies. We wondered about that, too. As hinted at in the preceding section, the answer is *yes.*

A Web-based course on brain and behavior at the University of New Mexico was the site of one of these experiments (McDaniel, Anderson, Derbish, & Morrisette, 2007). Students in the course, who were assumed to have completed 40-page weekly reading assignments, were assigned to the now-familiar four conditions: short-answer quizzes, multiple-choice quizzes, the opportunity to reread, and no intervention at all (control condition). Because this was a real class, of course, some students may have read the assignment multiple times, some once, and some not at all. Feedback was given after the quizzes and again for the third (read facts) condition in which students read the facts a second time to equate for exposure.

After three assignments had been completed, students took a multiple-choice unit test. The content was the same but the wording of the questions was changed, thus requiring different answers. For example, in the multiple-choice quiz, students were asked, "All preganglionic axons, whether sympathetic or parasympathetic, release _____ as a neurotransmitter." (The correct answer is acetylcholine.) On the unit exam, the question was "All _____ axons, whether sympathetic or parasympathetic, release acetylcholine as a neurotransmitter." Thus, students could not memorize answers from the quiz, but had to know the whole fact. Students in the two groups that had been quizzed did better on the exams (54 percent correct) than those in the other two groups (46 percent correct). Again, the short-answer format offered a better opportunity for retention than did the multiple-choice format, with the latter format leading to only slightly better retention than rereading, and rereading proving superior to no re-exposure at all. In short, the results of the classroom study agree remarkably well with those of the laboratory study, as well as with other laboratory results (see, for example, Butler & Roediger, 2007). Keep in mind that the lab experiment used short-answer items as the final test, whereas the classroom experiment used multiple-choice questions. We find it reassuring that the same pattern of results holds with both types of test.

In over a dozen experiments in middle-school (and some high-school) classrooms, we have also found strong testing effects (McDaniel, Thomas, Agarwal, McDermott, & Roediger, 2013; McDermott, Agarwal, et al., 2014; Roediger et al., 2011). Students in social studies, for example, achieved scores about 10 points higher on material on which they had been quizzed than on material that was not quizzed (Roediger et al., 2011). Quizzing helped raise grades one letter, from the level of about a B− or C+ to an A−.

Practical Implications for How to Study

One of us (KBM) teaches an undergraduate course on human memory, which meets twice a week for 1½ hours. As in most classes, readings are assigned for that day, and the lecture builds on and supplements the readings. However, unlike most classes, the last 5 to 10 minutes of the class are devoted to a quiz, with questions drawn from everything assigned as a reading for that day and from the lecture. Students also take three regular tests and a final exam. The news about the quiz schedule always leads a few faint-hearted students to drop the course. However, by the end of the semester, students' reactions are mostly quite positive.

Of course, as a student, you are in no position to tell the instructor how many tests to give, and it would take an unusually brave student to even broach the idea of an instructor giving more tests. How can you use the information we have provided to craft more effective study strategies for yourself? In providing advice, we draw on research not discussed in this essay (see Brown et al., 2014, and McDaniel & Callender, 2008, for a summary) to provide advice on how to read your textbook and get the most from it, how to best use lectures and lecture notes, and how to review prior to tests.

Reading a textbook may seem obvious and easy, but effective reading requires a strategy sometimes called the PQ4R technique: *Preview, Question, Read, Reflect, Recite, Review.*

- *Preview.* Skim through the chapter, looking at the headings and the figures to see what topics will be covered. If there are summaries, read them first to see where you will be heading. Also, see if there is a set of key terms and review questions at the end of the chapter, and possibly other study aids.

- *Question, Read.* If there were no key terms and no questions, make them up as you go along. List the important terms and write the definitions.

- *Reflect.* Read with an inquiring mind: Try to convert headings into questions that will be answered. So, if one heading is "Classical conditioning" ask yourself, "What is classical conditioning?" and your reading will answer that question. Jot down these questions to help you with later study and review. Some students find it worthwhile to outline chapters as they are reading, which forces them to think hard about the relationship among sections of a chapter and produce it in their own words.

■ *Recite, Review.* Reading carefully takes longer than simply blasting through the chapter with a highlighter, but studies show that students remember the material much better when they have carefully considered it this way. At the end of the chapter, review the key terms (either provided in the book or collected by you). Look up and restudy any terms about which you are unsure. If you can't remember it just after you have read it, what chance will you have on a test later? Similarly, review the study questions and try to answer them. Again, review (or give yourself feedback on) questions you cannot answer.

Paying careful attention and taking good notes in class is an art that some students master and others do not. We suggest regular class attendance, focused listening, copious note taking, and careful attention to the instructor's suggestions. Also, a recent study shows that taking notes by hand leads to greater comprehension and memory than typing on your computer (even if you have e-mail and other distractions turned off) (Mueller & Oppenheimer, 2014). Why? The reason seems to be that when students type, they tend to take dictation—just type the words they hear verbatim. Writing is slower so they have to think harder and paraphrase what they hear.

Many of these steps may seem obvious, but, surprisingly, many students view them as optional. After a class, read over your notes carefully. You were writing fast, at least some of the time, so you should go over the notes while the lecture is still fresh in your mind and flesh them out. Or, if you insist in taking notes on your laptop, you may need to edit them to extract key points. Think about what you have written.

Treat your notes the same way that you read the text: Cull out key terms and think of possible review questions. What the teacher covers in class is often what she or he considers most important and is therefore likely to include on the test. For some parts of the lecture that you might have found confusing, consult your notes, the Internet, or your instructor during office hours.

If you have thoughtfully studied your text and class notes each week, preparing for exams should be relatively easy. But, as should be clear by now, repeatedly rereading your text and notes is not a particularly effective strategy. Pre-exam time is the moment to put into practice our test-enhanced learning method. Test yourself on key terms and definitions. Examine the review questions in the book or the ones you created. If you are unsure of the meaning of a term or can't answer a question, review the book, your lecture notes, or both. Keep questioning yourself until you have the information down. Really make yourself answer the question, though; it is not enough to just think "that's familiar to me; I know I read all about that." Force yourself to generate an answer. By testing yourself, you can help gauge whether or not you know the material.

Repeated rereading can make information seem quite familiar without making it easy to retrieve when you need it—on the test. Repeated retrieval is the key to long-term retention (Karpicke & Roediger, 2007). So, even if you think you know the answers to questions, if you keep practicing retrieving them at spaced intervals, you will remember them better over the long term. Self-testing not only aids learning, but it also lets you know what you do not know and where you need to focus your efforts.

Conclusion

Repeated retrieval makes information more likely to be remembered in the future. Testing in the classroom accomplishes this goal, but so does studying by self-test. As William James wrote (1890, p. 646), "A curious peculiarity of our memory is that things are impressed better by active than by passive repetition. I mean that in learning (by heart, for example), when we almost know the piece, it pays better to wait and recollect by an effort from within, than to look at the book again. If we recover the words in the former way, we shall probably know them the next time; if in the latter way, we shall very likely need the book once more."

Acknowledgments The research reported here was supported by a James S. McDonnell Foundation 21st Century Science Initiative in Bridging Brain, Mind, and Behavior/ Collaborative Award and by the Institute of Education Sciences, U.S. Department of Education, through a series of grants to the authors at Washington University in St. Louis. The opinions expressed are those of the authors and do not represent views of the Institute or the U.S. Department of Education.

☐ Thinking Critically

1. Henry Roediger, Kathleen McDermott, and Mark McDaniel have shown that testing and retesting is a more effective way to learn than is studying and restudying. Why is that so?
2. Can you imagine *ever* asking an instructor for more tests? In what subjects do you think it would be helpful?

☐ Suggested Further Reading

Brown, P. C., Roediger, H. L., & McDaniel, M. A. (2014). *Make it stick: The science of successful learning.* Cambridge, MA: Harvard University Press.

Dunlosky, J., Rawson, K. A., Marsh, E. J., Nathan, M. J., & Willingham, D. T. (2013). Improving students' learning with effective learning techniques: Promising directions from cognitive and educational psychology. *Psychological Science in the Public Interest, 14,* 4–58.

Roediger, H. L., Putnam, A. L., & Smith, M. A. (2011). Ten benefits of testing and their applications to educational practice. In J. Mestre & B. Ross (Eds.), *Psychology of learning and motivation: Cognition in education* (pp. 1–36). Oxford: Elsevier.

☐ References

Brown, P.C., Roediger, H. L., & McDaniel, M. A. (2014). *Make it stick: The science of successful learning.* Cambridge, MA: Harvard University Press.

Butler, A. C., & Roediger, H. L. (2007). Testing improves long-term retention in a simulated classroom setting. *European Journal of Cognitive Psychology, 19,* 514–527.

Butler, A. C., Karpicke, J. D., & Roediger, H. L. (2008). The effect of type and timing of feedback on learning from multiple-choice tests. *Journal of Experimental Psychology: Applied, 13,* 273–281.

Callender A. A., & McDaniel, M. A. (2009). The limited benefits of rereading educational texts. *Contemporary Educational Psychology, 34,* 30–41.

Chan, C. K., McDermott, K. B., & Roediger, H. L. (2006). Retrieval induced facilitation: Initially nontested material can benefit from prior testing. *Journal of Experimental Psychology: General, 135,* 533–571.

James, W. (1890). *The principles of psychology.* New York: Holt.

Kang, S., McDermott, K. B., & Roediger, H. L. (2007). Test format and corrective feedback modulate the effect of testing on memory retention. *European Journal of Cognitive Psychology, 19,* 528–558.

Karpicke, J. D., & Roediger, H. L. (2007). Repeated retrieval during learning is the key to long-term retention. *Journal of Memory and Language, 57,* 151–162.

McDaniel, M. A., Anderson, J. L., Derbish, M. H., & Morrisette, N. (2007). Testing the testing effect in the classroom. *European Journal of Cognitive Psychology, 19,* 494–513.

McDaniel, M. A., & Callender, A. A. (2008). Cognition, memory, and education. In J. H. Byrne (Series Ed.) & H. L. Roediger (Vol. Ed.), *Learning and memory: A comprehensive reference: Vol. 2. Cognitive psychology of memory* (pp. 819–843). Oxford: Elsevier.

McDaniel, M. A., Roediger, H. L., & McDermott, K. B. (2007). Generalizing test-enhanced learning from the laboratory to the classroom. *Psychonomic Bulletin & Review, 14,* 200–206.

McDaniel, M. A., Thomas, R. C., Agarwal, P. K., McDermott, K. B., & Roediger, H. L. (2013). Quizzing in middle school science: Successful transfer performance on classroom exams. *Applied Cognitive Psychology, 27,* 360–372.

McDaniel, M. A., Wildman, K. M., & Anderson, J. L. (2012) Using quizzes to enhance summative-assessment performance in a web-based class: An experimental study. *Journal of Applied Research in Memory and Cognition 1,* 18–26.

McDermott, K. B., Agarwal, P. K., D'Antonio, L., Roediger, H. L., III, & McDaniel, M. A. (2014). Both multiple-choice and short-answer quizzes enhance later exam performance in middle and high school classes. *Journal of Experimental Psychology: Applied, 20,* 3–21.

McDermott, K. B., Arnold, K. M., & Nelson, S. M. (2014). The testing effect. In T. Perfect & D. S. Lindsay (Eds.), *Sage handbook of applied memory* (pp. 183–200). Thousand Oaks, CA: Sage.

Mueller, P. A., & Oppenheimer, D. M. (2014). The pen is mightier than the keyboard: Advantages of longhand over laptop note taking. *Psychological Science, 25,* 1159–1168.

Roediger, H. L., Agarwal, P. K., McDaniel, M. A., & McDermott, K. B. (2011). Test-enhanced learning in the classroom: Long-term improvements from quizzing. *Journal of Experimental Psychology: Applied, 17,* 382–395.

Roediger, H. L., & Karpicke, J. D. (2006). Test-enhanced learning: Taking memory tests improves long-term retention. *Psychological Science, 17,* 249–255.

6

Memory

Levels of Processing in Human Memory
Fergus I. M. Craik

Crimes of Memory: False Memories and Societal Justice
Elizabeth F. Loftus

Levels of Processing in Human Memory

FERGUS I. M. CRAIK Rotman Research Institute, Toronto

☐ Please describe your current position and research interests.

I am a senior scientist at the Rotman Research Institute in Toronto. My research interests focus on theoretical and experimental studies of human memory, using mostly behavioral techniques but also involving some neuroimaging. A second interest is in age-related changes in attention and memory.

☐ What got you interested in studying the effect of levels of processing on memory performance?

As a graduate student, I became interested in how attention, perception, and memory are interrelated, and this interest led to the development of the "levels-of-processing" ideas.

☐ What has been the real-world impact of this work?

These ideas have practical implications for investigations of *the memory trace.* Such investigations will take a different form if remembering reflects a dynamic pattern of cortical activity as opposed to the revival of a specific modular unit. The levels-of-processing ideas also have implications for education (how best to teach and learn) and for presurgical planning; for example, locating language areas by asking patients to carry out verbal processing tasks in an fMRI scanner.

How do you make a good memory? More technically, what is the best way to process information about an event if you wish to remember that event at a later date? Psychologists refer to the learning or acquisition stage of the memory process as encoding—the manner in which information is treated by the brain to form a stable representation that can be brought back to mind at a later time—and the remembering stage as retrieval. One central question about memory concerns the relations between encoding and retrieval processes. My research with colleagues in Toronto and elsewhere has focused substantially on the nature of memory-encoding processes, how they relate to retrieval processes, and, indeed, how they relate to other cognitive activities such as perception, attention, learning, and thinking.

When I was a graduate student and young faculty member in Britain in the 1960s, ideas about memory encoding were changing from the belief that the formation of associations between two mental events was key, to concepts derived from information-processing theory. Models of this latter type focused on a series of memory stores—sensory memory, short-term and long-term memory—with the idea that incoming sensory information was first passed to short-term memory by the processes of attention, and then transferred to a more permanent long-term memory store by repetition and rehearsal (Atkinson & Shiffrin, 1968, 1971).

This scheme was not without problems, however. Researchers talked about the capacity of the various stores, but the capacity of sensory buffers is difficult to assess, the capacity of the short-term store appears to vary substantially depending on the type of material being held, and the capacity of long-term memory has no apparent limits. As one example, the short-term store can hold only four to five unrelated words, but if the words form a sentence, it is relatively easy to reproduce strings of 20 to 25 words. Another problem arose when trying to determine the qualitative manner in which items are encoded in the short-term store. Work by Alan Baddeley and other British researchers had shown that short-term codes are auditory or phonological. (Letter strings such as PVGDCET are more difficult to remember than acoustically distinct strings such as APXIOQR.) However, other studies showed that codes could be visual or even semantic. Again, there seemed to be no one answer.

Treisman's Model of Attention

Much of the research in British experimental psychology around that time was concerned with the mechanisms of attention—how we are able to pay attention to one conversation in a room full of noisy conversations, for example. The eminent psychologist Donald Broadbent (1926–1993) had proposed a model involving an all-or-none selection device that could be tuned to accept messages of a particular type and reject others. This model was developed further by his colleague, Anne Treisman, from results she had obtained using the dichotic listening paradigm. In these experiments, participants wore headphones, and different messages were played to the two ears; the participant's task was to attend to one message and to repeat it back out loud, a method known as shadowing. Treisman found that when participants were shadowing continuous passages of prose, they could tell very little about the message being played to their unattended ear. They did not even realize that this message sometimes changed to a different language!

Participants in Treisman's studies could easily tell if the voice in the unattended ear switched from a male to a female speaker, leading her to theorize that sensory aspects of incoming signals are analyzed automatically, whereas the analysis of meaning requires attention. Accordingly, she proposed a model of selective attention in which incoming information is processed through a series of tests, or levels of analysis, in which the early levels were concerned with such sensory qualities as loudness, brightness, and pitch; later levels with detection of phonemes, syllables, or visual shapes; and the latest or deepest with meaning and implication (Treisman, 1964).

Treisman suggested that each successive level of analysis acts as a sort of pass-fail exam; only those messages that "pass the test" at any one level are sent on to be analyzed at the next deeper level. In school exams of this pass-fail type, two main factors determine whether a person passes or fails—how bright the student is and where the pass mark is set. A really bright student will pass the test even if the pass mark is set at 80 percent, but, of course, many students will fail. If the pass mark is set at 30 percent, on the other hand, virtually everyone will proceed to the next level. In her model, Treisman proposed that the bright-student factor is signal strength, so a loud or bright signal will pass many tests and be perceived regardless of attention. The pass-mark factor, on the other hand, is set from the *inside,* and reflects how probable or expected a particular signal is. Your own name is always important to you, for example, so the relevant tests are always set with a low criterion (pass mark), explaining why you hear your own name in noisy surroundings even when you can make out little else.

One intriguing result emerged from an experiment in which participants were shadowing a prose passage in one ear while, unknown to them, the *same* passage was played into the unattended ear, but staggered in time so that corresponding parts of the message were 10 seconds or more apart. The procedure could be modified so that the unattended message was gradually brought closer in time to the attended version until the participant realized "Hey, the same message is playing in my other ear!" Treisman's question was: How close in time must the unattended message be for that realization to occur? And the answer was: It depends on whether the unattended message precedes or follows the shadowed message. If the unattended message came *after* the version that had just been shadowed, participants detected the similarity when the messages were five seconds apart, but when the unattended message came first, it had to be moved to within one and one-half seconds of the attended version before participants realized that the messages were the same. Put another way, if the passage has just been attended to, analyzed, and understood, the following unattended message is also easily analyzed, and this facilitation lasts for at least five seconds. If the unattended message comes first, however, only its sensory aspects are analyzed, and the products of such analyses apparently disappear very quickly.

Our Levels-of-Processing Model of Memory

When I read Treisman's work in London in the early 1970s, it occurred to me that memory could be described in the same terms as her levels-of-analysis model of attention. Perhaps we don't have any "memory stores" as such, but memory may depend on how fully incoming information is attended to and how deeply it is processed on a continuum running from "shallow" sensory analyses through to the "deeper" analyses concerned with meaning and implication. About that time I moved from London to the University of Toronto and found that my Australian friend Bob Lockhart, who was already at Toronto, had been thinking about memory in very similar ways. Endel Tulving was the editor of the *Journal of Verbal Learning and Verbal Behavior* at that time; he liked the ideas and encouraged us to write them up for the journal in the summer of 1972. We did just that, with a lot of editorial help from Endel, and the article entitled "Levels of processing: A framework for memory research" (Craik & Lockhart, 1972) duly appeared at the end of that year.

The main points of the article included the idea, endorsed by many previous writers, that information processing consists of a hierarchy of processing stages, running from early sensory analyses, through more full-fledged perceptual analyses, to deeper conceptual analyses of meaning and implication. The other central notion was that the memory record was essentially a by-product of whatever perceptual/conceptual analyses had been carried out, with longer-lasting memory traces being associated with deeper levels of analysis. We assumed that processing could be extended or elaborated at any level but that the strength and persistence of the memory record reflected the greatest depth to which the stimulus or event had been processed. This scheme was applied to verbal materials (for example, phonological analysis, word identification, sentence comprehension, preparation for appropriate actions) but not *only* to verbal materials; the notion of levels or processing could also be applied to the perception and comprehension of pictures, faces, environmental sounds, tastes, and smells. In all these cases, the idea was that the quality and "strength" of a memory can be understood in terms of the specific analyses that have been carried out.

Our article made some further points also. One that became important later is the notion that memory performance would reflect the *amount* of processing at any level as well as the qualitative depth. We said, "After the stimulus has been recognized, it may undergo further processing by enrichment or elaboration" (p. 675). One example of this is the difference between proofreading and reading for gist—the former involves quite elaborate processing at the level of letters and words, whereas the latter involves relatively little processing at that level but much more at the level of meaning and implication. So, processing is flexible and guided by purposes and goals, but in all cases the memory record will reflect the operations that were carried out.

Another point concerned the sequence of processing operations within the analytic hierarchy. We discussed evidence suggesting that deeper analyses might sometimes precede analyses that are logically prior—for example, highly meaningful or expected events (say, simple pictures or highly probable words) may be processed rapidly to a deep level, with relatively slight amounts of sensory analysis. We commented that such stimuli "will be processed to a deep level more rapidly than less meaningful stimuli and will be well retained. Thus, speed of analysis does not necessarily predict retention" (p. 676). In fact, because of this "expectedness" or "meaningfulness" factor, neither processing time nor the amount of attention necessary for processing will serve as a reliable index of depth. This inconvenient truth got us into trouble later on with critics who (reasonably enough) wanted to see some objective index of processing depth.

A third point dealt with the concept of short-term memory. Despite what some textbooks tell you, the Craik and Lockhart article did *not* seek to abolish the distinction between short-term and long-term memory! In fact, we accepted the idea that information can be held in two different ways, but rejected the notion that short-term maintenance depended on a separate store. We suggested that in addition to the memories formed as a consequence of processing to various levels, "there is a second way in which stimuli can be retained—by recirculating information at one level of processing." In our view, maintaining information at one level is equivalent to continued attention to some aspects of the processed stimulus. In keeping with historical precedent, we termed this maintenance process *primary memory*, which in our case meant continued attention to such features as phonological properties of words, visual aspects of pictures, or even conceptual aspects of stimuli. So, rather than envisaging short-term memory as a store in which various types of items are held, we suggested that information can be retained temporarily in conscious awareness by the flexible allocation of attention to a variety of different analyzed features.

While writing the article, Lockhart and I alternated between feeling that we were really onto something, and feeling that the "something" might be rather trivial—a dichotomy later echoed by our fans and critics! One flash-bulb memory: Our fellow memory researcher Bennet Murdock came into our office late one evening and threw a book on the table and said, "You fellows should be interested in this!" The book was *Human Memory: Research and Theory* by Laird Cermak, a Boston researcher, and in it he laid out a scheme quite similar to ours. We joined forces later by organizing a conference on levels of processing in 1977, and the conference papers subsequently were published (Cermak & Craik, 1979).

Testing the Model

Meanwhile, I had been working in the lab to develop some empirical support for the levels framework. If the basic idea is correct, I reasoned, it should be possible to induce different levels of processing by asking different questions about the same stimulus. For example, if the stimulus word is TABLE, we can ask "Is the word printed in capital letters?" or "Does the word rhyme with fable?" or "Is the word a piece of furniture?" In our first experiments, we asked such questions before the word was presented briefly (for 200 milliseconds). Participants were told that we sought information on word processing and that they should answer each question as rapidly as possible after the following word appeared. They were *not* told anything about memory, so the instruction to recall or recognize as many words as possible after the list had been shown came as a surprise. This technique, known as incidental learning, ensured that participants would carry out only the type of processing induced by the question. Each word was presented very briefly to discourage further processing (although that turned out not to matter). The design crossed three levels (or types) of processing—case, rhyme, and semantic questions—with questions that led either to a "yes" response ("furniture?"—TABLE) or a "no" response ("written in small print?"—LION).

The results of this experiment are shown in line (a) in Table 1. The probability of recognizing a word correctly runs from 0.14 to 0.93—a factor of six!—despite the fact that all words were shown for the same length of time, were ordinary nouns, and, in fact, were the *same words* across conditions because each participant was presented with words under different encoding instructions. Line (b) in Table 1 shows a replication of the study using sentence frames for the semantic condition. Participants were shown a sentence with a blank space before each word, and had to decide whether the word was a meaningful fit. (For example, if the sentence was "The girl placed the __ on the table," the word *BOOK* would yield a positive response, whereas the response to the word *CLOUD* would be negative.) In this condition, recognition rates varied from 0.15 to 0.81; again a very large difference.

TABLE 1

Proportions of Words Recognized Correctly as a Function of the Initial Encoding Task

(a) Encoding Question:	Case	Rhyme	Category
"Yes" responses	0.18	0.78	0.93
"No" responses	0.14	0.36	0.63
(b) Encoding Question:	Case	Rhyme	Sentence
"Yes" responses	0.15	0.48	0.81
"No" responses	0.19	0.27	0.49
(c) Encoding Question:	Case	Rhyme	Category
"Yes" responses	0.23	0.59	0.81
"No" responses	0.28	0.33	0.62

Note: The figures in the table are probabilities of correct recognition following three types of encoding. In sections (a) and (b), words were initially shown for 200 milliseconds, with each word preceded by a question concerning either its visual appearance (case), sound (rhyme), or meaning (category or sentence frame). The questions led to either a positive (yes) or negative (no) response. In section (c), the words were initially shown for six seconds each. The results show that later recognition memory for words is greatly affected by the type of initial encoding, with deep levels of processing (semantic decisions) resulting in higher recognition levels than processing of sound or appearance. (Data from Craik & Tulving, 1975. Copyright © 1975 by the American Psychological Association. Reproduced with permission. The use of APA information does not imply endorsement by APA.)

Endel Tulving became interested in these studies and persuaded me that the 200-millisecond exposure was unnecessary. He predicted that he would obtain the same pattern if the target words were displayed for six seconds rather than 200 milliseconds, and even if the participants knew there would be a later memory test. Endel phoned me at home when the results were obtained (line (c) in Table 1) and I have another flashbulb memory of the event—the data seemed so amazing! The words and questions we used are given in the paper we subsequently published (Craik & Tulving, 1975). Try running the experiment on some friends; the levels-of-processing effect comes with a cast-iron guarantee!

One unexpected result was that the words associated with "yes" responses were much better recognized than those associated with "no" responses—for rhyme and semantic judgments at least. Our conjecture is that in the positive cases the word can be integrated with the preceding question, and perhaps elaborated by it, thereby forming a qualitatively richer record that is particularly well-recognized.

The first reaction of the experimental psychology community to these results was that they must reflect something else than the vaguely defined levels-of-processing model—maybe deeper processing simply takes longer to achieve? The theoretical ideas in the Craik and Lockhart article were also met skeptically by some critics; many of them were British friends of mine, which pained me slightly. After all, the ideas stemmed from such eminent British psychologists as Sir Frederic Bartlett, Donald Broadbent, and Anne Treisman! Probably the best critical paper is by Alan Baddeley (1978), and we presented some answers to the criticisms in Lockhart and Craik (1990) and Craik (2002). But the ideas were welcomed for the most part, and it is interesting to note that the Craik and Lockhart article is still reasonably well-cited—over 100 citations in 2008—36 years after publication!

It was exciting to work through the theoretical ideas and fun to devise experiments to test them. A research project is a bit like a detective mystery; the researcher hunts for clues that nature provides, pieces the fragments together to form a plausible story, and then confronts the suspect with a series of experiments. If you get it right, Mother Nature owns up with a smile, and the detective–researcher can file the story with satisfaction—and move on to the next case!

☐ Thinking Critically

1. What evidence supports Fergus Craik's theory that a deeper level of processing is associated with better memory performance?
2. Imagine yourself learning a foreign language or the vocabulary of a scientific discipline. What methods of elaboration would you use to enrich your memory for the new words?

☐ Suggested Further Reading

Craik, F. I. M. (2002). Levels of processing: Past, present . . . and future? *Memory, 10,* 305–318.
Craik, F. I. M., & Lockhart, R. S. (1972). Levels of processing: A framework for memory research. *Journal of Verbal Learning and Verbal Behavior, 11,* 671–684.

☐ References

Atkinson, R. C., & Shiffrin, R. M. (1968). Human memory: A proposed system and its control processes. In K. W. Spence and J. T. Spence (Eds.), *The psychology of learning and motivation: Advances in research and theory, Vol. II* (pp. 89–195). New York: Academic Press.
Atkinson, R. C., & Shiffrin, R. M. (1971). The control of short-term memory. *Scientific American, 225,* 82–90.
Baddeley, A. D. (1978). The trouble with levels: A re-examination of Craik and Lockhart's framework for memory research. *Psychological Review, 85,* 139–152.
Cermak, L. S., & Craik, F. I. M. (Eds.). (1979). *Levels of processing in human memory.* Hillsdale, NJ: Lawrence Erlbaum Associates.
Craik, F. I. M. (2002). Levels of processing: Past, present . . . and future? *Memory, 10,* 305–318.
Craik, F. I. M., & Lockhart, R. S. (1972). Levels of processing: A framework for memory research. *Journal of Verbal Learning and Verbal Behavior, 11,* 671–684.
Craik, F. I. M., & Tulving, E. (1975). Depth of processing and the retention of words in episodic memory. *Journal of Experimental Psychology: General, 104,* 268–294.
Lockhart, R. S., & Craik, F. I. M. (1990). Levels of processing: A retrospective commentary on a framework for memory research. *Canadian Journal of Psychology, 44,* 87–112.
Treisman, A. (1964). Selective attention in man. *British Medical Bulletin, 20,* 12–16.

Crimes of Memory: False Memories and Societal Justice

ELIZABETH F. LOFTUS University of California, Irvine

☐ **Please describe your current position and research interests.**

I am Distinguished Professor at the University of California, Irvine. I hold positions in psychology and social behavior and in criminology, law, and society. Also, I am Professor of Law.

☐ **What got you interested in studying the effect of leading questions on memory?**

I wanted to study a psychological problem that would have real-world applications. The problem of leading questions was obviously applicable to real court cases involving crimes, accidents, and other important events.

☐ **What has been the real-world impact of this work?**

Based not only on my work, but the work of many others in this field, the legal system has made changes. There are guidelines for how witnesses should be interviewed and handled in the legal system. There are courts that have decided that jurors should hear expert testimony from psychologists on the science of eyewitness testimony.

Memory. It's a paradox. Memory is the center of our identity. It defines who we are and where we come from. Without memory, life would not have the sense of continuity that it does. It would consist only of momentary experiences that do not relate to each other. Without memory we could not remember what we want to say. Nor would we have the sense of continuity to know who we are. At the same time, as my scientific research over the last 30 years has shown, memory is utterly malleable, selective, and changing. The malleable nature of memory doesn't matter when the changes are small and insignificant—as when I tell my friend I ate chicken last night when I really had beef. But sometimes the changes are so significant that they can lead to ruined lives.

Each year, my work brings me face to face with an important group of people—individuals falsely accused of crimes that someone else committed. Sometimes I meet people who are accused of crimes that never even happened. And when I learn more about the cases, I usually discover that faulty human memory is the major cause of these human tragedies. To put faces on some of these wrongfully convicted people, one need only visit the Web site of the Innocence Project (http://www.innocenceproject.org).

The project, initiated by two law professors, brings together lawyers, journalists, and institutions to tackle claims of innocence that can be proven (for example, by DNA evidence.) On the Innocence Project Web site, you can see the faces of actual innocence. One of the most famous, Ronald Cotton, had been identified by Jennifer Thompson, an attractive college student, as the man who raped her. Cotton served roughly 10 years of a life sentence before he was exonerated based on DNA evidence. Unlike many cases, the real perpetrator was found. To her credit, Jennifer accepted her mistake and used her newfound knowledge of faulty memory to crusade for the victims of mistaken memory—the wrongfully accused. Eventually Jennifer Thompson, a true victim, and Ronald Cotton, a different kind of victim, came together for a meeting. She apologized. He forgave her (Thompson-Cannino & Cotton, 2009).

Cases of actual innocence have been thoroughly studied by University of Virginia Law Professor Brandon Garrett (2011). It is clear that faulty eyewitness memory is the major cause of wrongful convictions, responsible in approximately 75% of the cases.

The Science of Memory Distortion

It was my scientific work on memory distortion that brought me face to face with the falsely accused. In the initial studies, conducted in the 1970s, I showed what can happen when a person sees a crime or an accident and is later questioned about the incident in a biased way. In one study, people who had seen simulated car accidents were asked, "How fast were the cars going when they smashed into each other?" This leading question led them to estimates of speed that were higher than those of people asked the more neutral question: "How fast were the cars going when they hit each other?" Moreover, the leading "smashed" question led more witnesses to later falsely remember that they had seen broken glass at the scene, when there was no broken glass at all (see Figure 1).

In another study, a simple question that referred to a stop sign (when it was actually a yield sign) led many people to believe they had seen a stop sign. In yet another study, we created a false memory for something as large and conspicuous as a barn. We asked some witnesses to a simulated

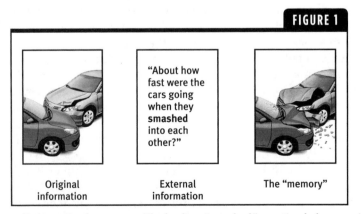

FIGURE 1

| Original information | External information | The "memory" |

"About how fast were the cars going when they **smashed** into each other?"

Two types of information in memory. The leading "smashed" question led more witnesses to later falsely remember that they had seen broken glass at the scene, when there was no broken glass at all. (Research from Loftus, 1979/1996.)

accident a leading question that made reference to a barn. Some of those witnesses later claimed to have seen a barn in the country landscape that contained no buildings at all. (See Loftus, 1979/1996, for a review of these early studies.)

In the years since my initial work, hundreds of studies have documented the ways in which exposure to misinformation can supplement, contaminate, or distort our memories. We pick up misinformation not only from biased and leading questions, but also when we talk with other people who (consciously or inadvertently) give an erroneous version of a past event (Loftus, 2005). Inaccuracy in memory caused by erroneous information provided after an event is known in psychology as the misinformation effect.

Based on this research, we know that the timing of misinformation is important. For example, if the original memory has a chance to fade, it becomes more prone to being altered by misinformation. Young children are especially susceptible to having their memories modified by misinformation. Once the modified version takes hold, people can be very confident about their misinformed memories, even though they may be totally wrong.

Eyewitness Identifications of People

It is not just memory for event details that can be changed, but so can memory for people we have seen before. Every day in the United States alone, hundreds of people are estimated to become defendants in criminal cases after having been identified by a witness from a lineup or photo spread. Thousands of studies have shown that certain conditions increase the chances that someone will be identified mistakenly (Wells, Memon, & Penrod, 2006). Even highly trained military personnel can be led, with a bit of suggestion, to misidentify a person who aggressively interrogated them for 30 minutes (Morgan, Southwick, Steffian, Hazlett, & Loftus, 2013). Some factors we simply have to live with because the justice system can't change them—for example, the comparatively low reliability of cross-racial identifications. But the justice system can change other factors, such as the instructions that are given to a witness before viewing a lineup.

Concerned about the growing number of proven cases of wrongful conviction based on faulty memory, the U.S. Department of Justice released a national guide for collecting and preserving eyewitness evidence (Technical Working Group for Eyewitness Evidence, 1999). The authors of the guide relied on findings from scientific memory research to shape their recommendations. The guide, for example, instructs investigators to use open-ended questions ("What can you tell me about the car?"), augmented by more specific ones ("What color was the car?"), rather than leading questions ("Was the car red?"). The guide offers advice about what instructions to give witnesses before they view lineups, how many fillers should be in the lineup, and how those fillers should be selected. Although at times arduous, the process of eliciting agreement among prosecutors, defense attorneys, police, and scientists ultimately resulted in a landmark product that surely is a major step toward reducing the chances of wrongful convictions (Doyle, 2005).

Planting Wholly False Memories

In the early 1990s, North America began to see an altogether more extreme sort of memory phenomenon. Some individuals were going into therapy with one kind of problem, like depression or anxiety, and leaving with another problem—"memory" of horrific abuse, perpetrated against them by loved ones, often involving satanic rituals that included bizarre and sometimes impossible elements. One woman recalled being impregnated by her father even though she was ultimately shown to be a virgin and he was sterile. Hundreds of the accused found themselves being prosecuted or sued civilly based on these suspect memories. Hundreds of the accusers would eventually retract their memories, and some of them sued their former therapists for malpractice, charging that they had planted false memories. Monetary settlements for the retractors were often high, topping $10 million in one case.

Where could these bizarre "memories" have come from? Highly suggestive therapy procedures, such as guided imagination, dream interpretation, hypnosis, and exposure to false information became the suspects.

To explore whether such techniques could in fact lead to rich false memories, researchers developed procedures that were inspired by some of the problematic therapies. Using suggestion, my colleagues and I initially got people to believe that when they were children they had been lost in a shopping mall for an extended time. The lost-in-the-mall technique used information obtained from their mothers and fathers to help create scenarios that described some true events and also the false event about getting lost. The scenarios were then fed to the participants as if they were entirely true. In that initial work, about a quarter of participants fell sway to the misinformation and claimed to have gotten lost in the suggested fashion.

Later research using the lost-in-the-mall technique showed that people would also accept suggestions that they experienced events that were more bizarre and upsetting. In one Tennessee study, about a third of participants were persuaded that as children, they had nearly drowned and had to be rescued by a lifeguard. In a study done in Canada, researchers succeeded in convincing half of the participants that something as horrible as being a victim of a vicious animal attack had occurred in their childhood (see Loftus, 2003 for a review of this work).

Telling people that their parents are the source of biographical information is a strong form of suggestion, without a doubt. But subsequent work showed that comparatively subtle suggestions may also lead people to develop false beliefs and memories. One such technique, common in some psychotherapy offices, is guided imagination, in which a therapist says something like, "You don't remember your abuse, but you have all the symptoms. Why don't you just close your eyes and try to imagine who might have done it?" The guided imagination technique persists despite good evidence that imagining an event that didn't happen (like breaking a window with your hand) can lead people to think that it did happen. Researchers call this phenomenon imagination inflation.

Who is susceptible to inflation by manipulation? Probably, we are all susceptible to some degree. But some individuals are somewhat more susceptible than others—for example, people who tend to have lapses in memory and attention and people who have vivid visual imagery. The implications for clinical practice are obvious: Professional therapists who use techniques involving any form of imagination need to better appreciate its capacity for distorting memory.

A common complaint about false memory research is the suggestion that reviving a true memory rather than planting a false one may occur. Perhaps the individual really did break a window, forgot it, and the imagination exercise revived it. Perhaps the individual really did get attacked by an animal, forgot it, and the strong suggestion revived the memory. To address this concern, researchers sought to plant implausible or even impossible memories. In one set of studies, people were led to believe that they had witnessed a person being possessed demonically as a child. Even though participants entered the experiment thinking this was not very plausible, many of them ended up, after strong suggestion, with increased confidence that this had occurred to them before the age of three. In another set of studies, many people were led to believe that as children they had met and shaken hands with Bugs Bunny on a trip to a Disney resort. This event is impossible because Bugs Bunny is a Warner Brothers character and would not be seen at a Disney resort. Nevertheless, some participants even embellished their "memories" with unique sensory details, such as remembering that they hugged Bugs, or touched his tail, or heard him say, "What's up, Doc?"

The sensory details are especially important to memory scientists because people typically use sensory detail to assist in distinguishing between true memories and those that are products of imagination, dreams, or some other process. And when we listen to the stories of others, which we do as therapists, or police officers, or jurors, or friends, we use sensory detail as a cue to tell us that we are hearing a report that is based on authentic memory. But these studies show that false memories can be detailed. In fact, false memories not only can be detailed, but they can be held with confidence, and expressed with emotion—other cues that usually make us think that memory reports are true.

False Memories Have Consequences

People who have developed false beliefs about relatives brutalizing them in childhood often act on those beliefs. They sever ties with their family members. They sometimes initiate criminal prosecutions or civil litigation against those whom they have accused. They frequently fail to get the kind of professional help that might restore their health (McNally, 2003). Sometimes they end up with a diagnosis of what used to be called multiple personality disorder and is now called Dissociative Identity Disorder. One famous case, a woman known by the name Sybil, may have been a product of suggestive therapy, or, less generously, a complete fabrication (Nathan, 2011).

Although ethical barriers prevent researchers from experimentally producing such dire consequences, they have devised harmless ways of collecting evidence about the consequences of false beliefs. In one set of studies, researchers planted a false belief that as children, participants had gotten sick eating dill pickles, hard-boiled eggs, strawberry ice cream, and other foods (Bernstein, Laney, Morris, & Loftus, 2005). Not only were researchers successful at planting these beliefs in a significant minority of subjects (sometimes as many as 40 percent), but those who fell for the suggestion later reported a decreased interest in the specified foods.

These techniques can work not only with food, but also with alcohol. In one study, people were led to believe that they had become ill drinking a particular type of alcohol (like vodka), and later they showed a tendency toward diminished preference for that particular type of drink (Clifasefi, Bernstein, Mantonakis, & Loftus, 2013). This particular line of research has unique implications for nutritional selection (and, perhaps, the obesity problem facing our society, or the drinking problems that some people face) demonstrating that false beliefs affect later thoughts, intentions, and behaviors. Of course with this ability to modify memory and control behavior comes some serious ethical and societal issues. Who should engage in this type of activity? Should we ever ban its use?

False Memories and Society

The Science of False Memory is a 557-page tome published by Oxford University Press (Brainerd & Reyna, 2005). Thousands of researchers have contributed to the solid science reported in this book. Despite more than a quarter century of investigation, however, false memories remain a problem for society. Hundreds of individuals—most of whom landed in hot water because of someone's faulty memory—have been convicted wrongly of crimes. While they were imprisoned, the real culprit was free—often committing further crimes. Hundreds, if not thousands, of fathers and mothers and uncles and grandparents and neighbors have been accused of crimes that may not have occurred at all. Some of the accused remain in prison. False memory is the root cause.

The science of false memory teaches us much about innovations that can reduce these tragedies, and police, mental health professionals, and others are already implementing some of the changes (Cutler, 2013). Communicating what we have learned to the broader public will go a long way toward minimizing the damage that false memories can cause. If there is one lesson to be learned from our findings, it is this: Just because a memory is expressed with confidence, just because it contains detail, just because it is expressed with emotion, doesn't mean it really happened. We cannot reliably discriminate true memories from false ones yet; we still need independent corroboration. Advances in neuroimaging and other techniques may someday aid in this endeavor (Schacter & Loftus, 2013). But in the meanwhile, we as a society would do well continually to keep in mind that memory—like liberty—is fragile.

Acknowledgments Funding for much of the underlying research described was provided by the U.S. National Science Foundation, the U.S. National Institute of Mental Health, the University of California, Irvine, and the Grawemeyer Prize in Psychology awarded to Elizabeth Loftus.

☐ Thinking Critically

1. Elizabeth Loftus has said, "[W]hat we think we know, what we believe with all our hearts, is not necessarily the truth." What is her evidence that misinformation can invade our memories?

2. Think of a distorted memory in your own life. What led to its creation? How did you learn it was false? What has been its impact on you and on others?

☐ Suggested Further Reading

Cutler, B. L. (Ed.). (2013). *Reform of eyewitness identification procedures.* Washington, DC: American Psychological Association Press.

Loftus, E. F. (2003). Make-believe memories. *American Psychologist, 58,* 864–873.

Wells, G. L., Memon, A., & Penrod, S. D. (2006). Eyewitness evidence: Improving its probative value. *Psychological Science in the Public Interest, 7,* 45–75.

☐ References

Bernstein, D. M., Laney, C., Morris, E. K., & Loftus, E. F. (2005). False beliefs about fattening foods can have healthy consequences. *Proceedings of the National Academy of Sciences, 102,* 13724–13731.

Brainerd, C. J. & Reyna, V. F. (2005). *The science of false memory.* New York: Oxford University Press.

Clifasefi, S. L., Bernstein, D. M, Mantonakis, A., & Loftus, E. F. (2013). "Queasy does it"; False alcohol beliefs and memories may lead to diminished alcohol preferences. *Acta Psychologica, 143,* 14–19.

Cutler, B. L. (Ed.). (2013). *Reform of eyewitness identification procedures.* Washington, DC: American Psychological Association Press.

Doyle, J. M. (2005). *True witness.* New York: Palgrave MacMillan.

Garrett, B. L. (2011). *Convicting the innocent.* Cambridge, MA: Harvard University Press.

Loftus, E. F. (1979/1996). *Eyewitness testimony.* Cambridge, MA: Harvard University Press.

Loftus, E. F. (2003). Make-believe memories. *American Psychologist, 58,* 864–873.

Loftus, E. F. (2005). A 30-year investigation of the malleability of memory. *Learning and Memory, 12,* 361–366.

McNally, R. J. (2003). *Remembering trauma.* Cambridge, MA: Harvard University Press.

Morgan, C. A., Southwick, S., Steffian, G., Hazlett, G. A., & Loftus, E. F. (2013). Misinformation can influence memory for recently experienced, highly stressful events. *International Journal of Law and Psychiatry, 36,* 11–17.

Nathan, D. (2011). *Sybil exposed.* New York: Free Press.

Schacter, D. L., & Loftus, E. F. (2013). Memory and law: What can cognitive neuroscience contribute? *Nature Neuroscience, 16,* 119–123.

Technical Working Group for Eyewitness Evidence. (1999). *Eyewitness evidence: A guide for law enforcement* [Booklet]. Washington, DC: U.S. Department of Justice, Office of Justice Programs.

Thompson-Cannino, J., & Cotton, R. (2009). *Picking cotton.* New York: St. Martin's Press.

Wells, G. L., Memon, A., & Penrod, S. D. (2006). Eyewitness evidence: Improving its probative value. *Psychological Science in the Public Interest, 7,* 45–75.

Language and Thought

Creating and Learning Language by Hand
Susan Goldin-Meadow

Thinking without Language
Herbert S. Terrace

Creating and Learning Language by Hand

SUSAN GOLDIN-MEADOW University of Chicago

☐ Please describe your current position and research interests.

I am the Beardsley Ruml Distinguished Service Professor in the Departments of Psychology and Comparative Human Development at the University of Chicago. In my current research, I am exploring three questions: (1) In rural Nicaragua, where the absence of oral schools for deaf children means that hearing parents provide a different kind of gestural model than do hearing parents of deaf children in the United States, I am asking whether this model makes a difference in the children's homesign systems; (2) In my continuing observation of the gestures that hearing children produce as they learn language, my goal is to figure out the moment when gesture no longer replaces single words but begins to convey larger propositions and thus looks more adult-like; and (3) In studies of whether gesturing plays a role in learning by encouraging children to either gesture or act during instruction, my hypothesis is that because gesture grounds thought in action, it is at least as effective as action (and maybe even more effective) in bringing learning about.

☐ What got you interested in studying deaf children's spontaneous sign systems?

I was interested in where language comes from and whether not having a language would affect the way a person thinks. I therefore wanted to study children who had not been exposed to language, and had heard that deaf children who were orally trained nevertheless used their hands to communicate. This seemed an ideal situation to explore the roots of language. But to explore the effect of language on thinking, I needed to first describe how much of language these deaf children could and could not invent.

☐ What has been the real-world impact of this work?

My studies of gesture in deaf children suggest that children are likely to express themselves in structured ways even if they are not using the language of the community. Clinicians and teachers can use the deaf children's gestures as a starting point for teaching them conventional language, either signed or spoken. More generally, because hearing children often express thoughts in gesture, teachers and parents can use their gestures to find out more about what is on their minds. Because gesturing may itself promote learning, adults can encourage children to gesture in learning situations. At the least, these gestures will give adults an additional window into what children are thinking—and the act of gesturing itself may change the way children think.

I magine what it would be like if you had no exposure to language and you wanted to make your desires and thoughts known to another person. How would you get someone to do something as simple as help you open a jar? You might instinctively turn to your hands—perhaps pointing to the jar and twisting your hand in the air. That is, in fact, the strategy adopted by children who cannot learn the language of their community.

Although many profoundly deaf children are exposed to a conventional sign language at an early age, some are not. These children lack a usable model for language: They can't hear the oral language that their hearing parents are using, and they don't have access to a language manual like *American Sign Language.* You might guess that, under circumstances such as these, a child would not try to communicate at all. But this guess would be wrong. The child will indeed try to communicate and will use one or both hands to do so. The child will gesture.

What's interesting about this finding, however, is not that deaf children gesture (everyone gestures), but that their gestures have properties in common with natural languages handed down from generation to generation. Indeed, the deaf children's spontaneously invented gestures are similar enough in structure to signed and spoken languages to have earned the label *homesign.* Homesign tells us just how resilient language is in humans.

Using the Hands to Create Language

When deaf children are exposed to sign language from birth, they learn that language as naturally as hearing children learn spoken language. However, 90 percent of deaf children are not born to deaf parents who could provide early access to sign language. Instead, they are born to hearing parents, some of whom choose to expose their children solely to speech. Unfortunately, deaf children with profound hearing losses are unlikely to acquire spoken language, even with specialized instruction.

My colleagues and I have studied 10 profoundly deaf, young homesigners in the United States, 4 in Taiwan (Goldin-Meadow, 2003a), and 4 in Turkey (Goldin-Meadow, Namboodiripad, Mylander, Ozyurek, & Sancar, in press). We are also studying deaf individuals in Nicaragua who, as adults, still use only homesign to communicate with the hearing people in their worlds (Goldin-Meadow, 2010). The deaf children's hearing parents chose to educate them in oral schools where sign language was neither taught nor encouraged, and they made little progress in oral language. With no exposure to sign language, they knew neither sign nor speech.

Interestingly, homesigners use gesture not only to get others to do things for them (to ask someone to open a jar), but also to share ideas and solicit information (to tell someone about a trip to the zoo or to inquire why a toy isn't working). These children even use their gestures to serve some of the relatively sophisticated functions of language—to tell stories, to comment on their own and others' gestures, and to talk to themselves. In this sense, the children's communications are qualitatively different from those produced by nonhuman primates: Language-trained apes use the signs and symbols they are able to develop only to change people's behavior and not to change their minds.

In Taiwan, we observed Qing, a deaf child of hearing parents, use her gestures to make a generic statement about swordfish. While looking at a picture of a swordfish, she produced five distinct gestures, illustrated in Figure 1, to make four general propositions about swordfish: They can poke people in the chest (proposition 1) and the people then become dead (proposition 2—the bent index finger is a stylized gesture used by hearing speakers in Taiwan to mean *dead*); they have long, straight noses (proposition 3); they swim (proposition 4). After gesturing about swordfish in general, Qing went on to invent a fantasy, motivated perhaps by sibling rivalry. She produced the *poke* gesture again, but this time aimed toward her hearing sister's chest rather than her own, and then gestured *dead*.

This example nicely illustrates two of the many properties of natural language found in homesign: *recursion* (the child has expressed several propositions, each about swordfish, within a single gesture sentence) and *displaced communication* (the child has described events that are not taking place in the here and now).

When attempting to determine which properties of language are found in each deaf child's homesign system, we first describe all of the gestures that the child produces, using a system developed to code the forms of signs in languages like *American Sign Language*. We then use the form of the gesture and the context in which it's produced to assign a meaning. For example, if a child produces a twisting motion in the air after trying unsuccessfully to open a jar of bubbles, we assign the meaning "twist" to the gesture. If the child relaxes her hand or pauses before producing another gesture, we consider the twist gesture to be a "one-gesture" utterance. If, however, the child does not relax her hand but moves seamlessly into the next gesture, we consider the gestures to

FIGURE 1

A Chinese homesigner gesturing about swordfish. The child produces five gestures in response to a picture of a harmless swordfish playing a xylophone in the picture (not spearing people): She points at the picture of a swordfish (= *swordfish*). She jabs at her own chest as though piercing her heart (= *poke-in-chest*). She crooks her index finger and wiggles it in the air (this is a stylized gesture in Taiwan that hearing speakers use to mean *dead*). She holds her index finger on her nose and extends it outward (= *long-straight-nose*). She wiggles her palm back and forth (= *swim*). Reprinted from Goldin-Meadow (2003a). Republished with permission of Taylor and Francis Group LLC Books. Permission conveyed through Copyright Clearance Center, Inc.

be a "two-gesture" string. We thus consider a string of gestures to be a single sentence-like unit if the child does not pause or relax her hand between gestures.

Using this system, we find that the deaf homesigners use their gestures to refer to the same range of objects, people, and places as do (1) young hearing children using words and (2) young, sign-language-exposed deaf children using signs—and in the same distribution. They refer most often to inanimate objects, followed by people and animals. They also refer to body parts, food, clothing, vehicles, furniture, and places, however less frequently.

We also find that frequently homesigners combine their gestures with other gestures. They use their gesture strings to convey sentence meanings that are the same as those of hearing children acquiring spoken language from their hearing parents (Brown, 1973) and as those of deaf children acquiring sign language from their deaf parents (Newport & Meier, 1985).

Even though homesigners do not have an explicit model to guide them in constructing their gesture systems, they produce gesture strings that are structured in sentence-like ways. For example, their gesture sentences are consistently ordered—when gesturing about beating a drum, the gesture for the object-acted-upon, the *drum,* will precede typically the gesture for the action, *beat.* In addition (as illustrated in Figure 1), the gesture sentences can be complex, containing several propositions. As another example, we observed a child produce the gesture sentence, *drum beat straw sip,* to describe a scene in which a soldier was beating a drum (proposition 1) and a cowboy was sipping from a straw (proposition 2).

Although they had not observed people signing, the deaf children in our studies were exposed to the gestures that their hearing parents—like all hearing speakers—produce as they talk. These gestures could have served as a model for the structure in the children's gesture systems. To explore this possibility, we analyzed videotapes of the gestures that the hearing mothers of our deaf children produced when talking to the children. However, we looked at them not as they were meant to be experienced (that is, with speech), but with the sound turned off, as the deaf child would see them. Using the analytic tools that we had used to describe the children's gestures, we found that the hearing mothers' gestures did *not* have language-like structure (see, for example, Goldin-Meadow & Mylander, 1998).

In sum, the children received speech-accompanying gestures as *input* that were not language-like in form, but they produced as *output* gestures that resembled language.

Using the Hands to Learn Language

The deaf children in our studies were in a unique situation—most children *are* exposed to a usable model for language from birth and have no trouble acquiring that language. But even children who are acquiring a spoken language like English use gesture and, in fact, many produce gestures several months before they produce their first words. The interesting finding is that hearing children seem to use their hands to help them learn their language.

The early gestures that children produce not only predate their words, they predict them. For example, the words that will eventually appear in a child's spoken vocabulary can be predicted by looking at that child's earlier point-ing gestures (Iverson & Goldin-Meadow, 2005). In fact, one of the best ways to predict the size of a child's spoken vocabulary at 42 months is to look at the number of different meanings the child conveys via gesture at 14 months.

In addition to predicting the shape of children's eventual spoken vocabu-laries, gesture also paves the way for early sentences. Children combine ges-tures with words to express sentence-like meanings ("eat" + point at cookie) months before they can express these same meanings in a word + word com-bination ("eat cookie"). We can even predict when a child will first produce a two-word utterance like "eat cookie" just from knowing the age at which that child first produced a gesture + speech combination like "eat" + point at cookie (Iverson & Goldin-Meadow, 2005). Gesture thus serves as a signal that a child will soon be ready to begin producing multi-word sentences.

Moreover, the types of gesture + speech combinations children produce change over time and predict changes in their speech. For example, children produce gesture + speech combinations conveying more than one proposi-tion (akin to a complex sentence, for example, "I like it" + *eat* gesture) several months before producing a complex sentence entirely in speech ("I like to eat it") (Ozcaliskan & Goldin-Meadow, 2005). Gesture thus continues to be at the cutting edge of early language development, providing stepping stones to increasingly complex linguistic constructions.

Finding that gesture predicts the child's initial steps into language learning raises the possibility that gesture could help bring about that learning. Gesture has the potential to play a causal role in language learning in at least two ways.

First, children's gestures could elicit from their parents the kinds of words and sentences that the children need to hear in order to take their next lin-guistic steps. For example, a child who does not yet know the word "dog" might refer to the animal by pointing at it. His obliging mother might say in response to the point, "Yes, that's a dog," thus supplying him with just the word he is looking for.

Or, a child in the one-word stage might point at her father while saying "sock." Her mother replies, "That's daddy's sock," thus translating the child's gesture + word combination into a simple (and relevant) sentence. It turns out that mothers often "translate" their children's gestures into words, thus providing timely models for how one- and two-word ideas can be expressed in English (Goldin-Meadow, Goodrich, Sauer, & Iverson, 2007). Gesture thus offers a mechanism by which children can point out their thoughts to others, who then calibrate their speech to those thoughts and potentially facilitate language learning.

The second way in which gesture could play a causal role in language learning is through its cognitive effects (Goldin-Meadow & Wagner, 2005). In studies of older school-aged children solving math problems, we have found that encouraging children to gesture while explaining how they (incorrectly) solved a math problem increases the likelihood that those children will end up learning how to solve the problem correctly. For example, a child who puts 11 in the blank of the problem $5 + 4 + 2 = \_\_ + 2$ is more likely to learn that 9 is the correct answer if he is told to move his left hand back and forth under the $5 + 4 + 2$ and his right hand back and forth under the $\_\_ + 2$ than if he is told to produce the verbal equivalent of these gestures: "To solve the problem, I need to make one side equal to the other side" (Cook, Mitchell, & Goldin-Meadow, 2008).

These findings suggest that the act of gesturing itself can promote learning. Extrapolating from these findings, we might predict that, for children in the early stages of language learning, the act of pointing to an object will increase the likelihood that the pointer will learn a word for that object—which is precisely what we find (LeBarton, Raudenbush, & Goldin-Meadow, in press). Gesture can thus promote language learning not only by allowing children to elicit timely input from their communication partners, but also by directly influencing their own cognitive state.

The Hands Can Provide the First Sign of Developmental Trouble

Because gesture and speech are so tightly intertwined, changes in gesture can predict, and may even help bring about, changes in speech. But what if a child is not following a typical language-learning path? Many, but not all, children with pre- or perinatal unilateral brain lesions have early language delays. These early delays are transient for some children but persistent for others. Can we use gesture to predict which children will sustain persistent delays and which children will not?

To find out, we calculated the number of different gestures and words children with brain injury produced during naturalistic interactions with their parents at 18 months, and we then assessed the children's spoken vocabulary on a standardized test at 30 months. Gesture use was highly variable in these children. But the important finding is that this variability predicts later spoken vocabulary: Children with brain injury who produced few gesture types at 18 months exhibited delays in vocabulary comprehension one year later; children who produced many gesture types did not (Sauer, Levine, & Goldin-Meadow, 2010).

These findings have both theoretical and practical implications. Theoretically, the fact that gesture and speech remain linked even when different brain structures underlie language functions suggests that early gesture may be inextricably linked to language learning. In terms of practice, the findings suggest that early delays in gesture production can be used to identify children whose language learning is likely to go awry in the future. If so, clinicians can use early gesture to diagnose which children are likely to have persistent language difficulties well before those difficulties appear in speech. We can then offer these children early interventions (perhaps in the form of more intensive gesture instruction) at a time when it really matters.

What Do the Hands Do Once Language Is Learned?

We have seen that children at the earliest stages of learning a spoken language use gestures to stand in for words—a gesture can take the place of a word that a child does not yet have in her spoken vocabulary, and combining gestures with words gives the child a way to express sentence-like meanings before those meanings can be expressed entirely in speech. Importantly, these early uses of gesture predict the entry of particular words into the child's spoken vocabulary and predict the onset of the child's earliest sentences. At the least, early child gesture reflects the child's readiness for learning language. At most, gesture plays a role in the learning process itself, either by eliciting targeted responses from the child's communication partner or by altering the child's own cognitive state.

We have also seen that gesture can function like words for deaf children who have not been exposed to a usable model for language and must invent their own. Gestures act like object-referring words in the homesign systems these deaf children create, and gestures are combined with each other to convey sentence-like meanings in structured ways. But because their gestures must carry the full burden of communication, homesigning deaf children need to continue to develop their gesture systems—and they do—building more and more linguistic properties into their gesture systems over time (Goldin-Meadow, 2003a).

Hearing children, in contrast, are learning the spoken language that surrounds them. Eventually, they will become proficient language users and will no longer need to substitute gestures for words. But they will continue to gesture. The question is—what form will those gestures take?

Speakers of all ages gesture when they speak, and those gestures are integrated in both timing and meaning with the speech they accompany (McNeill, 1992; Kendon, 1980). The gestures produced by proficient spoken-language users are comparable to those of children on the cusp of spoken language in the following sense—at times, those gestures convey information that is *different* from the information conveyed in speech. What is striking is that when both young language learners and older speakers use gestures that differ from speech to describe a problem, they are typically ready to learn how to solve that problem (Goldin-Meadow, 2003b).

The task facing the young, hearing language learner is spoken language itself. In these early stages, gesture is used as an assist into the linguistic system, substituting for spoken words that the child has not yet acquired. But once the basics of spoken language have been mastered, gesture is freed up for other purposes—for example, to frame the discourse (McNeill, 1992) or to help speakers grapple with ideas that they are having difficulty expressing in speech, ideas that rarely translate into a single word (see, for example, the math task described earlier). As a result, we see a change in the kinds of ideas expressed in gesture as children become proficient users of spoken language. The common thread, however, is that at every stage the gestures that accompany speech serve to enrich the ideas that speakers express.

To pull it all together, when young children do not have a model for language, they use gesture to fill the void. Even when children *do* have a model for language, they use gesture to help them take steps into language that they cannot yet take in speech. Indeed, gesturing may actually facilitate children's transition to language. The hands thus set the stage for language, be it created or learned.

Acknowledgments This work was supported by grants from the National Institute on Deafness and Other Communication Disorders (R01 DC00491) and the National Institute of Child Health and Human Development (R01 HD47450 and P01 HD40605). I thank the many colleagues and students without whom this research would not have happened: Lila Gleitman, Heidi Feldman, Carolyn Mylander, Cindy Butcher, Jana Iverson, Seyda Ozcalis-kan, Meredith Rowe, Whitney Goodrich, Eve Sauer, Susan Levine, Martha Alibali, Breckie Church, Michelle Perry, and Susan Wagner Cook.

☐ Thinking Critically

1. How do Susan Goldin-Meadow's findings support the idea that humans are born with an innate capacity to learn language?
2. How do you think gesturing can be brought into the classroom? Would you recommend that it should be?

☐ Suggested Further Reading

Goldin-Meadow, S. (2003). *The resilience of language: What gesture creation in deaf children can tell us about how all children learn language.* New York: Psychology Press.
Goldin-Meadow, S. (2003). *Hearing gesture: How our hands help us think.* Cambridge, MA: Harvard University Press.
Kontra, C. E., Goldin-Meadow, S., & Beilock, S. L. (2012). Embodied learning across the life span. *Topics in Cognitive Science, 4,* 731–739.

☐ References

Brown, R. (1973). *A first language.* Cambridge, MA: Harvard University Press.
Cook, S. W., Mitchell, Z., & Goldin-Meadow, S. (2008). Gesturing makes learning last. *Cognition, 106,* 1047–1058.
Goldin-Meadow, S. (2003a). *The resilience of language: What gesture creation in deaf children can tell us about how all children learn language.* New York: Psychology Press.
Goldin-Meadow, S. (2003b). *Hearing gesture: How our hands help us think.* Cambridge, MA: Harvard University Press.
Goldin-Meadow, S. (2010). Widening the lens on language learning: Language in deaf children and adults in Nicaragua. *Human Development, 53,* 235–312.
Goldin-Meadow, S., Goodrich, W., Sauer, E., & Iverson, J. (2007). Young children use their hands to tell their mothers what to say. *Developmental Science, 10,* 778–785.
Goldin-Meadow, S., & Mylander, C. (1998). Spontaneous sign systems created by deaf children in two cultures. *Nature, 91,* 279–281.
Goldin-Meadow, S., Namboodiripad, S., Mylander, C., Ozyurek, A., & Sancar, B. (in press). The resilience of structure built around the predicate: Homesign gesture systems in Turkish and American deaf children. *Journal of Cognition and Development.*
Goldin-Meadow, S., & Wagner, S. M. (2005). How our hands help us learn. *Trends in Cognitive Science, 9,* 234–241.
Iverson, J. M., & Goldin-Meadow, S. (2005). Gesture paves the way for language development. *Psychological Science, 16,* 368–371.
Kendon, A. (1980). Gesticulation and speech: Two aspects of the process of utterance. In M. R. Key (Ed.), *Relationship of verbal and nonverbal communication* (pp. 207–228). The Hague: Mouton.

LeBarton, E. S., Raudenbush, S., & Goldin-Meadow, S. (in press). Experimentally-induced increases in early gesture lead to increases in spoken vocabulary. *Journal of Cognition and Development.*

McNeill, D. (1992). *Hand and mind: What gestures reveal about thought.* Chicago, IL: University of Chicago Press.

Newport, E. L., & Meier, R. P. (1985). The acquisition of American Sign Language. In D. I. Slobin (Ed.), *The cross-linguistic study of language acquisition, Vol. 1: The data.* Hillsdale, NJ: Erlbaum.

Ozcaliskan, S., & Goldin-Meadow, S. (2005). Gesture is at the cutting edge of early language development. *Cognition, 96,* B01–113.

Sauer, E., Levine, S. C., & Goldin-Meadow, S. (2010). Early gesture predicts language delay in children with pre- or perinatal brain lesions. *Child Development, 81,* 528–539.

Thinking without Language

HERBERT S. TERRACE Columbia University

□ **Please describe your current position and research interests.**

I am Professor of Psychology and Psychiatry at Columbia University and the New York Psychiatric Institute. My colleagues and I at Columbia's Primate Cognition Laboratory focus on the cognitive abilities of nonhuman primates: their ability to learn lists of pictures and numerical stimuli and to evaluate their cognitive performance on various tasks.

□ **What got you interested in the intellectual abilities of nonhuman primates?**

I've always been interested in the evolution of language. Recently, my focus has been on the cognitive and social precursors of language.

□ **What has been the real-world impact of this work?**

Our findings offer the beginnings of understanding of the evolution of human cognition and its prelinguistic origins.

> It is a very remarkable fact that there are none so depraved and stupid, without even excepting idiots, that they cannot arrange different words together, forming of them a statement by which they make known their thought; while, on the other hand, there is no other animal, however perfect and fortunately circumstanced it may be, which can do the same.
>
> *Descartes (1637)*

Psychological science is the only life science that has not fully assimilated the theory of evolution. The main obstacle is the human mind—language, in particular. Many people are willing to accept the argument that nonhumans evolved according to the Darwinian principles of "descent with modification" as honed by "natural selection," but they balk at applying those principles to something as complicated as the human mind.

The human mind and language seem inseparable, and with good reason. Most people can't imagine that thinking can occur without language. During the last 50 years, however, many research programs on animal cognition have begun to obtain evidence that nonhuman animals might think without language, specifically by organizing information into cognitive maps. Additionally, since the 1970s, another line of research has focused on whether nonhuman animals can learn language. The consensus is that they cannot.

That leaves us with the question: How do animals think without language? I have addressed this question in two research programs: one concerned with the ability of a chimpanzee to learn language; the other, with the ability of rhesus macaques to memorize lists of the equivalent of nonsense syllables.

Project Nim

The goal of Project Nim was to teach a young chimpanzee to use American Sign Language (ASL), a complex, natural language used by thousands of deaf, English-speaking North Americans. Why ASL? The human and chimpanzee vocal apparatuses differ significantly, and chimpanzees' inability to articulate human sounds seemed to explain earlier failed attempts to teach chimpanzees to speak English by imitation (Terrace, 1979). The new idea was to use a human language that didn't depend on the vocal apparatus.

In 1973, I acquired a two-week-old infant chimpanzee from a colony in Oklahoma that I named Nim Chimpsky. I flew with him to New York, and then, with the help of a family who lived on the Upper West Side of Manhattan, raised him in an environment in which he was taught to use ASL. My project was modeled after one started by Beatrice Gardner and Allen Gardner (Gardner & Gardner, 1969) with a chimpanzee named Washoe.

My interest in the Gardners' project was based on their claim that Washoe was producing sentences in ASL. That claim was significant for two reasons: Descartes and other philosophers have argued that language is exclusively human. More recently, Noam Chomsky (1968), who is arguably the greatest theoretical linguist that ever lived, developed descriptive grammars that clarified the significance of human language. As opposed to a formal, prescriptive grammar that students learn in elementary school (grammars that tell them the proper way to speak), a descriptive grammar is an objective set of the rules for generating sentences that states how words, proper or not, should relate to other words in a sentence.

I shared with the Gardners the question—can a chimpanzee combine signs from ASL to generate sentences that differed in meaning? That approach was consistent with the general view of psycholinguists that human language makes use of two levels of structure: the word and the sentence. In contrast to the fixed character of various forms of animal communication (for example, bird songs that function as mating or "stay-out-of-my-territory" calls or bee "dances" that specify the location of a food source with respect to the hive), the meaning of a word is arbitrary. Birds cannot learn new mating calls, nor can bees learn new dances to communicate the distance and the direction in which other bees have to fly in order to obtain food.

No such restrictions limit human speakers: It doesn't matter if you refer to a particular color as *red, rouge, roit,* or any of the thousands of equivalents that can be found in other languages. However, the range of meanings of individual words pales in comparison to the essentially innumerable meanings that can be created by combining words. Although there was some evidence that chimpanzees and other animals share with humans the ability to learn individual symbols, there was none that showed that they could produce or understand sentences—an ability that requires knowledge of a grammar.

In an early diary report, the Gardners actually noted that Washoe combined signs to create particular meanings. For example, when her trainer, Roger Fouts, asked her "What's that?" in the presence of a swan, Washoe reportedly signed "water bird." That report prompted Roger Brown (1925–1997), a highly respected psycholinguist, to comment, "It was rather as if a seismometer left on the moon had started to tap out 'S-O-S'" (Brown, 1970).

I was also surprised when I read the Gardners' report, but I felt skeptical because I thought that any of the following simpler interpretations of *water bird* could apply: Washoe may have been prompted by Fouts to sign *water bird;* Washoe may have signed *bird water,* but Fouts may have recorded Washoe's utterance in the order we naturally speak; or Washoe may have signed *water* and *bird* as two separate utterances. To eliminate my doubts, I decided to run a project in which a chimp's signs and their contexts were recorded in diaries made by independent observers and then compared for reliability. Thus, the main goal of Project Nim was to obtain, for the first time, an accurate corpus of a young chimp's utterances.

In parallel with the Gardners' project, other efforts were underway to teach chimpanzees to use a language, but those researchers represented words with artificial stimuli. David Premack (1976) used plastic chips of different shapes, colors, and sizes to train a chimpanzee he called Sarah. For example, if Sarah wanted a piece of apple, as opposed to a piece of bread, she would have to give her trainer a blue triangle rather than the symbol for bread, a tan rectangle with a jagged edge. Sue Savage-Rumbaugh and Duane Rumbaugh (Rumbaugh, 1977) used "lexigrams" to teach symbols to their chimpanzee Lana. Each lexigram was a composite of an abstract geometric shape that was superimposed on a background of a particular color.

Once Sarah and Lana acquired a basic vocabulary of about 30 words, they were trained to make various requests by combining two words—for example, *give apple.* Eventually both learned to make four-item sequences—for example, Sarah: *Mary → give → apple → Sarah,* or Lana: *Please → machine → give → drink.* As compared to the free-flowing nature of Projects Washoe and Nim, the more rigorous nature of Premack's and the Rumbaughs' projects allowed them to keep comprehensive records of the sequences their chimps produced.

By the late 1970s, much evidence had accumulated purporting to show that apes could create sentences—specifically, that an ape could create new meanings by combining words according to grammatical rules. It turned out, however, that those "sentences" could be explained without reference to grammatical competence. My associates and I analyzed 20,000 of Nim's combinations of two or more signs. Superficially, many of his combinations appeared to be generated by the rules of a simple finite-state grammar—for example, *More + x; transitive verb + me* or *Nim,* and so on. Taken by themselves, such combinations provided the strongest evidence that apes could create a sentence. Indeed, many of Nim's multi-sign utterances resembled a child's initial multi-word utterances (Nelson, 1981).

However, further analyses provided a simpler explanation of Nim's signs. A frame-by-frame analysis of videotapes of his signing, however, revealed that Nim responded mainly to his teacher's unwitting prompts and that most of what he signed was a full or partial imitation of his teacher's immediately prior utterance(s). Although young children also imitate many of their parents' utterances, the relative frequency of imitated utterances is substantially lower than Nim's. Also, Nim never moved beyond the imitative phase of language development (Terrace, Petitto, Sanders, & Bever, 1979). Analysis of the available films of other signing apes showed that the patterns of their signing were similar to Nim's; specifically, that their signs were highly imitative.

The conclusions of Project Nim were criticized on various methodological grounds by other investigators attempting to teach an ape to use sign language. Importantly, however, my conclusions did not depend on the data I collected from Nim. I could have reached the same conclusions by looking at videotapes of other chimps using ASL. My conclusions could be refuted by unedited videotapes of a chimpanzee signing with a human companion. However, during the almost 40 years that have elapsed since I published my conclusions, there hasn't been a single videotape that challenged them.

Different considerations lead to a rejection of the view that Sarah's and Lana's sequences were sentences. In an analysis of a corpus of approximately 14,000 of Lana's combinations, it was shown that they could be accounted for almost entirely as conditional discriminations (Thompson & Church, 1980). First, Lana learned, by rote, to use "lexigrams" such as *apple, music, banana,* and *chocolate* in sequences like *Please machine give X.* If there was no incentive in view, the appropriate sequence would be *Please put into machine X.* Typically, the symbol for a particular reward was inserted into the last position of the stock sentence. Although Lana clearly understood the meanings of the lexigrams that referred to a particular reward (in the sense that she could use them contrastively to make specific requests), there is no evidence that she understood the meanings of the other lexigrams that composed the stock sequences she learned to produce (for example, *please, machine, give, put,* or *piece of*).

Training Monkeys to Learn Sequences

I developed circumstantial evidence that Lana's and Sarah's sequences were not sentences in experiments that showed that monkeys can learn sequences composed of four arbitrarily selected photos to which they have to respond in a particular order (Terrace, 2005). Thus, one list might consist of the items, *fish → tree → mountain → person;* another, the items, *flower → bird → rodent → beach;* and so forth. Because the selection of the photos was completely arbitrary, as was the order of a particular sequence, any of these sequences could "mean," for example, *please machine give food.* We used rhesus macaques in these experiments because they were much less expensive than chimpanzees and because they did not require extensive socialization.

In these experiments we presented the photographs simultaneously on a touch-sensitive video monitor in configurations that varied from trial to trial to insure that the monkeys could not learn the sequence as a motor sequence. Because no differential feedback was provided as the monkey moved from one photo to the next, its performance on such *simultaneous chains* couldn't be explained by traditional *chaining theory,* which assumes that a sequence is composed of items that are independent of each other. An example of a monkey performing a simultaneous chain is shown in Figure 1.

FIGURE 1

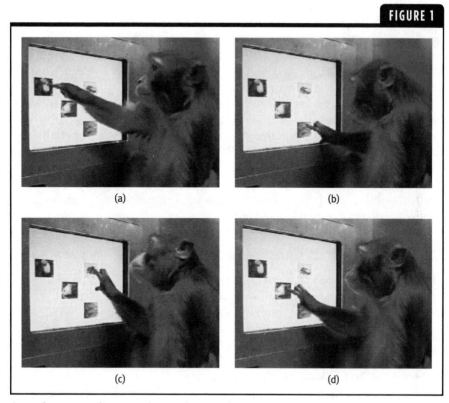

A monkey responding to each item during a four-item successive chain trial. The configuration of photographs changed after each trial. In each instance a reward occurred only after monkeys responded to all of the photographs in the sequence A→B→C→D. (Photos by Herbert S. Terrace)

In 1865, Ebbinghaus suggested that memory of lists was based on (1) associations of a particular stimuli and response as S-R units, and (2) the integration of distinct S-R units into linear chains in which each unit was linked to the next by virtue of extensive practice. It did not matter whether the sequence in question was a sentence or tying a shoelace.

In one of the most influential articles in modern psychology, Karl Lashley (1951) challenged chaining theory on the grounds that it could not explain a person's knowledge of relationships between items that are not adjacent to one another—for example, between words from different parts of a sentence. Because Lashley's arguments were based on examples of human behavior, his critique had less influence on ideas about animal cognition than it had on human cognitive theory. Indeed, critics have argued that Lashley's ideas do not apply to animals because their learned behavior does not approach the complexity of human skills and that the demands of their communication is simpler and less arbitrary than human language. That view is no longer tenable. Recent advances in our understanding of serially organized behavior in animals have confirmed that Lashley's criticisms of chaining theory apply with the same force to animal behavior as they do to human behavior.

The main impetus for my interest in serially organized behavior in animals was the now discredited claim that I described earlier that apes could create grammatical sequences and the success of a new paradigm for training monkeys to produce complex sequences without the benefit of any "linguistic" training (Terrace, 2005). Those sequences differed in many respects from the kind of sequences on which animals have been traditionally trained. To highlight those differences, I have referred to the former as simultaneous chains and to the latter as successive chains (Terrace, 2005). On *successive chains*—for example, a rat running through a maze—the choice points are spatially and temporally isolated from one another. A subject need only attend to the choice point on hand. As I will make clear in the following section, a *simultaneous chain* is much more similar to language than a successive chain. In the case of the former, all of the choice points are presented simultaneously, and an error is possible at any point of the sequence.

Thinking without Language

My negative conclusions about the linguistic abilities of chimpanzees supported Descartes' view that animals are incapable of communicating with language. But the ability of monkeys to recall difficult sequences challenged Descartes' view that, because animals cannot use language, they were incapable of thinking. In the remainder of this essay, I will describe some of the serial learning experiments I performed that provided unequivocal evidence that animals can think, albeit, without language.

What these experiments had in common was the need to represent a sequence. In humans, this is typically accomplished by thinking of the name of each item. But because animals don't have language, it was necessary to rule out chaining models in which the sequence was composed of S-R associations as an explanation of performance. It was also important to show that the sequence in question could be represented spatially.

In one experiment, four monkeys had to learn, by trial and error, the correct order in which to respond to four different lists, each composed of seven arbitrarily selected photographs. Each list was composed of novel photos. The monkeys had to guess the correct order in which to respond to the items of each list. The probability of guessing the correct sequence on a seven-item list is 1/5040 (Terrace, Son, & Brannon, 2003).

A Thought Experiment

To appreciate the difficulty of learning a single seven-item list, imagine trying to enter your seven-digit code, say *C-F-A-G-D-E-B,* at a cash machine on which the positions of the letters were changed each time you tried to operate it. You could not enter your code by executing a sequence of distinctive motor movements. Instead, you would have to locate each letter on the letter pad and mentally keep track of your position in the sequence as you pressed different buttons. This means that you would have to deduce your code by *trial and error.*

Any error would terminate a trial and result in a new trial in which the letters were displayed in a different configuration. To determine your code, you would have to recall the consequences of any of the 36 types of logical errors you might make while attempting to produce the required sequence (21 types of forward errors and 15 types of backward errors). Further, you would have to determine the first letter without getting any money from the cash machine. This is precisely the type of problem the monkeys had to solve at the start of training on each of the four seven-item lists on which they were trained. Instead of letters, the monkeys had to respond to photographs. Instead of cash, they were given banana pellets.

All four monkeys learned all four of the seven-item lists. Indeed, the monkeys became progressively more efficient at deducing the correct order in which to respond during the course of learning each list. As shown in Figure 2, they barely exceeded the minimum number of logical guesses needed to identify the first two items in the final seven-item list. When all of the lists were presented during the same session, a different list on each trial, the monkeys responded at high levels of accuracy to each list.

In a separate experiment, monkeys were tested on their ability to apply their knowledge of four different seven-item lists on a novel task. The monkeys were shown all of the 336 pairs that could be derived from the 28 items used to construct the four seven-item lists on which they were trained. The

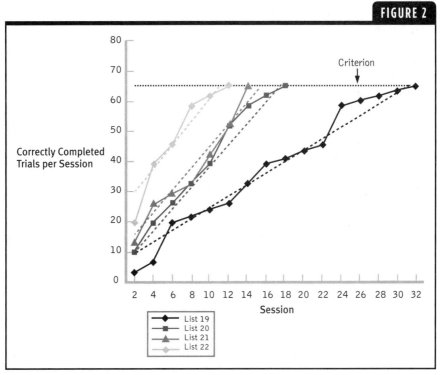

FIGURE 2

Acquisition of serial expertise. The mean accuracy of responding on each seven-item list during even-numbered sessions. The probability of executing a new seven-item list correctly by chance, assuming no backward errors, is $1/5040 = 1/7!$ Note that the X axis is session (not list). (Terrace, Son, & Brannon, 2003. Copyright © 2003 by BLACKWELL PUBLISHING LTD. Reprinted by permission of SAGE publications.)

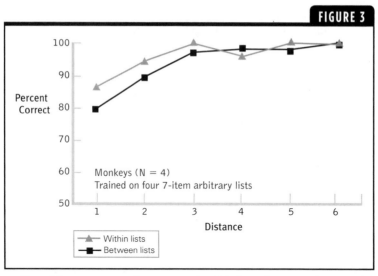

Distance effects. Mean accuracy to between- and within-list subsets as a function of distance between items on original lists in the Terrace, Son, and Brannon (2003) experiment. Copyright © 2003 by BLACKWELL PUBLISHING LTD. Reprinted by permission of SAGE publications.

pairs were always composed of items whose ordinal positions differed, for example, B_1-C_3, D_2-F_4, but never B_1-B_1 or C_3-C_3, and so on. Monkeys were rewarded for responding to the items in each pair in the order specified by their ordinal positions on the original list. As shown in Figure 3, monkeys responded at the same high level of accuracy (91 percent) on the *first* occasion on which each pair was presented, whether the items were drawn from the same or from *different* lists. For example, they were equally adept at responding in the correct order to the second item of the third seven-item list and the sixth item of the first seven-item list (a between-list pair) as they were to the second and the sixth item of the fourth seven-item list (a within-list pair).

Recent experiments on serial learning revealed that the representations that a monkey forms while learning a list is remarkably flexible. In one experiment, lists were trained by the transitive inference paradigm (TI), a paradigm that trains knowledge of lists of *n* items by presenting only two items on each trial. Consider a seven-item list, A→B→C→D→E→F→G. Subjects were never exposed to all seven items at the same time, as they would have been on a simultaneous training paradigm. Instead, they were trained on trials that only displayed two adjacent items (AB, BC, CD, DE, EF, or FG). The task was to choose the item that was "earlier" if all the items were presented simultaneously (for example, A on AB trials; B on BC trials, and so on). Following training on the six pairs of adjacent items that could be derived from a seven-item list, subjects were tested on all six adjacent and nine nonadjacent pairs. Accuracy of responding to nonadjacent items was at least as reliable as it was to adjacent items. These results showed that subjects could represent the ordinal positions of all of the items even though they were only trained on adjacent pairs.

Of greater relevance to our understanding of the serial knowledge of a nonhuman primate was their performance on transfer tests. In one experiment, transfer from TI training was tested on a simultaneous chaining paradigm with the same items (Jensen, Altschul, Danly, & Terrace, 2013). Transfer was immediate and virtually error-free, as compared with the performance of control subjects that had no prior training with those items. Transfer was also immediate when subjects were first trained on a simultaneous chaining paradigm and then tested with the same items on a TI paradigm.

The sequences that the monkeys learned in these experiments are by far the most difficult lists ever mastered by any nonhuman primate, including those trained in experiments on the linguistic and numerical abilities of apes. Indeed, their performance probably does not reflect the upper limit of a monkey's serial capacity. The ease with which they learned seven-item lists and the steady decrease in the number of sessions they needed to master new lists suggests that they could master longer lists. The monkeys' performance on the pair-wise test is significant because it showed that they could compare representations of the ordinal position of each item from each list and then apply that knowledge to solve a novel problem. Specifically, their performance shows that each monkey represented, in long-term memory, the ordinal position of items from each of the four seven-item lists they had learned and that they were able to compare, in working memory, the ordinal positions of any two items from any of the seven-item lists. Similarly, their performance on the transfer experiment showed that their knowledge of ordinal position is not specific to a particular training method. Such performance on serial tasks is beyond the scope of any contemporary theories of animal cognition.

Having observed monkeys perform so well on sequences based on arbitrary items, I felt encouraged to train them on various other tasks. For example, during the last 10 years, we have trained monkeys to learn lists based on numerical quantity (Brannon & Terrace, 1998) and to engage in a metacognitive task that requires them to indicate their confidence in the accuracy of their response (Kornell, Son, & Terrace, 2007). These and other experiments suggest that we have just scratched the surface of a monkey's ability to think without language.

☐ Thinking Critically

1. Why did Herbert Terrace choose macaques for his experimental subjects, and what cognitive-perceptual capacities underlie their remarkable ability to engage in high-level tasks without the aid of language?
2. The issue of ape language remains a controversial topic in psychology. Where do you stand, and what piece of evidence most persuaded you to take this stance?

☐ Suggested Further Reading

Terrace, H. S. (1979). *Nim.* New York: Knopf.

Wasserman, E. A., & Zentall, T. R. (2012). *The Oxford handbook of comparative cognition.* New York: Oxford University Press.

☐ References

Brannon, E. M., & Terrace, H. S. (1998). Ordering of the numerosities 1–9 by monkeys. *Science, 282,* 746–749.

Brown, R. (1970). *Psycholinguistics: Selected papers by Roger Brown.* New York: The Free Press.

Gardner, B. T., & Gardner, R. A. (1969). Teaching sign language to a chimpanzee. *Science, 162,* 664–672.

Jensen G., Altschul D., Danly E., & Terrace H. (2013). Transfer of a serial representation between two distinct tasks by rhesus macaques. *PLoS ONE, 8*(7).

Kornell, N., Son, L. K., & Terrace, H. S. (2007). Transfer of metacognitive skills and hint seeking in monkeys. *Psychological Science, 18*(1), 4–71.

Lashley, K. S. (1951). The problem of serial order in behavior. In L. A. Jeffress (Ed.), *Hixon symposium on cerebral mechanisms in behavior* (pp. 112–136). New York: John Wiley & Sons.

Nelson, K. (1981). Individual differences in language development: Implications for development and language. *Developmental Psychology, 17,* 170–187.

Premack, D. (1976). *Intelligence in ape and man.* Hillsdale, NJ: Lawrence Erlbaum Associates.

Rumbaugh, D. M. (1977). *Language learning by a chimpanzee: The Lana project.* New York: Academic Press.

Terrace, H. S. (1979). *Nim.* New York: Knopf.

Terrace, H. S. (2002). Serial expertise and the evolution of language. In Wray, J. H. A., & Newmeyer, F. J. (Eds.), *The transition to language* (pp. 64–90). New York: Oxford University Press.

Terrace, H. S. (2005). The simultaneous chain: A new approach to serial learning. *Trends in Cognitive Science, 9,* 202–210.

Terrace, H. S., Petitto, L. A., Sanders, R. J., & Bever, T. G. (1979). Can an ape create a sentence? *Science, 206,* 891–902.

Terrace, H. S., Son, L. K., & Brannon, E. M. (2003). Serial expertise of rhesus macaques. *Psychological Science, 14*(1), 66–73.

Thompson, C. R., & Church, R. M. (1980). An explanation of the language of a chimpanzee. *Science, 208,* 313–314.

Consciousness

Thinking About Consciousness

BERNARD J. BAARS The Neurosciences Institute

☐ Please describe your current position and research interests.

I work constantly to update my college textbook, *Cognition, Brain, and Consciousness: An Introduction to Cognitive Neuroscience.* I am also affiliated with the Neurosciences Institute, headed by Nobel Laureate Gerald Edelman, and I do collaborative research with Professor Stan Franklin at the University of Memphis on large-scale artificial intelligence systems that perform human-like functions, including approximations to computational consciousness. The ethical and legal implications of the return to the study of consciousness is another major focus of interest.

☐ How did you become interested in studying consciousness as such?

How could anybody who is interested in the human condition avoid it? I found it difficult as a student to understand why it was avoided so much. One of my hopes is to promote integration of the great philosophical and humanistic traditions of consciousness studies with science.

☐ What has been the real-world impact of this work?

The journal and scientific association I co-founded have helped to bring out a large amount of excellent scientific and medical research. For example, we are getting closer to a brain index for conscious processes—a very difficult feat. Medical research has also shown that diagnosed coma patients have intermittent conscious experiences about 40 percent of the time. We now know much more about consciousness in other species. The old saying is that "nothing is as practical as a good theory." We are beginning to see how that works in consciousness science.

We are all conscious beings, as we discover every morning when we wake up to a new day. But consciousness is not something that can be observed directly, at least not in the public domain of normal science. People can, of course, tell others about their conscious experiences, or they can signal their experiences through some voluntary action like pressing the accelerator in an automobile when the traffic light turns green. In brain science, we can record the activity of neurons and use the resulting overall record (an electroencephalogram, or EEG) to detect gross differences in brain activity between normal waking and deep (slow-wave) sleep (Crick & Koch, 2003; Edelman & Tononi, 2001).

In contrast to people's ability to report conscious events accurately, we have no access to the unconscious processes that are constantly ongoing in our brains. For example, over-learned habits, like the details of riding a bicycle, tend to become unconscious. Our own speech movements—of the tongue, lips, and vocal cords—are not under direct voluntary control, unless we get very clear conscious feedback about their movements. The cerebellum, a giant clump of neurons tucked under the back of the cortex, is believed to function unconsciously. People with bilateral damage to the cerebellum are conscious, but they lose the ability to control fine motor movement. And in the last 15 years or so, evidence has grown that the brain has an unconscious pathway through which visual information flows (called the dorsal stream), stretching from the visual cortex to the parietal regions, which is used for spatial framing and even visually guided reaching for objects within arm's reach. So even in the waking brain, many unconscious processes are active every second of the day.

The first obstacle in dealing with consciousness as a scientific topic arises from the tangled thicket of conflicting ideas that surrounds the topic. One philosophical debate alone, the mind-body debate, has a relevant literature extending from the Upanishads to the latest philosophical journals— 4,000 years of serious thought. But one time-honored strategy in science is to put aside philosophical issues for a time by focusing on empirically decidable ones.

The Evidence

How are we to discover empirical evidence about consciousness? Nineteenth-century psychologists like Wilhelm Wundt (1832–1920) and William James (1842–1910) believed that the nature of consciousness was the fundamental problem for psychology, but they had remarkably little to say about it as such. In a way, they took the reality of personal consciousness to be so obvious that it could not be doubted or explained. Freud and thinkers in the psychodynamic tradition have much to say about unconscious motivations, but they also took conscious experience largely for granted. Behaviorists working in the first half of the twentieth century tended to discourage a consideration of consciousness, and even cognitive psychologists avoided it until the last decade or two.

In truth, the facts of consciousness are all around us, ready to be studied. Practically all findings in psychology involve conscious experience, as you know if you've ever participated in an experiment. A psychologist can no more avoid consciousness than a physicist can evade gravity. A number of scientists have been focusing on consciousness by comparing conscious versus unconscious events—the ones people can tell us about versus the ones they can't.

This idea goes back to William James' *The Principles of Psychology* (1890). James proposed contrasting comparable conscious and nonconscious events as a way of focusing on the issue of consciousness as such. We call the resulting method contrastive analysis. One can think of contrastive analysis as an experiment in which consciousness is an experimental variable and everything else is held as constant as possible. A wealth of information has now accumulated based on this reasoning. In recent years, thousands of experiments have been published on the topic of human consciousness, many of them using this kind of comparison.

In one famous, well-studied technique, called binocular rivalry, one image is presented to the left eye, and a very different image is presented to the right eye. The two images are so different that the brain cannot fuse them into a single image, the way it does in normal vision when we look at a coffee cup on a table in front of us. Instead, the conscious part of the brain flips back and forth between the two images, often for several seconds each. We see one image (for instance, a smiley face) or another (a sunburst image). But when the smiley face is not conscious during binocular rivalry, it still is projected on the retina, just as before. The switch between the two stimuli takes place inside the brain.

Where and how does the brain decide which image is going to be conscious and which is not? Current evidence from animal and human studies suggests that visual objects "become conscious" when the brain is able to put together multiple maps of the visual input. You can think of the visual brain as a stack of maps of the scene your eyes are looking at at any given moment in time. Every fraction of a second, the retina takes a detailed snapshot, a "map" of the visual input, which is echoed at the next level of the thalamus and the first visual area of cortex. Next, the detailed map is taken apart into separate visual maps for colors, for edges between light and dark regions, for movement, and for shapes. All of those maps preserve the spatial location of the thing you are looking at, so that there is a point-to-point correspondence, a consistent stack of "visuotopic" maps. But we do not see a world of separate visual features—no points of light, no isolated patches of color, and not just one momentary snapshot at a time. Rather, we see a white cat jumping in a single graceful bound from the floor to the kitchen counter. Our conscious experiences are about an integrated world of objects in motion.

The best evidence we have today is that all the separate "feature maps" for visual location, color, shape, movement, and object identity are put together in the posterior half of the brain, terminating in the lower part of the temporal lobe. Studies of binocular rivalry in monkeys and humans show that this is where the information for the conscious stream comes together to make an integrated visual experience (Logothetis, 1998). Because all the visual maps are firing neurons in the same map coordinates, we find regular synchronized oscillations among the input maps, like a surfers' beach wave that just builds and builds on itself. In the brain, those oscillations among visual maps are believed to run around 30 Hz and higher. Like the surfers' wave, the activity in these maps becomes higher and higher as long as its locations and features are mutually consistent. A conscious visual object like a coffee cup seems to be made up of a lot of such visual maps synched together to produce high, synchronous waves, to bring the location, shape, and colors of the coffee cup into an integrated wave of brain activity (Varela, Lachaux, Rodriguez, & Martinerie, 2001).

But is that enough for conscious perception?

Global Workspace Theory: A Chat Room on the Brain Web

What about the rest of the brain? Is it enough for the visual cortex to have synchronized input maps of a visual coffee cup to make it conscious? Almost 30 years ago, I argued that stimulus integration is not enough for consciousness (Baars, 1983). After all, if you were to try to listen to your favorite music and understand this essay at the same time, you'll find out pretty quickly that you can't do both. Listening and studying interfere with each other. (I'm sorry, but it's true!)

And yet, why couldn't the brain, with its tens of billions of active neurons, just integrate those two streams of information at the same moment in time? If stimulus integration is enough for consciousness, you could be conscious of a textbook, a conversation with a friend, the heavy traffic around your car, and all the good things you might eat for lunch. Why can't we be conscious of everything all at once, even with different or contradictory streams of information?

The trouble with the "stimulus integration" explanation for conscious perception is that it doesn't explain the radical limited capacity of moment-to-moment conscious events. Consciousness is often compared to a stream, with one thought or percept coming after the next. And very careful experiments on the moment-to-moment limitations on conscious contents show that the window of consciousness is even smaller than we think. For example, the snapshots of the visual world that our eyes take in at any single moment are keyhole-sized. Our eyes jump from one place to another in the visual scene in front of us and take in narrow snapshots. The brain puts all of these foveal fixations, or snapshots, together, so that we have the sense of seeing the entire scene in front of us. But momentary input is remarkably small. That's why magicians can trick your eyes, by drawing your conscious vision in one place, while right in front of you (but outside of the fovea) the trickster is making tennis balls disappear or slipping new playing cards into a deck.

But notice a huge advantage of consciousness, namely its ability to access large amounts of information. An educated person may have a vocabulary of 100,000 words. Each word that we know can connect to a whole network of related ideas, sounds, and speech gestures. We can recognize literally thousands of different people (which doesn't mean we remember their names, of course). We can recognize a movie scene from many years ago, without trying to memorize it. Our access to information stored in the brain and in the world is huge even though our momentary conscious snapshots are small (Baars, 2002).

Do other systems have these properties? I believe so. Examples are the World Wide Web, radio stations, and gigantic stadiums. These systems involve massively parallel processing: Many complex and sophisticated things are happening at the same moment in time. The Web is constantly buzzing with activity all around the world. A radio station may broadcast a simple song, but it can be heard by thousands of people, all with their own thoughts and feelings associated with the song. Such massively parallel information-processing systems often operate through a narrow, limited capacity channel.

The radio station plays only one song at a time and, in fact, only one note of a song in any fraction of a second. A gigantic stadium might have tens of thousands of people all watching the same football player carry the ball across the field. All those systems combine massive capacity with a narrow focal series of events.

The brain looks like such a system. With 30 or 40 billion neurons, working away at the same time, with a massive highway system of connections between all the different regions of the cortex, and with literally trillions of axons firing, and even more synapses, the brain is of a level of complexity comparable to the World Wide Web.

But now imagine having a chat room with half a dozen people participating. Only one person can speak at any moment in time. Over time, as different people jump into the conversation and then start doing their own thinking because somebody else is talking, the chat room looks like a serial, one-at-a-time stream of events. But in fact, we know there are many parallel events happening. And if we imagine that the chat room discussion is being webcast to dozens or hundreds of other people, we have a huge "unconscious" system, with a very small "conscious" focal stream.

A Prediction That Seems to Be Working Out

In 1983, and in later publications, I predicted that conscious events should be "broadcast" in the brain, far beyond the stimulus-processing regions. I based my argument on what cognitive scientists already knew: Artificial intelligence architectures are built in precisely that way (Baars, 1983; Newell, 1992). And we knew that those systems—parallel-interactive ones, sometimes called society models—are very good at solving difficult problems, like computerized speech perception. Our knowledge of the brain is still very fragmentary. There are vast gaps in our knowledge about consciousness, but one testable prediction is that conscious events would trigger very widespread activation in the brain (Dehaene & Naccache, 2001).

That prediction has now been supported by brain imaging methods. Apparently, our consciousness of a coffee cup on a table in front of us requires more than just the visual brain. In addition to stimulus integration, consciousness seems to involve the forward spread of brain activity from the sensory regions at the back of the brain to the parietal and frontal lobes. That is at least what studies with functional magnetic resonance imaging (fMRI), magnetoencephalography (MEG), and EEG are showing. We always have to be aware of our limitations, and no doubt we will get more evidence that will force us to refine that hypothesis. But it is encouraging that we can make a rather surprising prediction about the role and effects of conscious events in the brain and obtain evidence suggesting that we are on the right path.

The Need to Understand Conscious Experience

Imagine the enterprise of scientific psychology as a great effort to solve a jigsaw puzzle as big as a football field. Several communities of researchers have been working for decades on the job of finding the missing pieces in the puzzle, and in recent years many gaps have been filled. However, one central missing piece—the issue of conscious experience—has been thought to be so difficult that many researchers sensibly have avoided that part of the puzzle. Yet the gap left by this great central piece has not gone away, and surrounding it are numerous issues that cannot be solved until it is addressed. If that is a reasonable analogy, it follows that the more pieces of the jigsaw puzzle we discover, the more the remaining uncertainties will tend to cluster about the great central gap where the missing piece must fit.

☐ Thinking Critically

1. For decades, Bernard Baars has argued that the scientific study of consciousness is possible. Why does he think mainstream psychology resisted his argument?

2. Imagine driving your car on a familiar route and on one that is unfamiliar. To what extent is consciousness involved in each task and what is its function?

☐ Suggested Further Reading

Baars, B. J., & Gage, N. M. (2010). *Cognition, brain and consciousness: An introduction to cognitive neuroscience* (2nd ed.). London: Elsevier/Academic Press.

Edelman, G. M., & Tononi, G. (2001). *A universe of consciousness.* New York: Basic Books.

☐ References

Baars, B. J. (1983). Conscious contents provide the nervous system with coherent, global information. In R. J. Davidson, G. E. Schwartz, & D. Shapiro (Eds.), *Consciousness and self-regulation: Vol. 3. Advances in research and theory.* New York: Plenum Press.

Baars, B. J. (1993). *A cognitive theory of consciousness* (Rev. ed.). New York: Cambridge University Press.

Baars, B. J. (2001). *In the theater of consciousness: The workspace of the mind.* New York: Oxford University Press.

Baars, B. J. (2002). The conscious access hypothesis: Origins and recent evidence. *Trends in Cognitive Sciences, 6(1),* 47–52.

Crick, F., & Koch, C. A. (2003). A framework for consciousness. *Nature Neuroscience, 6,* 119–126.

Dehaene, S., & Naccache, L. (2001). Towards a cognitive neuroscience of consciousness: Basic evidence and a workspace framework. *Cognition, 79,* 1–37.

Edelman, G. M., & Tononi, G. (2001). *A universe of consciousness.* New York: Basic Books.

James, W. (1890). *The principles of psychology.* NewYork: Holt.

Logothetis, N. K. (1998). Single units and conscious vision. *Philosophical Transactions of the Royal Society B: Biological Studies, 353,* 1801–1818.

Newell, A. (1992). SOAR as a unified theory of cognition: Issues and explanations. *Behavioral and Brain Sciences, 15(3),* 464–492.

Varela, F., Lachaux, J.-P., Rodriguez, E., & Martinerie, J. (2001). The brainweb: Phase synchronization and large-scale integration. *Nature Neuroscience, 2,* 229–239.

When You Put Things Out of Mind, Where Do They Go?

DANIEL M. WEGNER Harvard University

With great sadness, we acknowledge the passing of Dr. Daniel M. Wegner. We honor his scholarship and contributions to psychology in this volume.

☐ Please describe your current position and research interests.

I am Professor of Psychology at Harvard University. My research examines the role of thought in self-control and social life. This includes the study of thought suppression (why we have trouble keeping unwanted thoughts out of mind), transactive memory (how we remember things cooperatively with others), and apparent mental causation (what gives us the sense that we are causing our actions consciously). The past few years I've also become fascinated by mind perception—how people try to make sense of minds that are very different from their own, from the minds of animals to those of robots, infants, people in persistent vegetative states, fetuses, groups such as corporations, and even the nonliving or supernatural.

☐ How did you become interested in studying how we perceive and control the mind?

I'd have to say that the early seed of this interest was a sleazy politician. I noticed that when a headline aired someone's denial of an accusation (for example, "Mayor claims she took no bribes"), I often ended up thinking the accusation was true anyway. This got me to wondering if denials ever really work—if you can erase ideas or possibilities with denials once they are known and the "cat is out of the bag." Eventually, this led to experiments on what happens when people are asked specifically not to think about something.

☐ What has been the real-world impact of this work?

I'm not a clinical psychologist, but this work has real-world clinical implications. People who have unwanted thoughts—thoughts that make them anxious or depressed or disgusted or afraid—often come to clinical psychologists hoping that there will be treatments that can ease their struggle. Our studies of people who are simply asked in the lab to try to stop thinking about some neutral item provide a window into what people who are truly troubled by real-world unwanted thoughts can do to cope with them. And it turns out that people can sometimes overcome these thoughts by reversing the impulse to avoid them. Therapies that encourage people to talk about their unwanted thoughts, think about them, or otherwise confront them, often provide surprisingly useful pathways *away* from the thoughts. Research on the disclosure and acceptance of unwanted thoughts is helping to create useful new therapeutic strategies.

ave you ever tried to stop thinking about something? Try right now to stop thinking about your nose. Yes, the nose right there on your face. Put it out of mind. Really. Just stop everything for a minute and don't think about your nose.

Bet you couldn't. In fact, if you're like me, you may go a bit cross-eyed trying to sneak peeks at the darn thing. Fortunately, as soon as you give up the project of not thinking about it, the thought of your nose will settle back into the netherworld of things you've successfully *not* been thinking about all day. But the lesson is clear: Putting things out of mind brings them to mind. As Fyodor Dostoyevsky observed in *Winter Notes on Summer Impressions*, "Try to pose for yourself this task: not to think of a polar bear, and you will see that the cursed thing will come to mind every minute."

Dostoyevsky's Challenge

As it turns out, the Russian novelist was exactly right. My research team learned this a number of years ago in experiments that called for participants to accept the challenge of thought suppression (Wegner, Schneider, Carter, & White, 1987). We escorted individuals into a recording room and asked them to think aloud—saying anything that came to mind. After a while, we broke in and added a further instruction: Please try not to think about a white bear.

On average, people mentioned the bear about once per minute—just as Dostoyevsky had said. And, when we continued the experiment, we learned something new. After 5 minutes, we released participants from the suppression instruction and asked instead that they go ahead and *think* about the white bear. (See Figure 1.) During this release, we found a further effect of suppression—a kind of rebound effect in which participants talked almost continuously about the bear. In fact, they had much more to say about it than did others who had been asked to discuss it from the outset. If your nose suddenly has come to mind, you are experiencing the rebound.

Why then would anyone ever try to suppress a thought? It's useless, right? Dostoyevsky had a wise observation about this as well. In *Notes from the Underground,* he wrote, "Every man has reminiscences which he would not tell to everyone but only to his friends. He has other matters in his mind which he would not reveal even to his friends, but only to himself, and that in secret. But there are other things which a man is afraid to tell even to himself, and every decent man has a number of such things stored away in his mind." In other words, we all have thoughts that we may desperately want to suppress. We try not to think about that stupid boast to a friend, the little mole that could be cancer, the tempting ice cream in the freezer, the ridiculous fear that no one seems to share, or perhaps the pesky secret we promised never to reveal (Wegner, 1989).

One of Sigmund Freud's major discoveries was that people are driven by their emotions to try to put things out of mind (for example, Freud, 1915/1957). When thoughts make us anxious, sad, disgusted, afraid, or worse, we try to keep them at bay. Freud suspected that suppression might involve both conscious efforts and unconscious forgetting, which he called repression.

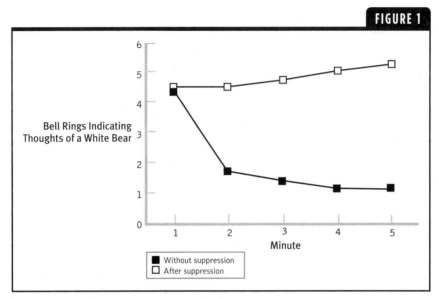

FIGURE 1

Rebound effect. Participants were asked to try not to think about a white bear, and then were asked to think about it and to ring a bell whenever it came to mind. Compared to those who were simply asked to think about the bear without prior suppression, those who first suppressed the thought showed a rebound of increased thinking (Wegner et al., 1987). Copyright © 1987 by the American Psychological Association. Reproduced with permission. The use of APA information does not imply endorsement by the APA.

Avoidance processes happen spontaneously when thoughts are too emotional, and that has made such processes notoriously opaque to scientific investigation. Freud and other psychoanalysts found it impossible to observe the way people put things out of mind because the observations could only start after the fact, when emotions had already led people to try to control their thoughts. Figuring out what had happened was a bit like trying to see whether the light is on after the refrigerator door is closed. Freud had to invent methods such as dream interpretation and free association to "uncover" thoughts he believed people might have actively avoided. My colleagues and I found a scientific solution to this problem: Our white bear technique—manipulating suppression by asking people to try not to think about an unemotional thought—offers a new experimental window on the mind.

Sticky Thoughts

What has the experimental study of thought suppression taught us? We now know that suppression can be superficially effective, in that people can keep things out of mind briefly or intermittently. Some people even tell us that they're pretty good at not thinking about things. Unfortunately, they happen to be the same sort of folks who claim that they floss daily, always wait for the green light to cross the street, and never get sad. Actually, almost anyone can succeed at suppression—if the target is a long list of unrelated items.

But research following up on the white bear studies (Najmi & Wegner, 2008; Rassin, 2005; Wenzlaff & Wegner, 2000) reveals that when you try to keep a single neutral thought out of mind:

- You are likely to notice it returning to mind for days.
- Distractions will make you think of it *more* rather than less often.
- Related ideas may remind you of it, but the thought itself is unlikely to remind you of those related ideas.
- You may think about it without even realizing it is on your mind but become conscious that you were thinking of it when someone asks.
- You may find it surfacing in your dreams, more so than if you had tried to think about it on purpose.
- The brain structure linked with remembering what you are doing (the dorsolateral prefrontal cortex) will be persistently activated even if you've pushed the thought out of mind.

One way to account for these findings is to suggest that part of the mind is *looking* for the very thought you are trying to suppress. This insight underlies the theory of ironic processes of mental control (Wegner, 1994). According to the theory, the attempt to stop a thought initiates two mental processes—a conscious operating process that searches for anything to think about other than the unwanted thought, and an automatic monitoring process that searches for the unwanted thought. The two processes work together normally to produce mental control.

When you try not to think of a white bear, for instance, the conscious operating process leads you to think of possible distracters: What's interesting in this room to think about? What will I be doing later today that I can review now? What's over there on the shelf that I can look at for a while? The automatic monitoring process must remain active too, so you can renew your efforts to find distracters if you happen to think of the white bear. This unconscious monitoring process alerts you when the unwanted thought enters consciousness. The two processes usually cooperate to keep the white bear out of mind, but, ironically, the monitoring process increases the mind's sensitivity to the unwanted thought and so increases the likelihood it will return.

Train Wreck

Does thought suppression begin to sound like a psychological train wreck? When profound motivation to suppress certain thoughts collides with an unconscious process that renders the effort useless, the result can be mental turmoil—cyclic attempts to suppress, punctuated by the thought's return. Unfortunately, this isn't even the worst part.

Suppression produces a cascade of additional unintended effects (Wenzlaff & Wegner, 2000). Many emotions associated with the unwanted thought re-emerge larger than life when the thought surges back to mind. When people try not to think about sex, for example, measures of skin conductance level indicate that their hands perspire and they get every bit as excited as if they were thinking about sex. When people who have no particular fear of visiting the dentist are asked not to think about it before a visit, they report increased anxiety and increased levels of intrusive distressing thoughts about what will happen. And when people are asked not to think about a past relationship with an old flame for whom they still are burning, their skin conductance levels rise to show increased emotionality as soon as they complete the suppression session.

Suppressing emotional thoughts seems to supercharge the thoughts, making them trigger the very emotion the person is trying to avoid through thought suppression. The eventual effect of suppressing thoughts, then, can be to leave the person overwrought, a bundle of emotions. This is not good. In fact, researchers examining the effects of thought suppression on the body have found that just a few hours spent suppressing emotional thoughts (for example, the feelings of depression and loneliness that come from moving away from home) can undermine bodily immune responses (Petrie, Booth, & Pennebaker, 1998). Perhaps thought suppression breaks down normal defenses and increases people's susceptibility to illness.

And, we've not even begun to talk about *mental* disorders. Some psychologists believe that thought suppression may be involved in psychological disorders such as depression, anxiety, and obsessive-compulsive disorder (OCD). People may develop these disorders because they are particularly poor at suppressing and so find that unwanted thoughts plague their minds. People with OCD who experience repetitive unwanted thoughts or find themselves performing compulsive behavioral rituals might have a deficit in mental control abilities. In fact, OCD sufferers have been found to be particularly poor at suppressing even a neutral thought. Perhaps this deficit precipitates their serious hassles with unwanted thoughts in everyday life.

For a wider range of psychological problems, however, thought suppression difficulties are more likely to be a *complication* rather than a cause. Doesn't it stand to reason that people who have unpleasant thoughts, emotions, or mental symptoms would try not to think about their problems? If you are hearing voices, for example, or are not able to stop crying, or are fearful of being outside, trying not to think about the disturbing symptom might at first seem like a sensible thing to do. Suppression may offer a flash of relief, a respite in the face of an alarming realization about oneself. So one possibility is that thought suppression is a common personal response to psychological disorders.

The Amplifier Hypothesis

The suppression response is not just a minor side effect of psychological disorders. Given what we know about the way suppression can echo in the mind, we might expect that suppression might help briefly but would eventually amplify the person's problem. The process could work like this: Thinking more about the problem would result in more frequent awareness of emotions associated with the problem. Alarmed by these snowballing difficulties and suppressing that response as well, the problem could grow even larger. Thus, a person who started with a minor fear of speaking in public could find that this fear has escalated into a full-blown social phobia.

There is evidence consistent with this amplifier hypothesis (Najmi & Wegner, 2008; Wegner & Zanakos, 1994). People who use conscious thought suppression chronically as a strategy for coping with distressing thoughts are more likely than others to be anxious and depressed and to report symptoms of OCD. This link between suppression and the severity of psychological symptoms is common in other disorders as well. For example, people who report engaging in self-mutilation or self-harm are more likely than others to engage in thought suppression, and people who use thought suppression as a strategy for quitting smoking are more likely to experience a return of thoughts about smoking when they are trying to quit. Children and adolescent victims of traumatic accidents who report using thought suppression are more likely than other accident victims to suffer from post-traumatic stress disorder.

Findings like these are evidence of an association between suppression and increases in the intensity of psychological disorders, but they cannot be interpreted to mean that suppression *causes* the amplification of disorders. In fact, experimental studies to test this idea could be unethical—the predicted effect of instructing people to suppress could possibly make a disorder worse! But an opposite strategy is ethically quite acceptable: In studies of what happens when people are encouraged to *relax* their attempts to suppress thoughts, researchers have reported the expected causal relationship: When people in psychotherapy are led to accept their symptoms and face the thoughts they've been striving to avoid, they can experience noteworthy alleviations of the symptoms of a disorder (for example, Marcks & Woods, 2005).

Facing unwanted thoughts isn't easy. The emotional motivation behind suppression can sometimes push so hard that there is no way to push back. If you fear spiders, for example, sitting and thinking about a spider even for a few minutes might be an emotional nightmare. People think of all kinds of ways to try to escape their unwanted thoughts because thinking such thoughts is exquisitely painful. Psychotherapists who help people stop knee-jerk suppression must often be masterfully persuasive and encourage clients to undertake change one step at a time.

Apparently, hypnosis can help people to suppress thoughts, but it's not an approach that we recommend. Overcoming the emotional urge to suppress is the key, and this can only be done by thinking the unthinkable. As Bertrand Russell (1930, p. 64) observed in *The Conquest of Happiness:*

> Now every kind of fear grows worse by not being looked at. The proper course is to think about it with great concentration until it has become completely familiar. In the end familiarity will blunt its terrors; the whole subject will become boring, and our thoughts will turn away from it, not, as formerly, by an effort of will, but through mere lack of interest in the topic. When you find yourself inclined to brood on anything, the best plan is always to think about it even more than you naturally would until at last its morbid fascination is worn off.

☐ Thinking Critically

1. Explain why Daniel Wegner uses the term "ironic processes" for the strategies that people use to control their own minds.
2. What lessons does research on unwanted thoughts have for people who are concerned about their weight and are considering dieting?

☐ Suggested Further Reading

Wegner, D. M. (1989). *White bears and other unwanted thoughts: Suppression, obsession, and the psychology of mental control.* New York: Viking/Penguin.

Wenzlaff, R. M., & Wegner, D. M. (2000). Thought suppression. In S. T. Fiske (Ed.), *Annual review of psychology, Vol. 51* (pp. 51–91). Palo Alto, CA: Annual Reviews.

☐ References

Dostoyevsky, F. (1955). *Winter notes on summer impressions* (R. L. Renfield, Trans.). New York: Criterion Books. (Original work published 1863)

Dostoyevsky, F. (2004). *Notes from the underground* (R. Pevear & L. Volkhonsky, Trans.). New York: Knopf. (Original work published 1864)

Freud, S. (1915/1957). Repression. In J. Strachey (Ed.), *The standard edition of the complete psychological works of Sigmund Freud, Vol. 14.* (pp. 146–158). London: Hogarth.

Marcks, B. A., & Woods, D. W. (2005). A comparison of thought suppression to an acceptance-based technique in the management of personal intrusive thoughts: A controlled evaluation. *Behaviour Research and Therapy, 43,* 433–445.

Najmi, S., & Wegner, D. M. (2008). Thought suppression and psychopathology. In A. J. Elliott (Ed.), *Handbook of approach and avoidance motivation* (pp. 447–460). Mahwah, NJ: Erlbaum.

Petrie, K. P., Booth, R. J., & Pennebaker, J. W. (1998). The immunological effects of thought suppression. *Journal of Personality and Social Psychology, 75,* 1264–1272.

Rassin, E. (2005). *Thought suppression.* New York: Elsevier.

Russell, B. (1930). *The conquest of happiness.* New York: Horace Liveright.

Wegner, D. M. (1989). *White bears and other unwanted thoughts: Suppression, obsession, and the psychology of mental control.* New York: Viking/Penguin.

Wegner, D. M. (1994). Ironic processes of mental control. *Psychological Review, 101,* 34–52.

Wegner, D. M., Schneider, D. J., Carter, S., & White, T. (1987). Paradoxical effects of thought suppression. *Journal of Personality and Social Psychology, 53,* 5–13.

Wegner, D. M., & Zanakos, S. (1994). Chronic thought suppression. *Journal of Personality, 62,* 615–640.

Wenzlaff, R. M., & Wegner, D. M. (2000). Thought suppression. In S. T. Fiske (Ed.), *Annual review of psychology* (Vol. 51, pp. 51–91). Palo Alto, CA: Annual Reviews.

Intelligence

The Theory of Multiple Intelligences

Howard Gardner

The Rainbow Project: Using Psychological Theory of Intelligence to Improve the College Admissions Process

Robert J. Sternberg

The Theory of Multiple Intelligences

HOWARD GARDNER Harvard Graduate School of Education

☐ Please describe your current position and research interests.

I am the Hobbs Professor of Cognition and Education at the Harvard Graduate School of Education and Senior Director of Harvard Project Zero. Since
the mid-1990s, colleagues and I have been studying the nature of good
work: work that is excellent technically, personally meaningful, and carried
out in an ethical manner. Since 2005, we have also been studying good play:
how young people are being changed by digital media.

☐ What led you to question the idea that intelligence is a single entity?

In the 1970s, I conducted research with two groups: adults who had suffered
brain damage and children who were artistically talented. Every day I saw
dramatic examples of jagged intellectual profiles: Individuals excellent in
some areas were average in others and had marked difficulties with some
materials. These daily experiences convinced me that the notion of a single,
uncomposable intellect could not possibly be correct.

☐ What has been the real-world impact of this work?

The real-world impact of this work is much greater than I could ever have anticipated. All over the world, educators found the ideas of interest and began
to institute changes that could better serve the "multiple intelligences" of
their students. My colleagues and I chronicle some of these educational experiments in *Multiple Intelligences Around the World* (see Suggested Reading). The work has also had influence in other institutions, such as museums,
and at the workplace, particularly in the areas of human resources and the
identification and cultivation of talent.

In 1969, while a graduate student in developmental psychology at Harvard University, I had one of those experiences that, in retrospect, changes
one's life. I was part of a research team at a fledgling research group called
"Project Zero"—a group concerned primarily with the nature of human artistic activity—headed by the renowned philosopher Nelson Goodman. Researchers at Project Zero were interested in artistic cognition—how artists
make and create worlds through the use of various symbol systems, and how
the rest of us relate to, make sense of, and fall in and out of love with symbolic
creations in several art forms.

Our team heard about the research of Boston-area neurologist Norman Geschwind, and so we invited him to give an informal seminar. This was the era
when nonspecialists first heard about the division of labor between the two
cerebral hemispheres. In most individuals, particularly right-handers, the left

hemisphere is "dominant" for language; an injury to areas in that part of the brain can cause aphasia (acquired loss of language). Language is seldom represented in the complementary right hemisphere; instead, injuries there typically impair spatial and musical capacities and produce an unusual emotional profile as well. Perhaps, we reasoned, this line of work might provide clues about human symbol-using capacities in the arts and other realms.

I was mesmerized by Geschwind's presentation—his impressive command of the field and (I must admit) his charismatic personality. At this time behaviorist ways of thinking were predominant, and I had never thought much about the organization of capacities in the human brain. As part of my work at Project Zero, I had been trying to understand the nature of artistic activities in artists and in ordinary persons, and particularly the relationships among different kinds of artistic skills. For example, I wondered about the connections between language and music: Did musical capacity piggyback on linguistic capacities, or vice versa, or were they largely independent from one another? I also was puzzling about the nature of artistic talent: From where did it come, how did it develop, and was it independent of other human capacities, other facets of intellect?

As I recall, the session with Geschwind lasted from early afternoon until well into the evening (we broke for dinner). I was particularly fascinated when, prompted by our questions, Geschwind told us about what had happened to famous artists—like the composer Maurice Ravel—after damage to the brain had been sustained. By the end of the session, I had become convinced that the representation of cognitive capacities in the brain might provide a clue to some of the issues about artistry that had puzzled me—and for which I had lacked a means for investigation.

And so, throwing caution to the wind, I decided to apply for a postdoctoral fellowship with Geschwind at the Harvard Medical School and the Aphasia Research Center of the Boston Veterans Administration Medical Center. I say "throwing caution to the wind" because most of my peers were applying for academic positions, and none of my professors thought that I could learn much from studying the cortical representations of human capacities. They still subscribed to the mid-twentieth-century dogma that the brain was off limits for psychology. The postdoctoral fellowship grew to 2 and then to 3 years; and it turned out that I ultimately spent 20 years carrying out neuropsychological research, in the process learning a great deal about the nature of artistic capacities and how they relate (and when they do not relate) to other human cognitive faculties.

But I did not abandon my work as a developmental psychologist, carried out under the auspices of Project Zero. While I was studying the breakdown of artistic (and other) capacities under conditions of damage to the brain, I was at the same time examining how various cognitive capacities developed in typical children, as well as children who showed unusual cognitive profiles (gifted children, prodigies, savants, and, on occasion, young persons with severe learning deficits). And so, in the aggregate, I was examining the human mind from three distinct vantage points: how abilities are organized in artists in their prime; how such symbol-using capacities develop under ordinary conditions; and how they can be disrupted by damage to the human brain—the "experiment of nature" caused by stroke and other kinds of trauma.

Among my colleagues in psychology, I am unusual. Nearly all empirically oriented psychologists spend the bulk of their time carrying out experiments and writing articles thereafter. Rarely do psychologists write books, and especially rarely before they earn tenure! And when they write books, they are often textbooks or popular accounts of their own work. From the first, however, I was a book writer. By the time I began my postdoctoral studies, I had finished three books, and I had begun a series of books about my favorite subject—the human mind. (By now, at least 10 of my books feature the word *mind* in the title.) In 1975, having spent a few years carrying out neuropsychological research, I published yet another mind-focused work: *The Shattered Mind: The Person After Brain Damage.*

By that time, thanks to my work with Norman Geschwind and other outstanding researchers in neurology and neuropsychology, I had become convinced already that the notion of the mind as a single, all-purpose computer could not be correct. Every day I saw young people who might be excellent in one area of study, art, or craft, while completely undistinguished in other spheres. Even more dramatically, daily I saw patients who exhibited unusual combinations of abilities and disabilities. One person might lose his ability to sing but be able to carry on ordinary conversation; a second might exhibit the reverse profile of symptoms. Similarly, the relation between proficiency in the visual arts and other competences was vexed; it even seemed, on occasion, that a stroke might free up artistic potential that had hitherto been latent.

And so I began to outline a book, provisionally entitled *Kinds of Minds,* in which I proposed to define the different spheres of human competence—as I might put it today, the several computers of the mind. Yet something told me that I was not quite ready to write this book, and so I put my notes aside and actually forgot this stalled project until 25 years later. Instead, I continued my parallel lines of research, contributing a few bricks to the edifices of developmental psychology and neuropsychology.

A New View of Intelligence

Enter another unexpected event. In 1979, the Harvard Graduate School of Education received a large grant from a Dutch foundation, the Bernard van Leer Foundation. I was chosen to be a Principal on The Human Potential Project. And I was given an intriguing assignment: Summarize what has been established about human cognition from the biological and cognitive sciences. The project lasted 5 years, covered much of my salary, provided research assistants, and, invaluably, gave me an opportunity to travel around the world, thereby broadening my notions of human cognitive potential.

In effect, I was picking up the pieces of *Kinds of Minds*. With a wonderful team of researchers, I embarked on a massive survey and synthesis of the various bodies of knowledge pertinent to human intellectual capacities: what was known from the realms of biology, psychology, anthropology, and other relevant disciplines. From my work with children and brain-damaged adults, I had a premonition of possible categories, the identity of the several "computers" that together constitute the human mind. But I was determined not to be aprioristic: I wanted to cut nature at its proper joints, come up with the optimal taxonomy, and so I was guided by what the data revealed.

I made a number of crucial decisions. First of all, I decided that I would not begin with the sensory organs. My work in neuropsychology had convinced me that the human intellect operates on information, irrespective of the particular sensory organs that happen to be involved in taking in that information. Thus, the language faculty can be activated by hearing (spoken language), sight (written language), and even tactilely (as in Braille). So, too, spatial capacities operate even in those who are blind.

Second, and fatefully, I decided to call these capacities human intelligences. I wanted to underscore the importance of the distinctions that I was making. I had a premonition that if I used a neutral word like *talent* or *capacity* or *faculty,* it would be easy to ignore what I was saying. ("Oh, for sure, there are many human talents.") But if I used the charged word *intelligence* I would be able to capture the attention of both psychologists and the general public—nearly all of whom have strong views of what human intellect is. As a tentative definition, I suggested that *an intelligence* is a competence to solve problems or fashion products that are valued in at least one culture. (Since then, I have refined the definition, but I am trying to be historically accurate.)

Third, I made an important methodological decision. I developed a set of eight criteria for what counts as intelligence; only those candidate abilities that scored reasonably well on these criteria would make the ultimate list. Here are the eight criteria:

- An intelligence should be discerned in relative isolation in prodigies, autistic savants, stroke victims, or other exceptional populations.
- It should have distinct representation in the nervous system.
- It should have a distinct developmental trajectory. Different intelligences should develop at different rates and with different patterns.
- It should have some basis in evolutionary biology. In other words, an intelligence should have putative survival value, and simpler manifestations of an intelligence should be discernible in other species.
- It should be susceptible to capture in symbol systems—some form of notation.
- It should be supported by evidence from psychometric measures.
- It should be distinguishable from other intelligences through experimental psychological tasks.
- It should contain core, information-processing capacities. For example, language includes core phonological and syntactic analyzing mechanisms.

Armed with a word, a definition, and a set of criteria, I proposed seven human intelligences. I have since added an eighth (Naturalist) and am considering a provisional ninth (Existential). In the accompanying Table 1, I have

TABLE 1

Eight Intelligences

Linguistic intelligence
Enables individuals to process information and create products involving language. Poets, novelists, and journalists exhibit this intelligence in abundance.

Examples: William Shakespeare, Toni Morrison

Logical-mathematical intelligence
Allows individuals to make calculations, consider hypotheses, and solve abstract problems. Engineers, scientists, and analytic philosophers are likely to possess a profile of intelligence high in logical-mathematical intelligence.

Examples: Isaac Newton, Marie Curie

Spatial intelligence
Enables individuals to navigate around complex terrains and to manipulate spatial images in their head. Sailors, pilots, architects, and painters stand out in their spatial abilities.

Examples: Frank Gehry, Georgia O'Keeffe

Musical intelligence
Allows individuals to produce and make meaning of different patterns of sound. Composers, conductors, and musical performers exhibit this intelligence.

Examples: Wolfgang Amadeus Mozart, Jay Z

Bodily-kinesthetic intelligence
Involves using one's body to create products or solve problems. Athletes, dancers, crafts-workers, and surgeons all draw upon bodily-kinesthetic intelligence.

Examples: Mikhail Baryshnikov, Serena Williams

Interpersonal intelligence
Reflects an individual's ability to recognize and interpret other people's moods, desires, skills, motivations, and intentions. Teachers, clinicians, and salespeople are likely to possess considerable interpersonal intelligence.

Examples: Martin Luther King, Jr., Oprah Winfrey

Intrapersonal intelligence
Allows individuals to recognize and assess these characteristics within themselves. Those who excel in introspection exploit this intelligence.

Examples: Sigmund Freud, Virginia Woolf

Naturalistic intelligence
Enables individuals to identify and distinguish among various types of plants, animals, weather formations, and so forth, that are found in the natural world. This form of intelligence is obviously important for those whose survival depends on direct interaction with the natural environment: hunters, farmers, and those who study the natural world. It is possible that this human faculty is now used by most of us chiefly to make distinctions among different consumer goods.

Examples: Charles Darwin, Rachel Carson

listed the intelligences, given a capsule definition, and proposed specimen individuals who excel in that particular intelligence.

There may be a ninth intelligence, which I call existential intelligence—I think of it as the intelligence of "big questions." Young people, religious leaders, artists, and philosophers ponder the nature of life, death, love, and war. We respond to leaders who embody existential intelligence. Before pronouncing this an "official" intelligence, however, I would like firm evidence that distinct brain systems have evolved to allow us to ponder those things that are too big, or too little, to be perceived directly.

These, then, are the set of intelligences that I proposed—initially in 1983 in *Frames of Mind* (Gardner, 1983/2011) and about which I've written and lectured in subsequent years. The theory makes two principal claims.

1. All of us have the full range of intelligences. The intelligences are what make us human beings in the cognitive sphere.

2. No two human beings, not even identical twins, exhibit exactly the same profile of intelligences—the same strengths, weaknesses, and patterns of interaction among the intelligences. And that is because even if two people are genetically identical, they have varied experiences and may well be motivated to distinguish themselves from one another. And so, in the end, they may turn out to be quite different from one another.

"Fifteen Minutes" of Fame for *Frames of Mind*

When *Frames of Mind* first appeared, I had certain expectations—none of which was met. First of all, I thought the book was addressed to my primary audience of psychologists—especially those in cognitive and developmental psychology. Second, having already published half a dozen books to modest reaction and equally modest sales, I expected little hubbub and a gradual silence.

What happened instead? First, this was—and remains—my only publication to receive a lot of immediate attention. Second, the primary response to my work came from educators (with whom I had only a modest amount of contact). Initially in the United States, and then throughout the world, educators latched onto the idea of multiple intelligences. And perhaps because I said little about the educational implications of the theory, these educators came up with their own applications—in teaching, in curriculum, and in tracking (or nontracking) of students. For the most part, I was impressed by the educational implementations of the theory, which included several schools built around the idea of multiple intelligences. Sometimes I was bemused by the applications. And a few times I was horrified—like when an educational program in Australia classified the major racial and ethnic groups in Australia in terms of the intelligences that they possessed and the ones that they lacked. Fortunately, that program was soon cancelled.

The harshest criticism by far came from the psychometric establishment—the individuals who developed the standard intelligence test, the IQ test, and who believed (and continue to believe) that they have the right to define intelligence, to determine how it is measured, and to resist efforts to pluralize the concept, or to assess it in ways that deviate noticeably from short oral or paper and pencil instruments.

Not having anticipated it, I walked into a buzz saw. The problem, I think, was my lack of training in the area of psychometrics: I rarely thought about IQ tests—in either a positive or negative vein. The choice of the term *intelligence* had been primarily strategic—based on calling attention to the idea, not on studied immersion in earlier work on intelligence. Although I did not like being attacked, I adjusted to it, and, hard as it is to admit it, I did learn from it . . . at least sometimes.

Looking back at this work from the vantage point of almost 30 years, what adjustments would I make? First, I learned to make important distinctions. Despite what many educators say, intelligences are not the same as learning styles. An intelligence is a capacity to compute information, not a way of approaching a range of tasks. Nor is an intelligence the same as a domain or a discipline. Any domain can involve several intelligences, and any intelligence can be drawn on for a variety of pursuits. More concretely, several intelligences are involved with mathematics; and someone with logical mathematical intelligence can apply it to a range of areas, from computing to gambling.

Second, if I don't create ways of assessing the intelligences, other people will—and indeed they have. Our own efforts to assess intelligences took the form of Project Spectrum: the development of a rich curriculum for preschool children. The Spectrum curriculum contains different materials that are attractive to young children; and by observing the young children as they interact with these materials (in the manner of a child making her way through a children's museum), one can infer their profile of intellectual strengths.

The best example of assessing intelligences that I've ever seen was developed with no input from me. Located in southwestern Denmark, Danfoss Universe is a 10-acre "science experience park" with more than 150 activities that strive to combine learning and fun ("About Universe," 2014). Its Explorama is a museum-sized building that houses more than 50 different activities. Each activity is designed to help participants learn about and focus on one of their specific intelligences. Importantly, the intelligences are probed directly, not through the screen of a multiple-choice, linguistic device. Here is a sample of a few exhibits found in the Explorama:

- A linguistic exhibit offers a recording of words spoken in Japanese. When participants mimic the Japanese words, the exhibit offers a visual representation of their vocalization superimposed over that of a native Japanese speaker. Through this comparison, participants can strive to improve the accuracy of their tone and pronunciation.

- A musical exhibit allows participants to create melodies on a theremin—an electronic instrument played without actually touching the instrument itself. Participants learn about melody by moving their hands within the vicinity of two antennae.

- An interpersonal exhibit called Teambot requires participants to work cooperatively to design a robot arm that can move an object from one location to another.

- An intrapersonal exhibit called Mindball asks that participants don electrode-equipped headbands attached to a computer that is, in turn, connected to a Ping-Pong table. If the participant can lower his or her stress level as measured by the electrodes, this reduction in stress can be converted by the computer into a force that propels a Ping-Pong ball to the other side of the table.

Before embarking on these and other MI-based activities, visitors to the museum are asked to complete a survey describing their beliefs about their own intellectual profile. After completing their visit to the Explorama, participants are invited to reflect upon whether their performance on the various exhibits bore out their initial beliefs about their profile of intelligences (Gardner, 2006a). In this way, many visitors conclude their visit to Danfoss Universe with a deepened understanding of their own intellectual strengths and weaknesses—and, in the process, have the opportunity to assess and perhaps enhance their own intrapersonal intelligence.

Looking Ahead

Seeing these various applications around the world has moved me deeply. Although I started out as a psychologist trying to map the mind as it is, now I am interested equally in the ways in which ideas are employed and the differences those applications might make in the world. At this point, determining the precise number and boundary of the intelligences has become less important than MI theory's overarching premise that intelligence is better understood as multiple rather than singular (Chen & Gardner, 2005; Gardner, 2006b). As research in the fields of neuroscience and genetics proceeds, our understanding of the ways in which different genes and areas of the brain impact specific intellectual capacities will increase dramatically. Currently identified constructs such as logical-mathematical intelligence will undoubtedly be found to be composed of specific subsets: perhaps subintelligences for processing small numbers, estimation, and deductive reasoning (Gardner, 2006a). Overall, however, I am confident that the concept of multiple intelligences will be substantiated. And I dare to think that its application in various domains—education, museums, the workplace—will be benevolent.

Nowadays, in our competitive global society, young persons feel pressured at increasingly young ages to make career decisions, even irrevocable ones. By the same token, young scholars often feel that they need to get the first job, define a focused area of research, and move straight to tenure and beyond. Reflecting on my own life, at a time when I am definitely a "senior" (as I write these words, I am 70), I am impressed by the extent to which my life trajectory could not have been predicted, and I am better for those chance events that make crucial differences. Had I not heard Geschwind speak; had we not received the grant from the Bernard van Leer Foundation; had I not used the word *intelligence*. . . . And even after *Frames of Mind* was published, I had no idea of the course that its ideas—its memes—would take. I love science and scientific explanations—but my own life's work is a testimony to the importance of history, culture, and, yes, chance.

Acknowledgment Thanks to Scott Seider for his help in preparing this essay.

☐ Thinking Critically

1. Resistance to Howard Gardner's theory of multiple intelligences has focused on the absence of statistical supporting data. What other kinds of data support his ideas?

2. You and seven other people get lost on a day-long trip. Imagine that you each excel in one of Gardner's intelligences. What methods would you use to find your way home?

☐ Suggested Further Reading

Chen, J., Moran, S., & Gardner, H. (2009). *Multiple intelligences around the world.* San Francisco: Jossey Bass.

Gardner, H. (2006). *Multiple intelligences: New horizons.* New York: Basic Books.

☐ References

About Universe. (n. d.) Retrieved May 1, 2014 from http://www.danfossuniverse.com

Chen, J., & Gardner, H. (2005). Multiple intelligences: Assessment based on multiple-intelligence theory. In D. Flanagan and P. Harrison (Eds.), *Contemporary intellectual assessment: Theories, tests and issues* (pp. 105–121). New York: Guilford Press.

Garder, H. (1975). *The shattered mind: The person after brain damage.* New York: Vintage Books.

Gardner, H. (1983/2011). *Frames of mind: The theory of multiple intelligences* (3rd ed.). New York: Basic Books.

Gardner, H. (2000). *Intelligence reframed: Multiple intelligences for the 21st century.* New York: Basic Books.

Gardner, H. (2006a). *Multiple intelligences: New horizons.* New York: Basic Books.

Gardner, H. (2006b). Response to my critics. In J. Schaler (Ed.), *Gardner under fire* (pp. 277–307). Chicago, IL: Open Court Publishers.

Gardner, H., Kornhaber, M., & Wake, W. (1996). *Intelligence: Multiple perspectives.* Fort Worth, TX: Harcourt Brace.

Kornhaber, M. (1995). *Multiple intelligences: Why and how schools use it.* Unpublished qualifying paper, Harvard Graduate School of Education.

Kornhaber, M., Fierros, E., & Veenema, S. (2004). *Multiple intelligences: Best ideas from research and practice.* Boston, MA: Pearson.

Olson, L. (1988). Children flourish here: Eight teachers and a theory changed a school world. *Education Week, 7*(8), 83–104.

The Rainbow Project and Beyond: Using a Psychological Theory of Intelligence to Improve the College Admissions Process

ROBERT J. STERNBERG Cornell University

☐ **Please describe your current position and research interests.**

I am Professor of Human Development at Cornell University. I am also Honorary Professor of Psychology at the University of Heidelberg. My main research interests are in intelligence, creativity, wisdom, and leadership.

☐ **How did you become interested in measuring practical and creative intellectual skills?**

I first devised my theory of successful intelligence as a result of my interactions with university students. These interactions made me realize that someone could be high in academic intelligence but not so high in the creative or practical aspects of intelligence, and vice versa. My colleagues and I have also done research on how to teach as well as assess for successful intelligence.

☐ **What has been the real-world impact of this work, or what do you envision that it will be?**

I hope that the world of education sees the light and adopts all or at least most of my ideas with great enthusiasm and energy, preferably before I either become senile or die.

Every scientific study has a story. The story of the Rainbow Project begins in the late nineteenth century, when British scientist Sir Francis Galton (1822–1911) proposed a theory of intelligence based on the notion that more intelligent people have keener sensory-motor capacities than less intelligent ones. He expected the more intelligent, for example, to have keener eyesight, a firmer grip, greater ability to distinguish between different tones, and so forth. Based on this notion, Galton developed a test of intelligence based upon sensory-motor skills.

As is always true in science, investigators have different ideas about how a story should develop and how it should end. French scientists Alfred Binet (1857–1911) and Theodore Simon (1873–1961) disputed Galton's claims about the nature of intelligence and how to measure it. Intelligence, they argued, is a matter of higher-level thinking and good judgment rather than sensory abilities (Binet & Simon, 1916). The tests they developed required people to demonstrate judgment, interpret proverbs, provide the meanings of words, and solve arithmetic problems, among other school-related skills. Their tests predicted school performance better than did Galton's and came, therefore, to serve as the basis for future intelligence-test development. In fact, Binet and Simon's assessment device became the first IQ test. The term IQ, a translation of the German word *Intelligenz-Quotient*, was coined by William Stern (1871–1938), who suggested that intelligence tests could be scored by using a ratio of mental age divided by chronological age $\times$ 100.

An American psychologist, Lewis Terman (1877–1956) of Stanford University, imported Binet and Simon's tests into the United States. He used them in his research and published a version and revisions (for example, Terman & Merrill, 1937). The fifth edition of this test—called the Stanford-Binet Intelligence Scale—is in use today. Binet and Terman had created tests to measure the intelligence of individuals, one at a time. However, soon others were taking mental measurement in another direction. Researchers such as Arthur Otis (1886–1964) and Carl Brigham (1890–1943) were interested in group testing of individuals. Brigham was the inventor, in the early twentieth century, of what is today called the SAT.

The SAT has a long history. Originally, the initials were an acronym for "Scholastic Aptitude Test." This name implied to many people that the test measured innate intellectual qualities, so the name was changed to "Scholastic Assessment Test." Perhaps because this name was too vague, the acronym was later made to be the test name. At present, "SAT" stands for nothing but itself!

Although its owner, the College Board, insists that the SAT is not an ability test, research suggests that scores on the test are very highly correlated with scores on tests of intelligence (Frey & Detterman, 2004). Indeed, the test is about as related to any one intelligence test as intelligence tests are related to each other. British psychologist and logician Charles Spearman (1863–1945) had argued as long ago as 1927 that all tests of mental abilities are positively related to each other, and the SAT is no exception.

The SAT has been a good predictor of college performance (Bridgeman, McCamley-Jenkins, & Ervin, 2000; Hezlett et al., 2001), but no test, including this one, provides perfect prediction. Moreover, there is another problem. Tests such as the SAT originally were introduced to counter decisions being made largely on the basis of social class. The world was changing. Whereas a person's last name, social standing, or private school had once mattered more to future outcomes than his or her ability, college was proving to be a gateway to a successful life. Thus, the goal underlying group testing was the introduction of a merit- rather than class-based system for admission to college. But as the diversity of the college applicant pool increased, an unfortunate fact emerged: Test scores are highly correlated with social class.

The SAT, ACT (the American College Testing Program, a national college admissions and placement exam), and similar tests are not based on any particular theory of abilities, and some psychologists argued that a test based more closely on a psychological theory, especially a broad theory of abilities, might improve prediction of performance beyond what the SAT yields currently (for example, Gardner, 1983; Sternberg, 1985). A related hope was that

such tests might better recognize the wide diversity of abilities students can bring to college life. So, in 2000, my collaborators and I initiated an effort to devise a test that might turn these hopes into reality.

The Rainbow Assessment: Underlying Theory

The Rainbow Project was carried out when I was a professor at Yale University. My collaborators and I called the project "Rainbow" to underscore the notion that abilities, like light, can be decomposed into different aspects like the spectrum of light. Intelligence, like light, may appear to be of just one "color." But it represents a rainbow of different kinds of abilities. Underlying the new assessment are ideas that I first proposed more than two decades ago. In a book called *Successful Intelligence* (Sternberg, 1997), I argued that intelligence is one's ability to achieve one's goals in life, within one's sociocultural context. Such success depends on capitalizing on one's strengths and compensating for or correcting one's weaknesses to adapt to, shape, and select environments through a combination of creative, analytical, and practical abilities. My theory distinguishes three aspects of intelligence: creative abilities to generate novel ideas, analytical abilities to evaluate whether the ideas are good ones, and practical abilities to execute one's ideas and to persuade others of their value.

I have argued that conventional tests of intelligence and the SAT measure primarily analytical abilities, as well as memory. Thus, a new, theoretically based test would contribute the most in its assessments of creative and practical abilities, the two kinds of abilities not directly measured by conventional tests.

The Rainbow Project Team

The team working on the Rainbow assessment was unusual in two ways. First, among its more than a dozen members from all around the United States were researchers with a range of viewpoints on what intelligence is and how to measure it. On most projects, collaborators share a single point of view, or at least their points of view differ relatively little. In contrast, the team's views varied all over the map! Second, the team was highly interdisciplinary, involving cognitive psychologists, measurement psychologists, educational psychologists, developmental psychologists, cultural psychologists, and others from outside psychology altogether. I was the team leader (Sternberg & The Rainbow Project Collaborators, 2006).

The College Board, publishers of the SAT, provided funding. Some collaborators were from the Board, but it made no attempt, ever, to influence the outcome.

Who Did We Test and How?

Roughly 1,000 participants—mostly college freshman—were attending a diverse group of schools, ranging from those that are not at all selective in their admissions procedures to some that are highly selective. Thirteen colleges and universities and two high schools were represented in the sample. Tests were administered at the universities by proctors under controlled conditions, either in paper-and-pencil format or over the Internet.

We used a variety of tests that measured analytical, creative, and practical skills. All of the analytical tests were multiple choice format, but only some of the creative and practical tests were of this kind. Other performance-based tests required participants to solve problems using relatively divergent thinking.

There were three creative-performance tests. In one, cartoons like those in the *New Yorker* magazine were presented without captions, and participants were asked to think up good captions. In a second test, participants were given unusual titles, such as *Beyond the Edge* or *The Octopus's Sneakers*, and were asked to write creative stories. In a third test, participants were shown visual collages, such as different pictures of musicians, and asked to dictate a story. The creative performance tests were scored for three attributes—the originality or novelty of a response, the quality of that response, and the extent to which the response was appropriate to what was asked on the assessment.

Three practical tests measured problem-solving skills. One presented participants with situations similar to those they might encounter in college—for example, resolving a dispute with a roommate. A second test was similar, but the scenarios were work related. A third test consisted of scenarios presented visually—for example, a video of a student entering a room filled with party goers, with the expression on his face suggesting that he did not know anyone at the party. Test takers had to figure out what to do. Various options were presented, and students had to rate their quality. They included options such as leaving the party, staying at the party but primarily observing what is going on, actively making efforts to meet people, and so on (see Table 1).

TABLE 1

Movies Used in the Rainbow Project to Assess Practical Intelligence

Title	Theme
The Party	Entering a party where you do not know anyone
A Fair Portion	Discussing shares of rental payments for an apartment
Professor's Dilemma	Asking for a letter of recommendation from a professor who does not know you very well
No Free Lunch	Having eaten a lunch and discovering that you do not have the money to pay for it
The Unwanted Guest	Dealing with a friend in need of help at a time when you are just seeing your significant other for the first time in a long time
Pressing Corporate Matter	Making a decision regarding proactive actions that can be taken before a wave of firings commences in your company
Jerry's "Beautyrest Sleeper"	Organizing your friends to move your furniture to a new apartment

Prediction of Freshman-Year Academic Success

In considering our findings, keep in mind that our goal was not excellent prediction of freshman-year performance but rather something even better: prediction of first-year grade-point average (GPA) *above and beyond* what we could get from SAT scores and high school GPA. In other words, we would measure the success of our venture in terms of what it added to existing predictors.

However, our decision to test students at community colleges and universities around the country introduced a kind of handicap: Because the dependent (predicted) variable was freshman GPA and colleges differ widely in their grading systems, we expected that our level of prediction would be lower than if only one college were studied.

We did not expect our analytical measures to add much prediction beyond what is obtained from the SAT because the SAT already is an analytical test. And, in fact, they added only 0.1% prediction over and above that of the SAT, raising the percentage of the variation in scores explained from 9.8% to 9.9%. (If you imagine a pie, where the whole pie represents perfect prediction and none of the pie represents no prediction, then our analytical measure added only 0.1% of the pie to our equation!)

We hoped, however, that our creative and practical measures would add significant predictive power, and they did. The creative measures increased prediction from 9.8% to 12.8%, and the practical measures increased prediction from 9.8% to 10.7%. If we allowed the measures we used to enter freely into the prediction equation, the combination of all our new measures increased prediction from 9.8% to 19.9%, roughly doubling our ability to predict freshman success. If we included high school GPA in the equation, our new measures increased prediction of freshman GPA 1½times (rather than double, as in the case of adding the new assessment to the SAT alone).

So, we now know our measures do seem to make a significant difference in predicting freshman academic success in college, at least in our sample. Among the roughly 1,000 students who took our tests, creative and practical abilities made a difference to academic success beyond the difference made by the analytical abilities as measured by the SAT and beyond what high school GPA measures.

Effect on Ethnic-Group Differences

An issue of concern for colleges and universities in general has been the persistence of gaps in SAT scores between racial and ethnic groups. A key question, therefore, was what would happen to differences among ethnic groups in their potential for admission if new tests were used. Would the new tests increase, decrease, or leave unchanged the level of diversity on college campuses? A test that decreased diversity would certainly be viewed as suspect for practical use.

In fact, use of the Rainbow assessment showed promise of *increasing* diversity. We assessed the impact of our tests on five ethnic groups: European Americans, Latino Americans, African Americans, Asian Americans, and Native Americans. Two different types of data analysis revealed the same results: Ethnic group differences, overall, *decreased* when assessments of creative and practical abilities were added to assessments of analytical ones. Why? Because, on average, backgrounds and methods of socialization differ among racial and ethnic groups, and so broader tests are more likely to capture the full range of their abilities than are narrower ones. For example, Native Americans (although limited in numbers in our sample), on average, did worse on the analytical tests than most other groups, but better on oral storytelling than did any other groups.

Kaleidoscope and Panorama

We had hoped for a second phase of the Rainbow Project, but the College Board did not provide funding, arguing that the tests were not practical on a large scale. I was disappointed because the data had been so good and because our empirical article had been published as the lead article in the leading journal in the field of intellectual abilities. Their argument led me to reflect on how one can turn data into action.

My arrival at Tufts University in the fall of 2005 gave me an opportunity to find out. As Dean of the School of Arts and Sciences at Tufts, I was interested in applying the latest findings in psychology to the education of students at Tufts. After all, we study psychology, at least in part, so that our findings can make a difference to the world. Beginning in the fall of 2006, Tufts added to its college-specific application a section that encourages students, on an optional basis, to select an activity that gives them an opportunity to demonstrate their creative, analytical, and practical skills in ways that conventional tests and college applications perhaps have not fully allowed (Sternberg, 2010; Sternberg, Bonney, Gabora, Karelitz, & Coffin, 2010; Sternberg, Bonney, Gabora, & Merrifield, 2012).

The project was called "Kaleidoscope" in order to emphasize the array of skills the assessments would measure. In addition to the creative, analytical, and practical skills measured in the Rainbow Project, we also assessed wisdom-based thinking. Our goal was to select future ethical leaders who would make a positive, meaningful, and enduring difference to the world. We did not necessarily expect to enhance prediction of grades in Kaleidoscope, but rather, to enhance prediction of leadership skills, in general. For example, one item asked applicants what book they would most like on their bookshelf and why (analytical). Another asked applicants to write a story with a title such as "The End of MTV" (creative). A nonverbal item allowed students to draw an advertisement for a new product (creative). Another item asked applicants how they would convince other students of an idea to which the other students did not initially respond favorably (practical). Yet another item asked students to state how a passion they have in high school could be applied to a common good later in life (wisdom). In carrying out these tasks, students had a fairly free opportunity to demonstrate a broad range of skills needed for college success— skills often hidden from college admissions officers. The essays we use are not the only ways to assess creative and practical skills, but they supplement other ways in providing a concrete opportunity for applicants to display these skills.

Putting the items on the college application rather than having them in a separate test (as in the Rainbow Project) had both advantages and disadvantages. An advantage was that students could ponder their responses rather than being forced to produce them rapidly—a situation particularly advantageous for creative thinking. A disadvantage, however, was that parents, counselors, or others could help the students write their answers. There was no way to know for sure. In measuring skills, no one perfect way exists that can produce a true reading of what anyone can do.

In the first year that we used Kaleidoscope, the number of applications, and the SATs and GPAs of our applicants rose. In particular, we had substantially fewer weaker applicants than we had in previous years. In that year, the number of applications by and acceptances of under-represented minorities increased substantially.

After the students' freshman year, we followed them to observe how they were performing at the university. We found that Kaleidoscope improved prediction of both college freshman GPAs and of meaningful participation in extracurricular activities beyond what we could obtain with SATs and high school GPAs. So we were able to enhance the leadership credentials of our students without adverse effects on academic performance. Students were more satisfied with the application process than they had been before.

I left Tufts and went to Oklahoma State University as Provost and Senior Vice President. Whereas Yale and Tufts were elite private institutions, Oklahoma State is a land-grant public institution. After my second year, we instituted a project called Panorama, similar to Kaleidoscope, which was designed to improve prediction of academic and leadership success (Sternberg, 2012). I only stayed at Oklahoma State for three years, however, so I did not get a chance to find out how Panorama worked.

Now some colleagues and I at Cornell are investigating ways of improving graduate admissions in psychology and related disciplines. Our goal is to help institutions choose the best applicants, but also to guide applicants in figuring out what program or programs might be the best fit for them.

Conclusion

Our goal was to devise assessments that were based on validated psychological principles and would build on already existing assessments. The kinds of abilities measured by the SAT and the ACT—primarily memory and analytical abilities—are important for success in school and in life. But they are not the only abilities that matter. Adults in our changeable environment also need to be able to adapt to rapidly changing environments (the creative aspect) and to apply what they learn in school to their everyday lives (the practical aspect). For example, 2008 and the years following presented a time of massive financial challenges not experienced by most people in their lifetimes. The "old rules" just no longer seemed to apply. People needed not only analytical but also creative and practical abilities to negotiate the new world that these challenges presented.

Every scientific study has a story. The story of the Rainbow Project began in a sense with Galton and Binet; but we have since gone beyond Rainbow, and it is hard to know where the endeavor will end!

☐ Thinking Critically

1. Robert Sternberg has said, "[A]bilities are not fixed but rather flexible . . . and anyone can transform their abilities into competencies, and their competencies into expertise." How is his point of view reflected in his theory and research?

2. What are some situations in which analytic abilities might actually interfere with successful functioning?

☐ Suggested Further Reading

Sternberg, R. J. (2003). *Wisdom, intelligence, and creativity synthesized.* New York: Cambridge University Press.

Sternberg, R. J. (2010). *College admissions for the 21st century.* Cambridge, MA: Harvard University Press.

Sternberg, R. J., & Grigorenko, E. L. (2007). *Teaching for successful intelligence* (2nd ed.). Thousand Oaks, CA: Corwin.

Sternberg, R. J., Jarvin, L., & Grigorenko, E. L. (2011). *Explorations of the nature of giftedness.* New York: Cambridge University Press.

☐ References

Binet, A., & Simon, T. (1916). *The development of intelligence in children* (E. S. Kite, Trans.). Baltimore, MD: Williams & Wilkins.

Bridgeman, B., McCamley-Jenkins, L., & Ervin, N. (2000). *Predictions of freshman grade-point average from the revised and recentered SAT I: Reasoning test.* (College Board Report No. 2000-1). New York: College Entrance Examination Board.

Frey, M. C., & Detterman, D. K. (2004). Scholastic assessment or g? The relationship between the scholastic assessment test and general cognitive ability. *Psychological Science, 15,* 373–378.

Gardner, H. (1983). *Frames of mind: The theory of multiple intelligences.* New York: Basic Books.

Hezlett, S., Kuncel, N., Vey, A., Ones, D., Campbell, J., & Camara, W. J. (2001). *The effectiveness of the SAT in predicting success early and late in college: A comprehensive meta-analysis.* Paper presented at the annual meeting of the National Council of Measurement in Education, Seattle, WA.

Spearman, C. (1927). *The abilities of man.* New York: Macmillan.

Sternberg, R. J. (1985). *Beyond IQ: A triarchic theory of human abilities.* New York: Cambridge University Press.

Sternberg, R. J. (1997). *Successful intelligence.* New York: Plume.

Sternberg, R. J. (2010). *College admissions for the 21st century.* Cambridge, MA: Harvard University Press.

Sternberg, R. J. (2012). College admissions: Beyond conventional testing. *Change, 44*(5), 6–13.

Sternberg, R. J., Bonney, C. R., Gabora, L., Karelitz, T., & Coffin, L. (2010). Broadening the spectrum of undergraduate admissions. *College and University, 86*(1), 2–17.

Sternberg, R. J., Bonney, C. R., Gabora, L, & Merrifield, M. (2012). WICS: A model for college and university admissions. *Educational Psychologist, 47*(1), 30–41.

Sternberg, R. J., & The Rainbow Project Collaborators. (2006). The Rainbow Project: Enhancing the SAT through assessments of analytical, practical, and creative skills. *Intelligence, 34*(4), 321–350.

Terman, L. M., & Merrill, M. A. (1937). *Measuring intelligence.* Boston, MA: Houghton Mifflin.

Emotion and Motivation

Reading Faces: The Universality of Emotional Expression

Paul Ekman and David Matsumoto

Human Self-Regulation and Emotion

E. Tory Higgins

Reading Faces: The Universality of Emotional Expression

PAUL EKMAN University of California, San Francisco
The Paul Ekman Group, LLC
DAVID MATSUMOTO San Francisco State University

☐ **Please describe your current position and research interests.**

PAUL EKMAN: Until I retired in 2004, I was Professor of Psychology in the Department of Psychiatry at the University of California at San Francisco. I am currently Manager, Paul Ekman Group, LLC. My research interests include emotion, nonverbal behavior, and deception.

DAVID MATSUMOTO: I am Professor of Psychology, San Francisco State University and Director of Humintell, LLC. My research interests include cross-cultural communication, nonverbal behavior and emotion, deception, and intergroup violence.

☐ **How did you become interested in the face and reading its expressions of emotion?**

PAUL EKMAN: The ability to detect signs of deception in psychiatric patients.

DAVID MATSUMOTO: Questions concerning why infants and young children could understand the emotional states of their parents and adults around them when they didn't understand language.

☐ **What has been the real-world impact of this work?**

As explained in the essay, we hope that our work will help to create a more humane, compassionate, and safe society for all people of the world.

The universality of facial expressions of emotion is perhaps the most important contribution that basic science has made to our understanding of emotional states in human beings. The idea that specific expressions accompany specific emotions and that these expressions occur in humans everywhere was first proposed by Charles Darwin (1872/1998) more than 100 years ago. Indeed, his ideas about emotions were central to his theory of evolution, suggesting that emotions and their expressions were biologically innate and evolutionarily adaptive, and that similarities could be seen as part of our primate heritage.

But, until the 1960s, the findings on this issue were admittedly inconclusive, and the dominant perspective in psychology at the time was exactly the opposite—that facial expressions were culture-specific, much like language. Darwin's claims were resurrected by Sylvan S. Tomkins (1962), who suggested that emotion was the basis of human motivation and that the seat of emotion was in the face. Tomkins and I (Paul Ekman) joined forces to conduct what are known in the field today as the original universality studies.

Four sources of evidence comprise these studies. In the first, we showed pictures of many different facial expressions to observers in different cultures and asked them to judge which emotion was portrayed in the face. If emotional expressions were universal, we expected to find high agreement within and across cultures in judgments. If emotional expressions were culture-specific, we thought we would find agreement within a culture, but disagreement across cultures. The results revealed high agreement both within and across cultures for six emotional expressions—anger, disgust, fear, happiness, sadness, and surprise. These data were the first systematic evidence for the universality of emotions and their expressions (Ekman, Sorenson, & Friesen, 1969).

Our next two studies assessed the possibility that the cross-cultural similarity in interpretation might be due to shared visual input. (All previous participants were from relatively industrialized countries and they might have learned to recognize emotion through mass media—television, movies, magazines, and so forth.) To address this issue, Wallace Friesen and I went to the highlands of southeast New Guinea to study an isolated, preliterate, stone-age culture devoid of mass media.

In one study, the tribespersons accurately matched the facial expressions of Western adults with stories depicting the relevant emotions (Ekman & Friesen, 1971). This finding was the second source of evidence for universality and addressed the concern about shared visual input; with no access to mass media, the tribespersons had never seen Westerners before. For the next study, we filmed the faces of individual tribespersons as they portrayed what they would look like if they were the person in the stories. We showed those film clips to Americans. Although they had never before seen anyone from the tribe, they accurately identified the emotions the New Guineans intended to portray. We now had two different, additional sources of evidence for universality of facial expression of emotion.

Still critical of our findings, opponents argued that our studies measured judgments of facial expressions, but that they did not show that people in different cultures actually produced those expressions when emotions were spontaneously aroused. We therefore conducted another study in which we videotaped individually American and Japanese participants alone in a room as each watched a highly emotion-provoking film. We analyzed the specific facial muscles that moved in the participants and showed that Americans and Japanese produced the same expressions of emotion—the same six universally recognized emotions (Ekman, 1972). These data provided the fourth source of evidence for universality of facial expression of emotion.

Since then, in judgment and production studies undertaken around the world, David Matsumoto and others have demonstrated convincingly that a small set of facial expressions are universally recognized, and when emotions are aroused, the same facial expressions of emotion are reliably produced by people from all walks of life everywhere (Matsumoto, Keltner, Shiota, Frank, & O'Sullivan, 2008). In other research, we demonstrated the existence of a seventh universal expression: contempt (Ekman & Friesen, 1986; Matsumoto, 1992). Even people who are congenitally blind—that is, blind from birth—spontaneously produce exactly the same facial expressions of emotion when placed in the same kinds of emotionally evocative situations (Matsumoto & Willingham, 2009). We now know that facial expressions are part of a coordinated response system that involves unique physiological responses, specific cognitive activities, preparation for motor behaviors, and specific feelings. Facial expressions are signals of a rich, complex response system we *all* have.

Microexpressions

A second important discovery was the existence of *microexpressions*, which are expressions of intense emotions that flash on and off the face in a fraction of a second, sometimes as fast as 1/30th of a second. They occur so rapidly that if you blink, you miss them. Microexpressions were first discovered by Haggard and Isaacs (1966) in their study of psychotherapy patients. A few years later, Wallace Friesen and I (PE) replicated their initial findings while investigating a problem that had long plagued psychiatric hospitals: determining the risk for suicide in depressed inpatients who had asked for weekend passes. We carefully reviewed films of inpatients who, although apparently improved, nonetheless attempted suicide during their leave. One patient admitted both to wanting to take her life and lying about it during the interview, but we could find nothing in the interview film that betrayed the lie. The patient smiled frequently, spoke optimistically, and was convincingly cheerful.

We then viewed the film in painstaking detail—frame by frame. With 24 frames per second and a 12-minute interview, it took literally over 100 hours to review the film. What we found was amazing: When the doctor asked the patient about her future plans, we noticed a brief but intense expression of anguish that lasted only two frames (1/12 of a second), followed by a smile. In freeze frame, her true emotion was obvious but then deliberately concealed. Finally knowing what to look for, we then found other examples of these extremely fast expressions in the same film. We did further research on microexpressions and found that microexpressions are signs of both deliberately concealed emotions (the person does not want to show his or her true feelings) and repressed emotions (the person does not know what he or she feels) (Ekman & Friesen, 1974).

Real-World Applications

Our rigorous demonstration that specific facial expressions reflect specific basic emotions in humans everywhere confirmed Darwin's insight that there are reliable, observable signs to any person's feelings, regardless of culture, race, ethnicity, gender, class, religion, or age. Our discovery of microexpressions meant that discerning people's true feelings—whether deliberately concealed or repressed from memory—is now possible. Two widely used training programs emerged from our discoveries: In one, people can learn to improve their emotional skills. The second involves improving the ability to evaluate truthfulness.

Improving Emotional Skills

The ability to understand basic emotions is important in many professions and improving those skills often increases the effectiveness of job performance. For example, health professionals skilled in reading others' emotions can develop better rapport with their patients—understanding and reflecting upon the patients' strong feelings about their illnesses, health care providers, caretakers, and themselves. Fortunately, our most recent studies demonstrate that people of various walks of life can learn to read microexpressions and that improvements in this ability are related to important real-world outcomes (Hurley, Anker, Frank, Matsumoto, & Hwang, 2014; Matsumoto & Hwang, 2011).

Physicians often need to have accurate information to make an accurate diagnosis. Yet, if their questions about sexual activity, alcohol consumption, and other behaviors arouse strong emotions (for example, embarrassment or fear), their patients may be unwilling or unable to disclose information essential to diagnosing their condition. Practitioners who can correctly assess a patient's emotional state and who can respond with empathy and compassion provide a comfortable and safe environment where accurate information is likely to emerge.

Learning to understand and regulate one's *own* emotions is key to becoming an effective health care practitioner. Blood, vomit, saliva, and excrement often elicit strong emotions. Burns and lacerations are common, and patients themselves may elicit strong emotions if they are dirty or out of control. Thus, professional and competent healers need considerable emotional control—as medical schools, other health care training institutions, and hospitals have come to realize recently. Our training programs have been delivered to many health care organizations including the world-renowned Mayo Clinic.

Emotional skills are also important in school settings. Teachers who accurately read the emotions of their students can more effectively adjust their lesson plans to students' needs. Burnout, a major issue, is less likely among teachers who understand their own emotions. And in schools where administrators have learned to read the emotions of the staff accurately, burnout is reduced and teacher effectiveness is improved. We have also found that administrators who undergo our training programs are better able to intervene effectively in cases of possible child abuse and other problematic situations. For these reasons our programs are a centerpiece of teacher training programs at institutions such as San Francisco's Center for Emotional Balance.

In the business world, success—whether you are a senior manager or the most junior assistant—depends on successfully nurturing mutually prosperous interpersonal relations and understanding one's own and others' emotions. Reading emotions in others incorrectly can lead to broken deals, destructive office politics, lost sales, and more. Our emotional skills training programs have been offered to businesses in several countries, as well as to organizational consultants including McKenzie Group Consulting, one of the largest organizational development consultants in the world. These programs deliver science-based information to a growing corporate market interested in the assessment and training of emotional intelligence.

Improving emotional skills is also important for moms and dads, husbands and wives, friends and neighbors, and anyone with a vested interest in building strong and constructive relationships. We receive inquiries about training almost daily, and interest is growing.

Evaluating Truthfulness

People are often very emotional when they lie, especially when the stakes are high, and facial expressions, especially microexpressions, can be signs of these emotions. Individuals and organizations with interests in detecting lies have used programs that we have developed. The programs are based on substantiated scientific research as well as the real-work experience of officers and agents who have worked with us. We have offered training to police interrogators not only in the United States but also in many other countries. Participants often discover after training that they see and better understand behavior that previously they misunderstood or misinterpreted. These additional skills invariably help them find ground truth in testimony, depositions, and interrogations. And our most recent research has documented these positive effects of our training as well (Matsumoto, Hwang, Skinner, & Frank, 2014).

We have also provided training to military intelligence officers who conduct interrogations of people encountered during military action, people who are suspected of intending harm against the United States. Military intelligence officers trained in our noncoercive methods for evaluating truthfulness have reported that our training was very useful in many highly charged settings, including use in detention centers and in the field. We have also taught counter-intelligence officers these same skills.

The U.S. State Department Foreign Service Institute has also used our programs to train personnel whose assignments are to conduct visa interviews with citizens of other countries seeking to visit the United States. Our training helps identify people who might be lying during an interview—trying to conceal the intention to work illegally, smuggle drugs, launder money, or engage in terrorist operations. The same skills are needed when interviewing Americans who come to an embassy or consulate to obtain advice, get a passport renewed, or arrange to take home an adopted child.

One trained Foreign Service Officer reported that when interviewing an American abroad, the "passport applicant's face drew up for a split second in a classic disgust microexpression when asked about his supposed hometown. It was enough to raise the suspicion of the Vice Consul, who investigated further and discovered that the true holder of the identity used by the applicant was locked up in a Florida prison. The applicant himself [was] a U.S. citizen wanted for robbery and rape in another state. He had been on the run for several years and previously had been issued a passport in the false identity. Dutch police arrested him."

The Transportation Security Agency (TSA) also includes our training on evaluating truthfulness. The program, called SPOT for "Screening Passengers by Observational Techniques," is currently used in many airports across the country. Thus, in addition to checking tickets, scanning baggage, comparing names to a watch list, and many new technologies, security procedures now include behavioral observation.

To be sure, despite all of the research our colleagues and we have done over the years, we cannot point to one single behavioral sign that on its own signifies deceit. Pinocchio may come to mind as a character with a reliable and observable sign of lying, but he is fictional! Instead, facial expressions can be evidence of emotions that don't match context; we call these hot spots. Our programs train individuals to identify hot spots and provide interviewers with advanced analytic interviewing skills to probe further the nature of the person's state and intent. In the SPOT program run by TSA, for example, when an individual shows a behavior of concern, a SPOT officer approaches the person and asks a few questions while the person remains in line. In many instances, they discover an innocent reason for the unusual behavior. For example, a person showing many signs of worry is trying to remember if he or she turned off the stove before leaving home or is concerned that he or she might miss the flight. In some instances, the person is detained for further interviews, and of those, a few turn out to be people who are wanted by local, state, or federal agencies.

Although very important, facial expressions are just one of several demeanor cues that reveal emotions associated with lying. Other cues include gestures and physiological responses (for example, sweating). When all of these cues are considered simultaneously, the hit rate for detecting lies is very high. We are currently conducting studies to determine the ceiling for this hit rate and how to reduce errors in detecting lies. We are also conducting studies that examine whether people can be trained to conceal the cues, and thus avoid detection.

Conclusion

The discoveries of universal facial expressions of emotion and microexpressions have opened the door to many applications in real-world contexts. We have been touched by the ways our lifework in basic science has been translated to real-world applications that can create a more fruitful partnership at work and home, more effective team performance, and help get the bad guys off the streets, helping to build a more humane, compassionate, and safe society. And, these real-world applications inform basic research of the future, in a healthy and productive cyclical relationship between science and practice. For example, we know everyone lies sometimes, and some people are better than others at detecting lies. But what makes one person better than another at lying or detecting lies? What do natural lie detectors see that we miss? And how exactly does culture influence universal emotions and their expressions? Although we have some ideas, research has yet to address these fundamental and important questions thoroughly. Although the basic findings we helped to create have been important in their own right, we look forward strongly to the future, where new findings will build on the old and create even further insights into the nature of emotions and expressions.

☐ Thinking Critically

1. The response to Paul Ekman's work has shifted from rejection to widespread acceptance. What changes in the field of psychology and in the social world are responsible for this change?

2. What are some practical advantages that result from emotions and their expression being the same for everyone everywhere?

☐ Suggested Further Readings

Ekman, P. (2007). *Emotions revealed* (2nd ed.). New York: Henry Holt.

Ekman, P. (2009). *Telling lies: Clues to deceit in the marketplace, politics, and marriage.* New York: W.W. Norton and Company.

Matsumoto, D., Frank, M., & Hwang, H. S. (Eds.) (2013). *Nonverbal communication: Science and applications.* Thousand Oaks, CA: Sage.

☐ References

Darwin, C. (1998). *The expression of emotions in man and animals.* New York: Oxford University Press. (Original work published 1872)

Ekman, P. (1972). Universal and cultural differences in facial expression of emotion. In J. R. Cole (Ed.), *Nebraska symposium on motivation, 1971* (Vol. 19, pp. 207–283). Lincoln, NE: Nebraska University Press.

Ekman, P., & Friesen, W. V. (1971). Constants across culture in the face and emotion. *Journal of Personality and Social Psychology, 17,* 124–129.

Ekman, P., & Friesen, W. V. (1974). Nonverbal behavior and psychopathology. In R. J. Friedman & M. Katz (Eds.), *The psychology of depression: Contemporary theory and research* (pp. 3–31). Washington, DC: Winston and Sons.

Ekman, P., & Friesen, W. V. (1986). A new pan-cultural facial expression of emotion. *Motivation & Emotion, 10*(2), 159–168.

Ekman, P., Sorenson, E. R., & Friesen, W. V. (1969). Pancultural elements in facial displays of emotion. *Science, 164*(3875), 86–88.

Haggard, E. A., & Isaacs, K. S. (1966). Micro-momentary facial expressions as indicators of ego mechanisms in psychotherapy. In L. A. Gottschalk & A. H. Auerbach (Eds.), *Methods of research in psychotherapy* (pp. 154–165). New York: Appleton-Century-Crofts.

Hurley, C. M., Anker, A. E., Frank, M. G., Matsumoto, D., & Hwang, H. C. (2014). Background factors predicting accuracy and improvement in micro expression recognition. *Motivation and Emotion.* doi: 10.1007/s11031-014-9410-9

Matsumoto, D. (1992). More evidence for the universality of a contempt expression. *Motivation & Emotion, 16*(4), 363–368.

Matsumoto, D., & Hwang, H. S. (2011). Evidence for training the ability to read microexpressions of emotion. *Motivation and Emotion, 35*(2), 181–191.

Matsumoto, D., Hwang, H. C., Skinner, L., & Frank, M. G. (2014). Positive effects in detecting lies from training to recognize behavioral anomalies. *Journal of Police and Criminal Psychology, 29*(1), 28–35. doi: 10.1007/s11896-012-9115-5

Matsumoto, D., Keltner, D., Shiota, M. N., Frank, M. G., & O'Sullivan, M. (2008). What's in a face? Facial expressions as signals of discrete emotions. In J. M. Haviland, M. Lewis, & L. Feldman Barrett (Eds.), *Handbook of emotion* (pp. 211–234). New York: Guilford Press.

Matsumoto, D., & Willingham, B. (2009). Spontaneous facial expressions of emotion of congenitally and noncongenitally blind individuals. *Journal of Personality and Social Psychology, 96*, 1–10. doi: 10.1037/a0014037

Tomkins, S. S. (1962). *Affect, imagery, and consciousness (Vol. 1: The positive affects)*. New York: Springer.

Human Self-Regulation and Emotion

E. TORY HIGGINS Columbia University

☐ **Please describe your current position and research interests.**

I am Stanley Schachter Professor of Psychology, Professor of Business, and Director of the Motivation Science Center at Columbia University. My current research addresses the general question, "Where does value come from?" Beyond the contribution of pleasure and pain to value, my lab is examining another source of value experience—how strongly we are engaged in what we do. Importantly, factors that strengthen engagement, such as obstacles and difficulties, can themselves be unpleasant, but by strengthening engagement, they can increase the value of the goal we are pursuing.

☐ **How did you become interested in self-regulatory processes in human motivation and emotion?**

My personal interest began when I suffered from depression and could not understand, as a psychologist, what was happening to me. After my recovery, I wanted to study what makes people depressed and how it differs from what makes people anxious.

☐ **What has been the real-world impact of this work?**

Over the last decade, new clinical treatments for depression have been developed and used that are directly based on self-discrepancy theory. Currently, my colleagues and I are developing new theory-based distinctions between the psychologies of depression and anxiety that we plan to translate into new and distinct treatments that will be tailored specifically for patients suffering from clinical depression or from generalized anxiety disorder.

Humans share with other animals the general motives of wanting to approach pleasure and avoid pain—the classic hedonic principle of motivation: We experience pleasant emotions when we are successful in our pursuit of goals and painful emotions when we are unsuccessful. But our motivations and emotions also differ from those of other animals in important ways. In this essay, I will consider two questions about these differences—questions that have shaped the course of my investigations into the sources of human vulnerability: What is special about the motivations of the human animal, and what are the emotional implications of these special motivations?

Most psychologists would argue that humans' capacity for reflective self-consciousness—our ability to think consciously about our self—distinguishes us from nonhuman animals. Although the cognitive consequences of this evolutionary development have received the most attention from researchers, significant motivational consequences have been demonstrated as well (see Higgins, 2012).

The ability of humans to engage in reflective self-consciousness is not the only motivationally significant aspect of our inner world, however. As Charles Horton Cooley (1864–1929) noted many years ago, "most of our reflective consciousness, of our wide-awake state of mind, is social consciousness, because a sense of our relation to other persons, or of other persons to one another, can hardly fail to be part of it" (1902/1962, p. 5). Such social consciousness involves awareness that the outcomes of our actions are determined by others' responses to those actions. People are motivated to behave in ways that result in the power and influence of others being used for them and not against them.

Importantly, human children by 3 to 6 years of age also recognize that the inner states of another person, such as a parent's beliefs, feelings, expectancies, and desires mediate that person's positive or negative response to their behavior. Equally significant, humans are aware that their own inner states—their own beliefs, competencies, and motives—can be the source of others' feelings, expectancies, and desires: Children have no difficulty, for example, in recognizing a parent's desire that they acquire a particular competency (for example, the ability to work hard). This crucial human discovery has profound effects on motivation (Grant Halvorson & Higgins, 2013; Higgins, 2012).

Perhaps because of this discovery, humans are unique in their capacity to imagine future-self competencies—whom they might become, hope to become, dream of becoming, fear becoming—and then using these future-self competencies as reference values for self-regulation in the present (Higgins, 1987; Markus & Nurius, 1986; Oettingen, 2012; Oyserman, 2013). Scholars have recognized for a long time that people imagine their future selves—their "potential" self (James, 1890/1948) or their "ideal" self (Rogers, 1961). Not until the late 1980s, however, did psychologists begin to investigate extensively two important functions of imagined future selves: (1) as goals or incentives that influence current planning and decisions, and (2) as standards or reference points for evaluating and interpreting the current self (Higgins, 1987; Markus & Nurius, 1986).

Imagined Future Selves as Goals or Incentives

In a landmark study of college students, Hazel Markus and Paula Nurius (1986) demonstrated the importance of future selves as an element in a person's self-knowledge. Two-thirds of their student–participants reported that they thought about their possible selves in the future a great deal of the time or all the time. The ratio of positive, "hoped-for" selves to negative, "feared" selves was almost 4 to 1. The positive and negative possible selves, these researchers argued, provide direction and impetus for action and change. Imagining that a desired future self—say, a successful self, a creative self, a loved and admired self—is possible is a form of optimism, and imagining that such selves are not possible is a form of pessimism, and, generally speaking, optimistic thinking about the future yields higher motivation and better performance than does pessimistic thinking. But imagining desired future selves alone or possible selves alone is not sufficient for effective self-regulation. What is effective is imagining future selves that are both desirable and possible.

Also effective is imagining not only desired future selves but also future difficulties and obstacles to attaining these desired selves. For example, commitment to and energizing of goal-directed actions increases when people both fantasize a desired (and possible) future self and imagine how to overcome realistic obstacles that could hinder their success (Oettingen, 2012). People are also more likely to experience an imagined desired self as being a truly possible self in the future if they can image themselves carrying out a strategy to reach that desired self. In one study, eighth graders from low-income families who possessed possible selves with a strategic self-regulator quality (that is, who believed that they could make it to high school by paying attention in class) had academic outcomes that were superior to classmates with purely self-enhancing possible selves (Oyserman, 2013).

Imagined Future Selves as Evaluative Standards or Reference Points

Imagined future selves function not only as directive goals but also as standards to evaluate current actual selves. This self-evaluation process also has major motivational and emotional effects as the self-evaluative process produces pleasant and painful emotions. Some of these self-evaluative emotions, such as pride or shame, are unique to humans because the self-evaluative process involves an awareness that one's actual self is, respectively, congruent with or discrepant from others' expectations (Grant Halvorson & Higgins, 2013; Higgins, 1987). Such socially conscious emotions can be highly motivating.

Emotional Consequences of Imagined Future Selves as Evaluative Standards

Fascinating questions arise when considering the emotional implications of human self-evaluation processes. In particular, why does success in achieving the same objective make some people feel happy or joyful while others feel relaxed or peaceful? Why does failure to achieve the same objective make some people feel sad or discouraged while others feel nervous or worried? Regarding emotional pain from failure, clinical psychologists, especially, have wondered why the same stressful life event, such as being divorced or being fired, can make some people clinically depressed while making others clinically anxious. Giants in the field, such as Sigmund Freud and Carl Rogers, described psychological mechanisms that underlie depression and anxiety. They did not, however, explain why the same failure or negative life event can cause depression in one person and anxiety in another. My self-discrepancy theory (Higgins, 1987) was developed specifically to address this issue.

I started with a consistent finding from several decades of psychological studies: When people experience a discrepancy between the kind of person they believe they are currently (their actual self) and the kind of person they want to be (their desired self), they feel bad. If the discrepancy is extreme and relates to a significant aspect of the desired self, then it can produce extreme negative feeling, such as depression and anxiety. Thus, the magnitude and significance of a discrepancy between an actual self and a desired self are major factors in the story of how failure or negative life events produce severe emotional distress. Clinicians have also known that the magnitude and significance of a congruency between an actual self and a desired self makes people feel good. Indeed, people's self-esteem depends on their having actual self/desired self congruencies.

Self-discrepancy theory introduced an additional factor critical for understanding the emotional impact of actual self/desired self congruencies and discrepancies—the notion that there are different types of desired states, or self-guides, that function as goals to attain or standards to be met. The theory distinguishes between two types of self-guides—an ideal self-guide, representing a person's hopes, wishes, and aspirations; and an ought self-guide, representing a person's beliefs about his or her personal duties, obligations, and responsibilities. The type of self-guide that is involved in self-regulation is the crucial factor in the differing emotional effects of the same life event on different people or on the same person at different times.

Specifically, self-discrepancy theory proposes that an actual self/desired self that is congruent or discrepant with people's ideal self-guides leads us to experiences along the cheerfulness-dejection dimension of emotions (for example, feeling happy after success and sad or even depressed after failure). In contrast, an actual self/desired self congruent or discrepant with people's ought self-guides results in emotions along the quiescence-agitation dimension (for example, feeling relaxed after success and nervous or even anxious after failure).

Most of the research on self-discrepancies and congruencies has focused on the distinction between ideal and ought self-guides. Research has shown that for self-guide discrepancies and congruencies to have emotional and motivational effects, they have to have high accessibility or high readiness to be activated. This condition could occur because some individuals have self-guides that are chronically high in accessibility. It can also occur because a situation temporarily makes people's self-guides high in accessibility. When this accessibility condition is clearly met, research has shown that, as predicted, congruencies and discrepancies from ideal self-guides produce emotions along the cheerfulness-dejection dimension, whereas congruencies and discrepancies from ought self-guides produce emotions along the quiescence-agitation dimension.

Importantly, researchers working with clinical patients (who typically have self-guides that are chronically accessible) have found that those who have mainly actual self-discrepancies to their ideal self-guides suffer from clinical depression, whereas those who have mainly actual self-discrepancies to their ought self-guides suffer from clinical anxiety. Applied research on clinical depression has demonstrated that interventions that reduce patients' ideal discrepancies produce a decrease in severity of their depressive disorder (Strauman et al., 2006).

Self-discrepancy theory considers congruencies and discrepancies from ideals and oughts in terms of particular types of psychological situations that people experience. An ideal congruency is experienced as the presence of a positive (that is, a gain). An ideal discrepancy is experienced as the absence of a positive (that is, a nongain). An ought congruency is experienced as the absence of a negative (that is, a nonloss). An ought discrepancy is experienced as the presence of a negative (that is, a loss). These different psychological situations underlie the different emotions associated with congruencies and discrepancies to ideals and oughts (see Figure 1). For example, when people experience the presence of a positive (ideal congruency), they feel happy; and when they experience the absence of a positive (ideal discrepancy), they feel sad. When people experience the absence of a negative (ought congruency), they feel relaxed; and when they experience the presence of a negative (ought discrepancy), they feel nervous.

Motivated-Cognition Consequences of Imagined Future Selves as Evaluative Standards

Research has shown that the different psychological situations associated with ideal and ought congruencies and discrepancies have implications beyond their emotional significance. These situations function like personal constructs—worldviews that influence how individuals perceive and remember the world around them (Kelly, 1955). Thus, for example, people remember better those events in a story that match their accessible self-guides (that is, they are more likely to recall story events involving the presence or absence of something positive when ideals are accessible than when oughts are accessible). People also remember better those events in their own lives that relate to whichever type of self-guide is more accessible for them.

Beyond their importance for people's emotional lives, research has shown, for example, that ideal and ought discrepancies relate to different physical problems, such as ideal discrepancies being associated with bulimia and stomach ailments and ought discrepancies being associated with anorexia and headaches. Individuals with ideal discrepancies have been found to have greater empathy for other people who suffer from dejection-related

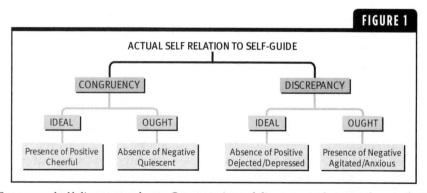

Summary of self-discrepancy theory. Congruencies and discrepancies between the actual self and the ideal or ought self-guides lead to characteristic feelings and have long-term effects.

problems, whereas those with ought discrepancies have greater empathy for those suffering from agitation-related problems.

In addition, recent research has shown that self-regulation operates differently when it serves different motives in decision-making situations. Ideal self-regulation serves a promotion focus, a concern with accomplishment and advancement. In contrast, ought self-regulation serves a prevention focus, a concern with security and safety. When promotion-focus ideals are relatively more accessible (whether situationally activated or chronically accessible), people are more open to change and are more creative than when their prevention-focus oughts are more accessible. Conversely, when people's oughts are more accessible, they are more accurate and analytic than when their promotion focus ideals are more accessible. And, importantly, it is possible for individuals to make either their promotion focus or their prevention focus more accessible in order to best fit what the immediate situation demands (for example, to be either more creative or more analytic), thereby enhancing success (Grant Halvorson & Higgins, 2013).

Conclusion

The emotional lives of humans vary depending on the personal standards toward which we strive. We are constantly asking ourselves: Are we the type of people we aspire to be in the future (promotion-focus ideals)? Are we the type of people we believe we should be in the future (prevention-focus oughts)? These kinds of self-regulatory processes underlie our entire strategic response to and views about the world. Thus, our unique characteristic—our ability to imagine the inner states that we want to attain (or maintain) in the future and the type of person that we want to be and become—is critical to human motivation and emotion.

___

☐ Thinking Critically

1. What is Tory Higgins's evidence that evaluating ourselves against inner standards can produce emotional states that have long-term consequences?
2. Experiencing discrepancies between how we see ourselves and how we want to be creates problems for most people. What could be helpful in dealing with such difficulties?

☐ Suggested Further Reading

Grant Halvorson, H., & Higgins, E. T. (2013). *Focus: Use different ways of seeing the world for success and influence.* New York: Penguin Press.
Higgins, E. T. (1987). Self-discrepancy: A theory relating self and affect. *Psychological Review, 94,* 319–340.

☐ References

Cooley, C. H. (1964). *Human nature and the social order.* New York: Schocken Books. (Original work published 1902)

Grant Halvorson, H., & Higgins, E. T. (2013). *Focus: Use different ways of seeing the world for success and influence.* New York: Penguin Press.

Higgins, E. T. (1987). Self-discrepancy: A theory relating self and affect. *Psychological Review, 94,* 319–340.

Higgins, E. T. (2012). *Beyond pleasure and pain: How motivation works.* New York: Oxford University Press.

James, W. (1948). *Psychology.* New York: The World Publishing Company. (Original work published 1890)

Kelly, G. A. (1955). *The psychology of personal constructs.* New York: W. W. Norton.

Markus, H., & Nurius, P. (1986). Possible selves. *American Psychologist, 41,* 954–969.

Oettingen, G. (2012). Future thought and behaviour change. *European Review of Social Psychology, 23,* 1–63.

Oyserman, D. (2013). Not just any path: Implications of identity-based motivation for disparities in school outcomes. *Economics of Education Review, 33,* 179–190.

Rogers, C. R. (1961). *On becoming a person.* Boston: Houghton Mifflin Company.

Strauman, T. J., Vieth, A. Z., Merrill, K. A., Kolden, G. G., Woods, T. E., Klein, M. H., et al. (2006). Self-system therapy as an intervention for self-regulatory dysfunction in depression: A randomized comparison with cognitive therapy. *Journal of Consulting and Clinical Psychology, 74,* 367–376.

Development

Cultural Variation in Children's Attention and Learning

Barbara Rogoff, Maricela Correa-Chávez,
and Katie G. Silva

Preserving Infant Memories

Carolyn Rovee-Collier

Cultural Variation in Children's Attention and Learning

BARBARA ROGOFF University of California, Santa Cruz
MARICELA CORREA-CHÁVEZ University of California, Los Angeles, now at California State University, Long Beach
KATIE G. SILVA University of California, Santa Cruz

☐ **Please describe your current position and research interests.**

BARBARA ROGOFF: I hold the UCSC Foundation Distinguished Professorship of Psychology at University of California, Santa Cruz. My research focuses on cultural aspects of how children learn, especially learning by observing and pitching in to family and community activities in Indigenous-heritage communities of North and Central America.

MARICELA CORREA-CHÁVEZ: I am Assistant Professor of Psychology at California State University, Long Beach. The focus of my research is the cultural organization of learning in communities with Indigenous North and Central American histories, cultural differences in attention and communication in learning, and tools and strengths that children from Latin American immigrant families bring to school contexts.

KATIE SILVA: I am a research associate in the Department of Psychology at the University of California, Santa Cruz. My research is on children's learning through observation, teasing with adults, and family stories, especially in Mexican-heritage communities.

☐ **How did you become interested in the social and collaborative nature of children's learning?**

Our interest in the cultural, social, and collaborative nature of children's learning comes from each of our experiences studying children's development and living in communities that vary in their cultural organization, including a Maya community in Guatemala; the highlands of Utah; eastern Australia; Santa Cruz and Los Angeles, California; several regions of Mexico; and a Mexican-American area in New Mexico.

☐ **What has been the real-world impact of this work?**

We hope that our research contributes to improving the well-being and learning of children, by encouraging greater opportunities for them to be present, observe, and contribute to important activities of their families and communities. In addition, we hope that the research enhances mutual understanding among people of varying cultural backgrounds.

At age 80, Caroline Pratt, a leader in education who grew up in the mid-1800s, thought back on her childhood community and the abundance of opportunities for learning through observing and participating in community activities:

> When I grew up in Fayetteville, New York, school was not very important to children who could roam the real world freely for their learning. . . . No one had to tell us where milk came from, or how butter was made. We helped to harvest wheat, saw it ground into flour in the mill on our own stream; I baked bread for the family at thirteen. There was a paper mill, too, on our stream; we could learn the secrets of half a dozen other industries merely by walking through the open door of a neighbor's shop. (Pratt, 1948, pp. xi–xii)

These experiences underline important cultural aspects of childhood that interest developmental psychologists who focus on the ways that social, cultural, and historical processes organize the lives of children and their communities. In this essay, we discuss our research revealing cultural differences in how children learn and pay attention.

Cultural research has inspired important innovations in the organization of children's learning opportunities. For example, the use of collaboration in classrooms was prompted in large part by observations of the home practices of native Hawaiian children, who spent much of their day in groups of children helping in their household. These observations sparked the inclusion of group work and other new approaches to learning in innovative classrooms in the Kamehameha schools in Hawaii, which then spread to many other schools. Such innovations are especially important for children whose community background differs from mainstream middle-class experience, and they have also improved learning opportunities for children from other backgrounds, including the "mainstream" middle class.

In our own research, we have studied cultural differences in how children pay attention to and learn from events going on around them. We focus on patterns of attention and learning that seem to be related to children's experience in two different learning traditions. One approach to learning emphasizes children's participation in a wide range of family and community activities; this approach is common in many Indigenous communities in North and Central America. Another approach to learning, which is common in middle-class communities, separates children from the range of family and community activities and instead presents exercises and lessons in specialized settings such as school.

Learning by Observing and Pitching In versus Lessons Out of the Context of Productive Activity

Indigenous communities of the Americas often use a way of organizing learning in which children are present during family and community activities and are expected and allowed to help out. This way of learning is called *Learning by Observing and Pitching In* ("LOPI," Rogoff, 2014; previously called *intent participation*, Rogoff, Paradise, Mejía Arauz, Correa-Chávez, & Angelillo, 2003).

In many traditional Indigenous communities of the Americas, children are embedded in community activities from a very young age. For example, in Zinacantán, Mexico, eight-month-old infants spend two-thirds of the day carried on a caregiver's back as she goes about her daily activities (de Leon, 2000). As children grow older, they continue to be present when adults engage in important daily activities such as buying and selling in the market, tending to fields and engaging in other work, conversing, and in most community activities. In such Indigenous communities, children notice surrounding events even while engaged in another activity like play (de Haan, 1999; Gaskins, 2000; Tsethlikai & Rogoff, 2013). They keenly observe and pitch in to ongoing events, many of which are not directed toward them or designed to instruct them. For example, a child accompanying a parent to sell items in the market can see how the parent makes change and can begin to help when ready. Children are expected to observe ongoing activities and develop keen attention to events around them.

By contrast, children in middle-class European-American communities are frequently segregated from the range of community social activities and work. For example, toddlers in two middle-class European-American communities were less often in the company of adults working and were more frequently engaged in specialized child-focused activities than children in a Mayan town in Guatemala and Efe foragers of the Democratic Republic of Congo (Morelli, Rogoff, & Angelillo, 2003). Thus, middle-class children have comparatively restricted opportunities to learn by observing the range of important community activities.

Instead, middle-class children are often involved in teachers' or parents' lessons or exercises that are separate from the productive activities of everyday life. Middle-class adults' interactions with children often involve lessons that do not include applying the skill being taught to accomplish something important in children's lives, such as lessons that teach words without actually using them to communicate. In such lessons and exercises, the children's attention and motivation are frequently managed by adults, rather than by the children themselves.

Cultural Comparisons of Attention

Is learning through wide, keen observation more common in Indigenous communities of the Americas than in middle-class U.S. communities? This idea comes from research that has reported impressive use of observation in Indigenous communities, with the assumption that it is more common than in the researchers' own middle-class communities.

Several systematic comparisons of cultural differences in attention support the idea of more frequent use of broad, keen attention in Indigenous communities of the Americas than in middle-class settings. These studies involve families from regions of Mexico and Guatemala where a family history of limited schooling may mean more (or more recent) family experience with traditional Indigenous practices such as Learning by Observing and Pitching In. For example, children whose families likely had experience with

Indigenous practices of Mexico and limited experience with school focused skillfully their attention on several events simultaneously more often than did European- and Mexican-heritage U.S. children whose mothers had extensive experience in Western schooling, who more often focused on one event at a time in rapid alternation (Correa-Chávez, Rogoff, & Mejía Arauz, 2005). Similarly, Guatemalan Mayan toddlers and their mothers attended simultaneously and skillfully to several events more often than did middle-class European-heritage toddlers and mothers, who tended to alternate attention between events (Chavajay & Rogoff, 1999).

These differences are consistent with the idea that children from families with experience with Indigenous practices of the Americas are more likely to broadly and keenly observe events than are middle-class children (a cultural group partially defined by extensive Western schooling). The differences also suggest that families with extensive experience with schooling may encourage children to learn in ways that resemble the learning approaches often used in schools.

Cultural Differences in Observing the Interactions of Others

Our work explores children's attention when they had the chance to observe the interactions of others without being addressed directly. All children learn from interactions that are not addressed to them directly. For example, they learn some aspects of language by overhearing others speak, and they learn to emulate violence by watching television shows that are not designed for them.

However, opportunities to learn by observing surrounding interactions are more common for children who are included in the range of their community's events—they are present but may not be involved directly when others are carrying out their work or social activities. Children with more experience of being included in a range of family and community activities, such as in many Indigenous American communities, may be more attentive when they are not addressed than children whose families have extensive experience with contrasting practices typical of Western schools and related institutions.

We conducted two studies that found especially keen attention and enhanced learning among children whose families had experience with Indigenous practices, particularly when they were present at an interaction that was directed to someone else. Children from families with extensive schooling experience were less attentive and learned less from nearby interactions.

In both studies, a research assistant showed one child how to make an interesting toy (a foam mouse that runs), while his or her sibling sat waiting at another table. The nonaddressed sibling sat near but not facing the research assistant and the child making the toy. The waiting sibling was shown a different toy (an origami jumping frog) that he or she would make soon and was invited to play with a distracter toy in the meantime. This way, the nonaddressed child was present during the toy-making demonstration and could watch but he or she was not told to observe and would not anticipate needing to observe in order to know how to make the toy he or she would soon make. We videotaped the children and coded the extent to which each child paid attention to their sibling's toy construction while they waited.

About a week later, we examined the children's learning from the instruction addressed to their siblings by unexpectedly inviting them to construct the toy that they previously had the opportunity to observe being constructed. When the children returned to pick up the toy they had made, the research assistant said, "Oh, it turns out we have some extra materials. Would you like to make the toy that your [brother/sister] made last week?"

The research assistant then offered the materials and sat back, seemingly occupied with some work. We videotaped the child's efforts and coded the amount of help needed from the research assistant. The research assistant followed a script that designated specific escalating steps of help they were to provide a child when he or she could not proceed alone.

In the first study, we compared the attention and learning of 120 children from three cultural backgrounds: (1) Guatemalan Mayan children whose mothers had extensive experience with traditional Indigenous practices and limited exposure to middle-class Western ways; (2) Mayan children from the same town whose mothers had more familiarity with middle-class Western ways through extensive schooling and related practices; and (3) European-American middle-class children whose families had extensive familiarity with middle-class Western ways through schooling and related practices (Correa-Chávez & Rogoff, 2009).

We found that the Mayan children of both backgrounds were more likely to sustain attention to interactions directed to their sibling than the European-American middle-class children. The Mayan children spent most of the time watching, whereas the European-American children spent most of the time not attending to the construction or only glancing at it briefly and casually. The differences between the Mayan children from more traditional families and the European-American children were especially pronounced; the extent of attention of Mayan children from families familiar with Western ways fell between the other two background groups. When the children were given the chance to make their sibling's toy, the Mayan children from more traditional families also showed that they had generally learned more—they commonly needed less help than the children from the other two backgrounds.

The second study, which involved children from two populations that were not living in an Indigenous community, showed similar results. This study examined the attention and learning of 80 children from two cultural backgrounds: (1) U.S. children from Indigenous-heritage regions of Mexico whose families were likely more familiar with Indigenous ways and less familiar with middle-class Western ways and (2) U.S. children from Mexico whose families were more familiar with Western ways through extensive schooling and related experience (Silva, Correa-Chávez, & Rogoff, 2010;

similar findings were also obtained by López, Correa-Chávez, Rogoff, & Gutiérrez, 2010).

The U.S. Mexican-heritage children whose families likely had more experience with Indigenous practices (and whose mothers had limited Western schooling) engaged more in sustained attention to the interactions directed to their sibling than the U.S. Mexican-heritage children whose mothers had extensive experience in Western schooling (and related practices). They also learned how to construct the toy with less help from the research assistant.

These results support the idea that children whose families have experience with Indigenous American community practices—where children are often present and expected to learn from surrounding events—observe more keenly in situations when they are not directly addressed than do middle-class children, from extensive schooling backgrounds. These findings fit with prior research that found that even when Indigenous Mexican children were playing, they monitored nearby adult activity for moments when their presence would be needed (de Haan, 1999; Gaskins, 2000). We also found that when children attend to events not addressed to them, they learn from observing.

Participation in Cultural Practices and Institutions

Children appear to develop patterns of attention related to the cultural practices of their families, communities, and the institutions in which they participate. The differences we found align with the idea that children from families from communities where children are present and expected to pitch in to a wide range of family and community activities observe more keenly nearby interactions, even when there is no obvious need to do so. These children may learn more from observing than children from families and communities that do not have such experience and instead have extensive experience in institutions with contrasting practices of attention and learning—especially Western schooling.

Involvement in the now-ubiquitous institution of schooling is a cultural experience. For those of us who have extensive schooling—almost all of the readers of this essay—it is easy to think of school as a "natural" feature of growing up. But mass, extensive schooling is a feature of children's lives only in some countries and has been available only for the last century or so, anywhere.

Although we refer to schooling as a key cultural experience, extent of schooling is only one part of a constellation of associated practices that fit together. Increases in experience with Western schooling in Indigenous-heritage communities are associated with many other changed practices—such as migration to urban settings or to the United States, new occupations, greater media access, reduced family size, and less involvement of extended family in children's lives (Rogoff & Angelillo, 2002; Rogoff, Correa-Chávez, & Navichoc Cotuc, 2005).

Thus, although we have examined schooling differences, we do not regard schooling as the only "active ingredient" in community differences. We see

differences in the extent of families' experience with Western school practices as potentially contributing, along with many associated practices, to
community differences in how children go about learning. Experiences with
school practices, along with many other cultural experiences, likely foster
certain ways of managing attention and provide expectations of what is considered a learning opportunity. Families with extensive experience in Western schooling—and related practices—may encourage children to depend on
adults to organize their attention and to expect that the primary source of
learning opportunities are adult-led lessons directed to them.

Implications of Cultural Differences in Learning by Observing

Cultural research on human development provides evidence of how children's lives vary in accordance with the practices of their communities. Cultural research also provides inspiration for changes in current practices to
make them more conducive to children's learning and well-being. In this final
section, we suggest some changes to improve children's learning in schools
and in the broader organization of family and community life.

We suggest that schools shift their organization to make greater use of
opportunities to learn by observing. In the usual organization of classrooms,
children have little opportunity to learn by observing their classmates or
teachers. Students are often discouraged from watching each other, and
teachers seldom actively participate in the exercises that they are teaching.
However, some innovative elementary schools (such as the "OC" in Salt Lake
City and Academia Semillas del Pueblo in Los Angeles) structure classroom
learning in a way that allows students to learn from observing the work of
adults and of other children on meaningful projects (Rogoff, Goodman Turkanis, & Bartlett, 2001). Enhancing children's opportunities to learn by observing others would benefit all children. Middle-class children could learn to
make more use of observation, and children from Indigenous-heritage backgrounds could make use of keen observation that they may be familiar with
in their families and communities.

In the United States, the organization of children's out-of-school lives also
provides limited opportunities to learn by observing and beginning to pitch
in to a wide range of family and community activities. The exceptions are
instructive. For example, Mexican immigrant children whose parents do
not speak English often accompany their parents in bureaucratic and other
complex U.S. institutional settings, helping as translators. Children in these
immigrant families thereby learn a great deal about a range of community
work and other activities, and they show impressive skill in handling them.
Although children's work as translators may be challenging, it also gives
them an opportunity to develop skills and to make important contributions
to their family (Dorner, Orellana, & Li-Grining, 2007).

On the basis of our research, we advocate decreasing the segregation of
middle-class children from the range of mature activities of their communities, giving them greater opportunities to learn by observing and beginning

to pitch in. When industrialized nations prohibited children from working in factories about a century ago, they were trying to prevent child exploitation; at that time many young children worked long hours in dangerous conditions. However, we feel that social policies and the organization of life in the United States have gone too far in excluding children from places where they can learn and from making contributions to their families and communities. Such contributions, we argue, are important not only for children's learning but also for their feeling of contributing something of value.

Of course, major structural changes in workplaces and changes to social expectations would be needed to undo the extreme segregation that children today often experience in middle-class settings in the United States (and around the world). However, on a small scale, some middle-class families in postindustrial nations manage to integrate children more fully in their work and social lives. For example, lawyers and real estate agents who manage their own offices sometimes organize their workplaces in ways that allow children to be present. Children of parents who telecommute have a chance to be present as their parents work.

Some occupations may be more conducive to very young children's actual contributions. However, observing even in settings that have fewer openings for young children to participate allows them to learn about those occupations and about work more generally. Children can pick up far more from observing and listening in on activities than we give them credit for. For example, one of the best predictors of children's early reading is the extent to which people around them read. If children see people reading, regardless of whether people read to them, they are more prepared to learn to read themselves. Relatedly, it is probably no accident that children of academics often have a relatively easy time in school, and children of doctors seem to become doctors at a level greater than chance.

If children are excluded from the range of their family's and community's activities, they have little chance to learn how to behave or contribute. However, if they can be present and begin to pitch in, they can learn how to blend with the community's social and work life. Allowing children to be present in a wide range of family and community activities permits them to develop an understanding of the valued work and other activities in their communities. On the basis of our research with families from communities where children have had wide opportunities to observe and pitch in, we argue that children everywhere deserve opportunities to be present to observe and learn how to fit in and to make meaningful contributions to their families and communities.

Author Note Author order does not reflect relative contribution to the development of this article; authorship was constrained by editorial policy to reflect seniority; all three authors contributed equally.

Acknowledgments We are grateful to the children, families, and teachers who participated in the research, and to our colleagues who have contributed work along related lines. The writing of this article was supported by a postdoctoral fellowship from the American Educational Research Association/Institute of Education Sciences to Maricela Correa-Chávez; a fellowship from the Center for Informal Learning and Schools

(NSF ESI# 0119787) to Katie Silva; and a sabbatical from UCSC, the UCSC Foundation Professorship, and a fellowship at the Center for Advanced Study in the Behavioral Sciences to Barbara Rogoff.

☐ Thinking Critically

1. How have your own ways of learning been influenced by practices in your own cultural community?
2. What effects might schooling have on children's roles in their family and society compared to the effects of ways of learning in communities where children are included broadly in their community's activities?

☐ Suggested Further Reading

Rogoff, B. (2011). *Developing destinies: A Mayan midwife and town.* New York: Oxford University Press.

Rogoff, B. (2003). *The cultural nature of human development.* New York: Oxford University Press.

Rogoff, B., Alcalá, L., Coppens, A. D., López, A., Ruvalcaba, O., & Silva, K. G. (2014). Learning by observing and pitching in to family and community endeavors. *Human Development, 57,* 65–170.

☐ References

Chavajay, P., & Rogoff, B. (1999). Cultural variation in management of attention by children and their caregivers. *Developmental Psychology, 35,* 1079–1090.

Correa-Chávez, M., & Rogoff, B. (2009). Children's attention to interactions directed to others: Guatemalan Mayan and European American patterns. *Developmental Psychology, 45,* 630–641.

Correa-Chávez, M., Rogoff, B., & Mejía Arauz, R. (2005). Cultural patterns in attending to two events at once. *Child Development, 76,* 664–678.

de Haan, M. (1999). Learning as cultural practice: How children learn in a Mexican Mazahua community. Indiana: Purdue University Press.

de Leon, L. (2000). The emergent participant: Interactive patterns in the socialization of Tzotzil (Mayan) infants. *Journal of Linguistic Anthropology, 8*(2), 131–161.

Dorner, L. M., Orellana, M. F., & Li-Grining, C. P. (2007). "I helped my mom," and it helped me: Translating the skills of language brokers into improved standardized test scores. *American Journal of Education, 113,* 451–478.

Gaskins, S. (2000). Children's daily activities in a Mayan village: A culturally grounded description. *Cross-Cultural Research, 34*(4), 375–389.

López, A., Correa-Chávez, M., Rogoff, B., & Gutiérrez, K. (2010). Attention to instruction directed to another by U.S. Mexican-heritage children of varying cultural backgrounds. *Developmental Psychology, 46,* 593–601.

Morelli, G. A., Rogoff, B., & Angelillo, C. (2003). Cultural variation in young children's access to work or involvement in specialized child-focused activities. *International Journal of Behavioral Development, 27,* 264–274.

Pratt, C. (1948). *I learn from children: An adventure in progressive education.* New York: Simon & Schuster.

Rogoff, B. (2014). Learning by observing and pitching in to family and community endeavors: An orientation. *Human Development, 57,* 69–81.

Rogoff, B., & Angelillo, C. (2002). Investigating the coordinated functioning of multifaceted cultural practices in human development. *Human Development, 45*, 211–225.

Rogoff, B., Correa-Chávez, M., & Navichoc Cotuc, M. (2005). A cultural-historical view of schooling in human development. In D. Pillemer & S. H. White (Eds.), *Developmental psychology and social change* (pp. 225–263). New York: Cambridge University Press.

Rogoff, B., Goodman Turkanis, C., & Bartlett, L. (2001). *Learning together: Children and adults in a school community.* New York: Oxford University Press.

Rogoff, B., Paradise, R., Mejía Arauz, R., Correa-Chávez, M., & Angelillo, C. (2003). First-hand learning through intent participation. *Annual Review of Psychology, 54*, 175–203.

Silva, K. G., Correa-Chávez, M., and Rogoff, B. (2010). Mexican-heritage children's attention and learning from interactions directed to others. *Child Development, 81*, 898–912. doi: 10.1111/j.1467-8624.2010.01441.x

Tsethlikai, M., & Rogoff, B. (2013). Involvement in traditional cultural practices and American Indian children's incidental recall of a folktale. *Developmental Psychology, 49*, 568–578.

Preserving Infant Memories

CAROLYN ROVEE-COLLIER Rutgers University

With great sadness, we acknowledge the passing of Dr. Carolyn Rovee-Collier. We honor her scholarship and contributions to psychology in this volume.

☐ Please describe your current position and research interests.

I am Professor II of Psychology at Rutgers University. I study learning and long-term memory in 2- to 24-month-old human infants, examining how they form new associations, how their memories are prolonged, and how new information updates their memory of a prior event.

☐ How did you come to study long-term memory in preverbal infants?

My graduate research with newborns was ongoing in the same lab when the first study of newborn classical conditioning was being conducted. Later, when I reported that 2½-month-olds could be operantly conditioned, it made a big impact because there was no evidence that infants could remember what they had learned longer than a few seconds to minutes at most. Without a capacity for long-term memory, how could infants' early experiences be important for their later behavior? I wondered why they had bothered to learn in the first place. This question motivated my research.

☐ What has been the real-world impact of this work?

First, by documenting the importance of early stimulation, enriched environments, and varied experience and their enduring impact on subsequent cognitive development, our findings have major implications for both caregivers and public policymakers. Second, our findings can inform parents, practitioners, and educators about how to introduce and program new information so that it can be learned most efficiently and remembered longer. Third, the findings make possible the formulation of personalized interventions to ameliorate the learning and memory deficits of cognitively impaired individuals of all ages, whether brain damaged or not, and have offered new insights into the elimination of undesirable behaviors.

For more than a century, scientists have believed that infants' early experiences have a lasting impact. Paradoxically, they also believe that young infants lack the capacity for long-term memory and cannot retain memories for more than a few seconds or minutes until late in the first year of life. Unless infants are able to preserve a relatively enduring record of their early experiences in some form or other, how could the impact of those experiences possibly last? Our research on infant memory has not only confirmed that the effects of early experiences are relatively enduring, but it also has revealed how infants remember them.

How Long Do Infants Remember?

The short answer to this question is longer than you think. The long answer is it depends on how the infant acquired the memory (that is, the original parameters of training or exposure to an event), the infant's age (older infants initially remember longer), and the infant's prior retrieval experience. Specifically, the more times the infant has retrieved a particular memory in the past, the longer it will be remembered in the future, and the longer the interval between one memory retrieval and the next, the longer the infant will remember the event in the future.

To document the development of long-term memory in infancy, we studied learning and retention among infants whose ages ranged from 2 to 18 months when the target memory was first acquired. Because infants' knowledge of the world and their repertoire of behaviors change dramatically over the first year-and-a-half of life, no single learning task could possibly be appropriate over this wide age range. We therefore developed two equivalent tasks—one to use with younger infants, and one to use with older ones. For 2- to 6-month-olds, we strung a ribbon between one ankle and an overhead crib mobile, and they learned to move the mobile by kicking; for 6- to 18-month-olds, we placed a large box housing a miniature train with a front lever, and the infants learned to move the train by pressing the lever.

Infants of these ages cannot tell us what they remember, and so their actions have to "speak" for them. During the long-term retention test, therefore, we simply show infants the same mobile or train they had seen before or one that differs in some way and "ask" them if they recognize it. If they do, then they say "yes" by kicking or lever pressing at a rate greater than their pretraining rate (baseline); otherwise, they do not respond above baseline. Because we disconnect the ankle ribbon and deactivate the lever during the test, infants' performance reflects only what they truly remember of their prior experience and not something new they might have learned at the time of testing.

Using these two procedures with infants of different ages, we tested groups of infants of each age after progressively longer delays until they finally forgot the task. Figure 1 shows that infants' retention increased linearly over the first year-and-a-half of life. Babies as young as 2 months of age remembered for 2 days that foot kicking activated the mobile, while 18-month-olds remembered for 13 weeks (Hartshorn et al., 1998). This pattern of results is not unique to these procedures.

Infants' retention in deferred imitation tasks also increases linearly with age, from 1 day at 6 months of age to 4 weeks at 18 months (Barr & Hayne, 2000). In deferred imitation tasks, an adult models novel actions and infants are given an opportunity to imitate those actions after a delay. In our task, the adult removes a same-colored mitten from the puppet's hand, shakes it to ring a jingle bell pinned inside, and replaces the mitten. Infants receive their first opportunity to imitate the actions during a deferred test. At that time, the puppet is presented within the infants' reach, and the number of target actions (remove the mitten, shake it, attempt to replace the mitten) that each

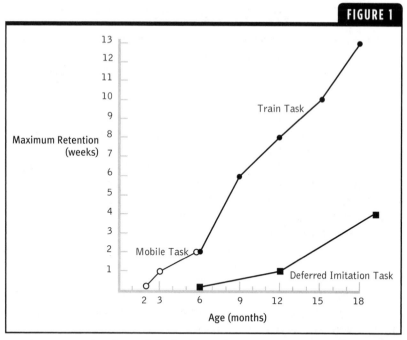

FIGURE 1

The maximum retention (in weeks) of infants who were trained in the mobile task at 2 to 6 months of age or the train task at 6 to 18 months of age and tested (only once) after increasingly longer delays until they forgot the task. Infants trained at 12 months, for example, remembered the task until they were 14 months old, or for a maximum of 8 weeks. (From Hartshorn et al., 1998.)

infant reproduces within 90 to 120 seconds of first touching the puppet is his or her imitation score (range = 0–3).

Although these findings reveal that even very young infants remember what they have learned for periods that are considerably longer than researchers previously thought, they still do not tell us whether an infant can remember a prior experience long enough for it to have a lasting impact. How that occurs is the subject of this essay.

How Do Memories of Early Experiences Become Enduring?

Reminders Restore Retention of Forgotten Memories

We found that briefly exposing infants to a reminder after a memory has been forgotten initiates an automatic, perceptual identification process that reactivates (primes) it and restores retention to the original level (Rovee-Collier, Sullivan, Enright, Lucas, & Fagen, 1980). Our finding that infants' forgotten memories are not permanently lost but can be recovered by a reminder changed the dialogue about the transient nature of infant memories.

Any isolated aspect of the original event, as long as it is represented in the original memory of that event, will reactivate the memory of the entire event.

We typically expose 3-month-olds to the moving mobile as the reminder, but the experimenter—not the infant—moves it. Similarly, we typically expose 6-month-olds to the moving train as the reminder, but a computer—not the infant—moves it.

When the memory is reactivated *within a week* of forgetting, infants of all ages remember the reactivated memory for the same duration that they had remembered the original one. In other words, a single reactivation *doubles the life of the memory* (Hildreth & Rovee-Collier, 2002). When the memory is reactivated after the longest delay possible (that is, at the upper limit of reactivation), a single reactivation *quadruples the life of the memory* (Hildreth & Hill, 2003). Three-month-olds initially remember the mobile task for almost 1 week after training, for example, and its forgotten memory can be reactivated 4 (but not 5) weeks afterward, while 9-month-olds initially remember the train task for 6 weeks, and its forgotten training memory can be reactivated 6 (but not 7) months afterward. Because 15- and 18-month-olds initially remember for so long, they actually outgrow the train task before they reach the upper limit of reactivation! When the forgotten memories of infants who were trained at 15 and 18 months are reactivated at approximately 2 years of age, the infants simply stop pressing the lever when the train doesn't move and tell their mother that the train is "broken" or needs "batteries" (Hsu & Rovee-Collier, 2006).

The preceding findings are summarized in Figure 2. The bottom curve in Figure 2 depicts the maximum duration for which infants of different ages remember the task after they originally learned it. The middle curve shows how long infants of the same ages remember the task when their memory is reactivated 1 week after they had forgotten it. The top curve in Figure 2 shows how long the same ages could remember the task when its forgotten memory was reactivated near or at the upper limit of reactivation. As you can see, the retention benefit of encountering a single reactivation reminder after a very long delay is huge at all ages.

Because exposure to a single reminder had such an impact in prolonging retention, we decided to examine the retention benefit of exposing infants to multiple reminders. We asked if exposure to multiple reminders might be the means by which early memories are maintained over significant periods of development. To answer this question, we trained 2-month-olds in the mobile task and reminded them every 3 weeks until they outgrew it. After five reminders, infants still exhibited significant retention 4½ months later, and after six reminders, all but one infant still remembered the task 5¼ months later, at 7¼ months of age. At that point, we discontinued testing because infants outgrew the task. When the study ended, all 2-month-olds except one were remembering longer than typical 2-year-olds who are trained for the first time, and the 2-month-old with the "poorest" memory had remembered almost as long as a typical 18-month-old. In contrast, infants who were not originally trained but received the same schedule of reminders exhibited no retention after any delay, confirming that the multiple reminders had not induced new learning that was mistaken for retention (Rovee-Collier, Hartshorn, & DiRubbo, 1999).

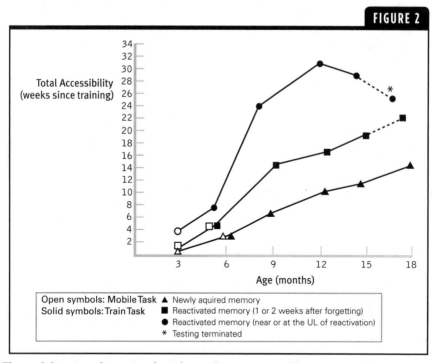

FIGURE 2

The total duration of retention for infants who were trained between 3 and 18 months of age. From bottom to top, the functions indicate how long infants remembered after original training (triangles), how long infants remembered after original training when the memory was reactivated a week after it was forgotten (squares), and how long they remembered after original training when the forgotten memory was reactivated near or at the upper limit of reactivation (circles). Dashes indicate that the verbal and operant indices of retention differed at the last data point; the asterisk indicates that further testing was discontinued. (Reprinted from Hsu & Rovee-Collier, 2006. Copyright © 2006, with permission from Elsevier.)

Because most infants were still remembering when the mobile study was terminated, Hartshorn (2003) repeated the study using the train task and beginning at 6 months of age. After five reminders, infants trained at 6 months still exhibited significant retention 1½ years later, when they were 2 years old! What's more, these infants had received only one reminder in the preceding year—at 18 months of age.

The successful use of multiple reminders to maintain infants' memories is not unique to conditioning procedures. The quintessential example comes from a study of deferred imitation. Recall that 6-month-olds can imitate a sequence of target actions 1 day after they are modeled. Because infants younger than 6 months lack the motoric competence necessary to perform the puppet imitation task, however, the question of whether they too are capable of deferred imitation remained unanswered. We attempted to answer this question by showing 3-month-olds the same demonstration that was shown to 6-month-olds and then using multiple reminders to maintain the memory of the demonstration until they were old enough to perform the puppet imitation task (Campanella & Rovee-Collier, 2005).

To determine whether our multiple reminder procedure even "worked," however, we first exposed 3-month-olds to two hand puppets (A, B), either simultaneously (paired) or at different times of day (unpaired), for 1 hour per day for 1 week. Next, we attempted to maintain the memory of the puppet A—puppet B association (presumably formed when the puppets were paired) by showing infants puppet A for 30 seconds as a reminder every 3 weeks (6 reminders in all) until they reached 6 months of age. At that time, an adult modeled the target actions on puppet A and, 24 hours later, tested infants' ability to imitate the actions on puppet B. Only infants who had seen the puppets paired at 3 months of age imitated the actions on puppet B; infants who had seen the puppets unpaired did not. This result confirmed that 3-month-olds had associated the two puppets and that the multiple-reminder procedure had successfully maintained the memory of the association for 3 months.

Therefore, we repeated the prior procedure for 3-month-olds with one major difference: One day after the last exposure to the paired puppets, an adult modeled the sequence of target actions on puppet A. At 6 months of age, 1 day after the last reminder, infants successfully imitated the modeled actions on puppet B! They had not seen either puppet B or the target actions for 3 months, and infants obviously had not imitated the actions immediately after they were modeled.

Most cognitive neuroscientists argue that the rapid forgetting exhibited by very young infants is due to the immaturity of their brains, which limits their ability to maintain and retrieve memories over the long term. Obviously, such conclusions are wrong. The preceding results clearly demonstrate that the brains of even very young infants are sufficiently mature to encode, maintain, and retrieve memories of events that had occurred months earlier—in fact, the equivalent of two to three *lifetimes* earlier!

Reminders Inoculate against Forgetting

Although a reminder can recover a forgotten memory after a remarkably long delay, in the interim, individuals undergo a relatively long period of sustained forgetting. In addition to reactivating memories that were forgotten, reminders forestall forgetting. Each reminder that is encountered before the memory is forgotten will retrieve it and extend its retention longer than it was remembered before. Moreover, the longer the interval since the memory was last retrieved, the longer it will be remembered in the future (Barr, Rovee-Collier, & Campanella, 2005).

When 3-month-olds received a brief reminder immediately after learning the mobile task, for example, they remembered the task for an additional day—6 days instead of 5 days; when they received the same reminder 3 days after training (at the midpoint of their original forgetting function), they remembered the mobile task for 10 days instead of 5 days; and when they received the same reminder 5 days after training (at the end of their original forgetting function), they remembered the mobile task for 21 days instead of 5 days (Galluccio & Rovee-Collier, 2006). In other words, the duration of retention increased exponentially as a function of the retrieval delay. Retention was doubled when infants were reminded after 3 days and was quadrupled when they were reminded after 5 days. We have obtained this same result many times with both conditioned and deferred imitation tasks with infants of all ages.

Are the Memories of Infants Like the Memories of Adults?

Discussion of our research often includes the disclaimer, "Of course, the memories of infants are very different from the memories of adults." The critics are correct to the extent that the memory contents of infants and adults differ both quantitatively (for example, adults have more memories and more links between them) and qualitatively (for example, what adults encode and the cues that retrieve it are different). The basic structure of memory in infants and adults, however, is fundamentally the same.

Table 1 lists the "rules" for prolonging infant memories that our research has turned up thus far, although I did not discuss all of our research that underlies these rules in this essay. Of particular importance is the fact that these rules apply equally well to individuals of all ages. Thus, anyone can enhance his or her learning and retention by following these rules—a matter that should be of particular interest to students. Moreover, clinicians and other practitioners can apply these same rules whether they are assisting healthy individuals overcome learning disabilities or are treating individuals whose memory is impaired as a result of acute brain damage or trauma (for example, in a car accident).

Back to the Future . . .

Regardless of the time, place, or circumstances of birth, infants begin learning about the structure of their particular environment from the earliest moments of life. Eventually, findings from basic research on what and how young

TABLE 1

Rules for Prolonging Retention

1. Distribute training or study sessions
2. Increase the number of training or study sessions
3. Increase the duration of the training or study sessions
4. Enhance attention during encoding
5. Increase the number of retrievals
6. Retrieve the memory nearer the end of its forgetting function
7. Remind periodically (reactivation, reinstatement) of the event
8. Increase the number of associations into which the memory enters
9. Associate shorter-lived memories with longer-lived memories

infants learn and remember will permit practitioners to detect and begin treating potential learning and memory problems long before their adverse effects have begun to snowball and become debilitating.

Resolution of the Paradox

As a result of systematic, basic research on infant learning and memory, we have finally resolved the paradox that was introduced at the beginning of this essay. Most of us had long believed that early stimulation plays a major role in cognitive development, but this belief was seriously challenged by the argument that early experiences cannot be important because infants cannot remember them. The evidence now shows that *memories of early experiences can be maintained over significant periods of development by occasional exposures to a reminder.* This evidence has major public policy implications for the funding of federal, state, and local programs that provide early stimulation and enriched environments.

Acknowledgments Preparation of this essay and the research described in it were supported by grant MH32307 from the U.S. National Institute of Mental Health.

☐ Thinking Critically

1. What is Carolyn Rovee-Collier's evidence that memories are preserved even in very early infancy?

2. What is your earliest true memory, and what age were you when the event occurred? Can you think of reasons why earlier memories are not accessible?

☐ Suggested Further Reading

Barr, R., Rovee-Collier, C., & Campanella, J. (2005). Retrieval facilitates retrieval: Protracting deferred imitation by 6-month-olds. *Infancy, 7,* 263–283.

Rovee-Collier, C. (1995). Time windows in cognitive development. *Developmental Psychology, 31,* 147–169.

☐ References

Barr, R., & Hayne, H. (2000). Age-related changes in imitation: Implications for memory development. In C. Rovee-Collier, L. P. Lipsitt, & H. Hayne (Eds.), *Progress in infancy research* (Vol. I, pp. 21–67). Hillsdale, NJ: Erlbaum.

Barr, R., Rovee-Collier, C., & Campanella, J. (2005). Retrieval facilitates retrieval: Protracting deferred imitation by 6-month-olds. *Infancy, 7,* 263–283.

Bjork, R. A. (2001). Recency and recovery in human memory. In H. L. Roediger, III., J. S. Nairne, I. Neath, & A. M. Surprenant (Eds.), *The nature of remembering: Essays in honor of Robert G. Crowder* (pp. 211–232). Washington, DC: American Psychological Association.

Campanella, J. L., & Rovee-Collier, C. (2005). Latent learning and deferred imitation at 3 months. *Infancy, 7,* 243–262.

Galluccio, L. D., & Rovee-Collier, C. (2006). Nonuniform effects of reinstatement within the time window. *Learning and Motivation, 37,* 1–17.

Hartshorn, K. (2003). Reinstatement maintains a memory in human infants for 1½ years. *Developmental Psychobiology, 42,* 269–282.

Hartshorn, K., Rovee-Collier, C., Gerhardstein, P., Bhatt, R. S., Wondoloski, T. L., Klein, P. J., et al. (1998). The ontogeny of long-term memory over the first year-and-a-half of life. *Developmental Psychobiology, 32,* 69–89, John Wiley and Sons.

Hildreth, K., & Hill, D. (2003). Retrieval difficulty and retention of reactivated memories over the first year of life. *Developmental Psychobiology, 43,* 216–229.

Hildreth, K., & Rovee-Collier, C. (2002). Forgetting functions of reactivated memories over the first year of life. *Developmental Psychobiology, 41,* 277–288.

Hsu, V. C., & Rovee-Collier, C. (2006). Memory reactivation in the second year of life. *Infant Behavior & Development, 29,* 91–107.

Rovee-Collier, C., Hartshorn, K., & DiRubbo, M. (1999). Long-term maintenance of infant memory. *Developmental Psychobiology, 35,* 91–102.

Rovee-Collier, C., Sullivan, M. W., Enright, M. K., Lucas, D., & Fagen, J. W. (1980). Reactivation of infant memory. *Science, 208,* 1159–1161.

Schmid, R. E. (2007). Infants form memories, but forget them. Associated Press, retrieved from *Yahoo! News* on February 16, 2007.

12

Personality

Products of Their Personalities or Creatures of Their Situations? Personality and Social Behavior Have the Answer

Mark Snyder

The Functional Significance of Temperament

H. Hill Goldsmith

Products of Their Personalities or Creatures of Their Situations? Personality and Social Behavior Have the Answer

MARK SNYDER University of Minnesota

☐ **Please describe your current position and research interests.**

I am McKnight Presidential Chair in Psychology and Director of the Center for the Study of the Individual and Society, University of Minnesota. How individuals create social worlds in which they can be true to their personalities at the same time as they are sensitive to their situations is the overarching theme of my research.

☐ **How did you become interested in the influence of personality and situations on the social behavior of individuals?**

The question of whether individuals are products of their personalities or creatures of their situations drew me into psychological research, when, as a student in psychology courses, I learned that the role of personality and situations was a matter of great debate in the psychological sciences, with strong proponents on either side of the issue. I have been especially intrigued by the processes whereby individuals construct and enact motivational agendas for action that draw upon and integrate features of their personal identities and their social settings and that guide and direct their pursuit of relevant life outcomes in diverse domains of functioning.

☐ **What has been the real-world impact of this work?**

Much of my research, conducted within the Center for the Study of the Individual and Society, focuses on understanding how and why people become actively involved in doing good for others and for society. Such involvement can take the form of volunteerism and philanthropy, social and political activism, and participation in community and neighborhood organizations. Among the questions being addressed are: What are the consequences of such action for individuals, for communities, and for society at large?

When the people of ancient Rome attended the theater, they watched performers wearing masks that told them what character each actor was playing. A performer who appeared behind a particular mask played a particular character, one who displayed a consistent pattern of behavior and attitudes (a villain, a hero, a friend, a foe, a wise man, a fool, and so forth). The Latin word for mask is *persona*. Originally, the term referred only to the theatrical mask. But, as time went by, it came to refer also to the character played by the wearer of the mask and eventually to the actor who played the character. Persona is also the Latin root of the psychological term *personality*. In the same way that persona referred to regularities and consistencies in the characters created by performers on the stage, so too does personality refer to regularities and consistencies in people's behavior in the course of their lives.

For example, someone who regularly behaves in a sociable and outgoing fashion across diverse situations (at work and at play), with different partners (friends and strangers), over time (yesterday, today, and tomorrow) is said to have an extraverted personality; by contrast, someone who is shy and retiring across situations, partners, and time is described as having an introverted personality. To the extent that such consistencies do exist, they distinguish some individuals from others (for example, separating extraverts from introverts), render actions predictable (for example, allowing us to forecast who will be the life of the party and who will be the wallflower), and determine adjustments to life circumstances (for example, influencing who will best fit into an occupational role that calls for much glad-handing and back-slapping and who will cope best in a working environment of solitude and isolation).

In what ways might regularities and consistencies in behavior be reflected in the concerns of psychological scientists? If, indeed, meaningful regularities and consistencies do exist in the behavior of individuals in the course of their lives, what are their origins? And what are their consequences? What are their implications for understanding human nature? It is to questions such as these that I and many other researchers in personality and social psychology have sought answers.

Persons, Situations, and Their Interaction

In contemplating these questions, let us first reflect further on the theater, the players, their masks, their roles, and their audiences. If the mask worn by the actor and the character played by the actor are appearances—outward displays of behavior and attitude—do these outward appearances reflect inner realities? Is the actor someone with exactly that personality, as we are tempted to infer in the case of actors who always seem to play the same role and to play it so naturally as to suggest that they are simply being themselves on the stage or screen? If we see the names of these actors—the Clint Eastwoods and John Waynes of the performing world—on a theater marquee, we immediately know exactly who they will be in the show.

Our expectations regarding this kind of actor, the one whose persona (in the sense of an underlying personality) is the same as the persona (in the sense of the part being played), has much in common with the view of human nature associated with the field of personality psychology. In defining personality, these psychologists usually include references to the quest to understand how the actions of individuals reflect stable and enduring traits and dispositions thought to reside within individuals and to move them to act in accord with their personalities. As Gordon Allport (1897–1967) defined it, "personality is the dynamic organization within the individual of those psychophysical systems that determine his unique adjustments to his environment" (1937, p. 48).

Of course, some actors simply play a role, their persona reflecting a script, with all of the demands and commands, specifications and instructions of its stage directors. These actors are chameleons, taking on the colors of their surroundings. They are highly flexible, role-playing creatures with great range and diversity, with such highly developed control of their verbal and nonverbal expressions that they literally can, in the course of their careers, become a cast of thousands, all roles played with equal conviction and equal persuasion. These actors are the Anthony Hopkinses and the Meryl Streeps of the dramatic arts; their names on a marquee assure us that they will give a great performance but don't tell us what role they will be playing.

This kind of actor, the one whose personas (that is, their public roles) are many and do not reflect an underlying persona (that is, their own personality), can serve as a metaphor for the view of human nature associated with social psychology. In characterizing personality, social psychologists view people as social animals, creatures of their situations, molding and tailoring their behavior with great flexibility and sensitivity to fit the shifting demands of their current situations, the pressures of their peers, the demands of their roles, and so forth. Thus, Allport said, ". . .with few exceptions, social psychologists regard their discipline as an attempt to understand and explain how the thought, feeling, and behavior of individuals are influenced by the actual, imagined, or implied presence of others" (1968, p. 3). In this view of human nature, to the extent that there are any consistencies in individuals' actions, they have their origin in regularities in the situations in which people find themselves. For example, people who seem forever to be the life of the party may behave that way precisely because they regularly spend time at parties and in other situations that bring out extraverted behaviors.

When faced with such different views of human nature, you might be tempted to ask: Which view is correct—that individuals are products of their dispositions or that individuals are creatures of their situations? In fact, it was this very question that drew me into psychological research, when as a student in psychology courses, I learned that the role of personality and situations was a matter of great debate in the psychological sciences, with strong proponents on either side of the issue. As is so often the case with either/or questions, the answer is that *both* views are correct, but neither view is wholly correct. For, each view captures *a part* of the truth. Dispositions are important, and so are situations. And curiously enough, dispositions are important in part because of the influence of situations, and situations are important in part because of the influence of dispositions. This intimate interplay between dispositions and situations has been revealed through the work of psychologists in a hybrid discipline that brings together both perspectives: personality and social behavior.

Personality Matters More in Some Situations than in Others

The evidence from research in personality is unequivocal: People's traits and dispositions are linked to their behavior. The linkages between personality and behavior are, however, stronger in some situations than in others. Thus, for example, the influence of personality is especially evident in those situations that actively encourage individuals to turn to their traits, dispositions, and attitudes as guides to action (for a review, see Snyder & Ickes, 1985). William Swann and I demonstrated this effect in a study of attitudes toward affirmative action employment policies. We set up a mock courtroom in which student "jurors" had to offer verdicts in a sex discrimination case. Jurors who were given time to think about their own general attitudes and values prior to hearing the evidence were more likely to reach verdicts that reflected these attitudes and values than were jurors who did not have this opportunity. Taking time to think about their attitudes may have made deciding the court case a matter of principle for these mock jurors (Snyder & Swann, 1976). More generally, life situations that involve consciousness raising, self-disclosure, taking a stand, and matters of principle may also be ones that are likely to foster high degrees of correspondence between personality and behavior.

By contrast, personality dispositions have minimal impact on behavior in situations that place very strong demands and constraints on people and that offer little latitude for people to respond in individualized ways. (These situations are sometimes called strong situations; for a review, see Snyder & Ickes, 1985.) Moviegoers familiar with the film *The Godfather* will understand this principle. Faced with an "offer that he couldn't refuse" (a gun to his head and the choice between his signature or his brains on the contract), the reluctant opponent signs the contract he had been refusing to sign. In a strong situation, individual differences in attitudes, values, temperament, and personality pale in comparison to the strong situational demands to which everyone responds in the same way. To pick a more mundane example than the Godfather's offer, in this culture, we *all* stop at red lights, whether or not we are characteristically inclined to be rule followers or rule benders in other circumstances.

Situations Matter More for Some Personalities than for Others

Research in social psychology provides clear evidence that individuals' behavior is sensitive to the guidelines provided by situations. However, the strength of these situational influences is greater for some people than for others. For example, the power of situations to guide behavior is especially evident for those people who characteristically turn to situational cues for guides to action; by contrast, the links between situations and behavior are considerably less pronounced for people who characteristically turn inward to their attitudes, traits, and dispositions as guides to action (for a review, see Snyder & Ickes, 1985).

Individual differences in the extent to which situations matter are captured in an aspect of personality trait known as self-monitoring, defined as the degree to which people can and do modify their behavior in response to situational pressures (see, for example, Snyder, 1987). For some people, known as high self-monitors, life is a series of public appearances molded and tailored to fit the situations in which they find themselves and the people with whom they are dealing. In a fashion not unlike the chameleon that takes on the colors of its physical surroundings, the high self-monitor takes on the social colors of his or her situations, with words and deeds carefully chosen to convey just the right image. For other people, known as low self-monitors, life is more a matter of finding ways to display and convey their own true selves, with actions chosen to reflect their own underlying attitudes, traits, and dispositions.

Individual differences in self-monitoring are identified with the Self-Monitoring Scale (Snyder, 1974); see Table 1 for sample items. Differences between high and low self-monitors manifest themselves across a wide range of life domains, including how people choose their friends, their romantic partners, their jobs, their consumer products, and their political candidates. The unifying theme across these diverse domains of life is responsiveness to the demands of social situations: The choices of high self-monitors are much more sensitive to considerations specific to particular situations than are the choices of low self-monitors (for a review, see Gangestad & Snyder, 2000). In other words, situations seem to matter more for high self-monitors than for low self-monitors.

The Interactionist View of Personality and Social Behavior

Taken together, these two propositions (that personality matters more in some situations than others and that situations have more influence on some personalities than others) have formed the basis for the interaction-ist view of the role of persons and situations in determining behavior (for example, Endler & Magnusson, 1976; Mischel & Shoda, 1995). This inter-actionist approach to personality and social behavior makes it possible to

---

TABLE 1

Sample Items from the Self-Monitoring Scale

ITEMS TYPICALLY ENDORSED BY HIGH SELF-MONITORS

- When I am uncertain how to act in a social situation, I look to the behavior of others for cues.
- In different situations and with different persons, I often act like very different persons.
- In order to get along and be liked, I tend to be what other people expect me to be rather than anything else.

ITEMS TYPICALLY ENDORSED BY LOW SELF-MONITORS

- My behavior is usually an expression of my true inner feelings, attitudes, and beliefs.
- I can only argue for ideas that I already believe.
- I would not change my opinions (or the way I do things) in order to please someone or win their favor.

specify *how* persons and situations work together in accounting for individual and social behavior.

In particular, the interactionist approach emphasizes the mutual interplay of persons and situations, with persons selecting situations conducive to the expression of relevant features of their personalities and with situations providing opportunities for people to act on traits and dispositions relevant to those situations (see, for example, Snyder & Cantor, 1998). That is, in some measure, situations are chosen and structured by people themselves, and people are motivated in their choices of situations by their own identities and personalities (for a review, see Ickes, Snyder, & Garcia, 1997). Thus, people with extraverted personalities may choose to spend time in situations such as parties that allow them to display their extraverted personalities; similarly, people with competitive dispositions may choose whenever possible to be in situations that provide opportunities to compete with others. More generally, through their choices of situations, people may create opportunities to act on their personalities.

Moreover, just as dispositions may influence the situations in which people live, so too can the situations in which people find themselves encourage and even enforce consistencies in people's behaviors and even in their personalities. Thus, for example, a lifetime spent in situations calling for success in public relations may produce a reliable record of sociability across situations, partners, and time—a pattern that, at a minimum, may reinforce an underlying extraverted disposition, or that may even be internalized to create an extraverted disposition to match a life spent in extraverted situations. More generally, people's personalities may be shaped and molded by regularities and consistencies in the situations in which they function (for further perspective on the influence of situations on individuals, see Snyder & Ickes, 1985).

Conclusion

Many years ago, Kurt Lewin (1890–1947), a psychologist so influential that he is claimed as a founding parent both of social psychology and personality psychology, observed, "Every psychological event depends upon the state of the person and at the same time on the environment, although their relative importance is different in different cases" (1936, p. 12). In accord with Lewin's fundamental proposition, those of us in the hybrid field of personality and social behavior have shown that if we are to understand people, we need to know something about them as individuals *and* as social beings, to understand their personalities *and* their situations. Moreover, the power of personality and the power of situations become particularly evident in their interaction. For personality is always important, but more so in some situations than others; and situations are always important, but more so for some people than others. And personality and situations are intricately interwoven, with people choosing situations conducive to their personalities, and situations affecting the personalities displayed in them. These interactionist propositions have provided the foundations for building a hybrid discipline of personality and social behavior, integrating the theoretical views and research approaches of personality and social psychology (for example, Snyder & Deaux, 2012; Deaux & Snyder, 2012).

This appreciation of the mutual interplay of persons and situations may pay dividends when it comes to understanding how people pursue important outcomes in critical domains of their lives. Thus, when it comes to understanding how people make critical choices in their lives—whether in choosing friends and romantic partners, or in selecting a career or a profession, or in getting involved in the affairs of their society—there may be value to looking at those choices from the perspective of the ways that those choices are guided by personality and how those choices in turn feed back on and influence their opportunities to express personality.

☐ Thinking Critically

1. Explain how Mark Snyder's research supports Kurt Lewin's famous statement, "Every psychological event depends upon the state of the person and at the same time on the environment, although their relative importance is different in different cases."
2. Consider an important choice that you recently made. How was it influenced by your personal disposition, and how was it influenced by the situation in which you found yourself?

☐ Suggested Further Reading

Snyder, M. (1987). *Public appearances/private realities: The psychology of self-monitoring.* New York: W. H. Freeman.
Snyder, M., & Cantor, N. (1998). Understanding personality and social behavior: A functionalist strategy. In D. T. Gilbert, S. T. Fiske, & G. Lindzey (Eds.), *The handbook of social psychology, Vol. 1* (4th ed., pp. 635–679). Boston: McGraw-Hill.

☐ References

Allport, G. (1937). *Personality: A psychological interpretation.* New York: Holt.
Allport, G. (1968). The historical background of modern social psychology. In G. Lindzey, & E. Aronson (Eds.), *The handbook of social psychology, Vol. 1* (2nd ed., pp. 1–80). Reading, MA: Addison-Wesley.
Deaux, K., & Snyder, M. (2012). *The Oxford handbook of personality and social psychology.* New York: Oxford University Press.
Deaux, K., & Snyder, M. (2012). Personality and social psychology: The state of the union. In K. Deaux & M. Snyder (Eds.), *The Oxford handbook of personality and social psychology* (pp. 830–836). New York: Oxford University Press.
Endler, N. S., & Magnusson, D. (1976). Toward an interactional psychology of personality. *Psychological Bulletin, 83*, 956–974.
Gangestad, S. W., & Snyder, M. (2000). Self-monitoring: Appraisal and reappraisal. *Psychological Bulletin, 126*, 530–555.
Ickes, W., Snyder, M., & Garcia, S. (1997). Personality influences on the choice of situations. In R. Hogan, J. A. Johnson, & S. R. Briggs (Eds.), *Handbook of personality psychology* (pp. 165–195). New York: Academic Press.

Lewin, K. (1936). *A dynamic theory of personality.* New York: McGraw-Hill.

Mischel, W., & Shoda, Y. (1995). A cognitive-affective system theory of personality: Reconceptualizing situations, dispositions, dynamics, and invariance in personality structure. *Psychological Review, 102,* 246–268.

Snyder, M. (1974). The self-monitoring of expressive behavior. *Journal of Personality and Social Psychology, 30,* 526–537.

Snyder, M. (1987). *Public appearances/private realities: The psychology of self-monitoring.* New York: W. H. Freeman.

Snyder, M., & Cantor, N. (1998). Understanding personality and social behavior: A functionalist strategy. In D. T. Gilbert, S. T. Fiske, & G. Lindzey (Eds.), *The handbook of social psychology, Vol. 1* (4th ed., pp. 635–679). Boston: McGraw-Hill.

Snyder, M., & Deaux, K. (2012). Personality and social psychology: Crossing boundaries and integrating perspectives. In K. Deaux & M. Snyder (Eds.), *The Oxford handbook of personality and social psychology* (pp. 3–9). New York: Oxford University Press.

Snyder, M., & Ickes, W. (1985). Personality and social behavior. In G. Lindzey & E. Aronson (Eds.), *The handbook of social psychology, Vol. 2* (3rd ed., pp. 883–948). New York: Random House.

Snyder, M., & Swann, W. B., Jr. (1976). When actions reflect attitudes: The politics of impression management. *Journal of Personality and Social Psychology, 34,* 1034–1042.

The Functional Significance of Temperament

H. HILL GOLDSMITH University of Wisconsin–Madison

☐ **Please describe your current position and research interests.**

I am Fluno Bascom Professor and Leona Tyler Professor of Psychology at the University of Wisconsin–Madison. I also chair the Department of Psychology and coordinate the Social and Affective Sciences Research Group at the University of Wisconsin's Waisman Center. My research focuses on temperament as a factor in human affective development and spans periods from infancy to adolescence. My students and I have studied genetic contributions to children's affective individuality and development. Some of my specific research topics are objective behavioral measurement of temperament, the functional significance of temperament for risk and resilience, pediatric sensory over-responsiveness, and the interplay of genes and environment in childhood and adolescent behavioral challenges.

☐ **How did you become interested in temperament?**

The genetics of childhood temperament was the topic of my dissertation in 1978, so temperament was one of my initial research interests. Modern temperament research was just getting started at that time, so I was in on the ground floor. Over the years, my professional identity has shifted through the fields of behavioral genetics, developmental psychology, personality psychology, developmental psychopathology, and affective science. It's not that my interests have changed much; rather, the relevant fields have evolved. One constant, however, is that temperament is part of each of these fields, and thus temperament has remained a cornerstone of my interests.

☐ **What has been the real-world impact of this work?**

Temperament research has led us to better appreciate emotional individuality, especially of infants and young children. Looking through the lens of temperament allows us to see trajectories of infant development differently, to discern reasons for the behavior of our social partners, and to view behavioral challenges in a different light.

The Meaning of Temperament

We could draw traditional definitions of temperament from the ancient Greek physicians or from Pavlov, but my vote for the best starting place is Gordon Allport's 1937 book on personality, *Personality: A Psychological Interpretation.* Allport defines temperament as the *emotional core* of personality traits, and he defined a personality trait as "a generalized and focalized neuropsychic system (peculiar to the individual), with the capacity to render many stimuli functionally equivalent, and to initiate and guide consistent (equivalent) forms of adaptive and expressive behavior." In other words, Allport's traits have three key properties:

- Traits are rooted in neural systems—of course, we now understand that all human experience and behavior has neural and biological underpinnings, so being rooted in neural systems is nothing distinctive.

- Traits lead us to react similarly to contexts that share incentives—for example, being ignored, being insulted, and being lied to are similar contexts that share similar incentives; they all involve being the object of some kind of social aggression.

- Traits motivate us to behave in coherent ways. If we reacted to every situation in a way that was divorced from our prior reactions in similar situations (for example, losing our backpack and losing our cell phone), then we would not be behaving coherently, and our friends would have trouble predicting our behavior.

Allport also believed that personality traits were largely stable in adulthood, despite being susceptible to change. That is, Allport anticipated contemporary researchers by recognizing both stability and change in temperament. As the emotional cores of personality traits, temperament traits should also show consistency across situations and stability over time, as well as motivate behavior. Saying that temperament motivates behavior means that temperament is not just a *style* of behaving; instead, temperament plays a causative role in producing behavior.

My eventual goal here is to skip forward to the mid-2010s and to explain how temperament research has impacted our daily lives. However, first we need a sense of the nature of that temperament research.

Trends in Temperament Research

What has happened in temperament research over the past four decades? The story is documented in many books, handbook chapters, and reviews (Kagan, 1994; Rothbart & Bates, 2006; Thomas & Chess, 1977; Strelau, 1998; Zentner & Bates, 2008). Below, I describe the major trends in the field:

- We—and when I say *we* I mean temperament researchers in general as well as my research group—learned to measure children's temperament in the lab without relying on their parents' report. My research group's Laboratory Temperament Assessment Battery (Lab-TAB) provides age-graded measures of temperament that are useful from early infancy to 7–8 years of age (Goldsmith & Gagne, 2012). Lab-TAB is widely used for early temperament assessment when an objective measure is needed. For research when a more subjective measure suffices, the field has also refined questionnaires and interviews that parents can use to describe their children's temperament.

■ We fit temperament conceptually into broader personality frameworks, such as the Five Factor Model. My research group found that the primary trait level, rather than the factor level, of temperament is best supported by the behavioral data (Gagne, Van Hulle, Aksan, Essex, & Goldsmith, 2011). In other words, we think that talking about *exuberance* and *contentment* advances scientific progress more than talking about *positive affect.*

■ We debated whether temperament made more sense as a *type* (for example, an inhibited child or a slow-to-warm-up child) as opposed to a *dimension* (for example, anger proneness, ranging from not-at-all prone to anger vs. extremely prone to anger). The dimensional perspective predominates in academics, but person-centered approaches have also proven scientifically valuable (Meehl, 1992) and easy to translate to the public.

■ We found that temperament was relatively stable over time, yet not remarkably so. For example, inhibited infants often become about average in behavioral inhibition as children, yet they rarely become highly uninhibited (Pfeifer, Goldsmith, Davidson, & Rickman, 2002).

■ We demonstrated genetic origins for most temperament traits (Gagne, Vendlinski, & Goldsmith, 2009), as well as some psychobiological and neural correlates of temperament. Most of these correlates have involved reactivity of the autonomic nervous system and neuroendocrine systems. Mostly recently, neuroimaging correlates of temperament are being discovered (Schwartz, Wright, Shin, Kagan, & Rauch, 2003).

■ Perhaps most importantly, we began to understand the functional significance of temperament traits. Generalizing over many studies, we have often found that temperament traits are moderator variables. For example, anger proneness acts as a moderator variable in specifying who would be more likely to be affected by an experience. Researchers have mostly studied noxious types of experience and they have mostly studied maladaptive outcomes. However, I anticipate that we will find that temperament also moderates the association of positive experiences with adaptive outcomes.

Although research has generally validated the trait-like conceptualization of temperament, many things have changed over the last four decades. For instance, the idea that temperament is *uniquely* influenced by biology has faded. Nontemperamental facets of personality such as attitudes and self-concept are also biologically influenced. In other words, researchers used to think that we could divide personality into biological parts, such as temperament, and nonbiological parts, such as self-concept. We now realize that this was a false dichotomy.

Another change is that we no longer expect a simple answer to the question of the breadth or narrowness of temperament traits. In Allport's terms, the impact of the "capacity to render many stimuli functionally equivalent" hinges on how diverse the "many stimuli" are. In the mid-2010s, we must conclude that temperament traits vary in their breadth. For example, no trait renders all stimuli with hedonically negative incentive values functionally equivalent—in other words, the proposed trait of *negative affectivity* is too broad. However, a trait of *anger proneness* does render many stimuli that incorporate goal blockage or assault functionally equivalent. And a trait of sadness renders many stimuli involving loss functionally equivalent; that is, we often react the same way when we experience loss, regardless of the type of loss.

The field has moved away from a focus on *difficulty* as the central construct in temperament. Instead, we embrace multidimensional reactivity and regulation as concepts that compose temperament. The revised Children's Behavior Questionnaire (Rothbart, Ahadi, Hershey, & Fisher, 2001) offers the set of temperament traits described in Table 1. Reading the descriptions in Table 1 illustrates the meaning of reactivity and regulation very clearly.

As Table 1 shows, each of these 15 dimensions carries a specific operational definition. We note that most of the dimensions, that is, 10 of the 15 traits, are overtly affective in nature. Those traits that are not overtly affective are mostly regulatory (for example, attentional focusing and inhibitory control). However, affective reactions play a role even for those traits that are predominately regulatory. For example, focusing attention is a way of regulating affective reactions. Thus, virtually the whole domain specified as temperamental by Rothbart and her colleagues is either directly or indirectly affective in nature. Some of these traits have been studied extensively (anger/frustration, fear, shyness), but others remain poorly understood and have only been sparsely studied (low-intensity pleasure, perceptual sensitivity).

So What? The Functional Significance of Temperament

With this review of the current status of the field, we are primed to ask about the functional significance of temperament. That is, we ask the question, *so what?*

What is the real-life relevance of temperament? I suggest four ways to answer this question.

Temperament helps us understand our children. The classic "what-to-expect" books provided to new parents were once filled with descriptions of the monthly developmental milestones attained by babies from one month, to nine months, and to twenty-four months. Although these books sometimes recognized variability in the onset of affective reactions such as the social smile and fear of strangers, they did not recognize patterns of individual affective differences that were not simply a matter of timing. With increasing public awareness of temperament research, contemporary "what-to-expect" books often describe patterns of temperament, such as Thomas and Chess's (1977) "slow-to-warm-up" infant, and suggest that parents first discern their child's temperament before setting expectations for behavior. This advice has the effect of normalizing a wide range of behavior and potentially relieving parents of unwarranted anxiety.

Understanding children's temperament not only helps parents reframe their interpretation of behavior, but also nurture their children in ways that respect temperamental differences. A basic parenting skill is anticipating how

TABLE 1

Rothbart's Set of Temperament Traits, as Measured by the Children's Behavior Questionnaire[1]

Activity Level	Level of gross motor activity including rate and extent of locomotion.
Anger/ Frustration	Amount of negative affect related to interruption of ongoing tasks or goal blocking.
Approach	Amount of excitement and positive anticipation for expected pleasurable activities.
Attentional Focusing	Tendency to maintain attentional focus upon task-related channels.
Discomfort	Amount of negative affect related to sensory qualities of stimulation, including intensity, rate or complexity of light, movement, sound, and texture.
Falling Reactivity and Soothability	Rate of recovery from peak distress, excitement, or general arousal.
Fear	Amount of negative affect, including unease, worry or nervousness related to anticipated pain or distress and/or potentially threatening situations.
High Intensity Pleasure	Amount of pleasure or enjoyment related to situations involving high stimulus intensity, rate, complexity, novelty, and incongruity.
Impulsivity	Speed of response initiation.
Inhibitory Control	The capacity to plan and to suppress inappropriate approach responses under instructions or in novel or uncertain situations.
Low Intensity Pleasure	Amount of pleasure or enjoyment related to situations involving low stimulus intensity, rate, complexity, novelty, and incongruity.
Perceptual Sensitivity	Amount of detection of slight, low intensity stimuli from the external environment.
Sadness	Amount of negative affect and lowered mood and energy related to exposure to suffering, disappointment, and object loss.
Shyness	Slow or inhibited approach in situations involving novelty or uncertainty.
Smiling and Laughter	Amount of positive affect in response to changes in stimulus intensity, rate, complexity, and incongruity.

[1]Descriptions from Rothbart, Ahadi, Hershey, & Fisher (2001), Appendix A. The Children's Behavior Questionnaire.

different children will react to the same challenge, such as introduction to new friends. An understanding of temperament helps parents to generalize their expectations.

The other side of the coin is how adult temperament relates to parenting behavior. Thomas and Chess popularized the contextual notion of *goodness of fit.* The idea behind goodness of fit is that a closer match between the child's temperament profile and the features of the context results in more successful adaptation. An important part of the context might be the temperament of another person who often interacts with the child, such as a parent or teacher.

Temperament helps us predict the behavior of those who are close to us. Anyone who has experienced arguments with roommates, family members, partners, or close friends knows that a postconflict cooling off period is often needed. But when is it "safe" to resume typical interactions? Some people recover so quickly that we can resume typical interactions in 15 minutes. For others, we learn to stay away until the next day. Recognition that recovery from frustration reflects a temperamental trait that is unlikely to change easily allows us to predict the likely behavior of those who are close to us.

The research trend of investigating the effects of temperament on interpersonal relationships is ripe with real-world implications. Interpersonal relationships vary along several dimensions, including security, expressiveness, exclusiveness, and stability. Understanding how individual temperamental differences interact with relationship dimensions is crucial for understanding the practical importance of temperament (Goldsmith & Harman, 1994).

Temperament helps us to understand risk and resilience. Generalizing across the literature on the functional significance of temperament traits, we can suggest their generic role: temperament traits are often moderator variables. Standing on a moderator variable (for example, how shy a person is) explains the association between a predictor and an outcome. For example, the same trauma experienced by people with different temperaments leads to different outcomes. The stressor that inoculates some people against further insults and thus fosters resilience may overwhelm other people and place them at risk for later adaptive problems.

A recent example of the temperament-as-moderator approach comes from longitudinal research by Schermerhorn et al. (2013), who showed that a temperamental combination of high unmanageability and high unadaptability early in life moderated the link between stressful life events and externalizing problems.

The same temperament-as-moderator principle should apply to adaptive outcomes; however, much less research has addressed this issue. For either adaptive or problematic outcomes, this simple contingent principle in the link from experience to outcome can help not only researchers, but also parents and teachers better appreciate and react to children's experiences.

Temperament might help us reconceptualize the nature of psychopathology. For decades, "abnormality" has been defined by the criteria described in the American Psychiatric Association's *Diagnostic and Statistical Manual* (DSM). For many scientists, the proliferation of disorders in the more recent editions of the DSM is problematic. Many of these disorders are common and they frequently co-occur in the same person, especially when we consider a person's full lifetime. The difficulty of finding specific genetic or neurological causes for DSM-defined disorders has also been a problem. So, in a nutshell, if mental disorders are defined so that most of us qualify for a disorder at some time during our lifetime, and if we often qualify for more than one disorder, and if we cannot find the causes of the disorders, then perhaps something is wrong with our basic conception of the disorders, at least as represented in the DSM. This state of affairs has led some scientists to search for entirely different ways to conceive of mental illness.

One of these alternatives to DSM centrally involves temperament. As a future alternative to our current conceptualization of psychopathology, the National Institute of Mental Health (NIMH) has proposed the Research Domain Criteria framework, or RDoC (Insel et al., 2010). RDoC specifies dimensions rather than categories of behavior; there is no judgment of whether the behaviors are "normal" or "abnormal." The current RDoC framework is only an initial vehicle to facilitate research. This framework with its emphasis on neuroscience has several shortcomings as a replacement for current systems, but these shortcomings don't concern us here. The major RDoC domains are negative valence systems, positive valence systems, cognitive systems, social processes, and arousal and regulatory systems. Of these, the negative valence systems and the positive valence systems (see Table 2), overlap substantially with contemporary views of temperament. Table 2 shows the subcomponents of the negative and positive valence systems and my interpretation of related temperamental dimensions.

As Table 2 shows, the proposed matches are neither precise nor unique; that is, the temperament dimensions are *related* to the RDoC constructs rather than synonymous with them. For instance, frustrative nonreward is more closely tied to aggression than anger, but aggressiveness is not a temperament

TABLE 2

Correspondence of RDoC Constructs with Temperament Constructs

RDoC CONSTRUCTS	RELATED TEMPERAMENT CONSTRUCTS
Negative Valence Systems	**Negative Affect**
Active threat ("fear")	Fearfulness
Potential threat ("anxiety")	Anxious temperament, shyness, behavioral inhibition
Sustained threat	Anxious temperament, shyness, sensitivity to punishment
Loss	Sadness, low positive affect
Frustrative nonreward	Anger proneness
Positive Valence Systems	**Positive Affect**
Approach motivation	Anticipatory positive affect, exuberance
Initial responsiveness to reward	Consummatory positive affect, reward sensitivity
Sustained responsiveness to reward	Reward sensitivity
Reward learning	Goal-oriented positive affect
Habit	Persistence

trait. Anger proneness, which is related to aggression, is thus the most closely related temperament trait to frustrative nonreward. Table 2 also hints that the negative affect systems are more closely tied to temperament than the positive affect systems, likely because the latter are strongly influenced by research on learning, which currently has more direct links to neuroscience than other areas of positive valence systems research. In other words, unsurprisingly, we know more about the neural bases of why and how rodents in cages respond to rewards of food than we know about the neural bases of why and how humans feel a sense of pleasure when they see a beautiful sunset.

Not only do dimensions of temperament coincide substantially with the constructs that compose negative and positive valence systems, but regulatory aspects of temperament, such as attentional focusing and inhibitory control (see Table 1) also are clearly related to some of the constructs under the RDoC cognitive systems and arousal and regulatory systems domains. The regulatory features are important to consider because an individual's strong regulatory abilities can compensate for otherwise risky reactive aspects of temperament.

Finally, temperament might in the future connect to our daily lives through its integration into RDoC. Whether the integration of temperament into RDoC is ultimately a good or bad development for our daily lives is up for debate. On the one hand, if we associate psychological disorders with temperament traits familiar to all of us, that might help destigmatize the disorders and generate empathy for those with these disorders. On the other hand, viewing mental disorders dimensionally might contribute to the trend of medicalization of ordinary behaviors, where shyness, childhood temper tantrums, mild memory loss related to aging, impulsivity, mourning and grief, and a host of other human experiences and feelings run the risk of becoming diagnosable as abnormalities.

Temperament provides us with a framework with which to understand the variation in our emotional behavior, including its extremes, without resorting to the label of psychopathology.

Acknowledgments Preparation of this essay was partially supported by NIMH grants R01 MH101504 and P50 MH100031. Infrastructure support was provided by P30 HD03352.

☐ Thinking Critically

1. Examine the list of temperament traits in Table 1 and rate yourself as high, medium, or low on each. Then, rate a roommate, a parent, or another significant person in your life. Do your ratings help you make sense of your pattern of interactions with that person?

2. Temperament is intended as a value-neutral concept. That is, it's not inherently good or bad to be high on any temperament trait, although a culture may attempt to foster high or low standing on certain temperament traits. Try to think of positive (useful, adaptive) features of scoring either high or low on the traits discussed in Goldsmith's essay.

☐ Suggested Further Reading

Goldsmith, H. H., Buss, A. H., Plomin, R., Rothbart, M. K., Thomas, A., Chess, S., et al. (1987). Roundtable: What is temperament? Four approaches. *Child Development*, 505–529.

Kagan, J., & Snidman, N. C. (2009). *The long shadow of temperament*. Cambridge, MA: Belknap of Harvard University Press.

☐ References

Allport, G. W. (1937). *Personality: A psychological interpretation*. Oxford: Holt.

Gagne, J. R., Van Hulle, C. A., Aksan, N., Essex, M. J., & Goldsmith, H. H. (2011). Deriving childhood temperament measures from emotion-eliciting behavioral episodes: Scale construction and initial validation. *Psychological Assessment, 23*(2), 337.

Gagne, J. R., Vendlinski, M. K., & Goldsmith, H. H. (2009). The genetics of childhood temperament. In Y-K Kim (Ed.), *Handbook of behavioral genetics*. New York: Springer.

Goldsmith, H. H., & Gagne, J. R. (2012). Behavioral assessment of temperament. In M. Zentner & R. L. Shiner (Eds.), *Handbook of temperament* (pp. 209–228). New York: Guilford.

Goldsmith, H. H., & Harman, C. (1994). Temperament and attachment, individuals and relationships. *Current Directions in Psychological Science, 3,* 53–57.

Insel, T., Cuthbert, B., Garvey, M., Heinssen, R., Pine, D. S., Quinn, K., et al. (2010). Research domain criteria (RDoC): Toward a new classification framework for research on mental disorders. *American Journal of Psychiatry, 167*(7), 748–751.

Kagan, J. (1994). *Galen's prophecy: Temperament in human nature*. New York: Basic Books.

Meehl, P. E. (1992). Factors and taxa, traits and types, differences of degree and differences in kind. *Journal of Personality, 60,* 117–174.

Pfeifer, M., Goldsmith, H. H., Davidson, R. J., & Rickman, M. (2002). Continuity and change in inhibited and uninhibited children. *Child Development, 73,* 1474–1485.

Rothbart, M. K., Ahadi, S. A., Hershey, K. L., & Fisher, P. (2001). Investigations of temperament at 3–7 years: The Children's Behavior Questionnaire. *Child Development, 72*(5), 1394–1408.

Rothbart, M. K., & Bates, J. (2006). Temperament. In W. Damon, R. Lerner, & N. Eisenberg (Eds.), *Handbook of child psychology: Vol. 3. Social, emotional, and personality development* (6th ed., pp. 99–166). New York: Wiley.

Schermerhorn, A. C., Bates, J. E., Goodnight, J. A., Lansford, J. E., Dodge, K. A., & Pettit, G. S. (2013). Temperament moderates associations between exposure to stress and children's externalizing problems. *Child Development, 84*(5), 1579–1593.

Schwartz, C. E., Wright, C. I., Shin, L. M., Kagan, J., & Rauch, S. L. (2003). Inhibited and uninhibited infants "grown up": Adult amygdalar response to novelty. *Science, 300* (5627), 1952–1953.

Strelau, J. (1998). *Temperament: A psychological perspective*. New York: Springer.

Thomas, A., & Chess, S. (1977). *Temperament and development*. Philadelphia: Brunner/Mazel.

Zentner, M., & Bates, J. E. (2008). Child temperament: An integrative review of concepts, research programs, and measures. *International Journal of Developmental Science, 2*(1), 7–37.

Psychological Disorders

Predisposed to Understand the Complex Origins of Behavioral Variation

Irving I. Gottesman

Lost in Thought: The Perils of Rumination

Susan Nolen-Hoeksema

Predisposed to Understand the Complex Origins of Behavioral Variation

IRVING I. GOTTESMAN University of Minnesota

☐ Please describe your current position and research interests.

I am semi-retired and enjoy being appointed a senior fellow in the Department of Psychology, University of Minnesota, and Sherrell J. Aston Professor of Psychology Emeritus, University of Virginia. International research connections in the United Kingdom have led to honorary fellowship statuses in the Royal College of Psychiatrists and King's College London. My research interests continue to be in psychiatric and behavioral genetics, including new strategies from epigenetics, focused on schizophrenia and bipolar disorder.

☐ How did you become interested in studying and resolving psychiatry genetics?

It was a mountain (of ignorance) needing to be climbed and a rather empty niche when I began graduate school in 1956.

☐ What has been the real-world impact of this work?

One concrete example can be seen in the number of times my work has been cited in Google Scholar: Both my textbooks and my journal articles have been heavily cited and that has led to numerous national and worldwide prizes for advancing my three fields (psychology, psychiatry, and genetics). The recognition comes both from scientific organizations and from organizations advocating for the mentally ill (NAMI, Brain & Behavior Research Foundation). My formulations in genetic counseling for the families of the mentally ill have brought relief from exaggerated fears of mental illness "running in the family." Prizes from the Lieber Foundation for Outstanding Schizophrenia Research and the University of Louisville Grawemeyer Award in Psychology guarantee a longer half-life for my data-informed theories.

Had I been born two centuries ago, I might have ended up pursuing a career as a naturalist, happy enough but without the means to live well and to educate my children. The field of behavioral genetics, arising at the interfaces of the biological and behavioral sciences with essential support from medicine, mathematics, and the philosophy of science, has been very, very good to me, and satisfying. My childhood curiosity about nature took the form of collecting rocks, leaves, bird eggs, and pond water, and really escalated with birthday and Christmas gifts of junior microscopes and expansions of starter chemistry sets, supplemented by trips to the pharmacy. Before completing elementary school, my mother had to constrain my expertise at bad smells emanating from the basement as well as the potential self-harm of homemade fireworks.

The Journey to Psychology via Physics

Success in high school biology, physics, and chemistry led to the strong advice to major in physics in college, as it had a future. Reading the novel *Arrowsmith* by Sinclair Lewis about biomedical researchers also made a deep impression on my career fantasies. It only took one course in abnormal psychology for me to switch majors and to focus on psychopathology as a way to reconcile my interests. After a three-year interlude on active duty as a naval officer during the Korean War, I was fortunate to be accepted into the scientist-practitioner-model training program in clinical child psychology at the University of Minnesota on the G.I. Bill. Mandatory core courses on the psychology of individual differences, taught by Donald G. Paterson and James J. Jenkins, exposed me to the classical twin studies of schizophrenia and other psychoses conducted by F. J. Kallmann in this country and by E. T. Slater in the United Kingdom, with their unambiguous conclusions that hereditary factors play major roles in their distal etiologies—unambiguous, that is, to those not bitten by the psychodynamic bug endemic in post-World War II psychiatry, psychology, and clinical social work.

Paterson, an eminent applied psychologist who had shaped military cognitive testing for literate and illiterate draftees during World War I, and an avid civil libertarian, introduced me to his friend in the department of zoology, Sheldon C. Reed. The latter was a fruit fly geneticist whose interests had shifted to human psychopathology (mental retardation and the psychoses), conceptualized as continuously distributed traits, with his new appointment to head the Dight Institute for Human Genetics. He coined the term "genetic counseling," and it was one of the functions of the Dight. Conversations with him and members of the clinical program quickly gave rise to the design of my doctoral dissertation initiated in 1957: I would somehow collect a sample of adolescent identical and fraternal same-sex twins from the public high schools of Minneapolis and Saint Paul, determine their zygosity objectively, administer objective tests of their personality traits and intelligence, and then delve into the "psychogenetics of personality"—not a popular topic in that day.

One instrument, of course, would be the locally invented but world-renowned Minnesota Multiphasic Personality Inventory (MMPI). This paper-and-pencil test consisting of 550 true-false questions was developed by the psychologist Starke R. Hathaway, a member of my dissertation committee, and his neuropsychiatrist friend and colleague, J. C. McKinley, to assess symptoms and prodromal features of mental disorders along Kraepelinian lines in time for its deployment in evaluating the millions of draftees in World War II in a cost-effective manner. The giant intellect of Paul E. Meehl, a student of Hathaway, influenced and shaped the thought processes about clinical psychology of all the graduate students and faculty in the Ph.D. program.

The objective results were very reinforcing to a would-be behavioral geneticist (the term would not be used until 1960 with the publication of the textbook by J. Fuller and W. R. Thompson) in that they showed 4 of the 10 clinical scales were reliably more similar for identical than fraternal twins, even in a small sample of 68 pairs. The scales implicated to contain appreciable genetic variance had been derived from psychiatric patient criterion groups with diagnoses of affective disorders, schizophrenia, and antisocial personality disorders. Such findings, especially when replicated a few years later in my Harvard sample twice the size and in a different locale, helped to usher in a paradigm shift in the study of psychopathology and personality two decades later, wherein genetic factors, including genes and SNPs (single-nucleotide polymorphisms, which are DNA sequence variations), would become targets of large-scale research using new tools from molecular genetics and medicine.

Escalating the Degree of Difficulty: Twin Studies of Schizophrenia

One of the major goals of psychopathologists who study people in the general population, such as the normal adolescent twins described earlier, is that our assumptions are correct about there being a continuum from normality into psychiatrically noteworthy symptom domains and disorders, and that awareness of such a dimensional approach will shed light on the causes of abnormal behavior. Studying the diseases themselves, such as schizophrenia, in adult twin samples is a demanding, time-consuming, and expensive enterprise. All such studies in the literature were conducted before the use of fertility-enhancing drugs, when the overall twinning rate in this country was 12 pairs per 1,000 deliveries. The current rate of twinning overall is now about 31 per 1,000 deliveries. The older schizophrenia projects starting in 1928 allowed researchers to verify the representativeness of their samples if they came close to 12/1,000, with about 1/3 being identical twins (monozygotic, MZ, or one-egg), 1/3 being fraternal twins (dizygotic, DZ) of the same gender, and 1/3 being opposite-gender fraternal pairs.

How often might we expect to encounter a pair of identical twins in the adult population where at least one in the pair has a valid diagnosis of schizophrenia? This is the calculation: 4/1,000 multiplied by the age-adjusted base rate of schizophrenia, 1/100, yields an expectancy of 4/100,000 persons in the general population meeting our needs to locate the uranium in the pitchblende, the tortuous journey mapped out by Nobelist Curie. The task of assembling a decent-sized sample of both identical (MZ) and fraternal (DZ) twins meeting the criteria is facilitated by having national population and twin birth registries such as those in Australia, the Netherlands, and the Scandinavian countries, or by having special records of twinships in large teaching hospitals in countries with a form of national health insurance that records admissions and treatment for mental disorders in both inpatients and outpatients.

When James Shields and I, under the guidance of Eliot Slater, commenced our London, United Kingdom study in 1962 of schizophrenia in twins consecutively admitted to the joint Bethlem Royal Hospital and the Maudsley Hospital, we could identify all same-gender twin pairs from some 45,000 patients admitted between 1948 and 1965. After personal and record follow-up of the 479 patients who were twins to determine their most valid diagnoses, we accumulated a sample of 62 index cases (probands) with a diagnosis of schizophrenia ascertained independently of one another in our hospitals from 57 pairs equally divided by gender. Further research showed that we had 24 pairs of MZ twins and 33 pairs of DZ.

Ninety-one of the 114 twins were seen by us for tape-recorded, semi-structured interviews and, when consented to, testing with the MMPI. We did not rely on either our own diagnosis or that in the hospital charts; we chose to prepare case histories, without mentioning zygosity, and presented them in random order to a panel of six expert diagnosticians from varied "psychiatric cultures." The next task was to make use of the consensus diagnoses from the panel to calculate the most accurate summary rates for the MZ and DZ samples, still without an attempt to correct for age among the younger co-twins, still at risk for developing the disease in their future. The probandwise rate for a schizophrenia-related psychosis in MZ twins was 58%, while that for the DZ pairs was 12%. Allowing for the usual age correction would have had little effect on these uncorrected rates, that is, 62% and 15%.

The fact that these results have been replicated in more than a dozen studies across the globe means that an irrefutable foundation has been established for moving forward on an enlightened neuroscience frontier, recognizing the priority to be accorded to gene finding, gene expression, and epigenetics (changes in gene function that occur without a change in the sequence of DNA), identifying endophenotypes (Gottesman & Gould, 2003; Ritsner, 2009), and probing the brain pathophysiology with the newest imaging strategies (White & Gottesman, 2012) that can lead to new treatments. The term *endophenotype* was introduced by Gottesman and Shields (1972) to specify variables mediating the long chain of events in the complex pathways between gene expression and the precursors of psychiatric symptoms, which, in combination, usher in the disease itself. The term *enlightened* means a necessary sensitivity to probable gene by environment interactions as well as to measured environments, pre- or postnatal, that may be triggers to, or inhibitors of, varying degrees of predisposition (Glahn et al., 2014). I am reminded of the powerful rhetoric of Sir Winston Churchill in 1942 when the tide began to turn in favor of the Allied forces against the Nazi forces, as an analogy to our war against the ignorance surrounding the causes of schizophrenia and other psychoses: "Now this is not the end. It is not even the beginning of the end. But it is, perhaps, the end of the beginning."

Variations on the Classical Twin Design

The straightforward contrasting of MZ concordance rates (or correlations) with DZ concordance rates (or correlations) for a disease or trait, while of fundamental value to advancing knowledge about causes and their proper weights, far from exhausts the other kinds of information that can be derived from the study of twins. I would caution against just searching in Google for "twins" as it would drown you in some 56 million hits; the field is narrowed to a mountain of 4 million by asking for the combination "twins, psychology, psychiatry." Contemplating variations on the classical theme will open your mind: A focus on MZ twin pairs discordant for diseases and traits generates a list of vulnerability factors and another for contributions to resistance; studying the adult offspring of twins concordant or discordant for disorders may reveal unexpressed genotypes in the healthy MZ co-twin; MZ and DZ twins reared apart (often a practice of adoption agencies) allows for the assessment of the power, or lack of power, of environmental factors/rearing styles on behavioral outcomes (Segal, 2012); and a last example, collaboration with epigeneticists will allow the exploration at the molecular genetic level for factors impacting gene regulation on behavioral outcomes for which twins are discordant or differ greatly. A serious concern for the role of epigenetics on behavioral features is relatively recent, opening a window on sources of variation in behavior not directly attributable to either environment or to DNA-sequence changes or to gene by environment interactions. An appreciation of epigenetics will perhaps be analogous to the introduction of the Hubble Space Telescope into earth orbit and its impact on our old ideas about the solar system.

Complexity, Complexity, and Complexity

No one has ever been so bold as to believe that understanding why one human differs from another across behaviors would be easy. Even formulating the best questions to ask requires a talented, judicious, and multi-disciplinary task force, as discovered when The Hastings Center and the American Association of Science garnered funding from the Ethical, Legal, and Social Implications (ELSI) division of the National Human Genome Research Institute to reconnoiter the intellectual territory (Parens, Chapman, & Press, 2006). The fruits of the labors are well worth deep exploration. (See suggested readings at the end of this essay for titles and how to locate them.) A sampling of the disciplines convened to generate ideas and understanding (sometimes) in a confrontational (often) atmosphere would include several flavors of theology, philosophers of science, ethics and bioethics, law, psychology, psychiatry, molecular genetics, chemistry, human genetics, animal genetics, mathematics, sociology, neurobiology, journalism, anthropology, and the lay public—quite an assemblage of sharpened minds. But even more variety is needed to do justice to the complexities.

How can we approximate our dilemma of describing and explaining the sources of variation in human behavior, normal and deviant, to the point of requiring therapeutic interventions without obtaining, say, three different higher degrees, field experiences, and spending the majority of our adult lives in universities or medical schools? Don't answer. One suggestion I will proffer is to look for analogous questions elsewhere, tackling other complexities, and then examine partial answers that may have been discovered. For example, what causes floods or car crashes or divorce or 50 percent drops in the stock market in one year, and how could partial answers to those questions help with finding the causes of schizophrenia?

Let's start with floods such as the one that decimated New Orleans during Hurricane Katrina and see how far and where it takes us. The list of variables on our list, looked at both cross-sectionally at the time of the flood and historically, would include current local rainfall, rainfall upriver feeding into all the tributaries of the Mississippi, saturation levels of the earth from the previous season's snowfall, current wind velocities from the hurricane, the condition of the protective dikes, the presence or destruction of upriver and tributary dams, and so forth. The point is that both cross-sectional and

FIGURE 1

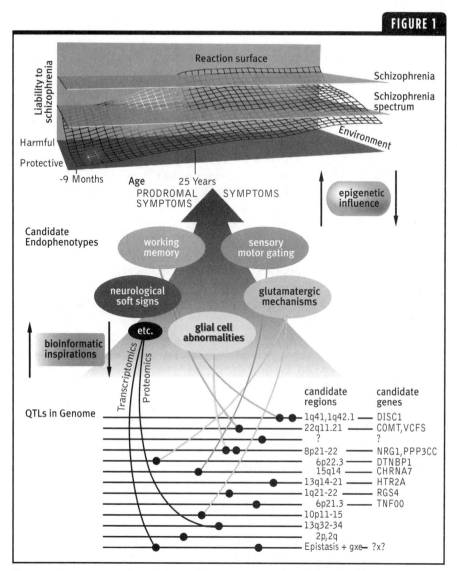

Gene regions, genes, and candidate endophenotypes are implicated in a biological systems approach to psychosis research. Endophenotypes are characterized theoretically as having simpler structural antecedents than the psychiatric phenotypes themselves. This schema (genes to endophenotypes to symptoms to disease), allowing for epigenetic, environmental, and stochastic influences, can be applied to other complex diseases as well. None of the components in the figure can be definitive; many more elements exist or await discovery. (© I. I. Gottesman & T. D. Gould, 2008. Used by permission.)

"developmental" histories of the land, river, behavior of the Corps of Engineers and of political decisions over the previous *n*-years will all enter into one big prediction equation, and it must be a dynamic one. I would make the same argument for understanding and predicting schizophrenia. We know less about which elements will be the puzzle pieces for schizophrenia than we do for floods, but we can begin with a schema for organizing those in which we have some confidence. Let's call the schema "an endophenotype strategy" and the cartoon/sketch could look like Figure 1 (Gottesman & Gould, 2003).

The schema has provisions for the roles of specific genes or SNPs implicated as distal contributors to the phenotype of schizophrenia and those to be discovered; it implies just a few of the many endophenotypes already in the literature from different domains of brain functioning; it suggests the need to consider the essentiality of developmental processes over time; it allows for the interplay of genes, environments, and epigenetic factors over time coming together pre- and postnatally with the additional schema of the "reaction surface" promoted by Turkheimer, Goldsmith, and Gottesman (1995) and, in passing, reminds us of the importance of bioinformatics, proteomics, and transcriptomics for the big picture. I can only hope that I have whet your appetite for complexity with this brief essay and the clues it has provided along the trail from my own interests to examples of some of the research I have pursued for the past 57 years. Those clues and the recommended readings may lead some of you to a nontraditional career in psychology, one that has permeable borders with other disciplines and one that prepares you for working collaboratively for the betterment of our species on projects akin to those that led to the Manhattan Project and putting an astronaut on the moon.

☐ Thinking Critically

1. In their classic study, what evidence did Irving Gottesman and James Shields uncover that supports the idea that genetics influences people's susceptibility to schizophrenia?
2. How has psychiatric genetics brought relief to people worried about mental illness "running in their family"?

☐ Suggested Further Reading

Carey, G. (2003). *Human genetics for the social sciences.* Thousand Oaks, CA: Sage.
DiLalla, L. F. (Ed.). (2004*). Behavior genetics principles: Perspectives in development, personality, and psychopathology.* Washington, DC: American Psychological Association.
Kaminsky, Z. A., Tang, T., Wang, S. C., Ptak, C., Oh, G., Wong, A. H. C., et al. (2009). DNA methylation profiles in monozygotic and dizygotic twins. *Nature Genetics, 41,* 240–245.
McGuffin, P., Owen, M. J., & Gottesman, I. I. (Eds.). (2004). *Psychiatric genetics and genomics* (Rev. ed.). Oxford, U.K.: Oxford University Press.
Plomin, R., DeFries, J. C., Knopik, V. S., & Neiderheiser, J. M. (2012). *Behavioral genetics* (6th ed.). New York: Worth.

☐ References

Glahn, D. C., Knowles, E. E., McKay, D. R., Sprooten, E., Raventos, H., Blangero, J., Gottesman, I. I., & Almasy, L. (2014). Arguments for the sake of endophenotypes. *American Journal of Medical Genetics Part B: Neuropsychiatric Genetics, 9999,* 1–9.
Gottesman, I. I., & Gould, T. D. (2003). The endophenotype concept in psychiatry: Etymology and strategic intentions. *American Journal of Psychiatry, 160,* 636–645.

Gottesman, I. I., & Shields, J. (1972). *Schizophrenia and genetics: A twin study vantage point.* New York: Academic Press.

Parens, E., Chapman, A. R., & Press, N. (Eds.). (2006). *Wrestling with behavioral genetics: Science, ethics, and public conversation.* Baltimore, MD: Johns Hopkins University Press.

Segal, N. L. (2012). *Born together—reared apart: The landmark Minnesota twin study.* Cambridge, MA: Harvard University Press.

Ritsner, M. S. (Ed.). (2009). *The handbook of neuropsychiatric biomarkers, endophenotypes, and genes: Promises, advances, and challenges.* Frankfurt: Springer.

Turkheimer, E., Goldsmith, H. H., & Gottesman, I. I. (1995). Commentary (on G. Gottlieb). *Human Development, 38,* 142–153.

White, T. J., & Gottesman, I. I. (2012). Brain connectivity and gyrifications as endophenotypes for schizophrenia: Weight of the evidence. *Current Topics of Medicinal Chemistry, 12*(21), 2393–403.

Lost in Thought: The Perils of Rumination

SUSAN NOLEN-HOEKSEMA Yale University

With great sadness, we acknowledge the passing of Dr. Susan Nolen-Hoeksema. We honor her scholarship and contributions to psychology in this volume.

☐ **Please describe your current position and research interests.**

I am Professor of Psychology at Yale University. My research interests are depression, gender differences in psychopathology, and adolescent psychopathology.

☐ **How did you become interested in studying the style of thinking you call rumination and its impact on mood?**

While working with depressed patients, I was impressed by their tendency to ruminate about their past and about their current problems in a way that was nonproductive and decided to study it as a causal factor in depression.

☐ **What has been the real-world impact of this work?**

The work has led to innovations in treatment for depressed people. I have also written self-help books that people who ruminate tell me have been helpful.

When something unpleasant happens—you fail a test or have an argument with a friend—do you ever find yourself going over and over what happened, questioning why it happened, how you could have prevented it, what the consequences might be, and how upset you feel? If your answer is "yes," you're like most people. We analyze unpleasant events to understand them, hoping that questioning will lead to solutions to ongoing problems, prevent bad things from happening in the future, or both. However, some people never move into a problem-solving mode. Instead, they remain stuck, rehashing events or situations, microanalyzing them, contemplating their deep meaning. They also tend to worry about future events, imagining all the ways that things could go wrong. We call this process rumination—repetitively thinking about difficult situations and all their possible causes, consequences, and meanings without moving into problem solving.

The Consequences of Rumination

Although most of us ruminate occasionally, some people—we call them ruminators—ruminate very frequently. In other words, the tendency to ruminate appears to be a stable trait in some individuals. Some years ago, colleagues and I developed a questionnaire, the Response Styles Questionnaire, to assess rumination (Nolen-Hoeksema & Morrow, 1991). Our questionnaire asks people what they tend to do when they feel sad, blue, and depressed. For examples of items from this questionnaire, see Table 1.

TABLE 1

Sample Rumination Items

Instructions

People think and do many different things when they feel sad, blue, or depressed. Please read each of the items below and indicate whether you never, sometimes, often, or always think or do each one when you feel sad, down, or depressed. Please indicate what you generally do, not what you think you should do.

	never	sometimes	often	always
1. I think "What am I doing to deserve this?"	1	2	3	4
2. I think "Why do I always react this way?"	1	2	3	
3. I think "Why do I have problems other people don't have?"	1	2	3	4
4. I think about a recent situation, wishing it had gone better.	1	2	3	4
5. I think "Why can't I handle things better?"	1	2	3	4

Respondents who endorse many items such as those in Table 1 are designated as ruminators. Ruminators tend to ruminate even when their lives are going relatively smoothly.

Ruminators are at increased risk for a number of mental health problems including depression, a problem we have studied closely. In several studies, we have found that ruminators are more likely than those without this trait to experience severe and prolonged symptoms of depression after difficult events and even to be diagnosed with major depressive disorder, one of the most severe forms of depression. For example, we studied the effects of rumination on depression among people who had recently lost a loved one to cancer (Nolen-Hoeksema & Larson, 1999). Recently bereaved people often feel quite depressed, but the severity and duration of bereavement-related depression varies greatly from one person to another, with bereaved ruminators having relatively longer and more severe episodes of depression following the loss of their loved one.

Similarly, in a study of reactions to the 1989 earthquake that rocked the San Francisco Bay Area, we found that ruminators experienced more symptoms of depression and anxiety after the earthquake than did nonruminators (Nolen-Hoeksema & Morrow, 1991). In a fortuitous coincidence for our research, about 140 Stanford University students had taken the Response Styles Questionnaire 2 weeks before the earthquake. When we assessed their mental state after the quake, those students who had previously scored as ruminators were found to be more depressed and anxious 10 days after the quake and 7 weeks after the quake than those who were not ruminators, regardless of how much stress they had endured as a result of the earthquake (for example, whether they were in a safe building or a building that literally fell down around them).

In other studies, we have found that rumination predicts not only depression and anxiety but also substance abuse (for example, binge-drinking alcohol), binge eating and bulimia nervosa, and self-harming behavior (for example, cutting) (for a review, see Nolen-Hoeksema, Wisco, & Lyubomirsky, 2008). We think that these diverse behaviors all represent maladaptive attempts to escape from the aversive self-awareness and negative emotions that rumination brings about.

Mechanisms Linking Rumination with Negative Outcomes

How does rumination lead to all these negative consequences? In laboratory studies designed to answer this question, our method has been to compare two groups: people who are experiencing depression or dysphoria and people who are not at all depressed. We ask participants to ruminate, or we distract them from any natural ruminations by requiring them to focus their attention on a series of phrases. In the rumination-induction condition, the phrases direct their attention to thoughts about themselves, how their bodies feel, and how their lives are going—for example, "think about your level of motivation right now" or "think about your character and who you strive to be." In the distraction-induction condition, the phrases direct their attention to thoughts and images that are not self-focused—for example, "think about a truckload of watermelons" or "think about the face on the Mona Lisa."

Notice that both the rumination and distraction phrases are neutral in emotional tone. We don't specifically ask participants to focus on negative aspects of themselves or negative images in the environment. Thus, we don't expect the rumination phrases to have any effect on the mood of nondepressed participants, whereas we expect the rumination phrases to *increase* the depressed mood in the short term in depressed participants because they are more likely to be thinking negatively about themselves and feeling badly. In contrast, we expect the distraction phrases to *decrease* the depressed mood in the short term because these phrases draw the attention of the depressed participants away from their negative ruminations. And this is just what we have found. In a few dozen studies using this paradigm, rumination induction has been found to increase depressed mood in depressed participants and have no effect on mood in nondepressed participants. In contrast, the distraction induction decreases depressed mood in depressed participants but does not affect mood in nondepressed participants (see Nolen-Hoeksema et al., 2008).

What's particularly interesting, however, is how rumination induction affects the quality of depressed people's thoughts, increasing negativity about the past, present, and future (see Nolen-Hoeksema et al., 2008). Specifically, we have assessed thoughts about past, present, and future events in four groups—depressed people who have ruminated, depressed people who have been distracted, nondepressed people who have ruminated, and nondepressed people who have been distracted. Depressed/ruminators on average generate more negative memories of the past and rate these negative events as having been more frequent than do those in the other three groups. When thinking about the present, the depressed/ruminators as a group focus more on their problems, engage in more self-blame for their problems, and express less self-confidence about overcoming their problems compared with the other three groups. When thinking about the future, depressed/ruminators are on average less optimistic and predict fewer happy events in their future, compared to the other three groups. In turn, these negative thoughts about the past, present, and future feed the depression of the depressed/ruminators, prolonging it and worsening it.

Ruminators often tell us that they ruminate in an attempt to understand and solve their problems. But, paradoxically, rumination appears to interfere with good problem solving. In other experimental studies, we have given participants sticky, interpersonal problems to solve after they have ruminated or been distracted. The problems are typical of the kinds of interpersonal issues that arise in the life of a depressed person, such as a friend avoiding you. We find that depressed people who have been ruminating generate solutions to such problems that are significantly lower in quality (as rated by impartial judges) than the solutions generated by depressed people who were distracted or nondepressed people who either ruminated or were distracted. For example, in response to the friend-is-avoiding-you problem, individuals in the depressed/rumination group generate "solutions" such as "I guess I would avoid them, too." In contrast, members of the other three groups tend to generate solutions such as "I would ask a mutual friend if I had done anything to upset my friend, and if so, I would apologize."

Even when ruminators generate reasonable solutions to problems, rumination seems to get in the way of their implementation of these solutions. In another study, for example, we asked ruminators and nonruminators (defined by answers to our questionnaire) to generate solutions to a concrete problem, such as revising the curriculum for their school or solving the housing problem on their campus. For such noninterpersonal problems, the ruminators generated solutions that were just as good as those generated by the nonruminators. But when it came time to commit to a solution and present it to a panel of judges, the ruminators had less confidence than the nonruminators in the quality of their solution and were more likely to ask for additional time to work on it. And at the presentation, the ruminators appeared less confident in their presentations than did the nonruminators (Ward, Lyubomirsky, Sousa, & Nolen-Hoeksema, 2003). Thus, ruminators may become immobilized in indecision and self-doubt and fail to implement solutions to their problems, even when those solutions are good ones.

Finally, ruminators may drive away social support, perhaps when they need it the most, because people become weary and frustrated at the ruminator's inability to let go of their concerns and move on. In our bereavement study, we found that ruminators were reaching out to others for social support even more than were nonruminators. This makes sense because ruminators were feeling more depressed and had a lot on their minds. Over time, however, the ruminators reported that others were becoming annoyed with their constant need to talk about their loss and their feelings of grief and critical of their inability to get on with their lives. In turn, this loss of social support and increase in criticism gave ruminators more to ruminate about and fueled their depression (Nolen-Hoeksema & Davis, 1999).

What Drives Rumination?

If rumination leads to such misery, why do ruminators continue to ruminate? One reason may be that rumination saps motivation. In one study using our rumination and distraction inductions in depressed and nondepressed participants, we asked how useful several pleasant, simple activities—for example, "go for coffee with a friend" or "take a walk in the hills"—would be in improving mood. The depressed/rumination group rated these activities as just as useful as the other three groups (depressed/distraction, nondepressed/rumination, and nondepressed/distraction) for lifting mood. But when we asked the four groups how likely they would be to get up immediately and actually go for coffee or take a walk, the depressed/rumination group rated themselves as less likely to do so, compared the other three groups. It was as if they said, "Yes, I know doing one of these activities would make me feel better, but I'm not going to do it." The content of depressed rumination—the focus on how tired and blue you feel, and on compelling problems in your life—may drain any motivation individuals have to do things they can intellectually acknowledge would improve their moods.

Basic cognitive deficits associated rumination may make it difficult for ruminators to pull out of rumination once it starts. Jutta Joormann (2006) has used tasks that assess participants' ability to inhibit negative information when instructed to do so; she finds that ruminators have more difficulty on these tasks compared to nonruminators. So, once ruminators get going, turning off negative thoughts may be very difficult, even if they are motivated to do so. Similarly, in a neuroimaging study, we found that ruminators showed sustained activity in areas of the brain associated with self-related thought even when given distractions. In other words, compared to nonruminators, they could not redirect their attention to the distractions and continued to show activity in brain regions associated with self-related thought (Johnson, Nolen-Hoeksema, Mitchell, & Levin, 2009).

These cognitive deficits may have genetic roots. In a group of adolescent girls and their mothers, we examined the relationship between rumination and a specific gene abnormality (Val/Val genotype for BDNF) that is associated with difficulties in inhibiting information (Hilt, Sander, Nolen-Hoeksema, & Simen, 2007). We found that participants with the Val/Val genotype were more likely to be ruminators than participants with other variants of this genotype. Thus, genetic factors may play a role in who becomes a ruminator, perhaps by affecting the brain regions involved in the ability to inhibit information voluntarily.

Overcoming Rumination

Are there strategies for overcoming rumination? Our experimental studies provide some clues. We have found if depressed/ruminators spend just 8 to 10 minutes engaged in a pleasant, distracting activity, their negative mood decreases and their thinking improves. A wide range of activities can break the cycle: physical exercise, engaging in hobbies such as gardening or cooking, spending time with others, or meditating on pleasant images. The key is to find activities that are engaging and distracting but that are not in themselves maladaptive or dangerous (such as binge drinking). Because depressed/ruminators are not motivated to engage in pleasant activities, they may need extra encouragement. Actually scheduling such activities in their date book can increase commitment.

Distraction only has short-term effects on mood and thinking, however. People prone to ruminating also need to do something about the situations or problems they frequently ruminate about: They must engage in active problem solving around these issues once their mood has lifted and their thinking has cleared. Starting small is important; focusing on actions that are simple and relatively easy can have a positive impact on the problem. For example, if you are afraid of losing your job, a possible solution would be to increase relevant skills, so that you become a more valuable employee. This big goal could seem distant and overwhelming to a ruminator, but a small step toward that solution would be to look into community college classes. Then the next small step would be to actually enroll in a class, and so on. Taking small steps toward solutions can increase a person's sense of control and counter ruminations.

Sometimes ruminators do not have a specific problem they need to solve. Instead, they need to change their perspective on a situation. For example, a woman whose parents were emotionally abusive might understandably ruminate about why they were so cruel to her, whether they loved her, how much they damaged her self-esteem, and so on. This problem cannot be solved with concrete actions. But gaining a different perspective on the emotional abuse might help this woman stop ruminating about it. How to do this? One strategy would be to imagine talking with a good friend who had the same background—that is, to try to look at the situation as if it were happening to someone else who needed helpful advice. She might say, "I'd tell my friend that you'll never know why they behaved the way they did. But you can choose to focus on your life right now, and to not let your past haunt you."

Studies show that interventions that include teaching depressed people to use positive distracting activities to break their rumination cycles, to engage in active problem solving, and to work toward different perspectives on their life situations help to reduce their ruminations and relieve their depression (Watkins et al., 2007). Even if they are not depressed, people prone to ruminate can benefit from self-help strategies involving positive activities, problem solving, and gaining new perspectives (Nolen-Hoeksema, 2003).

Conclusion

Rumination can certainly be destructive. It leads to more negative thinking about the past, present, and future. It interferes with good problem solving and carrying through with solutions to your problems. It drives friends and family away. Ultimately, it can lead to serious depression, anxiety, binge drinking, binge eating, and other escapist behaviors. But rumination can be overcome. The first task is to break rumination cycles through pleasant distractions. Then you must begin to solve the problems you frequently ruminate about, or try to gain a new perspective on the situations that fuel rumination.

☐ Thinking Critically

1. Susan Nolen-Hoeksema's research explores the self-destructive cycle of rumination. What keeps people in a cycle of rumination, and how can they break this cycle?
2. How does rumination affect people's relationships with others?

☐ Suggested Further Reading

Nolen-Hoeksema, S. (2003). *Women who think too much: How to break free of overthinking and reclaim your life.* New York: Holt.

Nolen-Hoeksema, S., Wisco, B., & Lyubomirsky, S. (2008). Rethinking rumination. *Perspectives on Psychological Science, 3,* 400–424.

☐ References

Hilt, L. M., Sander, L. C., Nolen-Hoeksema, S., & Simen, A. A. (2007). The BDNF Val66Met polymorphism predicts rumination and depression differently in young adolescent girls and their mothers. *Neuroscience Letters, 429,* 12–16.

Johnson, M. K., Nolen-Hoeksema, S., Mitchell, K., & Levin, Y. (2009). Emotional distress, rumination, and medial cortex activity during self-reflection. *Social Cognitive and Affective Neuroscience, 4,* 313–327.

Joormann, J. (2006). Differential effects of rumination and dysphoria on the inhibition of irrelevant emotional material: Evidence from a negative priming task. *Cognitive Therapy and Research, 30,* 149–160.

Nolen-Hoeksema, S. (2003). *Women who think too much: How to break free of overthinking and reclaim your life.* New York: Holt.

Nolen-Hoeksema, S., & Davis, C. G. (1999). "Thanks for sharing that": Ruminators and their social support networks. *Journal of Personality and Social Psychology, 77,* 801–814.

Nolen-Hoeksema, S., & Larson, J. (1999). *Coping with loss.* Mahwah, NJ: Erlbaum.

Nolen-Hoeksema, S., Larson, J., & Grayson, C. (1999). Explaining the gender difference in depressive symptoms. *Journal of Personality and Social Psychology, 77,* 1061–1072.

Nolen-Hoeksema, S., & Morrow, J. (1991). A prospective study of depression and post-traumatic stress symptoms following a natural disaster: The 1989 Loma Prieta earthquake. *Journal of Personality and Social Psychology, 61,* 115–121.

Nolen-Hoeksema, S., Wisco, B., & Lyubomirsky, S. (2008). Rethinking rumination. *Perspectives on Psychological Science, 3,* 400–424.

Ward, A., Lyubomirsky, S., Sousa, L., & Nolen-Hoeksema, S. (2003). Can't quite commit: Rumination and uncertainty. *Personality and Social Psychology Bulletin, 29,* 96–107.

Watkins, E. R., Scott, J., Wingrove, J., Rimes, K. A., Bathurst, N., Steiner, H., et al. (2007). Rumination-focused cognitive behaviour therapy for residual depression: A case series. *Behaviour Research and Therapy, 45,* 2144–2154.

Treatment of Psychological Disorders

The Development and Evaluation of
Psychological Treatments for Panic Disorder
David H. Barlow

Treatments for Children with Severe
Aggressive and Antisocial Behavior
Alan E. Kazdin

The Development and Evaluation of Psychological Treatments for Panic Disorder

DAVID H. BARLOW Boston University

☐ **Please describe your current position and research interests.**

I am Professor of Psychology and Psychiatry and Founder and Director Emeritus of the Center for Anxiety and Related Disorders at Boston University. I received my PhD from the University of Vermont in 1969 and have published over 500 articles and chapters and 60 books, mostly in the area of the nature and treatment of emotional disorders. I have received numerous awards, including the Distinguished Scientific Award for Applications of Psychology from the American Psychological Association, and the James McKeen Cattell Award for Lifetime Achievement in Applied Research from the Association for Psychological Science, and I continue to attempt to develop a deeper understanding of emotional disorders as well as improved treatments.

☐ **How did you become interested in studying the effectiveness of treatments of anxiety disorders?**

Following a fascination that developed in high school with why people do the things they do, I became aware that many people had fears and anxieties focused on objects or situations even though they knew there was nothing to be afraid of. This is called the "neurotic paradox," and I've been studying it ever since.

☐ **What has been the real-world impact of this work?**

Individual mental health clinicians and health services around the world have adopted our new treatments for panic and related disorders based on our deeper understanding of the nature of these chronic problems, and we hope to further improve these tools to relieve human suffering and enhance functioning.

Early in my career, a middle-aged woman called my office and asked if I would make a house call on her elderly mother who lived alone in a small flat in the middle of a medium-sized city. When I mentioned that it would be better for her mother to come to the clinic where she would get the full attention of all of our staff, the daughter replied that the mother had not been out of her apartment for 20 years. The daughter went on to say that in the early years when her mother attempted to leave her flat to go anywhere, she suffered from uncontrollable episodes of severe anxiety. After a number of years, the attempts to leave decreased and finally stopped altogether.

When I arrived at the apartment, I rang the bell, was buzzed in and, over the intercom, asked to walk up a flight of stairs. As I reached the door to the second-floor flat and knocked, I heard an elderly woman's voice asking me to let myself in. I found the woman sitting in a chair in the middle of her living room. She apologized for not greeting me at the door, but explained that she had not been near the front door of her apartment for at least 5 years, nor could she go to the back of her kitchen or the back porch beyond. She was living out her life in a portion of her living room, the front portion of her kitchen, and her single bedroom and bath.

I realized that the woman was suffering from a severe case of panic disorder and agoraphobia, a condition in which people experience sudden surges of fear for no apparent reason at unpredictable times. I knew without asking that these unexpected surges of fear would be characterized by sharply increased heart rate, blood pressure, muscle tension, and other physical signs of the flight/fight syndrome, in which the body gears up to handle an imminent threat or danger. In situations of real danger, this surge in the sympathetic nervous system prepares us to be at our physical best: We see more acutely, run faster, perform feats of incredible strength. (Newspapers occasionally feature stories of these extraordinary deeds—for example, a 90-pound woman lifting a car off of a trapped child.)

If the fear is groundless, this reaction is called a panic attack. With nothing dangerous happening, individuals who are susceptible to developing panic disorder experience the attack as a mysterious jolt out of the blue, which they attribute to a heart attack or some equally terrible bodily affliction, with death soon to follow. They believe that if somehow they survive that first attack, the next one will surely get them. Because panic attacks occur unpredictably, affected individuals soon learn not to venture far from a safe place (or safe person) where help might be available if the worst happens. This avoidant behavior is called agoraphobia. In severe cases, the individual becomes housebound, which is what had happened to the elderly woman. Limited by her fears to a small area of her apartment, she had everything delivered or brought to her by her adult daughter, who came by every few days. She wiled away the long days reading and watching television, utterly alone.

What Causes Panic Disorder?

Panic disorder seems to be caused by an interaction of three factors, referred to as triple vulnerabilities (Barlow, 2000; Suárez, Bennett, Goldstein, & Barlow, 2009; see Figure 1).

1. A generalized biological vulnerability in the form of an inherited anxious temperament can result in a high-strung or easily stressed individual. Although this genetic vulnerability does not cause panic disorder, it does make the problem more likely.

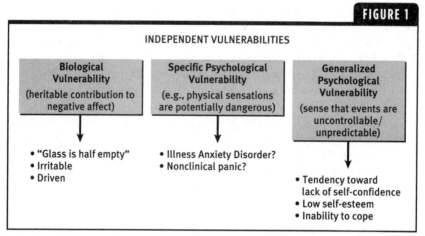

Triple vulnerabilities in the etiology of panic disorder. These three vulnerabilities, or diatheses, must all be present for an individual to develop panic disorder. (Based on Barlow, 2002)

2. A generalized psychological sense, while growing up, that the world is a potentially dangerous place can produce a pervasive belief that coping with all of the challenges and threats that come along might be difficult indeed. This sense of the unpredictability and uncontrollability of future threats does not focus on any one threat but becomes a broad-based disposition to experience the world as dangerous. This psychological vulnerability also does not cause panic disorder but can contribute to its formation.

3. A belief, developed at an early age, that physical sensations are particularly dangerous and that one must be on guard for unexplained somatic (bodily) events or illnesses. For example, when they were children, some individuals who later developed panic disorder were rushed to the doctor at the first sign of unexplained physical symptoms. Others witnessed chronic illness and were sensitized to the dangers of illnesses or injuries. That these individuals would become vigilant for any unexplained somatic symptoms is not surprising. This third factor is referred to as a *specific* psychological vulnerability because the individual learns to be anxious about a very specific set of circumstances; in this case, bodily sensations.

The three vulnerabilities, when they occur in the same individual, set the stage for the development of panic disorder.

Why Do Panic Attacks Occur Initially?

Stressful events trigger panic attacks in approximately 10 percent of the population. In fact, panic is a common reaction to stress, as are headaches, high blood pressure, and a "nervous" stomach. These "nonclinical" panic attacks pass quickly for most people. But in approximately 3 percent of the population, the panic attack activates the three vulnerabilities, and these individuals, believing that they are dying or losing control, may develop panic disorder and possibly agoraphobia.

Psychological Treatments for Panic Disorder

In the 1980s, a physical problem—some kind of a brain dysfunction—was thought to cause panic disorder. The leading candidate was a "chemical imbalance," which was believed to cause heightened sensitivity in the brain stem. But research in the 1990s ruled this out as the sole underlying cause (Barlow, 2002; Gorman et al., 1990), and investigators agreed that an interacting web of biological and psychological factors, such as those just described, contribute to the onset of panic disorder.

When the cause of panic disorder was thought to be solely biological, drugs were the first choice for treatment. In the 1980s, the most popular drugs for panic disorder were high-potency tranquilizers, known by brand names such as Xanax and Klonapin. These drugs could be effective for panic disorder, but many patients developed a dependence, such that attempts to stop taking them produced serious side effects. Because of this problem with dependence and addiction, other drugs, such as selective serotonin reuptake inhibitors (SSRIs), have become the preferred drugs for treating panic disorder. These drugs include brand names such as Paxil and Prozac. Approximately 60 percent of patients with panic disorder respond at least somewhat (and some very well) as long as they continue to take the medication. But relapse rates are high once the medication is stopped (Craske & Barlow, 2014).

Around 1990, Michelle Craske and I developed a psychological treatment for panic disorder that focused directly on the sensitivity of these individuals to their own physical sensations, such as fluctuating heart rate, skin temperature, and dizziness (Barlow & Craske, 2007; Craske & Barlow, 2007). In people who are susceptible, these sensations are very frightening because they come to trigger the next panic attack through the psychological process of learning and association called conditioning (Bouton, Mineka, & Barlow, 2001).

Based on this insight, we experimented with a treatment in which individuals with panic disorder were exposed to mild versions of the physical sensations. In the protected setting of our clinic, we had them exercise vigorously to produce fluctuations in heart rate, spin around in a chair to produce slight dizziness, and so forth. We chose a person's induced symptoms based on an assessment of the mix of physical sensations that were closely associated with their panic attacks. (These vary from one person to another.)

In a psychological process called extinction, our patients—by experiencing these physical sensations repeatedly—learned that the sensations don't lead to a terrible outcome, such as a heart attack. Of course, their rational self knew this all along, but the emotional brain, where these fear responses reside, tends to override the rational brain in cases of panic or any emotional disorder. Hence, these specialized treatments reach the emotional brain.

To assist in strengthening the "rational brain," the patients' basic faulty attitudes and perceptions about the dangerousness of these sensations are also identified and modified. Patients may also be taught calming techniques such as breathing and meditation to help them cope with stress and anxiety. A number of studies demonstrated subsequently that this treatment, a cognitive-behavioral approach called panic control treatment (PCT), is effective for panic disorder (Barlow & Lehman, 1996).

Combined Psychological and Pharmacological Treatments

My colleagues and I then sought to test the hypothesis that combining drugs and psychological treatments might prove more effective than either individual treatment alone. We conducted a large clinical trial that treated 312 patients with panic disorder at four different sites. Two of these sites were known for their expertise with drug treatments, and two were known for their expertise with cognitive-behavioral treatments. Patients at all sites were administered either the psychological or drug treatment alone, or in combination, along with appropriate comparison conditions such as a drug placebo condition. The experiment was also double blind, which means that neither the therapists nor the patients knew whether they were getting the actual medication or the placebo (sugar) capsule (Barlow, Gorman, Shear, & Woods, 2000).

We found that both the drug and the psychological treatments were effective, as we expected, with each better than the placebo. But, much to our surprise, the combination treatment was not any better than the individual treatments. Thus, our hypothesis was not proven, and the widespread practice of administering both treatments simultaneously for panic disorder was called into question. Furthermore, after all treatments were stopped, the psychological treatment was found to be more durable. That is, among those patients who received psychological treatment either alone or combined with placebo, fewer people relapsed in the 6 months after treatment as compared with patients who received either drug treatment alone or drug plus psychological treatment.

We concluded from this evidence that combining treatments offered no advantages, and, that given a choice, the preference would be for the psychological treatment because it is more durable and less intrusive. (Drug treatments are almost always considered more intrusive than psychological treatments due to side effects or drug interactions that can occur.) Of course, some patients prefer to take a drug, or the cognitive-behavioral treatment may not be available, in which case drug treatment is a good alternative.

Keeping People Healthy

In a second study (White et al., 2013), colleagues and I evaluated the best strategies for maintaining long-term health after treatment. We began with the working hypothesis that once patients received cognitive-behavioral therapy and were essentially cured, they would not need any further treatment sessions. We based this assumption on the view of most of our therapists that no further intervention is needed if patients have learned all the concepts that the therapists teach and have implemented them well in daily life.

Not all of our therapists agreed, however. Some argued that occasional booster sessions would prove useful in preventing relapse over the long term in this chronic condition. To test this notion, we treated 256 patients with panic disorder and agoraphobia of varying degrees of severity, using the same cognitive-behavioral therapy that we employed in our first study. Many of these patients (157, or 61.3%) did very well with treatment and were cured essentially. To evaluate the advantage of booster sessions, half of these patients ($n = 79$) went on to receive nine additional sessions spaced every month for 9 months, and they then were followed for another year with no further treatment. The other half of the patients ($n = 78$) received no further treatment.

When the results were assessed after the 1-year period without any treatment, the majority view was proved wrong. That is, there *was* an advantage to having booster sessions. Among the group that did not have booster sessions, 18% had some relapse or recurrence of panic disorder during the 1-year follow-up and 82% stayed well. By contrast, only 2.7% of the group that experienced booster sessions evidenced a relapse or recurrence during that year, and fully 97.3% stayed well. This significant difference demonstrates the value of some continued attention to these patients, who are, after all, suffering from a chronic condition that waxes and wanes.

Of the remaining patients—individuals who did not meet our criteria for "responding" to treatment to the point where they were essentially cured—some dropped out along the way for a variety of reasons, such as moving away or just feeling they didn't need treatment anymore. Others finished treatment with varying responses, from just missing our criteria for being all but "cured" to having no benefit whatsoever. In this latter group, we evaluated the benefits of then giving them a medication for panic disorder, and while the results haven't been fully analyzed yet, sequencing the treatments in this way looks like a promising treatment approach.

Conclusion

Scientific discoveries about the nature of panic disorder led us to develop a specifically tailored psychological treatment. The two experiments I've described confirm that we have an effective psychological treatment for panic disorder—a treatment that has become a first-line choice based on recommendations from national health services around the world. Of course, we still have a long way to go to make our treatments powerful enough to benefit the largest number of people.

Interestingly, our studies also confirm that a number of our assumptions were incorrect. First, we proved ourselves wrong that combining drug and psychological treatments would be better than simply providing patients with one treatment or the other. Second, we now know that individuals who do well need further attention after treatment has ended to ensure that they have the best chance to stay well. Without close scientific examination of the effects of psychotherapy, we would have been unaware of these important treatment issues, and patients with panic disorder would not be getting the best care possible.

☐ Thinking Critically

1. How does David Barlow's research on panic disorder demonstrate the value of science in developing effective treatment interventions for emotional disorders?

2. How serious are panic attacks? What are the consequences for those who have them?

☐ Suggested Further Reading

Barlow, D. H., Sauer-Zavala, S., Carl, J. R., Bullis, J. R., & Ellard, K. K. (2014). The nature, diagnosis, and treatment of neuroticism: Back to the future. *Clinical Psychological Science, 2,* 344–365.

Gallagher, M. W., Payne, L. A., White, K. S., Shear, M. K., Woods, S. W., Gorman, J. M., & Barlow, D. H. (2013). Mechanisms of change in cognitive behavioral therapy for panic disorder: The unique effects of self-efficacy and anxiety sensitivity. *Behavior Research and Therapy, 51,* 676–777.

☐ References

Barlow, D. H. (2000). Unraveling the mysteries of anxiety and its disorders from the perspective of emotion theory. *American Psychologist, 55*(11), 1245–1263.

Barlow, D. H. (2002). *Anxiety and its disorders: The nature and treatment of anxiety and panic* (2nd ed.). New York: Guilford Press.

Barlow, D. H., & Craske, M. G. (2007). *Mastery of your anxiety and panic: Client workbook* (4th ed.). New York: Oxford University Press.

Barlow, D. H., Gorman, J. M., Shear, M. K., & Woods, S. W. (2000). Cognitive-behavioral therapy, imipramine, or their combination for panic disorder: A randomized controlled trial. *JAMA, 283,* 2529–2536.

Barlow, D. H., & Lehman, C. L. (1996). Advances in the psychosocial treatment of anxiety disorders: Implications for national health care. *Archives of General Psychiatry, 53,* 727–735.

Bouton, M. E., Mineka, S., & Barlow, D. H. (2001). A modern learning-theory perspective on the etiology of panic disorder. *Psychological Review, 108,* 4–32.

Craske, M. G., & Barlow, D. H. (2007). *Mastery of your anxiety and panic: Therapist guide* (4th ed.). New York: Oxford University Press.

Craske, M. G., & Barlow, D. H. (2014). Panic disorder and agoraphobia. In D. H. Barlow (Ed.), *Clinical handbook of psychological disorders* (5th ed.). New York: Guilford Press.

Gorman, J. M., Goetz, R. R., Dillon, D., Liebowitz, M. R., Fyer, A. J., Davies, S., et al. (1990). Sodium D-lactate infusion of panic disorder patients. *Neuropsychopharmacology, 3,* 181–189.

Suárez, L., Bennett, S., Goldstein, C., & Barlow, D. H. (2009). Understanding anxiety disorders from a "triple vulnerabilities" framework. In M. M. Antony & M. B. Stein (Eds.), *Oxford handbook of anxiety and related disorders.* New York: Oxford University Press.

White, K. S., Payne, L. A., Gorman, J. M., Shear, M. K., Woods, S. W., Saksa, J. R., Barlow, D. H. (2013). Does maintenance CBT contribute to long-term treatment response of panic disorder with or without agoraphobia? A randomized controlled clinical trial. *Journal of Consulting and Clinical Psychology, 81,* 47–57.

Treatments for Children with Severe Aggressive and Antisocial Behavior

ALAN E. KAZDIN Yale University

☐ **Please describe your current position and research interests.**

I am the John M. Musser Professor of Psychology and Child Psychiatry and the Director of the Yale Parenting Center. My interests are in developmental psychopathology, which consists of the study of psychiatric disorders and impairment among children and adolescents. My research has focused primarily on aggressive and antisocial behavior and depression. The study of child dysfunction invariably leads to other topics including parent, family, and contextual factors that are often linked with child functioning. For example, we have also studied parent psychiatric dysfunction, interpersonal violence in the home, child-rearing practices, and stress to help understand child and parent functioning.

☐ **How did you become interested in this area of work?**

My primary interest has been on developing treatments for clinical dysfunction. This interest in treatment began in graduate school. I became interested in applying methods and findings from psychological science, particularly learning research, to treat clinical dysfunction. There also was an overarching zeitgeist in clinical psychology to place psychotherapies on much firmer empirical ground than was the case at the time. Added to that, experiences including a part-time job during and after graduate school and then a mid-career job change guided me toward intervention research, as I highlight further later in this essay. In each case, there was a need and even explicit demand to do something to help individuals with significant psychological impairment.

☐ **What has been the real-world impact of this work?**

We have developed two effective psychosocial treatments for children with severe aggressive and antisocial behavior. Other researchers have worked with this population and now there is a well-supported set of interventions that can be used with children ranging in age from preschool through late adolescence and from mild to extreme aggressive and antisocial behavior. As for impact, the personal suffering mental disorders cause for children and their families and the societal monetary costs are enormous. We have made a direct impact in addressing these burdens with the couple thousand children with whom we have worked. Of course, we hope that the children who did not participate in our work will see the benefits of it through evidence-based treatments of our work as well as that of other researchers. To extend our impact, we train mental health professionals throughout the world to carry out the treatments; we work with television, radio, newspapers, and print and online magazines to disseminate information about available options for parents; and we provide resources for clinicians in practice and parents.

A few times in my career, I have been in a position where there is a need to change the behavior of children or adults who are not functioning well in everyday life. These individuals have difficulties getting along with others, meeting the demands of school or work, and managing to stay out of trouble. I found myself in this position for the first time in graduate school when I took a part-time job at a facility for children, adolescents, and adults with a range of emotional and behavioral problems and developmental disabilities. At the job interview, the director asked me to develop interventions that would make genuine differences in the functioning of the clients and to begin working with adolescents and adults in the sheltered workshop part of the facility. I eagerly confessed I was quite interested in behavior change, but as a graduate student I knew little (maybe even less) about the clinical problems experienced by the clients, let alone how to change them. The director reassured me by noting that the staff included the full range of mental health professionals, but added that none of them was focusing on actually changing functioning of the clients in concrete ways. He invited me to take the job and sit in my office for as many weeks or months as it took to learn what I needed and then to come out and actually try to change the clients' behaviors. I did what graduate students do—I read many articles from key leaders throughout the country, and began to study the budding literature on interventions, especially those based on applications of operant conditioning. The most familiar of these interventions provide reinforcing consequences after specific behaviors to increase the likelihood of these behaviors in the future. However, there is much more to operant conditioning including what is done before the behavior (*antecedents*), how the *behavior* is gradually developed to achieve the goals, and *consequences* used along the way to achieve them. Within each category there are many different techniques, but for them to be effective, they have to be provided in a very systematic way. For example, rewarding a specific behavior almost every time the behavior occurs—at least in the beginning of the program, reinforcing consistency in performance, and explicitly specifying what behavior led to the consequence, is much more effective than rewarding a behavior once in a while.

After a few months, I began some modest programs with individual clients. The programs were carried out by the staff in the setting and we collected data to see if behaviors of the clients were changing. I began with the use of token reinforcement programs in which individuals earn tokens (which can be points, stars, chips, and checkmarks) for specific behaviors that are to be developed. We used plastic (colored but otherwise blank) credit cards as the tokens that individuals could use to exchange for back-up reinforcers such as free time, use of various games, purchase of magazines, and so on. Depending on the individual and the goals of the program, behaviors that earned the tokens included socializing with others (for someone who was isolated and withdrawn), speaking respectfully (for someone who was regularly sarcastic and swore when speaking to staff), and handling change by being calm (for someone who had an explosive tantrum in response to even the slightest change in her activities or routines).

We paired the tokens with praise because both together are likely to be more effective than either one used individually. The tokens and praise need to be timed carefully to be effective. In some cases, tokens and praise can be provided when the desired behavior occurs; at other times they can be provided as the behavior moves closer and closer to the desired behavior. This process is a lot like learning a musical instrument where the learner practices small segments of behaviors (playing notes, scales, chords), then simple pieces, and then more complex musical pieces. In other cases, the individual practices the desired behaviors in role-play or simulated situations to increase the likelihood that the behaviors will occur in real life. The key to this approach is not in the tokens or the praise. Rather, we want the individual to practice and engage in the behavior repeatedly and under different circumstances to lock in the behavior. Tokens and praise help foster that repeated practice.

We collected data to see how, whether, and the extent to which changes occur in this approach. This means that we could identify when the intervention is not working or not working very well and adjust it as needed. We focused on interpersonal behaviors because these behaviors usually precluded individuals from functioning in community settings. Often we were able to change behavior in ways that had a clear impact on individual functioning.

A superintendent of schools invited me to evaluate several elementary school classrooms and implement similar interventions on a larger scale. Disruptive behavior was a problem in these classrooms. For example, children walked on desks during lessons, destroyed other students' work, threw things at the teacher, and shouted out whenever they wanted. Coincidentally, I was looking for a dissertation topic and was able to use these classrooms to test various hypotheses about interventions and how they could be implemented to change behavior. I began by training teachers to carry out token economies, training observers to record disruptive classroom behavior reliably, and monitoring the classrooms daily to ensure the interventions were implemented correctly. So at this time, still in graduate school, I had moved down a path of intervention research.

A decade later, I faced another situation that provided an even greater challenge in changing behavior. I moved from an academic psychology department to a psychiatry department at a medical school. I was placed in charge of an inpatient service (Children's Psychiatric Intensive Care Service) for children 5–12 years of age. The children were referred for severe psychiatric problems such as attempted suicide, major depression, and violent behavior, all of which required hospitalization and intensive care. No inpatient program, group or individual therapy, or medication had been shown to be effective with these children. We tried virtually all reasonable options including novel medications (because standard medications for various psychiatric problems did not work); group sessions that focused on social skills; developing a close relationship in individual therapy sessions with a therapist;

a structured milieu with routines, unlike many of the environments from which these children had come; and an attentive and caring staff. Occasionally we even allowed parents to try options they viewed as reasonable, but for which there was no scientific evidence, such as exorcism. There was no evidence that exorcism would do anything at all, but humility was required. There was not much in the way of evidence for what we were doing either. Trying to help and great intentions can only go so far.

The goals of our interventions were to improve child functioning at home, at school, and in the community. Setting goals was the easy part. But how could we alter deeply ingrained antisocial behavior patterns and replace them with prosocial behavior? I remembered well the lesson from my undergraduate days, namely, that the difference between psychologists and magicians is that psychologists pull habits out of rats! Maybe I could do that—psychology knows a great deal about building habits!

Aggressive and Antisocial Behavior

Consider for a moment the problem of antisocial behavior and its challenges. Antisocial behavior or actions that violate social norms include hitting others, breaking other people's possessions, vandalism, theft, cruelty to animals and people, lying, setting fires, and running away from home. Some of these behaviors, such as lying and vandalism occur, at least occasionally, as part of development among children who do not have any clinical problems. For some children, however, these behaviors are frequent, intense, enduring, and impair daily functioning. These children become difficult and sometimes impossible to manage at home or at school.

The extremes of antisocial behavior constitute a recognized psychiatric disorder referred to as Conduct Disorder (CD) (American Psychiatric Association, 2013). Many of the behaviors noted earlier and those exhibited by the children I studied make up the criteria for CD. Individuals receive a diagnosis of CD if these behaviors continue for months at a time (up to 12 months). Indeed, the children we saw usually had long histories of these behaviors.

CD is associated with a variety of other outcomes such as academic failure, expulsion from school, and poor peer relations. Adults with a history of CD are at great risk for psychiatric disorders, substance abuse, criminal behavior, financial problems, chronic job loss, and violence (for example, spouse/partner or child abuse). Moreover, such individuals are more likely to have a compromised immune system, a condition that may have emerged early in life from prolonged stress, conflict, or exposure to violence. A compromised immune system places them at risk for early death and makes them more susceptible to cancer, heart disease, and chronic respiratory diseases.

As a psychiatric disorder, CD is one of the most expensive. During childhood and adolescence, monetary costs mount due to placement in special education classes or schools, hospitalizations, emergency room visits, encounters with the law, visits to the home by family service agencies, and foster placement. If left untreated or ineffectively treated, the problems and costs associated with CD can be enduring. In addition, many children exhibit behaviors associated with CD. In the United States, for example, the lifetime prevalence of CD is approximately 9.5 percent. This amounts to millions of children who will suffer from the dysfunction at some point and need treatment.

What are the causes of CD? Surely if we knew, we could move toward effective treatment and prevention. The disorder encompasses many different symptoms and symptom combinations. In fact, an individual can meet the psychiatric diagnostic criteria of CD with over 32,000 possible combinations of symptoms. Consequently, few researchers believe CD is a single disorder. Research tries to break down the large category into subtypes and investigate salient symptoms such as aggression and its causes. For example, it appears now that children who have CD beginning early in life are more aggressive and have a greater likelihood of psychiatric impairment in adulthood than individuals who develop CD in adolescence. Child versus adolescent onset of CD may have important implications for understanding the disorder and what treatments will be effective. In relation to the CD and its subtypes, understanding how the environment, genes, and the brain interact is crucial in understanding clinical dysfunction including CD.

What Can Be Done in the Way of Treatment?

My research team and other researchers have taken on the challenge of developing effective interventions. The Children's Psychiatric Intensive Care Service admitted an endless stream of severely disturbed children, who were often brought to our locked ward strapped to a gurney by an ambulance team or by the police. Once admitted, the children and their parents completed many psychological measures to describe systematically the scope and nature of the child's symptoms and functioning at home, at school, and in the community. Parents also completed several measures to evaluate their own functioning, such as their history of psychiatric disorder and treatment, home life, conflict and exposure to violence, and child-rearing practices. This information enabled us to understand functioning of the child (for example, problems at school, more than one psychiatric disorder), potential influences that might need to be addressed (for example, marital conflict, child abuse), and also helped us to identify whether some children and families are more responsive to treatment.

Children lived in the hospital for 4–8 weeks and participated in a milieu that included several activities such as group therapy and school classes. We developed two treatments for children with severe antisocial and aggressive behavior: parent management training and cognitive problem-solving skills training for children. We devoted the next decade to investigating these treatments and refining them based on our clinical experience and research findings.

Parent management training (PMT) teaches parents very concretely on ways of interacting with their children in the home. The procedures draw on several principles and techniques derived from human and nonhuman animal research in operant conditioning. The techniques focus on how to eliminate behaviors through reinforcement and very mild punishment; how to develop desired behaviors through positive reinforcement and how to maintain the behaviors once they are developed. Parents met individually with a therapist and without the child. In the sessions, parents learn how to administer antecedents, such as instructions, prompts, or cues on how to perform the behavior; to focus the child on practicing the behavior by gradually reinforcing approximations of the behavior; and about consequences to increase prosocial behaviors by delivering praise and tokens. Training parents in how to understand and administer specific techniques to develop and eliminate behavior is the core part of treatment. Individual sessions use role playing of parent–child interactions, repeated practice, modeling of the desired parent behaviors by the therapist, feedback to the parent, and praise to shape parent behavior. The therapists focus on the parents' behaviors; as in PMT, the parents are the ones who actually change the child's behaviors by implementing the techniques they have. Occasionally, the child joins the session so the therapist can observe the parent–child interaction and refine the parents' skills.

Therapists adjust the focus of treatment as children improve a behavior that was problematic (for example, aggression at school) or more intensively focus on areas that have not responded to change or have yet to be addressed (for example, stealing). The critical feature of treatment is reinforced practice; that is, the therapist's goal is for the parent to practice the desired behavior and to this end, the therapist works with parents, offering praise and guidance to improve parenting behavior, very much the way a coach works with an athlete. In effect, the parent is trained to do this with their children, but with careful coaching by a therapist.

PMT had been used with children who engage in antisocial behavior in pioneering work by Gerald Patterson and his colleagues (Patterson, Reid, & Dishion, 1992). Among the pioneering contributions were studies in the home showing that parent and child interaction can develop and maintain aggressive child behavior. We expanded on the intervention procedures to apply them to a severely impaired population. That expansion included drawing on a broad range of behavior-change techniques including my own research on methods of changing behavior. In my prior work, I had evaluated interventions with children and adults in rehabilitation, special education, and institutional settings for individuals with intellectual disabilities.

We found that PMT worked well as a treatment for children who had a parent or guardian (for example, grandparent serving in the parental role). Yet, many children we saw did not have a parent or guardian with whom we could work. The parent or guardian was seriously debilitated—he or she was on drugs or had a psychiatric disorder; was in and out of prison; or engaged in illicit activities, such as selling drugs or prostitution. For these children, we focused on cognitive problem-solving skills training (PSST) as an individual treatment that did not require parent participation.

Cognitive problem-solving skills training (PSST) is a treatment in which a therapist meets individually with the child. The child engages in a sequence of steps or self-statements designed to help the child look carefully at the demands of the situation, consider what might be alternative positive (rather than aggressive) ways of responding, consider the consequences of different actions, select one of those responses, and actually act out the solution in a role-play situation in the treatment session. We developed these steps to guide behavior based on research indicating that children with aggressive and antisocial behavior have deficits in how they identify social cues, in how they consider their options in responding, and then of course in how they respond. PSST focuses on these thought processes, but also on practicing positive behaviors in the treatment sessions and in everyday situations outside of treatment.

The steps are self-statements, or what children learn at the beginning of treatment to break down social situations and to respond prosocially. The steps include questions such as: What am I supposed to do? What could I do (identifying solutions) and what would happen (consequences)? I need to make a choice (selecting one of the solutions), and I need to find out how I did (self-evaluation). The child states the sequence of statements out loud while role playing the situation with the therapist. In the sessions, the child and therapist practice many different social situation scenarios, including being bullied, being threatened, and being asked to steal something by a friend. The therapist models how to apply the self-statements to situations the child may encounter and how to complete the sequence of steps. Over time, the child is instructed to eliminate the self-statements gradually (first to a whisper, then saying them to oneself silently), and he or she continues to practice in more role-play situations. PSST sessions include intensive practice in using the steps and in responding to increasingly more complex social situations. Over the course of treatment, children have "homework" assignments (called supersolvers) to solve problems using the steps at home, at school, and at any other place where the child exhibits behavior problems. Points are provided for homework practice and they can be exchanged for small prizes.

To evaluate the effectiveness of treatment, we began a series of randomized controlled trials—studies in which children are randomly assigned to receive one of the treatments or one of the control conditions. In our studies, control conditions included usual hospital care only or usual hospital care and individual sessions of play therapy with a therapist. In this way, we could evaluate whether the treatments actually improved behavior or if the behavior would have improved anyway over time or with more routine care. Table 1 summarizes the results from some of our studies.

Essentially, the two treatments made a difference not only by reducing symptoms, but also by improving positive prosocial behaviors in interactions with parents, siblings, teachers, and peers. Children in the various control groups did not show these changes. But are the changes enough to make a real difference? That is hard to tell because there is no agreed-on measure or definition of "real difference." To approximate that, we looked at whether the symptoms and social behaviors of children in our treatment program fell within the range of these behaviors among children of the same age and sex functioning well in everyday life. Many children who received the treatment fell within this normative range, but certainly not all. Are the effects of treatment enduring and will they make the adult lives of these children better? We do not know. What we do know from our work is that the benefits of treatment continue for at least two years, but we have not made longer-term evaluations.

The overview of our treatments and studies belies several challenges in developing and providing treatment. Families of children with antisocial

TABLE 1

The Effects of Parent Management Training and Cognitive Problem-Solving Skills Training

- Reduction in aggressive and antisocial behavior and increase in prosocial behavior among children referred for inpatient or outpatient treatment;

- Gains that surpass the effects of other treatment conditions (for example, routine hospital care by itself, play, and relationship therapy);

- Changes in behavior that are evident at home, at school, and in the community immediately after treatment and up to 2 years later;

- Clinically significant changes (that is, many individuals fall within normative levels of functioning for same sex and age peers by the end of treatment);

- Effective with children who have multiple disorders (in addition to CD) and with families with severe stressors, parent clinical dysfunction, and socioeconomic disadvantage; and

- Additional positive changes not specifically targeted that include improvement in peer relations at school, parental decreases in depression, decreases in stress at home, and improvements in family member relations.

To read more about these findings, see Kazdin (2010).

behavior often suffer enormous stressors (for example, financial, marital), have little or no social system support (for example, single parents with no relatives or friends to help), and may experience psychiatric dysfunction themselves. The lack of financial resources often means they are suffering both physical and mental health problems that are not treated. These obstacles often result in families canceling appointments or not showing up for treatment, and dropping out of treatment. These challenges have prompted us to conduct related lines of research to:

- identify child, parent, and family factors that influence who carries out the treatment procedures well and who profits from treatment;

- understand who drops out of treatment and why;

- treat (reduce) parental stress as a means to improve treatment outcomes of the children; and

- understand the relationships between parent and therapist and child and therapist during the course of treatment and how these relationships influence participation in treatment and therapeutic change (see Kazdin, 2010 for a review).

Conclusion

My work has developed PMT and PSST for children with severe aggressive and antisocial behavior. In the past 30 years, researchers have developed many psychosocial treatments for a wide range of psychiatric disorders among children, adolescents, and adults. A recent count noted over 320 psychosocial treatments that have a strong evidence base (U.S. Department of Health and Human Services, 2014). The treatments focus on many different disorders and their subtypes including anxiety, depression, bipolar disorder, eating disorders, autism spectrum disorders, and attention-deficit/hyperactivity disorder, among others.

A current challenge is to disseminate treatments from clinical research settings where the treatments are developed and carefully evaluated to clinical practice where they are applied. At the Yale Parenting Center where we study treatment, we also provide training opportunities for mental health professionals through webinars, in-service training, direct case supervision, and online training with the goal of sharing what we have learned about treatment well beyond the confines of our setting. To help professionals, we have developed detailed guidelines for treatment sessions (Kazdin, 2009). To help parents, we offer materials they can use on their own as a first line of intervention to overcome the challenges of raising a child with conduct problems or in handling the everyday challenges of parenting (Kazdin & Rotella, 2008, 2013). I work with television, radio, and online and print news services and prepare magazine articles to present to parents options to help with both the common challenges of child rearing (for example, getting children to eat vegetables, complete their homework, and go to bed on time, or getting teenagers to stop eye-rolling, swearing at their parents, or treating them as if they had the plague), as well as more severe clinical problems that impair the children's everyday lives.

There is an enormous unmet need to provide psychological services to children and their families. This need is related to CD but applies more generally to children, adolescents, and adults with psychological problems. For example, in the United States, approximately 70 percent of individuals in need of psychological services receive no treatment at all. Worldwide too, most individuals who need care for their emotional, cognitive, or behavioral problems receive nothing. Another challenge is to deliver treatment in novel ways, such as through the use of technology and social media (for example, texting, apps) and training nonprofessionals to deliver treatment (Kazdin & Rabbitt, 2013). Our work for families has evolved to providing our interventions online—live, face-to-face, to families anywhere where there is access to the Internet. Online delivery is a way to bring treatment into peoples' homes, and in many circumstances it is more convenient than bringing people to clinics. Another means to extend treatment is to train nonprofessionals (laypeople including other parents and adults without a background in mental health) to deliver the treatments. Evidence related to treatments of psychological problems other than CD indicates that nonprofessionals are often as effective as mental health professionals in providing psychological services. Our emphasis is now shifting from developing techniques for treatments to developing novel ways of delivering those treatments.

Acknowledgment The research highlighted here was supported in part by grants (R01s, MERIT, and Research Development and Career Awards from the National Institute of Mental Health, The Lowenstein Foundation, The Rivendell Foundation of America, and The William T. Grant Foundation). I am extremely grateful for that support.

☐ Thinking Critically

1. The treatments that Kazdin describes develop prosocial behavior in children by training behaviors gradually, having the children repeatedly practice approximations of the behaviors and until they perform the desired behaviors, modeling the behaviors by the therapist, providing feedback and praise to refine and lock in performance, and applying the skills to new situations and contexts. How do Alan Kazdin's treatments to encourage prosocial behavior in children with CD resemble teaching individuals to learn to play a musical instrument or learn to dance?

2. Therapy does not solely change a specific, narrow human behavior—its effects often lead to many changes that affect many areas of the client's life. Apart from changes in antisocial and aggressive behaviors, how else did Kazdin's treatments affect children, parents, and families?

☐ Suggested Further Readings

Kazdin, A. E. (2010). Problem-solving skills training and parent management training for oppositional defiant disorder and conduct disorder. In J. R. Weisz & A. E. Kazdin (Eds.), *Evidence-based psychotherapies for children and adolescents* (2nd ed., pp. 211–226). New York: Guilford Press.

Kazdin, A. E. (2011). Evidence-based treatment research: Advances, limitations, and next steps. *American Psychologist, 66,* 685–698.

☐ References

American Psychiatric Association. (2013). *Diagnostic and statistical manual of mental disorders* (5th ed.). Arlington, VA: American Psychiatric Publishing.

Kazdin, A. E. (2009). *Parent management training: Treatment for oppositional, aggressive, and antisocial behavior in children and adolescents.* New York: Oxford University Press.

Kazdin, A. E. (2010). Problem-solving skills training and parent management training for oppositional defiant disorder and conduct disorder. In J. R. Weisz & A. E. Kazdin (Eds.), *Evidence-based psychotherapies for children and adolescents* (2nd ed., pp. 211–226). New York: Guilford Press.

Kazdin, A. E., & Rabbitt, S. (2013). Novel models for delivering mental health services and reducing the burdens of mental illness. *Clinical Psychological Science, 1,* 170–191.

Kazdin, A. E., & Rotella, C. (2008). *The Kazdin Method for parenting the defiant child: With no pills, no therapy, no contest of wills.* Boston: Houghton Mifflin.

Kazdin, A. E., & Rotella, C. (2013). *The everyday parenting toolkit: The Kazdin Method for easy, step-by-step lasting change for you and your child.* Boston: Houghton Mifflin Harcourt.

Patterson, G. R., Reid, J. B., & Dishion, T. J. (1992). *Antisocial boys.* Eugene, OR: Castalia.

United States Department of Health and Human Services. (2014, March). *Substance Abuse and Mental Health Services Administration's National Registry of Evidence-Based Programs and Practices.* http://www.nrepp.samhas.gov

Stress and Health

Positive Psychology: Cultivating Resilience and Health through Everyday Positive Emotions

Barbara L. Fredrickson

Positive Illusions: How Ordinary People Become Extraordinary

Shelley E. Taylor

Positive Psychology: Cultivating Resilience and Health through Everyday Positive Emotions

BARBARA L. FREDRICKSON University of North Carolina at Chapel Hill

☐ **Please describe your current position and research interests.**

I am Kenan Distinguished Professor in the Department of Psychology at the University of North Carolina at Chapel Hill. My research centers on positive emotions and well-being, including the biological, cognitive, psychological, and social underpinnings of each.

☐ **How did you become interested in this area of research?**

I've long been drawn in by uncharted scientific terrain. I was a post-doctoral trainee when the science of emotions took hold in the early 1990s, and noticed immediately that virtually all of the research targeted negative emotions, whereas almost none of it targeted positive emotions, such as joy, gratitude, interest, serenity, and the like. The sheer intellectual challenge of exploring the unknown captivated me.

☐ **What has been the real-world impact of this work?**

I've been immensely gratified to learn that the results of my research in positive psychology have been deployed to improve lives and communities, both nationally and internationally. The U.S. Army now trains all soldiers—and their family members—in how to use positive emotions judiciously, even in tough circumstances, to build resilience. In Australia, programs for the unemployed that teach about the merits of day-to-day positive emotions have had remarkable success in helping people move into employment. These are just two of the many interventions that have applied the science of positive emotions to educational, business, health care, military, and community settings to create results that matter.

Why Care about Positive Emotions?

Can people make themselves more resilient? Can they become healthier simply by changing their daily diets of emotions? Are emotional habits malleable? These are reasonable questions to ask. Emotional upsets at best, inconvenience, and at worst, disrupt and derail our daily lives. Unforeseen obstacles, incivilities, rebuffs, insults, and arguments abound. These and other upsets often ignite the pains of anger, anxiety, or sadness with their attendant downward spirals and destructive behaviors.

The link between negative events and negative emotions may seem automatic and altogether inescapable, but people actually have enormous choice in how they respond to the slings and arrows of daily life. What does it take to experience these and other upsets *without* inner turmoil or outer destructiveness? How can people become resilient and healthy despite the inevitable challenges life presents? Is it possible?

It is indeed possible. Resilience requires the ability to regulate your own attention and cognition in the service of recognizing and appreciating emotional states—both pleasant and unpleasant. Stepping back and attending to your negative emotions in a mindful and accepting way provides a strong foundation for cultivating more open and optimistic inner states—states that till the soil for positive emotions to take root, ranging from serenity and inspiration, to joy, gratitude, and more. The experience of positive emotions, research shows, is key to being able to bounce back in tough situations. This essay, anchored in empirical evidence, outlines why the ability to self-generate positive emotions is so important, as well as how this ability can be learned.

The Beneficial Correlates of Positive Emotions

People who frequently experience positive emotions seem successful, well-adjusted, and full of verve. Indeed, scientific evidence documents that such people are more resilient to life's adversities, more socially connected, and more successful in their personal and work lives. They are also healthier; they have lower rates of hypertension and cardiovascular disease. They even contract viruses, like the common cold, less often. Plus, they even live up to 10 years longer than those who experience positive emotions less often (Fredrickson, 2013).

If you believe the folk wisdom that positivity is an inborn, biologically programmed trait, these research findings can be disheartening (if you are not the most positive person). Don't lose hope too quickly, though. When this bit of folk wisdom is subjected to scientific scrutiny, the evidence suggests that only about 50% of individual differences in trait affect are genetically determined, with the remaining 50% reflecting a combination of life circumstances and daily habits (Lyubomirsky, Sheldon, & Schkade, 2005), which can change, especially with age. Indeed, age-related changes in emotions are striking; younger adults favor negative information and older adults more often dwell on the positive. For example, in studies that show people a variety of pictures that range from negative and neutral to positive, older adults show a clear preference for positive images, both in how they direct their attention and in what they remember, findings that are backed up by brain imaging (Carstensen & Mikels, 2005). To the extent that positivity forecasts success, health, and longevity, there may be wisdom in this age-related preference for the positive. Positive emotions seem to hold survival advantage.

A theory I formulated two decades ago explains why this may be so. The *broaden-and-build* theory of positive emotions states that pleasant emotional states evolved because they aided the survival of our human ancestors. They did so by creating a form of consciousness marked by a broad scope of awareness that momentarily includes a wider array of thought and action tendencies than is typical. This broadened mindset aided the discovery of new knowledge, new alliances, and new skills, and thereby helped our human ancestors build their reserves of personal resources that might later make the difference between surviving or succumbing to various threats to life and limb. Resources built through positive emotions also increased the odds that our ancestors would experience subsequent positive emotions, with their additional benefits, thus creating an upward spiral toward improved odds for survival, health, and flourishing. The broaden-and-build theory and its two tenets—that positive emotions (1) broaden awareness and (2) build resources—identified positive emotions as key drivers of personal growth, resilience, and health, not simply as the products of these valued outcomes. Through incremental broaden-and-build processes, moments of positive emotions grow into stable affective dispositions that foster people's physical health and render their lives more meaningful and satisfying. In short, positive emotions help us reach our full potential.

Positive Emotions As Means, Not Ends

The first tenet of the broaden-and-build theory is that positive emotions expand people's awareness, temporarily allowing them to take in more of the contextual information around them than they would during neutral or negative emotional states. My lab and other researchers have demonstrated the ways positive emotions broaden awareness in tightly controlled experiments. In one experiment, we showed participants one of five emotionally evocative film clips to induce one of two positive emotions (joy or contentment), one of two negative emotions (fear or anger), or no emotion (the control condition). While in these states, participants listed all the things they would like to do right then. Compared with those experiencing no emotion, those experiencing fear or anger listed fewer things they would like to do right then. By contrast, and again compared with those experiencing no emotion, those experiencing joy or contentment named more things they would like to do right then, consistent with a broadened action repertoire (Fredrickson & Branigan, 2005). Other researchers have used eye-tracking technology and brain imaging and discovered that positive emotional states literally expand people's peripheral vision, allowing them to see more of what surrounds them (for a review, see Fredrickson, 2013). Positive emotions, then, quite literally widen people's outlook on the world.

The expanded awareness that comes with positive emotions is theorized to be as subtle and as short-lived as the emotion itself. Yet, however, short-lived research shows that expanded awareness accounts for positivity-related increases in creativity (Rowe, Hirsh, & Anderson 2007), and may well account for increases in autobiographical memory and integrative decision making; improvements in test and work performance, teamwork, and negotiation outcomes; and increases in coping and resilience, interpersonal trust, and social connection (for a review, see Fredrickson, 2013). In short, open and flexible awareness is a core cognitive attribute of positive emotional states that accounts for a wide range of valued life qualities.

Positive Emotions Transform Lives

The second tenet of the broaden-and-build theory is that, over time, the momentary states of expanded awareness sparked by positive emotions aggregate to build personal and social resources that ultimately reshape people's lives for the better. In other words, people who acquire skills to self-generate positive emotions are able to increase their day-to-day experiences of positive emotions that promote resources and resilience to overcome adversity and generate health and well-being. In a recent longitudinal experiment, we tested the effects of learning an ancient mind-training practice called *loving-kindness meditation* as a means to self-generate positive emotions more frequently. Loving-kindness meditation involves extending heartfelt wishes for another's well-being. The results of this study show that, relative to a control group, loving-kindness meditation reliably elevated participants' positive emotions. Most importantly, however, we observed that the increase in positive emotions among those who practiced loving-kindness meditation strengthened these people's personal resources, including their mindfulness, resilience, relationships, and self-reported health. In turn, these strengthened resources accounted for decreases in depressive symptoms and improvements in life satisfaction (Fredrickson, Cohn, Coffey, Pek, & Finkel, 2008). The accumulating evidence on the long-term psychological and health benefits of cultivating positive emotional states provides a compelling rationale for learning to self-generate more frequent positive emotions in daily life.

Upward Spirals Counter Downward Spirals

All emotions—positive or negative—affect people's attention, thinking, motivation, and behavior. As such, both pleasant and unpleasant emotional states can trigger self-perpetuating dynamics—or spirals—that can either lift people up or drag them down. To illustrate, the negative emotions of anger, anxiety, or sadness narrow people's attention and reinforce emotion-consistent thinking, such as blame, threat, or loss, that feed further bouts of anger, anxiety, or sadness with attendant social friction or isolation. These self-perpetuating cycles produce the downward spirals all too familiar to anyone who has experienced life's challenges.

The broaden-and-build theory holds that positive emotions create upward spiral dynamics that counteract negative spirals. The expanded awareness that accompanies positive emotions enables people to take a step back from their stressful circumstances and consider them from a broader perspective and in a more positive light. This broader perspective often triggers more positive emotions. For example, the positive emotion of gratitude broadens people's awareness to enable them to see aspects of their experience as gifts to be treasured, and this appreciative lens helps them spot even more goodness in their circumstances. As this upward spiral unfolds, it creates resilience, well-being, health, and greater social connection. A number of prospective studies document this upward spiral dynamic and emerging evidence suggests that upward spirals might drive lasting brain changes that can be productively applied within psycho-therapy to change people's emotional habits and increase their well-being (Garland et al., 2010).

Shared Positive Emotions Carry Particular Health Benefits

Think about a time when you and another person shared an experience of a positive emotion, such as joking around with a friend, hugging a relative with compassion, or playing with and smiling at a baby. These moments of joint positive emotion appear to be especially valuable. Our most recent tests of the effects of learning to self-generate positive emotions through loving-kindness meditation included daily measures of social connection together with objective measures of cardiovascular functioning (Kok et al., 2013). The results suggest that the positive emotions that you feel *in connection with another person* may carry particular benefits for your physical health. I've called moments like these *positivity resonance*, because during these moments a re-markable dance unfolds between you and the other person, wherein your smiles, gestures, and postures mirror each other. So too do your biochemi-cal cascades and neural firings. For instance, when a parent shares smiles and laughs with his or her infant, each shows a similar spike in oxytocin, a neuro-peptide central to trust and bonding (Feldman, Gordon, & Zagoory-Sharon, 2010). The more two people become synchronized, the more a single, positive emotion rolls like a wave through two brains and bodies at once, creating a momentary resonance of good feeling and good will.

Our research showed that a steady diet of positivity resonance has measur-able health benefits (Kok et al., 2013). The vagus nerve, which emerges from your brainstem to tether your brain to your heart, is at the center of positiv-ity resonance. One of its jobs is to return your racing heart to normal after a fright. When your vagus nerve is functioning especially well, it also slows your heart a tiny amount each time you exhale, creating a healthy rhythm to your heart rate.

Studies have shown that this healthy heart rhythm reflects your overall health, including your body's ability to regulate glucose and inflammation. It also reflects your biological capacity for connection, including your ability to track another's voice, make eye contact, and mimic any facial expressions.

Scientists used to think that vagus nerve functioning was stable, like your height once you reach adulthood. Yet my team and I have discovered that when people learn loving-kindness meditation and create more moments of positive connection in daily life, their vagus nerve functioning improves: Their habitual heart rhythms become healthier (Kok et al., 2013).

Our work suggests that beat-by-beat, your heart records your recent his-tory of positivity resonance. Intriguingly, these moments of positive con-nection seem to function like positive health behaviors, such as eating your vegetables and exercising regularly. But this isn't just about *your* health; the other person's heart gets a mini "tune-up" at the same time!

In short, we are wired to connect, and the vagus nerve is a key part of that wiring. This wiring is adaptive—how we connect and our experiences of positivity resonance can change the strength of this wiring. The more we connect with others over positive emotions, the more we lower our odds of having a heart attack and increase our odds of a long, happy, and healthy life.

Practical Implications for Everyday Life

Even before you began to read this essay, you knew that positive emotions feel good. Yet now you also know that good feelings do far more for you than simply provide pleasant distractions. Your day-to-day experiences of joy, gratitude, inspiration, and serenity—especially when co-experienced with others—broaden your outlook and put you on trajectories of growth that build your resilience and health. Put differently, day-to-day positive emotions give you a leg up on survival.

Be warned, though: A little knowledge of positive psychology can be a dangerous thing. Research shows that when people excessively value happiness, or simply try to force their way into feeling good, they ironically make themselves feel worse (Mauss, Tamir, Anderson, & Savino, 2011). The pursuit of happiness is a delicate art. My team's research suggests that more effective ways to cultivate positive emotions involve adopting habits and making regular plans to engage in activities that reliably elicit positive emotions (Catalino, Coffey, Algoe, & Fredrickson, in press).

One such habitual activity is meditation. My team has studied the ancient meditation practice called *metta* (in Pali) or *maître* (in Sanskrit). Often translated as loving-kindness meditation, this practice involves learning authentic ways to self-generate positive emotions in daily life by extending heartfelt wishes to others, and to ourselves. The traditional phrases that are repeated silently as the touchstone of this practice are *"May you feel safe. May you feel happy. May you feel healthy. May you live with ease."* Yet these sentiments can be rephrased; the words themselves don't matter as much as the feelings of goodwill they generate. In our research, we've seen that people who devote about an hour each week to the practice of loving-kindness meditation measurably boost their happiness, resilience, and health. Readers interested in learning more about this practice can find additional information and access free, guided meditations at www .PositivityResonance.com.

Of course, paths other than meditation practice can also help you increase your daily diet of positive emotions and reap attendant benefits. You might choose to spend time volunteering to help others, or pursuing meaningful projects or healthy passions, either on your own or with others. In theory, any activity that reliably triggers caring, positive emotions can produce similar benefits. What's most important is to recognize that positive emotions are the tiny engines of a powerful positive psychology. They can transform your life—and others' lives—for the better, helping all of us reach our higher ground.

☐ Thinking Critically

1. Positive emotions predict longevity. What types of evidence suggest that positive emotions play a causal role in extending life?

2. When you smile in a genuine and friendly way, what effects does it have on others? What effects does it have on you?

☐ Suggested Further Reading

Fredrickson, B. L. (2009). *Positivity.* New York: Three Rivers Press.

Fredrickson, B. L. (2013). *Love 2.0.* New York: Plume.

Fredrickson, B. L. (2013). Positive emotions broaden and build. *Advances in Experimental Psychology, 47,* 1–53.

☐ References

Carstensen, L. L., & Mikels, J. A. (2005). At the intersection of emotion and cognition: Aging and the positivity bias. *Current Directions in Psychological Science, 14,* 117–121.

Catalino, L. I., Coffey, K. A., Algoe, S. B., & Fredrickson, B. L. (in press). Prioritizing positivity: An effective approach to pursuing happiness? *Emotion.*

Feldman, R., Gordon, I., & Zagoory-Sharon, O. (2010). The cross-generational transmission of oxytocin in humans. *Hormones & Behavior, 58,* 669–676.

Fredrickson, B. L. (2013). Positive emotions broaden and build. *Advances in Experimental Psychology, 47,* 1–53.

Fredrickson, B. L., & Branigan, C. (2005). Positive emotions broaden the scope of attention and thought-action repertoires. *Cognition and Emotion, 19,* 313–332.

Fredrickson, B. L., Cohn, M. A., Coffey, K. A., Pek, J., & Finkel, S. M. (2008). Open hearts build lives: Positive emotions, induced through loving-kindness meditation, build consequential personal resources. *Journal of Personality and Social Psychology, 95,* 1045–1062.

Garland, E. L., Fredrickson, B. L., Kring, A. M., Johnson, D. P., Meyer, P. S., & Penn, D. L. (2010). Upward spirals of positive emotions counter downward spirals of negativity: Insights from the broaden-and-build theory and affective neuroscience on the treatment of emotion dysfunctions and deficits psychopathology. *Clinical Psychology Review, 30,* 849–864.

Kok, B. E., Coffey, K. A., Cohn, M. A., Catalino, L. I., Vacharkulksemsek, T., Algoe, S. B., Brantley, M., & Fredrickson, B. L. (2013). How positive emotions build physical health: Perceived positive social connections account for the upward spiral between positive emotions and vagal tone. *Psychological Science, 24,* 1123–1132.

Lyubomirsky, S., Sheldon, K. M., & Schkade, D. (2005). Pursuing happiness: The architecture of sustainable change. *Review of General Psychology, 9,* 111–131.

Mauss, I. B., Tamir, M., Anderson, C. L., & Savino, N. S. (2011). Can seeking happiness make people unhappy? Paradoxical effects of valuing happiness. *Emotion, 11,* 807–815.

Rowe, G., Hirsh, J. B., & Anderson, A. K. (2007). Positive affect increases the breadth of attentional selection. *Proceedings of the National Academy of Sciences of the USA, 104,* 383–388.

Positive Illusions: How Ordinary People Become Extraordinary

SHELLEY E. TAYLOR University of California, Los Angeles

☐ **Please describe your current position and research interests.**

I am Distinguished Research Professor of Psychology at UCLA. My research concerns antecedents of responses to stress, such as early environment and psychosocial resources, and their impact on psychological and biological stress responses.

☐ **How did you become interested in studying positive illusions and the factors that regulate them?**

My interest in positive illusions was sparked by seeing how cancer patients often hold positive, though erroneous, beliefs about their illnesses that nonetheless help them cope successfully.

☐ **What has been the real-world impact of this work?**

Research on positive illusions tells researchers that the errors and biases seen commonly in human thought often serve vital functions, and so one must look beyond their risks to understand why they occur. For clinicians, the message underscores the realization that false beliefs may, nonetheless, be adaptive and that human beings have deep capacities for self-restoration and renewal.

Our investigations of stress and health began in the 1970s when I was invited to participate in a cancer conference to address social psychology's contribution to understanding psychological responses to breast cancer. My first reaction was that social psychologists had little to say, but I soon realized that there were many bases for hypotheses, especially in the social cognition literature. Accordingly, in 1980, Rosemary Lichtman, Joanne Wood, and I conducted an investigation with breast cancer patients in an attempt to understand what factors helped them cope with the stress of their illness and get back to normal (Taylor, Lichtman, & Wood, 1984). Initially, we were operating with a homeostatic concept in mind. That is, our implicit thinking was that stress temporarily disturbs psychological functioning, which is then restored by coping efforts that help people return to their previous psychological state.

We were quickly disabused of this naive idea. In account after account, we heard not how these women had gotten back to normal but how their lives had changed, often for the better. Many women told us that the experience had forced them to develop or draw on strengths they did not know they had

(Taylor, 1983). Many also told us that the experience had forced them to identify what was truly of value in their lives, and that relationships, especially with children, were chief among those discoveries. Other women expressed the feeling that they had discovered what was meaningful in life, and they expressed regret that anyone would have to go through such a stressful experience to achieve those insights.

But there was a disturbing component to these stories as well. In many cases, the women were exhibiting what we came to call positive illusions, namely, falsely positive beliefs about their abilities to stave off a recurrence of the illness or to combat an advancing metastatic condition. We asked a clinician whether these false beliefs were worrisome and were assured that they were normal and not indicative of an underlying psychological problem. However, it was this aspect of coping with illness—positive illusions—that captured our enduring interest.

These insights were first published in a 1983 paper on cognitive adaptation to illness (Taylor, 1983). I suggested that the ability to cope successfully with cancer depended heavily on restoring a sense of mastery, gaining a sense of meaning, and restoring self-enhancing self-perceptions. All of these beliefs typically suffer during the acute illness experience, and so coping efforts seem to focus heavily around these three themes.

Subsequent to our work with breast cancer patients, Jonathon D. Brown and I investigated whether positive illusions could be identified in ordinary people not going through intensely threatening health experiences, and, if so, whether the illusions are similarly adaptive. And, indeed, we did document the existence of very similar positive beliefs in normal people (Taylor & Brown, 1988). We reported evidence that people hold self-aggrandizing self-perceptions, an illusion of control, and unrealistic optimism about the future. Far from being maladaptive, we argued, these positive illusions are associated with the criteria normally associated with mental health: the ability to be happy or contented; the ability to care for and about others; the capacity for creative and productive work; and the ability to meet setbacks, challenges, and stressors of everyday life with equanimity and adaptive coping efforts. Our theoretical perspective generated many dozens of empirical investigations, and the article proved to be highly influential: More than 3,000 researchers have cited it in their publications to date.

The significance of positive illusions and their beneficial effects stems, in part, from the challenges they pose to traditional models of mental health. In these models, departures from rationality were regarded primarily as errors to be corrected. We showed that certain forms of irrationality have their functions and can be adaptive, leading to better outcomes than more realistic perceptions would afford.

Our initial findings prompted us to undertake several lines of empirical work. We identified the conditions under which positive illusions are most likely to exist and how they exert beneficial effects on motivation and performance (for example, Taylor & Gollwitzer, 1995). We uncovered how social comparison activities under threat are motivated to maximize both their informational value and their ability to restore or maintain positive self-perceptions (Taylor & Lobel, 1989). We also showed, not only how unrealistic optimism is associated with positive outcomes, but how it can be reconciled with the need to monitor reality effectively (Armor & Taylor, 1998).

Critiques of Positive Illusions

Nonetheless, the concept of positive illusions came under considerable fire. Some of the criticisms stemmed from misinterpretations. For example, the idea that more illusion is better is not a part of the positive illusions perspective. We argue that positive illusions typically stay within quite modest bounds largely because the feedback of the world is corrective. Illusions that are too extreme will be corrected into more modest proportions by feedback from the environment.

A particularly surprising paper reported evidence that people who have overly positive views of the self can be considered maladjusted when clinical interviews are the adjustment criteria (Shedler, Mayman, & Manis, 1993). The researchers also suggested that people with "illusory mental health" (that is, who claim psychological health that is contradicted by clinical evidence) have comparatively stronger biological responses to stress, suggesting potential health risks of positive illusions. This evidence contradicted pilot data from our cancer investigation, which suggested that people who held positive illusions about their ability to keep the cancer from coming back, in fact, lived longer, controlling for initial prognosis (although these data had remained unpublished due to a small sample size).

Accordingly, we replicated the Shedler et al. (1993) procedures and doubled the sample size. Contrary to their findings, we showed that self-enhancers were evaluated as well-adjusted and well-liked by clinicians, peer judges, and friends (Taylor, Lerner, Sherman, Sage, & McDowell, 2003a) and that self-enhancing cognitions were associated with healthier biological responses to stress (Taylor, Lerner, Sherman, Sage, & McDowell, 2003b).

The realization that self-enhancement, feelings of mastery, and unrealistic optimism not only have psychological effects on well-being but actually influence biological processes to affect health makes you realize how truly meaningful the act of psychological construal is and how important the psychological and biological effects of beliefs can be (see Taylor & Broffman, 2011, for a review).

Origins of Positive Illusions

In recent years, we have explored the origins of positive illusions—that is, the factors that lead people to see themselves, the world, and the future in a positive, optimistic manner. At least some of the variance in positive beliefs is accounted for by genetic factors, although the specific genes have not yet been identified. This is an area of our current work. The origins of positive beliefs also lie in early family environment (Taylor, 2010). Early nurturant experience helps to shape children's responses to stress, conferring the ability to respond to stress with positive beliefs and low biological reactivity. Correspondingly, a conflict-ridden, neglectful, or harsh family environment in childhood has been linked to a high rate of mental and physical health disorders in adult-hood (Repetti, Taylor, & Seeman, 2002).

To examine these processes, we undertook a series of studies focusing on the interaction between family background and response to stress. We assessed participants' socioeconomic status (a contributor to chronic stress during childhood) and, to determine whether aspects of their early environment put participants at risk for later health problems, we interviewed them and asked them to complete questionnaires about their childhood family experience. We also examined their psychosocial functioning as adults (looking at the quality of their social contacts and their emotional health and distress), and we obtained data on the functioning of their biological stress regulatory systems (for example, blood pressure). Our work to date has shown that our model has predictive power for explaining health outcomes. Specifically, we find that high socioeconomic status and a positive family environment lead to the development of positive resources, such as optimism and social support, which are, in turn, tied to lower autonomic and neuroendocrine stress responses—that is, for example, lower heart rate and slower breathing in stressful situations and lower production of such stress hormones as cortisol, lower risk for metabolic syndrome (which is a risk factor for heart disease and diabetes, among other conditions) (Lehman, Taylor, Kiefe, & Seeman, 2005), and lower levels of C-reactive protein (which is prognostic for heart diseases and depression, among other conditions) (Taylor, Lehman, Kiefe, & Seeman, 2006).

Current Directions

Our current work explores the genetic, early environmental, and neuro-cognitive origins of these resources in conjunction with their beneficial consequences. Specifically, we examine genes related to the serotonin and dopamine neurotransmitter systems; childhood socioeconomic status and early family environment as indicators of childhood environment; and neural mechanisms (anterior cingulate cortex, amygdala, hypothalamus, and prefrontal cortex) that link socioemotional resources to low psychological and biological (cardiovascular, immunological, and neuroendrocrine) stress responses. As such, our current work integrates perspectives from genetics, psychoneuroimmunology, health psychology, and social neuroscience (Taylor, 2011).

We have also shown that variations in the nurturance of early family environments can lead to dramatically different expressions of a common genotype. Specifically, people with the s/s variant (s: short; l: long) of the serotonin transporter gene 5-HTTLPR who were in early or are in current environments that are intensely stressful, experience an elevated risk for depressive symptoms; however, those with the s/s variant of the 5-HTTLPR who experienced early or current nurturant environments actually have a reduced risk for depressive symptoms as compared with those who have s/l or l/l variants of the 5-HTTLPR gene. Thus, the impact of the social environment can completely reverse the effects of a genetic risk factor (Taylor, Way, Welch, et al., 2006).

Implications

We believe that our work helps scientists and clinicians to understand how ordinary people become extraordinary. The most powerful aspect of our findings, at least to me, has been to see how people hold within themselves the abilities to construe circumstances that would seem to be inherently threatening, even traumatic, and not only adjust to them successfully but achieve a degree of heroism. We have used our research program of the past 25 years to try to identify the very best of human attributes and the power that those attributes have for achieving extraordinary human outcomes.

Acknowledgments Preparation of this manuscript was supported by grants from the National Institute of Mental Health (MH056880) and the National Institute of Aging (AG30309).

☐ Thinking Critically

1. What is Shelley Taylor's evidence for the psychological benefits of positive illusions in people dealing with stressful life problems?
2. Explain how positive illusions are adaptive and not mental errors that need to be corrected. How might have positive illusions contributed to our species' survival by being passed on to future generations?

☐ Suggested Further Reading

Taylor, S. E. (2010). Mechanisms linking early life stress to adult health outcomes. *Proceedings of the National Academy of Sciences, 107,* 8507–8512.

Taylor, S. E., & Broffman, J. I. (2011). Psychosocial resources: Functions, origins, and links to mental and physical health. In J. M. Olson & M. P. Zanna (Eds.), *Advances in experimental social psychology* (pp. 1–57). New York: Academic Press.

☐ References

Armor, D. A., & Taylor, S. E. (1998). Situated optimism: Specific outcome expectancies and self-regulation. In M. P. Zanna (Ed.), *Advances in experimental social psychology* (Vol. 30, pp. 309–379). New York: Academic Press.

Lehman, B. J., Taylor, S. E., Kiefe, C. I., & Seeman, T. E. (2005). Relation of childhood socioeconomic status and family environment to adult metabolic functioning in the CARDIA study. *Psychosomatic Medicine, 67,* 846–854.

Repetti, R. L., Taylor, S. E., & Seeman, T. E. (2002). Risky families: Family social environments and the mental and physical health of offspring. *Psychological Bulletin, 128,* 330–366.

Shedler, J., Mayman, M., & Manis, M. (1993). The illusion of mental health. *American Psychologist, 48,* 1117–1131.

Taylor, S. E. (1983). Adjustment to threatening events: A theory of cognitive adaptation. *American Psychologist, 38,* 1161–1173.

Taylor, S. E. (2010). Mechanisms linking early life stress to adult health outcomes. *Proceedings of the National Academy of Sciences, 107,* 8507–8512.

Taylor, S. E. (2011). Pathways linking early life stress to adult health. In J. Decety & J. Cacioppo (Eds.), *The handbook of social neuroscience* (pp. 776–786). New York: Oxford University Press.

Taylor, S. E., & Broffman, J. I. (2011). Psychosocial resources: Functions, origins, and links to mental and physical health. In J. M. Olson & M. P. Zanna (Eds.), *Advances in experimental social psychology* (pp. 1–57). New York: Academic Press.

Taylor, S. E., & Brown, J. D. (1988). Illusion and well-being: A social psychological perspective on mental health. *Psychological Bulletin, 103,* 193–210.

Taylor, S. E., & Gollwitzer, P. M. (1995). The effects of mindset on positive illusions. *Journal of Personality and Social Psychology, 69,* 213–226.

Taylor, S. E., Lehman, B. J., Kiefe, C. I., & Seeman, T. E. (2006). Relationship of early life stress and psychological functioning to adult C-reactive protein in the Coronary Artery Risk Development in Young Adults Study. *Biological Psychiatry, 60,* 819–824.

Taylor, S. E., Lerner, J. S., Sherman, D. K., Sage, R. M., & McDowell, N. K. (2003a). Portrait of the self-enhancer: Well-adjusted and well-liked or maladjusted and friendless? *Journal of Personality and Social Psychology, 84,* 165–176.

Taylor, S. E., Lerner, J. S., Sherman, D. K., Sage, R. M., & McDowell, N. K. (2003b). Are self-enhancing cognitions associated with healthy or unhealthy biological profiles? *Journal of Personality and Social Psychology, 85,* 605–615.

Taylor, S. E., Lichtman, R. R., & Wood, J. V. (1984). Attributions, beliefs about control, and adjustment to breast cancer. *Journal of Personality and Social Psychology, 46,* 489–502.

Taylor, S. E., & Lobel, M. (1989). Social comparison activity under threat: Downward evaluation and upward contacts. *Psychological Review, 96,* 569–575.

Taylor, S. E., Way, B. M., Welch, W. T., Hilmert, C. J., Lehman, B. J., & Eisenberger, N. I. (2006). Early family environment, current adversity, the serotonin transporter polymorphism, and depressive symptomatology. *Biological Psychiatry, 60,* 671–676.

Social Psychology

Reducing Prejudice and Building Empathy in the Classroom

Elliot Aronson

When Good Things Happen to Good People: Capitalizing on Personal Positive Events in Relationships

Harry T. Reis

Reducing Prejudice and Building Empathy in the Classroom

ELLIOT ARONSON University of California, Santa Cruz

☐ Please describe your current position and research interests.

I am professor emeritus at the University of California, Santa Cruz. My long-standing research interests include social influence and attitude change, cognitive dissonance, research methodology, and interpersonal attraction. My experiments are aimed both at testing theory and at improving the human condition by influencing people to change dysfunctional attitudes and behaviors.

☐ How did you become interested in studying and resolving social conflict?

Social psychology has always thrilled me because it is such a wonderful blend of art and science. I believe that with sufficient ingenuity, almost any phenomenon can be tested in the laboratory. But I don't want simply to observe. I want to determine precisely what's causing a phenomenon, and if it's a situation that is impacting people's lives negatively, I want to take the next step and create an intervention that makes things better.

☐ What has been the real-world impact of this work?

Schools all over the country have adopted the jigsaw classroom process described in this essay. By encouraging listening, engagement, and empathy, and by giving each member of a student group an essential part to play in its activity, the process creates an environment in which racial, gender, and socioeconomic divisions can be overcome.

Prejudice is ubiquitous. In our own country, it has existed at least since the Puritans emigrated from England in 1620 to escape intolerance and eventually began practicing intolerance against everybody else in sight. It is not easy to change. In this essay, I will tell you a story about one successful attempt to reduce prejudice among elementary school children.

My story begins in 1954, when the United States Supreme Court outlawed school segregation. At that time, most social psychologists believed that when youngsters from various ethnic and racial backgrounds came to share the same classroom, negative stereotypes would gradually be reduced and cross-ethnic friendships would develop under the glow of face-to-face contact. Ultimately, these young people would grow into adults who would be relatively free of racial and ethnic prejudice.

The decision reversed the 1896 ruling (*Plessy* v. *Ferguson*), which had held racial segregation permissible as long as equal facilities were provided for both races. In 1954, in *Brown* v. *Board of Education,* the Court held that, psychologically, there could be no such thing as "separate but equal" education because the forced separation, in and of itself, implied to the minority group in question that its members were inferior to those of the majority. To quote from the 1954 decision:

> Does segregation of children in public schools solely on the basis of race, even though the physical facilities and other "tangible" factors may be equal, deprive the children of the minority group of equal educational opportunities? We believe that it does . . . to separate [Negro school children] from others of similar age and qualifications solely because of their race generates a feeling of inferiority as to their status in the community that may affect their hearts and minds in a way unlikely ever to be undone. . . . We conclude that in the field of public education the doctrine "separate but equal" has no place. Separate educational facilities are inherently unequal.

The implication of the ruling is that, because segregation *lowers* self-esteem, desegregation would produce an increase in the self-esteem of minority students. Furthermore, because segregation was depriving minorities of equal educational opportunities, the implication is that desegregation would lead to improved education for these students. Thus, the Court's decision was not only a humane interpretation of the Constitution, it was also the beginning of an exciting social experiment with three clear hypotheses: Desegregation will (1) reduce prejudice, (2) raise the self-esteem of minority students, and (3) improve the classroom performance of minority students.

Unfortunately, things did not work out exactly as supporters of the ruling had hoped. For example, in the 15 years following the implementation of the 1954 ruling, not a single study showed an increase in the self-esteem of minority children following desegregation; in fact, several studies showed that desegregation was followed by a significant *decrease* in their self-esteem. Moreover, if anything, according to the early studies, desegregation produced an increase rather than a decrease in racial prejudice, and the academic performance of minority students did not improve (Stephan, 1978).

In short, the results were incredibly disappointing. What went wrong? Why was desegregation failing to have the positive effects that most social psychologists had predicted?

What We Observed in Desegregated Classrooms

As luck would have it, I got a chance to find out first hand what was happening in the newly desegregated schools. In 1971, I was teaching at the University of Texas at Austin when the Austin public schools were finally desegregated—and all hell broke loose. Because Austin had been segregated residentially, youngsters of various ethnic and racial groups were encountering one another for the first time. A lot of suspicion and stereotyping existed prior to this contact, and it seems to have exacerbated the problem. In any case, taunting frequently escalated into fistfights. The situation was both ugly and dangerous.

The school superintendent knew that I had some experience in resolving social conflict, and he asked for my help. All he really wanted was for me to find a way to end the violence. But I had a more ambitious agenda: My students and I entered the system, not to smooth over the unpleasantness but rather to see if there was anything we might do to help desegregation achieve some of the positive goals envisioned for it originally. The first thing we did was to observe systematically the dynamics taking place in various classrooms. By far, the most common process we observed was typified by this scenario in a fifth-grade class:

> The teacher stands in front of the room and asks a question. Most frequently, seven or eight youngsters strain in their seats and raise their hands—some waving them vigorously in an attempt to attract the teacher's attention. Several other students sit quietly with their eyes averted, as if trying to make themselves invisible. When the teacher calls on one of the students, there are looks of disappointment, dismay, and unhappiness on the faces of those students who were eagerly raising their hands but were not called on. If the student comes up with the right answer, the teacher smiles, nods approvingly, and goes on to the next question. This is a great reward for that student. At that moment, however, an audible groan can be heard coming from the youngsters who were striving to be called on but were ignored. It is obvious they are upset.

Through this process, students learn several things in addition to the material being covered. First, they learn there is only one expert in the classroom: the teacher. The students also learn that the payoff comes from pleasing the teacher by actively displaying how smart they are. There is no payoff for consulting with their peers. Indeed, many learn that their peers are their enemies—to be defeated.

In this highly competitive dynamic, if you are a student who knows the correct answer and the teacher calls on one of your peers, chances are you will hope that he or she will come up with the wrong answer so you will have a chance to show the teacher how smart you are. Those who fail when called on, or those who do not even raise their hands and compete, usually resent those who succeed. The successful students, for their part, often hold the unsuccessful students in contempt; they consider them to be stupid and uninteresting. This process discourages mutual understanding. Indeed, it tends to create enmity, even among students of the same racial group. When this competitive classroom dynamic is added to a situation already strained by interracial distrust, it sets the stage for the kind of turmoil we encountered in Austin. We began to understand why desegregation was not producing the desired consequences.

Although competitiveness in the classroom was nearly universal, as social psychologists, we realized that alternative dynamics were possible. We reasoned that a cooperative process might be precisely what was needed in this situation.

Our Jigsaw Classrooms

Within a few days, my students and I invented a simple, cooperative method for the classroom. We designed it so that, in order to learn the material and do well on an upcoming exam, students had to work *with* each other and not push against one other. Trying to win at the expense of your classmates became dysfunctional. We called our method the "jigsaw classroom" because it works very much like a jigsaw puzzle.

An example will clarify: In a fifth-grade classroom, the children were studying biographies of famous Americans. The upcoming lesson happened to be a biography of Joseph Pulitzer, the famous journalist. First, we divided the students into groups of six—making certain that each group was as diverse (in terms of race and gender) as possible. Then, we constructed a biography of Pulitzer consisting of six paragraphs. Paragraph one was about Pulitzer's ancestors and how they came to this country; paragraph two was about Pulitzer as a little boy and how he grew up; paragraph three was about Pulitzer as a young man, his education, and his early employment, and so forth.

Each major aspect of Joseph Pulitzer's life was contained in a separate paragraph. We mimeographed our biography of Joseph Pulitzer, cut each copy of the biography into six one-paragraph sections, and gave every child in each of the six-person learning groups one paragraph about Pulitzer's life. Thus, each learning group had within it the entire biography of Joseph Pulitzer, but each student had no more than one-sixth of the story. In order to get the whole picture, each student needed to listen carefully to the other students in the group as they recited.

The teacher informed the students that they had a certain amount of time to communicate their knowledge to one another. She also informed them that they would be tested on their knowledge at the end of that time period.

The students eventually learned that none of them could do well without the aid of each person in the group. They learned to respect the fact that each member (regardless of race, gender, or ethnicity) had a unique and essential contribution to make to their own understanding and subsequent test performance. Now, instead of only one expert (the teacher), each student was an expert on his or her own segment. Instead of taunting each other, they began encouraging each other—because it was in each student's own best interest to make sure that the youngster reciting was able to communicate his or her material in the clearest possible way.

It wasn't easy. During their previous years in school, the students had grown accustomed to competing. For the first few days, most of them tried to compete against each other—even though competitiveness was now dysfunctional. Let me illustrate with an actual example that was typical of the way the children stumbled toward learning the cooperative process. In one of our groups there was a Mexican-American boy, whom I will call Carlos. Carlos's task was to report on Joseph Pulitzer's young adulthood. He knew the material, but he was very nervous and was having a very hard time. During the past few weeks, some of the Anglo students had taunted him about his accent, and he was afraid that this might happen again.

He stammered, hesitated, and fidgeted. Sure enough, the other kids in the circle were not very helpful. Well-versed in the rough-and-tumble tactics of the competitive classroom, they knew what to do when a kid stumbled—especially a kid whom they believed to be stupid. They ridiculed him. During our experiment, a girl we'll call Debbie was observed saying: "Aw, you don't know it, you're dumb, you're stupid. You don't know what you're doing."

The groups were being monitored by a research assistant who was float-ing among them. When this incident occurred, the assistant made one brief intervention, saying: "Okay, you can do that if you want to. It might even be fun for you. But it's *not* going to help you learn about Joseph Pulitzer's young adulthood. By the way, the exam will take place in about 20 minutes."

Notice how the reinforcement contingencies had shifted. No longer did Deb-bie gain much from rattling Carlos; in fact, she now stood to lose a great deal.

After a few similar experiences, the students in Carlos's group realized that the *only* way they could learn about the segment Carlos was trying to teach them was by paying attention to what Carlos had to say. Gradually, they began to develop into good listeners. Some even became pretty good interviewers. Instead of ignoring or ridiculing Carlos when he was having a little trouble communicating what he knew, they began asking gentle, prob-ing questions—the kinds of questions that made it easier for Carlos to com-municate what was in his mind.

Carlos began to respond to this treatment by becoming more relaxed; with increased relaxation came an improvement in his ability to communicate. After a couple of weeks, the other children realized that Carlos was a lot smarter than they had thought he was. Because they were paying attention, they began to see things in him they had never seen before. They began to respect him. For his part, Carlos began to enjoy school more and began to see the Anglo students in his group not as tormentors but as helpful and respon-sible people. Moreover, as he began to feel increasingly comfortable in class and started to gain more confidence in himself, his academic performance improved. The vicious cycle had been reversed; the elements that had been causing a downward spiral were changed—the spiral now began to move upward. Within a few weeks, the entire atmosphere in that classroom had changed dramatically. We then randomly assigned several classrooms in Austin to the jigsaw condition and compared them with classrooms using traditional methods. The results were clear and consistent. Children in jigsaw classrooms performed better on objective exams, grew to like each other bet-ter, and developed a greater liking for school and greater self-esteem than children in traditional classrooms. The increase in liking among children in the jigsaw classroom crossed ethnic and racial barriers, resulting in a sharp decrease in prejudice and stereotyping. We replicated the same experiment in dozens of classrooms in several cities—always getting similar results (Aron-son, Stephen, Sikes, Blaney, & Snapp, 1978; Aronson & Goode, 1980; Aronson & Patnoe, 1997).

What Are the Benefits of the Jigsaw Classroom?

Over the years, dozens of experiments have shown that the jigsaw method's effectiveness is not limited to either Americans or to young children. Jigsaw has been used with great success in Europe, Africa, the Middle East, and Australia—with students at all levels, from elementary schools to universities.

We speculated that one of the processes underlying the success of the method is empathy—the ability to experience what your group member is experiencing. In the competitive classroom, the primary goal is simply to show the teacher how smart you are. You don't have to pay much attention to the other students. But the jigsaw situation is different. In order to participate effectively in the jigsaw classroom, each student needs to pay close attention to whichever member of the group is reciting. In the process, the participants begin to learn that great results can accrue if each of their classmates is approached in a way that is tailored to fit his or her special needs. For example, Alice may learn that Carlos is a bit shy and needs to be prodded gently, while Phyllis is so talkative that she might need to be reigned in occasionally. Peter can be joked with, while Serena responds only to serious suggestions.

If our analysis is sound, then it should follow that working in jigsaw groups would lead to the sharpening of a youngster's general empathic ability. To test this notion, Diane Bridgeman (1981) conducted a clever experiment with 10-year-old children. Prior to her experiment, half of the children had spent two months participating in jigsaw classes; the others spent that time in traditional classrooms. Bridgeman showed the children a series of cartoons aimed at testing a child's ability to empathize—to put themselves in the shoes of the cartoon characters. For example, in one cartoon, the first panel shows a little boy looking sad as he waves good-bye to his father at the airport. In the next panel, a letter carrier delivers a package to the boy. In the third panel, the boy opens the package, finds a toy airplane inside, and bursts into tears. Bridgeman asked the children why they thought the little boy burst into tears at the sight of the airplane. Nearly all of the children could answer correctly—because the toy airplane reminded him of how much he missed his father. Then Bridgeman asked the crucial question: "What did the letter carrier think when he saw the boy open the package and start to cry?"

Most children of this age make a consistent error; they assume that everyone knows what they know. Thus, the youngsters in the control group thought that the *letter carrier* would know the boy was sad because the gift reminded him of his father leaving. But the children who had participated in the jigsaw classroom responded differently. Because of their experience with jigsaw, they had developed the ability to take the perspective of the letter carrier; they realized that, not having witnessed the farewell scene at the airport, he would be confused at seeing the boy cry over receiving a nice present.

Schools are conservative organizations. As such, they are slow to change. In spite of jigsaw's success, it is being used in approximately 15 percent of the schools in this country. In those schools, desegregation works the way it is supposed to work.

☐ Thinking Critically

1. As Elliot Aronson demonstrated, cooperation can reduce intergroup conflict. What conditions did he set up in his experiment that made cooperation work?

2. Interdependence reduced prejudice and improved performance in jigsaw classrooms. Can you think of other real-world contexts in which cooperation can break down social barriers?

☐ Suggested Further Reading

Aronson, E. (2011). *The social animal* (11th ed.). New York: Worth.

Aronson, E. (2000, May/June). Nobody left to hate: Developing the empathic schoolroom. *The Humanist, 60,* 17–21.

☐ References

Aronson, E., Bridgeman, D. L., & Geffner, R. (1978). The effects of a cooperative classroom structure on students' behavior and attitudes. In D. Bar-Tal & L. Saxe (Eds.), *Social psychology of education: Theory and research.* Washington, DC: Hemisphere.

Aronson, E., & Goode, E. (1980). Training teachers to implement jigsaw learning: A manual for teachers. In S. Sharan, P. Hare, C. Webb, & R. Hertz-Lazarowitz (Eds.), *Cooperation in education* (pp. 47–81). Provo, UT: Brigham Young University Press.

Aronson, E., & Patnoe, S. (2011). *Cooperation in the classroom: The jigsaw method* (3rd ed.). London: Pinter & Martin, Ltd.

Aronson, E., Stephen, C., Sikes, J., Blaney, N., & Snapp, M. (1978). *The jigsaw classroom.* Beverly Hills, CA: Sage.

Bridgeman, D. L. (1981). Enhanced role taking through cooperative interdependence: A field study. *Child Development, 52,* 1231–1238.

Stephan, W. G. (1978). School desegregation: An evaluation of predictions made in *Brown v. Board of Education. Psychological Bulletin, 85,* 217–238.

When Good Things Happen to Good People: Capitalizing on Personal Positive Events in Relationships

HARRY T. REIS The University of Rochester

☐ **Please describe your current position and research interests.**

I am a professor of Psychology at the University of Rochester. My research concerns the factors that lead people to perceive that their partners are responsive to them. More broadly, I am interested in the ways in which relationships affect human behavior in nearly all domains of activity.

☐ **How did you become interested in positive factors that influence the quantity and closeness of social interactions?**

I felt that the clinic-inspired psychology of relationships was much too heavily focused on conflict. People don't seek out relationships because they are low in conflict or because they can "fight well" with this person; they seek out partners who help them feel good about themselves, who make them feel listened to and supported, and who inspire them. That is what we are trying to get at.

☐ **What has been the real-world impact of this work?**

My hope is that from this work people will pay more attention when their partner tells them about good news and that they will make their appreciation more evident. This is a very modest goal but in my mind it is one with great potential.

> *A happiness shared is a happiness doubled.*
>
> —*Navajo proverb*

> *Whenever a friend succeeds, a little something in me dies.*
>
> —*Gore Vidal*

Let's consider two friendships. In the first, Jacques has just won a prestigious, all-expenses-paid fellowship to a major university. His friend Jules is excited and enthusiastic, giving him high fives, asking questions about the details, and suggesting a celebratory dinner. Another friend, Jalen, has won the same fellowship. However, when he informs his friend Jon, he gets a half-hearted response. "That's nice," Jon says and quickly changes the topic to a concert they plan to attend that evening. What's the difference between these two reactions, and why does it matter?

For the past several years, my colleagues and I have investigated the process embodied in these examples. We call it "capitalization." The term refers to the attempt to get the most out of a positive event—that is, to capitalize on good news. There are many ways in which this might be done. One of the most common is sharing the news with a relationship partner (Langston, 1994). You've probably had this experience: Something good happens, and your first impulse is to call, e-mail, or text a friend, significant other, or family member. How the news is received, our research has shown, turns out to be important to the quality of the relationship and to how the sharer feels about the news.

Our involvement in this line of research grew out of our interest in the difference between what we call "appetitive" and "aversive" processes in close relationships. For many years, researchers and practitioners alike had viewed responses to stressful events and undesirable outcomes as critical in determining relationship success. In the arena of social life, these aversive phenomena include rejection, insecurity, rudeness, criticism, jealousy, loneliness, betrayal, and conflict. Many relationship researchers, in fact, have viewed conflict and its management as the defining attribute of relationship success.

Psychological research on aversive processes has far outweighed consideration of the impact of appetitive processes on relationship functioning. Appetitive processes refer to desired outcomes and goals, such as intimacy, love, shared fun, and a feeling of meaningful connection. For my colleagues and me, the capitalization situation has been a natural prototype for our broader interest in these appetitive processes. Ideas about capitalization derive directly from research on the importance of self-disclosure and social support in close relationships. But there is a key difference. Social support, which is characterized by some researchers as an appetitive process, is usually sought when people are in a negative state—that is, when they are distressed or worried and need assistance, guidance, or comfort to help diminish their distress. By contrast, when capitalizing on good news, the goal is to savor and otherwise maximize the positive aspects of that news.

First Studies on Capitalization

We began our research with a daily diary study (Gable, Reis, Impett, & Asher, 2004). For one week, 154 college students reported the most important positive and negative event or experience of each day and whether they had told someone about the event. They then rated the event's importance. Approximately 70 percent of the positive events were recounted to another person. We applied to the data multi-level analysis, a statistical procedure that controls for differences between people who are inclined to share and people who are not. After further controlling for the importance of the positive event and for whatever negative events had occurred during the day, we found that on days in which the most positive event had been related to another person, our respondents' positive affect and life satisfaction were significantly higher than on days in which those positive events were left untold. In plain language, relating a positive event to another person was strongly associated with having a better day.

Correlation is not causality, of course, and this important distinction led us to develop an experimental paradigm for examining the capitalization process. We first ask participants in our experiments to describe and rate the three best things "that have happened to you in the past two years." We then randomly select either the second- or third-most positive event and ask participants to spend about eight minutes describing it to an interviewer trained to respond enthusiastically and supportively. (For example, the interviewer smiles, makes eye contact, uses a lively tone of voice, and says things like "Your friends must be really proud of you.") After these conversations, participants are asked again to rate all three of their best-in-two-years events. The results of one experiment are shown in Figure 1. We found that ratings

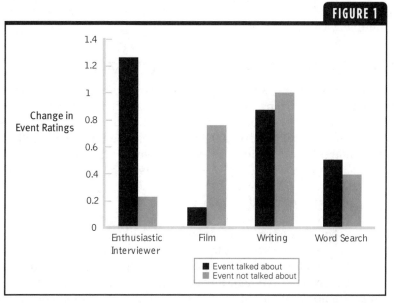

FIGURE 1

From pre to post in four experimental conditions. Change in ratings of best-in-two-years events. (From Reis et al., 2010, Study 1. Copyright © 2010 by the American Psychological Association. Reproduced with permission. The use of APA information does not imply endorsement by the APA.)

of the event discussed increased significantly, whereas ratings of the event not discussed stayed steady (Reis et al., 2010, Study 1).

To rule out other possible causes of the capitalization effect, this study included other conditions asking participants for ratings of their best-in-two-years events after they had undergone one of three different experiences. In one condition, participants wrote an essay describing their thoughts and feelings about the target event. (Other researchers have shown that this kind of expressive writing can help people cope with traumatic events [Pennebaker, 2003]). In a second condition, participants watched a humorous clip from the film *Austin Powers: International Man of Mystery* to see if similar results might be obtained from being in a good mood (Fredrickson, 1998). The final control condition involved doing word-search puzzles. As Figure 1 shows, none of these conditions yielded differential increases for the event discussed over the event not discussed, suggesting that the *act of recounting* an event with an enthusiastic listener is responsible for the benefits of capitalization.

Does capitalization depend on an enthusiastic listener? To find out, in another experiment we compared a condition in which the listener was enthusiastic (as in the previous study) with one in which the listener adopted a more passive, disengaged, but not hostile orientation (Reis et al., 2010, Study 2). For example, throughout the participant's recounting, the listener slouched and fidgeted, mostly avoided eye contact, maintained a steady and fairly dry tone of voice, and said things like "Oh yeah, that's nice." Enthusiastic listening again led to a significant capitalization effect; passive responses yielded no significant findings. This result dovetails with research showing that inattentive, distracted listening (but not attentive, responsive listening) may undermine people's ability to find personal meaning in oral narratives (see, for example, Pasupathi & Rich, 2005).

The Interpersonal Benefits of Capitalization

Capitalization is not only about savoring good news; it also contributes to the well-being of relationships. We theorize that this occurs because enthusiastic responses demonstrate emotional engagement, and such responsiveness is at the core of close relationships. For example, when one person discloses personal thoughts and feelings, responses seen as understanding, validating, and caring foster warm, supported feelings in the speaker and intimacy between the partners (Reis & Shaver, 1988).

Psychologists have tended to study responsiveness in terms of negativity— for example, after disclosures of fears, anxieties, and embarrassing moments, or in conflict-laden communications. But perceived responsiveness can also be revealed in responses to a person's aspirations, goals, and ideals. For example, romantic partners' behavioral and psychological support has been found to foster movement toward personal goals and aspirations and thereby to promote individual growth and the well-being of the relationship, a phenomenon dubbed the "Michelangelo phenomenon" (Rusbult, Finkel, & Kumashiro, 2009).

Of course, friends, relatives, and even romantic partners do not always respond to a retelling of personal good fortune with visible pride and enthusiasm. In some circumstances, partners respond with envy or distance (Beach & Tesser, 1995). For example, when good news has meaning that is personally relevant for the partner, it may provoke anxiety. Imagine hearing about something that threatens your self-esteem or security in a relationship or that involves new activities or responsibilities that potentially compete with the relationship for time or attention. You'd have to put your personal feelings aside for the good of the relationship to respond enthusiastically.

Ironically, relationship-threatening good news from a romantic partner can create more ambivalence and make it harder to respond enthusiastically than if the same news were being related by an acquaintance. Capitalization attempts may also be hampered by the third-party experience. All other things being equal, close friends expect to learn each other's news firsthand. Thus, learning about a close friend's good fortune from a less close other (the third party) may undermine closeness and the capitalization process. Learning the same news about the same person from a third party who is closer to the target than oneself does not have this effect (Tsai, 2006).

My colleagues and I have examined the benefits of capitalization in both correlational studies and experiments. We do so for several reasons. One reason is methodological: Experiments are better for asking questions about causality, whereas correlational studies are better for examining these processes from the perspective of the individuals involved. Another, more general reason is that we believe that capitalization applies not only to transitory interactions among strangers but also to ongoing relationships, including friendship, marriage, and families. To examine these processes in romantic relationships, some of our studies have used a questionnaire that looks at the way partners are perceived to respond to a person's capitalization attempts. Are these responses experienced as active and constructive ("My partner usually responds to my good fortune enthusiastically"), passive ("My partner says little but I know he/she is happy for me"), or destructive ("Sometimes I get the impression that he/she doesn't care much" or "He/she points out the potential downsides of the good event")? Correlations consistently reveal that the active-constructive responses are associated with higher levels of well-being in both partners and in the relationship. (These associations are obtained after controlling for general levels of satisfaction with the relationship, indicating that perceived responsiveness to capitalization attempts represents something more particular than general happiness.)

In one study conducted with 89 heterosexual couples who had been married between 1 and 43 years, we asked spouses to keep daily records of their interactions with each other. Spouses who perceived their partners' responses as active-constructive reported higher levels of daily satisfaction than did couples who perceived passive or negative feedback, and they reported more shared fun and relaxing activities, higher intimacy, and fewer conflicts. Interestingly, passive responses, which nominally might not seem destructive, were associated with *worse* outcomes (Gable et al., 2004). Another study, using carefully controlled laboratory observations, similarly showed that active-constructive responses to capitalization attempts (as rated by the individual or independent observers) were associated with higher relationship well-being and stability (Gable, Gonzaga, & Strachman, 2006). Interestingly enough, these active-constructive responses to capitalization attempts have been shown to better predict the durability of relationship well-being than responses in conversations about stressful events (Gable, Gosnell, Maisel, & Strachman, 2012).

Providing an enthusiastic response to a partner's effort to capitalize on good news may also benefit the responder. In one experiment, we trained listeners to provide enthusiastic feedback as research participants recounted positive experiences (Reis et al., 2010, Study 3). In a different condition, we provided an opportunity for "fun"; this involved the participant describing in words a series of ambiguous pencil drawings that the trained listener had to draw without seeing. In both conditions, the confederate was liked equally well, but in the capitalization condition, trust was higher and participants were more willing to self-disclose.

Enthusiastic positive feedback even affects brief encounters between strangers, as we found when our lab assistants, posing as interviewers, approached people on the street and asked them to describe (for $1) the best thing that had happened to them during the previous week (Reis et al., 2010, Study 4). As before, we set up three response conditions—enthusiastic, passive, and disparaging—and we also added a fourth: The interviewer offered a piece of candy from a box that she said she had just received from her grandmother. After the interviews, participants received an envelope containing $2 and a receipt (hidden from the interviewer's vision). If capitalization builds social resources, we would expect that participants in the enthusiasm condition would be more likely than those in the other groups to return the unexpected additional dollar. And indeed they did. Sixty-eight percent of the enthusiastic response group returned the extra money, significantly more than in the candy (51%), neutral (48%), and disparaging (36%) conditions.

Translating Capitalization Research to Everyday Relationships

What can we learn from our findings that can be applied in everyday relationships? Most apparent is the insight that relationships benefit when partners respond with enthusiasm and visible pride to each other's good fortune. We believe that two general processes are operative. First, enthusiasm signals people's genuine appreciation for the event in question, as well as high regard for the other person. As hundreds of studies have shown, we humans are inherently social creatures whose attitudes, beliefs, and self-evaluations are profoundly influenced by the feedback we receive from others, especially from valued others. A positive response from a valued partner allows one to savor the event, enhances its meaningfulness, and makes it more memorable—all parts of the upward cycle in well-being that positive emotions foster (Fredrickson, 1998). It also likely fuels gratitude, another positive relationship behavior (Algoe, Gable, & Maisel, 2010).

The second process is relational in nature and involves a defining feature of close relationships—cognitive interdependence. When we are really close to someone, attributes of the other person become linked cognitively and emotionally to our own attributes; in a psychological sense, we include the other in the self (Aron, Aron, Tudor, & Nelson, 1991). By responding with pride rather than envy and with enthusiasm rather than disengagement, one partner signals mental inclusion of the other in their own self-representation and enhances their feelings of closeness. "Basking in reflected glory," or displaying pride in the accomplishments of relationship partners, is associated with closeness and the desire for continued closeness (Beach & Tesser, 1995). An enthusiastic response, then, is a sign of closeness and appreciation.

In conclusion, recounting one's personal good fortune is not just a strategic attempt to brag; it creates an opportunity for friends, relatives, and romantic partners to support and affirm, or alternatively to undermine or disparage. Although we have not yet identified the numerous personal and situational factors that encourage partners to share good news in relationship-promoting ways and to provide enthusiastic responses, a few brief principles from the social psychological literature suggest promising possibilities. For example, traits that foster responsiveness and genuine openness toward others, such as attachment security, high self-esteem, and agreeableness, would seem relevant, as would skills such as empathic accuracy (the ability to accurately perceive how others are thinking and feeling) and perspective-taking. Traits only tell part of the story (and a small part at that); situational factors are also important, suggesting that people can learn to do better. Some situational factors that are likely to be relevant include other-focused (as opposed to self-focused) attention, commitment, and the absence of threats to the security of the relationship. Moreover, we see these processes as promising candidates for intervention. We suspect that in long-term relationships, rather than reflecting malign intent, capitalization failures may reflect mindlessness and inattention, processes that occur commonly as partners become habituated to their relationships and instead direct their attention to stresses and strains. If so, interventions that foster mindful attention to what is transpiring within our relationships and other responsive listening skills may have merit.

Finally, our work to date suggests that fostering the positive aspects of close relationships merits as much attention as is typically devoted toward repairing the negative side. A large majority of therapies and interventions teach skills for talking about negative emotions and resolving conflicts constructively, and these are certainly important. But people do not engage in friendships and close relationships to avoid their destructive potential. They enter relationships for positive reasons, including the desire to share life's many wonderful moments with another person. Maintaining and expanding that desire represents a new opportunity for capitalizing not just on good news, but on our rewarding connections with others.

☐ Thinking Critically

1. How does Harry Reis's approach to understanding relationship issues differ from traditional ways researchers have looked at relationships?
2. Do you think active-constructive responding is likely to be easy or difficult? Try it for a few days, and then evaluate its impact on you and those close to you.

☐ Suggested Further Reading

Reis, H. T., Clark, M. S., & Holmes, J. G. (2004). Perceived partner responsiveness as an organizing construct in the study of intimacy and closeness. In D. Mashek & A. Aron (Eds.), *The handbook of closeness and intimacy* (pp. 201–225). Mahwah, NJ: Erlbaum.

Reis, H. T., Smith, S. M., Carmichael, C. L., Caprariello, P. A., Tsai, F. F., Rodrigues, A., & Maniaci, M. R. (2010). Are you happy for me? How sharing positive events with others provides personal and interpersonal benefits. *Journal of Personality and Social Psychology, 99*, 311–329.

☐ References

Algoe, S., Gable, S., & Maisel, N. (2010). Everyday gratitude in romantic relationships. *Personal Relationships, 17,* 217–233.

Aron, A., Aron, E. N., Tudor, M., & Nelson, G. (1991). Close relationships as including other in the self. *Journal of Personality and Social Psychology, 60,* 241–253.

Aron, A., McLaughlin-Volpe, T., Mashek, D., Lewandowski, G., Wright, S. C., & Aron, E. N. (2004). Including others in the self. *European Review of Social Psychology, 15,* 101–132.

Beach, S. R. H., & Tesser, A. (1995). Self-esteem and the extended self-evaluation maintenance model: The self in social context. In M. H. Kernis (Ed.), *Efficacy, agency, and self-esteem* (pp. 145–170). New York: Plenum Press.

Fredrickson, B. (1998). What good are positive emotions? *Review of General Psychology, 2,* 300–319.

Gable, S. L., Gonzaga, G. C., & Strachman, A. (2006). Will you be there for me when things go right? Supportive responses to positive event disclosures. *Journal of Personality and Social Psychology, 91,* 904–917.

Gable, S. L., Gosnell, C. L., Maisel, N. C., & Strachman, A. (2012). Safely testing the alarm: Close others' responses to personal positive events. *Journal of Personality and Social Psychology, 103,* 963–981.

Gable, S. L., Reis, H. T., Impett, E., & Asher, E. R. (2004). What do you do when things go right? The intrapersonal and interpersonal benefits of sharing positive events. *Journal of Personality and Social Psychology, 87,* 228–245.

Langston, C. A. (1994). Capitalizing on and coping with daily-life events: Expressive responses to positive events. *Journal of Personality and Social Psychology, 67,* 1112–1125.

Pasupathi, M., & Rich, B. (2005). Inattentive listening undermines self-verification in personal storytelling. *Journal of Personality, 73,* 1051–1086.

Pennebaker, J. W. (2003). Writing about emotional experiences as a therapeutic process. In P. Salovey & A. J. Rothman (Eds.), *Social psychology of health.* New York: Psychology Press.

Reis, H. T., & Shaver, P. (1988). Intimacy as an interpersonal process. In S. Duck & D. F. Hay (Eds.), *Handbook of personal relationships: Theory, research, and interventions* (pp. 367–389). New York: John Wiley & Sons.

Reis, H. T., Smith, S. M., Carmichael, C. L., Caprariello, P. A., Tsai, F. F., Rodrigues, A., & Maniaci, M. R. (2010). Are you happy for me? How sharing positive events with others provides personal and interpersonal benefits. *Journal of Personality and Social Psychology, 99,* 311–329.

Rusbult, C. E., Finkel, E. J., & Kumashiro, M. (2009). The Michelangelo phenomenon. *Current Directions in Psychological Science, 18,* 305–309.

Tsai, F. F. (2006). *Why didn't you tell me first?: The third-party experience.* Unpublished doctoral dissertation, University of Rochester.

Psychology at Work

Work and the Art of Motivation Maintenance

ADAM M. GRANT The Wharton School, University of Pennsylvania

☐ **Please describe your current position and research interests.**

I am the Wharton Class of 1965 Professor of Management, as well as Affiliated Professor of Psychology. I study work motivation, the design of meaningful jobs, what encourages people to proactively create change in their organizations, and why people are driven to help others—and what happens to their careers when they do.

☐ **What got you interested in studying organizational psychology?**

Growing up, I was surprised that although most people spend the majority of their waking hours at work, few find their work to be the most meaningful and motivating part of their lives. When I began studying psychology, I wanted to do research that could make a difference, and I was excited about the prospect of collaborating with organizations to improve the quality of work life.

☐ **What has been the real-world impact of this work?**

My favorite studies have motivated doctors and nurses to wash their hands more often, lifeguards to focus more attention on protecting the safety of swimmers, and fundraisers to bring in more money for universities and non-profits. This work has also led to the design of a program that significantly increased the happiness and job performance of Google employees and managers, as well as a series of programs to improve motivation and engagement in a wide range of organizations, from the military and the government to call centers, schools, and investment banks.

Employees without a Cause

In college, my first real job was in advertising for the "Let's Go" travel books. We sent hundreds of Harvard students to scale mountains and hike through monsoons in search of the best-kept secrets about what to do, where to stay, and how to eat on the road. In the office back in Cambridge, teams of editors had three months to deliver a complete book. They started out highly motivated, often working 100-hour weeks, but the dream of writing a travel book gave way to the reality of deciphering chicken scratch (often written on a chicken bus) and transforming it into prose. I decided this would make for a fascinating undergraduate thesis: What keeps some editors highly motivated to produce successful books, whereas others burn out?

When I surveyed the editorial teams and asked their managers to rate their effectiveness, the most consistent predictor of success was the perception that the work had a positive impact on others. Because they were all doing the same work, I was puzzled that some editors had a much clearer grasp of its importance than others. This became the focus of my doctoral research, and I stumbled upon an opportunity to explore it at a call center.

The callers were contacting University of Michigan alumni and trying to persuade them to donate money to the university. It was a mundane, repetitive job using a standardized script with many more rejections than successes, and most callers quit within two months. One caller posted a sign next to his desk: "Doing a good job here is like wetting your pants in a dark suit. You get a warm feeling, but no one else notices."

The callers were raising millions of dollars for the university, but had no idea where the money went. Managers tried to solve the problem by delivering inspiring speeches, waxing poetic about athletic teams supported, buildings funded, and faculty and staff salaries provided. A team of students and I realized that it was the right message, but the wrong source. What if the callers heard from the people who were directly affected by the money they raised?

Connecting the Dots

We identified a scholarship recipient, Will, who was willing to share a compelling story about how the scholarship had improved his life. We designed an experiment, randomly dividing the callers into three groups. One group of callers met Will face-to-face, a second group read a letter from him, and the control group had no exposure to him (Grant et al., 2007).

After spending five minutes with Will, a full month later, the average caller in the first group spiked 142% in weekly minutes on the phone and 171% in weekly revenue. There were no significant gains in effort or performance among the callers in the second group who read Will's letter or the control group who had no contact with him. We ended up replicating the effect five times—one of the virtues of high turnover is that each semester brought new employees for new experiments. In one version of the experiment, a graduate student spoke about how the callers had funded archeological digs, and the average caller increased 406% in weekly revenue, from raising an average of $411 before meeting her to $2,083 afterward. In total, the 23 callers who met her raised an extra $38,451 in a single week (Grant, 2008a).

This research solved the "Let's Go" puzzle. The editors were producing travel books that helped readers have life-changing experiences in foreign lands, but stuck in an office disconnected from readers, many of the editors lost sight of their impact. This is true in many jobs: software developers, scientists, engineers, and accountants all perform work that makes a difference but never have direct contact with the ultimate beneficiaries of their products and services.

We conducted a number of experiments to figure out why face-to-face contact with beneficiaries is so powerful. It turns out that there's a big difference between knowing that your work helps others and seeing the impact on a living, breathing human being. When we interact directly with the people who benefit from our work, we develop a stronger conviction that our work matters and is valued and appreciated, and we become committed to working harder, smarter, longer, and productively on behalf of the people we're trying to help.

It's Not All About Me

These studies highlighted a new way of thinking about motivation. Traditionally, when we wanted to motivate employees, we focused on providing incentives or making the work itself more interesting. These approaches overlook the importance of interactions and relationships in motivation. We're driven to do our best work not only when our tasks are engaging and we expect to be paid well, but also when we can see that our work will have a lasting impact on others.

More recent research has extended these ideas into health and safety jobs where lives are on the line. When lifeguards read stories about how other lifeguards had rescued drowning swimmers, they became more aware of the impact and value of their work, and increased 43% in monthly hours worked and 21% in supervisor ratings of efforts to help keep swimmers safe (Grant, 2008b). When nurses assembled surgical kits, those who met a health care professional who would use the kits worked 64% longer than a control group, achieving more than double the output and making 15% fewer errors (Belle, 2012).

In high-stakes health care settings, even a photograph or a word that signals the impact of our work can be enough to boost motivation. When radiologists scanned an x-ray, including a photo of the patient, it was enough to increase their reports by 29% and their diagnostic accuracy by 46% (Turner, Hadas-Halperin, & Raveh, 2008). And consider the important behavior of hand washing in hospitals, which is the single most effective way to prevent the spread of infections and illnesses (Grant & Hofmann, 2011). When doctors and nurses saw a sign that said "Hand hygiene prevents you from catching diseases," their behavior didn't change. But when we changed the word "you" to "patients," they increased their hand washing by over 10% and their soap and gel usage by over 45%. Medical professionals often believe that they're immune to diseases: They don't get sick very often, and when they do, how can they be sure it was due to poor hand hygiene? By contrast, patients are a vulnerable population.

It's not all about me: People often engage in more health and safety behaviors when they focus on others rather than themselves. We found similar effects with fundraisers and lifeguards: Highlighting the personal benefits of the job did no good. They only became more motivated when they saw how their work benefited others.

Givers, Takers, and Matchers

Motivation climbs when we can see how our work helps others, but people differ in their motivation to help others. How do these differences influence our professional success?

To paraphrase the humorist Robert Benchley, there are only two kinds of people in the world: those who divide the world into two kinds of people, and those who don't. So often, psychologists make the mistake of oversimplifying people by breaking them down into two categories. In this case, we can gain more insight by examining three styles.

Extensive research shows that across industries and cultures, people typically have one of three dominant motivations when interacting with others (Grant, 2014). On opposite ends of the spectrum, we have people who I call takers and givers. Takers are self-serving: Their goal is to get as much as possible from others while contributing little in return. Givers are other-oriented: They enjoy giving more than they get, and helping others without strings attached. In the middle are matchers, people who aim to keep a fair, even balance of giving and taking. Most people are matchers at work: When they do a favor, they expect an equal one back, and when they receive a favor, they feel like they're in debt until they've settled the score.

Being a matcher is a safe way to operate, but is it ultimately the most productive way to live your professional life? To find out, I examined studies of three different jobs with very different ways of measuring success: engineering productivity, medical school grades, and sales revenue. Across each setting, among the takers, givers, and matchers, there was one group that consistently achieved the lowest performance.

No Good Deed Goes Unpunished

The givers sank to the bottom. In engineering, the lowest productivity belonged to the engineers who were rated by their colleagues as doing more favors than they received in return. They were so busy helping others that they ran out of time and energy to get their own work done. In medicine, the lowest grades belonged to the students who agreed most strongly with statements such as: "I love helping others." In sales, the lowest revenue was attained by the salespeople who reported dedicating the most time and energy to helping their colleagues and customers.

This is sad news for givers. It's also sad news for organizations, because we now have several decades of evidence that shows when groups of employees act like givers, organizations are better off. In one comprehensive analysis of more than 3,600 business units, for example, the more frequently employees helped each other, the better those units did in terms of profits, customer satisfaction, employee retention, and operating expenses (Podsakoff, Whiting, Podsakoff, & Blume, 2009). Givers contribute to organizations by sharing knowledge, making introductions, providing mentoring, and solving problems, but they appear to make their organizations better at their own expense. So if givers are the worst performers, who are the best performers?

When I analyzed the data, it wasn't the takers. They were too self-serving, and their colleagues penalized them for it—especially the matchers. If you're a matcher, you believe in a just world, and you can't stand to see people get away with acting selfishly. When you encounter a taker, you might feel that it's your mission in life to punish that person (Feinberg, Willer, Stellar, & Keltner, 2012). Most people expect that the matchers are the best performers, but the data showed that it wasn't the matchers either.

Good Returns

When I looked at who attained the highest performance, it was the givers again. They were more likely to finish last, but they were also more likely to finish first. The most productive engineers were the ones who did more favors than they received in return. Somehow, they managed to balance helping others with doing their own work efficiently and effectively. The matchers who traded favors evenly—and the takers who got more favors than they gave—didn't have terrible results, but they rarely had extraordinary results. It's a fascinating paradox: helping others can sink your career or accelerate it.

In medicine and sales, time was a key factor. In the first year of medical school, the givers fell behind. They admitted that when it was time to study for a big exam, they would teach what they already knew to their friends instead of filling the gaps in their own knowledge. But by the second year, the givers caught up and gained a slight advantage. The program shifted: Now, instead of being evaluated on exam performance, students were graded on their abilities to work with colleagues and care for patients. Once the work became interdependent rather than independent, the givers thrived. Each year, as their grades depended more heavily on collaboration and service, the givers pulled further and further ahead. Ultimately, the positive correlation between the motivation to help others at the beginning of medical school and grades at the end of medical school was stronger than the effect of smoking on the odds of getting lung cancer.

A similar pattern unfolded in sales. The givers were reluctant to deliver aggressive pitches, and often struggled in the first quarter or two. However, by taking a sincere interest in their customers, they learned more about customers' interests and built more trust. Over time, this meant that they could deliver pitches that were tailored to customers' needs, and they generated more repeat business and more referrals. By the end of the year, on average, the givers averaged 68% higher sales revenue than the takers and matchers.

This body of research raised two exciting questions. First, what do successful givers do that takers and matchers can learn? Second, what differentiates the givers at the top from those at the bottom—how do they avoid burning out and becoming doormats?

On the first question, research has shown that givers tend to build deeper and broader networks than takers and matchers. By being willing to help others without strings attached, they create strong relationships and engage with a wide range of people. By contrast, takers and matchers tend to create a transactional impression and limit their exchanges to people who seem able to help them. As a result, givers tend to receive greater support from others and benefit from stronger reputations. People are threatened by successful takers, whereas, they root for successful givers. In addition, givers tend to think more creatively: They're motivated to take others' perspectives, which enables them to make connections between different ideas and figure out how to make novel ideas useful to others.

On the second question, the available evidence points to two kinds of givers (Helgeson & Fritz, 1998). Selfless givers tend to be self-sacrificing: They make the mistake of helping all of the people all of the time with all of the requests. This makes them vulnerable to burnout and to being exploited by takers. There's another group of givers, "otherish" givers, who strive to integrate their own ambitions with their desires to help others. They put others first often, and help without the expectation of reciprocity, but they keep their own interests in the rearview mirror. This means being more cautious when dealing with takers and blocking out time in their calendars to get their own work done. It also involves becoming specialists rather than generalists when it comes to giving: helping in one or two key ways that align with one's interests and unique expertise, so that giving is more likely to be energizing and efficient than exhausting and distracting.

What inspires me most about successful givers is that they manage to lift others up, rather than cutting them down. They open the door to a broader definition of success that includes helping others succeed. Instead of trying to sink all of the other ships in the sea, givers are the rising tide that lifts all boats.

☐ Thinking Critically

1. Adam Grant identifies three types of people in organizations: takers, matchers, and givers. Explain the paradox of the high performance of organizations with many givers as employees and the low individual performance of these givers.
2. Looking at a student's whole college experience, how might it be possible to give more to others and achieve more success at the same time? What might you do differently to increase your giving and your performance in college now that you've read Grant's essay?

☐ Suggested Further Reading

Dominus, S. (2013, March 31). Is giving the secret to getting ahead? *New York Times Magazine*. Retrieved May 30, 2014, from www.nytimes .com/2013/03/31/magazine/is-giving-the-secret-to-getting-ahead .html?pagewanted=all

Grant, A. (2014). *Give and take: Why helping others drives our success*. New York: Penguin.

☐ References

Belle, N. (2012). Experimental evidence on the relationship between public service motivation and job performance. *Public Administration Review, 73*, 143–153.

Feinberg, M., Willer, R., Stellar, J., & Keltner, D. (2012). The virtues of gossip: Reputational information sharing as prosocial behavior. *Journal of Personality and Social Psychology, 102*, 1015–1030.

Grant, A. M., Campbell, E. M., Chen, G., Cottone, K., Lapedis, D., & Lee, K. (2007). Impact and the art of motivation maintenance: The effects of contact with beneficiaries on persistence behavior. *Organizational Behavior and Human Decision Processes, 103*, 53–67.

Grant, A. M. (2008a). Employees without a cause: The motivational effects of prosocial impact in public service. *International Public Management Journal, 11*, 48–66.

Grant, A. M. (2008b). The significance of task significance: Job performance effects, relational mechanisms, and boundary conditions. *Journal of Applied Psychology, 93*, 108–124.

Grant, A. M. (2014). *Give and take: Why helping others drives our success.* New York: Penguin.

Grant, A. M., & Hofmann, D. A. (2011). It's not all about me: Motivating hospital hand hygiene by focusing on patients. *Psychological Science, 22*, 1494–1499.

Helgeson, V. S., & Fritz, H. L. (1998). A theory of unmitigated communion. *Personality and Social Psychology Review, 2*, 173–183.

Podsakoff, N. P., Whiting, S. W., Podsakoff, P. M., & Blume, B. D. (2009). Individual- and organizational-level consequences of organizational citizenship behaviors: A meta-analysis. *Journal of Applied Psychology, 94*, 122–141.

Turner, Y. N., Hadas-Halperin, I., & Raveh, D. (2008, November). *Patient photos spur radiologist empathy and eye for detail.* Paper presented at the annual meeting of the Radiological Society of North America.

Work Motivation: From Processes to Purpose

RUTH KANFER Georgia Institute of Technology

☐ Please describe your current position and research interests.

I am a Professor of Psychology at the Georgia Institute of Technology. My research interests focus on the determinants and dynamics of adult motivation and achievement striving related to work. I am interested in how individuals develop and sustain motivation to accomplish goals related to achievement and work across the lifespan and in the context of learning, job search, job performance, and teams.

☐ How did you become interested in studying motivation, in particular motivation in the context of work?

As a graduate student in clinical psychology, I became interested in understanding the psychological processes by which individuals gain control over their own behavior, often in the context of environments that provided little or no support for desired behavior change. That led me to study self-regulation. During my clinical internships, I also noticed the profound importance of employment and the work environment in shaping client activities, self-concept, and psychological well-being. After graduate training, I narrowed my focus to understanding the motivational system in the context of work-related achievements, namely, how person and situational factors affect the goals an individual chooses, the self-regulatory strategies that contribute to goal accomplishment over time, and how motivation contributes to an individual's sense of competence, agency, and performance.

☐ What has been the real-world impact of this work?

My early work was guided by two questions, namely: (1) how do individual differences in cognitive abilities and personality traits jointly affect task motivation?, and (2) how do individuals regulate their motivation in the context of an ever-changing and often unsupportive environment? First, I considered how different task demands affect motivation over time using expectancy models of motivation (Kanfer, 1987). Then, working with Phillip Ackerman, we proposed an attentional resource allocation model of motivation and performance to predict learning and performance during skill training. The model integrated cognitive ability and motivation theories by defining attentional resources in terms of individual differences in cognitive abilities and motivation in terms of the dynamic processes by which individuals allocate attentional resources to on-task performance, off-task performance, and self-regulatory activities (Kanfer & Ackerman, 1989). To test the model, we constructed an air traffic controller simulation task that allowed us to examine our predictions in the lab as well as in the field. As expected, we found that the positive effect of performance goal assignments on learning and performance depended jointly on both the attentional demands of the task as well as the individual's cognitive and self-regulatory resources. For trainees with lower cognitive ability, difficult performance goals had a negative effect on learning outcomes compared to trainees with higher cognitive ability. Based on these and related findings using the attentional resource allocation model, we constructed a new battery of tests for the selection of Air Traffic Controllers that has been used by the Minnesota ATC training program for the past two decades.

In the early twentieth century, work motivation research focused largely on how reward practices and job design affected an individual's motivation on the job. During the mid-to-late twentieth century, researchers focused on identifying the psychological processes through which individuals established work goals, and on the self-regulatory strategies used to accomplish difficult goals. In the twenty-first century, as more jobs involve interpersonal communications and greater emphasis is placed on innovation rather than performance quantity, work motivation research has shifted again from a performance-centric to a person-centric perspective. In the latter perspective, optimal levels of motivation at work are proposed to occur when individuals perform personally interesting and meaningful tasks that provide not only extrinsic rewards (such as pay), but also a positive sense of self. In this perspective, analysis of work motivation requires greater consideration of the sociocultural context in which work is performed. From an organizational perspective, the person-centric perspective is better suited for managing a workforce that is increasingly diverse in age, gender, and culture.

Accordingly, during the past decade, I have focused greater attention on specific motivational problems that arise as a consequence of the changing nature of work and the workforce. One stream of research examined factors that influence effective self-regulation during the job search. Another stream of research examines the determinants of motivation to work among older workers. A third stream of research investigates the influence of team dynamics on team member motivation and performance. Finally, a fourth stream of inquiry examines the generalizability of job design to enhancing work motivation among low-earning workers in developing countries.

Motivational Traits, Self-Regulatory Skills, and Performance

Decades of research on achievement motivation show that individuals with strong motives to excel tend to adopt higher, more challenging performance goals than individuals with lower levels of achievement motivation. Individual differences in these broad tendencies for mastery and achievement are called motivational traits. In the workplace, however, accomplishment of job goals, such as writing a computer program or being a top salesperson, involves more than just an intention. To accomplish difficult performance goals that occur over time, individuals must monitor their behavior, evaluate their progress, minimize the occurrence of off-task disruptive thoughts and feelings, and adjust their resource allocations over time as needed. In other words, individuals must develop effective self-regulatory skills and strategies that promote the allocation of their attentional resources and time to improving and sustaining performance (Kanfer & Heggestad, 1997). In high-stakes student testing, for example, long tests may contribute to cognitive fatigue, daydreaming, and lower task performance over time. However, we found that for some students, feelings of fatigue served as a reminder to allocate more effort to test performance. Students who frame their goals in terms of mastery and who use self-regulatory skills to inhibit disruptive negative emotions appear able to sustain higher levels of task effort over time than students who frame their goals in terms of performance or fail to use self-regulatory strategies to maintain task effort.

Self-Regulation During Job Search

Self-regulation is particularly important in job search, which can often take months or even years. During job search, individuals must set and adjust employment goals, monitor the effectiveness of their search strategies, and sustain their effort in the face of failure and feelings of discouragement. Whereas job search in the twentieth century occurred primarily at the start of adult work life, adults in the twenty-first century can expect to hold many different jobs over the span of a work life lasting five decades or longer.

To better understand the factors that influence effective job search, I conceptualized job search as a motivated, self-regulatory process that begins with the adoption of a goal to obtain employment. In collaboration with Connie Wanberg, we conducted a series of studies that looked at the impact of different person and situation variables on self-regulation during job search, job search behavior, and employment outcomes. Our review and meta-analysis of the literature using the self-regulation perspective showed that self-efficacy and person variables were positively related to the level of job search activity, and that job search activity, in turn, was positively related to successful employment (Kanfer, Wanberg, & Kantrowitz, 2001). In subsequent research (Wanberg, Zhu, Kanfer, & Zhang, 2012) we extended our model by investigating weekly self-regulatory and job search activities among laid off mid-life workers over a period of five months. We found that individuals who were higher in success-oriented motives engaged in greater job search activity than did persons low in these traits. Even so, job search intensity declined over time for most people. Perhaps the most interesting finding in this study was that job search intensity for all participants varied each week in direct relation to the individual's level of negative emotion. Individuals who reported higher negative affect at the beginning of the week were less likely to engage in job search the following week than individuals who reported lower negative affect at the start of the week. These findings suggest that the use of interventions to help job seekers more effectively regulate negative affect, particularly after initial search efforts, have proven unsuccessful.

Work Motivation and Aging

The graying of the workforce in the United States and in other developed countries represents one of the most pressing challenges of the twenty-first century for societies, organizations, and individuals. On the one hand, improved health care, increased longevity, the termination of mandatory retirement laws, and changing social norms represent trends that encourage employment beyond traditional retirement age. On the other hand, there is increasing evidence that older individuals differ from younger and mid-life individuals (in ways both positive and negative) in terms of job-related competencies and work motives (Kanfer & Ackerman, 2004; Kooij, de Lange, Jansen, Kanfer, & Dikkers, 2011). Consistent with these findings, we proposed that age-related declines in work motivation were not due to a reduction in motivation "to work," but instead to a decline in motivation "at work" as a consequence of an increasing mismatch between what the individual wants from work and the opportunities and rewards that most organizations offer employees. Results of our meta-analysis on the relationship between age and motivation to work provide partial support for this idea, showing a significant negative correlation between age and promotion-related rewards, but a significant positive relationship between age and motives for skill utilization and task enjoyment. For example, we found that the importance of work roles that allow the individual to train or help co-workers increased with age, while the importance of promotions decreased with age.

The impending retirement of members of the Baby Boomer cohort (born 1946–1964) has also broadened the scope of work motivation beyond questions of motivation "at work" to increasingly include questions about motivation "to work" (Kanfer, Beier, & Ackerman, 2013). For example, what person and contextual factors might encourage individuals to retire later or to seek employment after retirement? Are there age-related/cohort differences in the attractiveness of different job features or conditions? To date, we have focused on "to work" questions in terms of predicting motivation to continue working past normative retirement age, and employment motivation after retirement. For example, we found that among working engineers, neither health nor retirement attitudes affected intended retirement age or postretirement work intentions. However engineers with higher levels of motivation for success reported intentions to retire later and more frequent plans to work after retirement than did engineers with lower levels of the motivational trait. In the domain of motivation "at work," my colleagues and I are investigating how an individual's orientation toward the future, job crafting opportunities in the workplace, and supervisory support affect older adult work motivation and well-being. To date, these studies have focused on how aging affects work motivation; we are also planning research to better understand the impact of life course on work motivation, for example, how one's work history (for example, number of unemployment spells) and occupation (for example, construction worker versus computer programmer) affects motivation to work and an individual's job goals following retirement.

Work Motivation, Teams, and the Developing World

Many organizations use teams to accomplish goals that cannot be accomplished easily by a single employee or employees working independently. In the health care industry for example, patient care is accomplished by teams of physicians, nurses, social workers, and other support staff who share information and coordinate efforts. Working as a team provides team members with a common "mental model" of the patient's needs, and can improve patient outcomes by enabling team members to share information more quickly and effectively. In the sciences, project teams are increasingly used to promote cross-fertilization of ideas across disciplines that can contribute to the development of innovative and creative solutions to major problems, such as disease and climate change. Research findings on team motivation emphasize the importance of social dynamics among team members in the development of effective teamwork processes and team performance. Extending individual models of motivation and self-regulation to this context, Gilad Chen and I developed a multi-level model of motivation in and of teams that describes how team goals, teamwork activities, and team member behavior can enhance or hinder team member motivation and team performance (Chen & Kanfer, 2006). Consistent with the model, our findings to date show that emergent team motivational states (such as collective efficacy) and individual motivation are interconnected, with higher levels of team motivation exerting a positive effect on individual motivation (Chen, Kanfer, DeShon, Mathieu, & Kozlowski, 2009). In the health care setting, my colleagues and I have also found that the adoption of team-level goals, such as patient well-being, increases teamwork motivation and coordination among employees who do not typically work together, such as physicians and nurses.

Until recently, most research on team motivation has been conducted in the United States and Europe. Over the past few decades, however, globalization has led to new opportunities to study team-based goals and incentives in cultures and environments that are dramatically different from those in the developed world. My research in this area has focused on motivation among hospital and frontline health care worker jobs in rural communities in Jordan, the Republic of Georgia, and India. In these countries, health care workers are often paid relatively little (and often not on time), with little or no opportunity for advancement. Findings in these contexts have shown that motivational strategies, such as team-based goal setting, also improve job performance in developing countries. Although the pathways by which these strategies affect work motivation remain unclear, our findings among front-line health care workers in India suggests that the adoption of common, team-level goals increased information exchange and social support among team members, which in turn facilitated job performance.

Conclusion

Motivation plays a major role in nearly all aspects of behavior related to work. At any given point in time, both person and situational factors influence where and how much time and effort an individual will devote to accomplishing a specific work-related goal. Over a lifespan, age-related changes in motives further affect an individual's motivation to continue working in later adulthood, as well as the types of jobs older adults seek. During job training, an individual's goal orientation and self-regulatory skills play a key role in learning complex tasks and routines. On the job, the social context in which work is performed can increase or decrease an individual's motivation to work toward a team goal.

Although we have learned a great deal about motivation related to work over the past century, many important theoretical and practical questions remain. These questions pertain to understanding work motivation from a person-centric perspective; in other words, understanding work motivation in the context of human development as well as the individual's life and work experiences. For example, although we know a great deal about normative changes in motives over a lifespan, we know little about how decades of work in a particular occupation or different employment histories affect the centrality of work in the individual's life or the development of self-regulatory skills. We also know relatively little about how the social forces that operate in the workplace affect the direction of an employee's efforts, the factors that influence how employees choose to distribute their time and effort across tasks and teams, or the work conditions that foster high levels of employee creativity. Answers to these questions have direct implications for helping human resource managers and leaders develop programs that not only improve organizational productivity but also enhance and sustain the quality of work life across the globe.

Acknowledgments Funding for much of the research described in this essay has been provided by the U.S. National Science Foundation, the U.S. Air Force Office of Scientific Research, the U.S. National Institutes of Health, the U.S. Office of Naval Research, and the Society for Human Resource Management Foundation.

☐ Thinking Critically

1. How might person and situational factors differ for younger and older workers, and how might these differences affect motivation "at work" and "to work"?

2. How might teams contribute to more successful self-regulation and job search outcomes in student job search?

☐ Suggested Further Reading

Kanfer, R. (2012). Work motivation: Theory, practice, and future directions. In S. W. J. Kozlowski (Ed.), *The Oxford handbook of industrial and organizational psychology* (pp. 455–495). Oxford: Blackwell.

Parker, S. K. (2014). Beyond motivation: Job and work design for development, health, ambidexterity, and more. *Annual Review of Psychology, 65,* 661–691.

Pinder, C. C. (2008*). Work motivation in organizational behavior* (2nd ed.). New York: Psychology Press.

☐ References

Chen, G., & Kanfer, R. (2006). Toward a systems theory of motivated behavior in work teams. *Research in Organizational Behavior, 27,* 223–267.

Chen, G., Kanfer, R., DeShon, R. P., Mathieu, J. E., & Kozlowski, S. W. J. (2009). The motivating potential of teams: Test and extension of Chen & Kanfer's (2006) cross-level model of motivation in teams. *Organizational Behavior and Human Decision Processes, 110,* 45–55.

Kanfer, R. (1987). Task specific motivation: An integrative approach to issues of measurement, mechanisms, processes, and determinants. *Journal of Social and Clinical Psychology, 5,* 237–264.

Kanfer, R., & Ackerman, P. L. (1989). Motivation and cognitive abilities: An integrative/aptitude-treatment interaction approach to skill acquisition. *Journal of Applied Psychology—Monograph, 74,* 657–690.

Kanfer, R., & Ackerman, P. L. (2004). Aging, adult development and work motivation. *Academy of Management Review, 29,* 1–19.

Kanfer, R., Beier, M., & Ackerman, P. L. (2013). Goals and motivation related to work in later adulthood: An organizing framework. *European Journal of Work and Organizational Psychology, 22,* 253–264. doi: 10.1080/1359432X.2012.734298

Kanfer, R. & Heggestad, E. (1997). Motivational traits and skills: A person-centered approach to work motivation. *Research in Organizational Behavior, 18,* 1–57.

Kanfer, R., Wanberg, C., & Kantrowitz, T. M. (2001). Job search and employment: A personality-motivational analysis and meta-analytic review. *Journal of Applied Psychology, 86,* 837–855.

Kooij, D., de Lange, A., Jansen, P., Kanfer, R., & Dikkers, J. (2011). Age and work-related motives: Results of a meta-analysis. *Journal of Organizational Behavior, 32,* 197–225.

Wanberg, C. R., Zhu, J., Kanfer, R., & Zhang, Z. (2012). After the pink slip: Applying dynamic motivation frameworks to the job search experience. *Academy of Management Journal, 55,* 261–284.

Lie Detection in the Interrogation Room and the Courtroom

MARK COSTANZO Claremont McKenna College and Claremont Graduate University

☐ Please describe your current position and research interests.

I am Professor of Psychology at Claremont McKenna College and Co-Director of the Center for Applied Research. I am also a member of the Plenary Faculty at Claremont Graduate University.

I am interested in the application of psychology to the legal system. I have conducted research on a variety of law-related topics, including the death penalty, sexual harassment, attorney argumentation, and jury decision making. Most of my current research focuses on the consequential and psychologically rich areas of police interrogations and false confessions.

☐ How did you get interested in the application of psychology to the legal system?

As a social psychologist, I am interested in basic psychological processes including persuasion, nonverbal communication, and decision making. The legal system is a fascinating, high-stakes context for studying these processes. Interrogators attempt to detect deception in the nonverbal behavior of suspects, and try to persuade suspects to admit to crimes. Attorneys attempt to persuade jurors to convict or acquit, and jurors attempt to persuade each other to reach a particular verdict decision.

☐ What has been the real-world impact of this work?

The research conducted by psychologists interested in the legal system has been influential in changing how evidence is collected and evaluated in areas such as eyewitness identification, police interrogations, and the interviewing of child victims and witnesses.

You are a liar. In fact, all humans are liars. We tell a variety of lies for a variety of reasons. We lie for honorable reasons (for example, to make other people feel good) and for dishonorable reasons (for example, to conceal our own bad behavior). We might create an elaborate, false account of a past event, or we might simply omit important information from an otherwise true account of an event. The lies we tell may be improvised or carefully planned and rehearsed. Sometimes we tell lies to lubricate our interactions with others or to avoid conflict (for example, "I was stuck in traffic" or "I love your new haircut"). At other times, we lie to make ourselves seem more attractive or accomplished. Most lies are relatively minor and inconsequential, but some—like those told by people who have committed crimes—are important for the legal systems to detect.

Criminals are usually highly motivated to tell convincing lies as a means of avoiding arrest, prosecution, and prison. Those criminals must confront a legal system that is highly motivated to find ways of exposing lies. Imagine the implications of a device that could tell with certainty whether a criminal suspect is lying or telling the truth. Such a device would transform the legal system. Instead of relying on police interrogations, courtroom trials, and jury deliberations to separate lies from truth, we could simply ask criminal suspects a few critical questions: "Did you shoot him?" or "Did you attack her?" or "Did you steal the money?" The device would deliver the verdict and enable us to release all innocent suspects and to send all guilty suspects to prison. Indeed, such a device would render many parts of our current legal system obsolete.

Because there is no perfect lie detection device, most attempts to detect lies rely on human powers of observation. Police and jurors simply watch and listen to suspects or witnesses and then make judgments about whether the person being observed is being truthful or deceptive. But how effective is this approach? There are now hundreds of studies investigating how accurately we are able to detect lies. In most of these studies, participants are shown videos of many people telling the truth or telling a lie. The task of the participants is to decide whether the person in the video is being honest or deceptive. Keep in mind that because there are only two choices (lie or truth), participants can achieve an accuracy rate of 50% simply by guessing or flipping a coin. In a major review, researchers combined data statistically from 384 studies using more than 24,000 participants. They found that the overall rate of accuracy was 54%—only 4% above pure chance (Bond & DePaulo, 2006). Rates of accuracy dropped about 2% when participants tried to detect lies that had been rehearsed in advance (this finding is relevant because criminals often plan and practice their lies before talking to police), and rates rose about 2% if participants were able to observe the same person being both truthful and deceptive.

The underwhelming accuracy of human lie detection has important implications for the legal system. Police officers often rely on their intuitive lie detection abilities—decisions about which suspects to interrogate are sometimes based on a police officer's suspicion that a criminal suspect is not being truthful. Based on a mistaken judgment that a suspect is lying, a police officer may subject an innocent suspect to a lengthy, high-pressure interrogation that may lead to a false confession (Costanzo & Leo, 2007). Many proven false confessions have followed this pattern. In the courtroom, a misreading of verbal and nonverbal cues can influence the trial process. At trial, the jury is responsible for assessing the credibility of witnesses who testify in court. Judges instruct jurors to pay careful attention to witnesses' "demeanor on the witness stand" and "manner of testifying" as a means of detecting whether a witness is lying or attempting to conceal information. If jurors mistakenly believe a witness is being deceptive, that judgment will influence the verdict.

There appear to be three main reasons why people have great difficulty recognizing the lies of others. First, when attempting to judge whether someone is lying, most people look for behaviors consistent with what has been called the "liar's stereotype." According to the liar's stereotype, which has been found to exist in more than 60 countries, people who are lying tend to fidget, stutter, avert their gaze, touch themselves more, and speak more slowly (Bond & DePaulo, 2008). Unfortunately for observers, these behaviors are not consistently associated with deception, and may merely be indicative of nervousness, discomfort, or uncertainty. Second, there is a "weak signal" effect, meaning that even when the liar exhibits verbal and nonverbal behaviors correlated with deception, those behaviors tend to be faint, fleeting, and difficult to notice. Finally, people differ in the verbal and nonverbal cues they emit while lying. There is individual variation—the behavior that indicates deception in one person may not be correlated with deception in another person.

The Effect of Training on Confidence and Accuracy

If we are generally bad at detecting lies, perhaps training can help improve our performance. In an early study of whether people would benefit from training, we used videos of several people lying about their personal history and then truthfully describing their personal history (Costanzo, 1992). Participants were asked to judge which statements were truthful and to indicate how confident they were about each of their judgments. After measuring pretraining accuracy, we then provided training on how to interpret verbal and nonverbal cues. This training was delivered using either a lecture format or a lecture plus practice format. We found that only the lecture plus practice training produced any significant improvements in performance. Interestingly, although the lecture only format did not improve accuracy, it did increase the participants' confidence in their judgments. This finding that confidence can be high while accuracy is low has important implications for interrogators.

Many training programs teach interrogators to look for signs of deception in verbal and nonverbal cues. Usually, the cues police are taught to look for are those associated with the liar's stereotype described earlier. In studies using actual interrogation training videos, researchers have found that although training increases confidence in lie detection ability, it usually does not improve accuracy (Vrij, Mann, Kristen, & Fisher, 2007). In one study, prison inmates gave true and false videotaped confessions to crimes they did or did not commit. Next, a group of police detectives and a group of college students judged the truthfulness of each confession. Although college students performed slightly better than chance when distinguishing between true and false confessions, police detectives did not. An even more interesting finding was that even though they performed worse than the students, the detectives were far more confident about the accuracy of their judgments (Kassin, Meissner, & Norwick, 2005).

This combination of high confidence and low accuracy can create serious problems in the interrogation room. Sometimes, based on a suspect's "suspicious" behavior, a police officer may confidently but mistakenly believe that an innocent suspect is guilty (Costanzo & Gerrity, 2009). Because of that mistaken but confidently held belief, the officer may wrongly interpret the suspect's ambiguous nonverbal behavior (for example, nervousness, gaze aversion, distress) as further evidence of deceptiveness and guilt. As a result, the interrogating officer may turn up the pressure on the "guilty" suspect possibly eliciting more nonverbal "guilty" behaviors. If the suspect eventually confesses, interrogators may view the confession as confirming their initial presumption of guilt, as well as justifying the use of questionable interrogation tactics (Leo, Costanzo, & Shaked-Schroer, 2009). As research on wrongful convictions indicates, police sometimes misperceive an innocent suspect as guilty because he "acts like a liar" when questioned (Leo, 2008).

Technology-Based Lie Detection

If humans are not very good at detecting deception, can technology do any better? The oldest and most widely used technology for detecting lies is the polygraph. The polygraph measures changes in blood pressure, respiration rate, heart rate, and skin moisture that are associated with physiological arousal. These changes are tracked and displayed as moving lines on a computer screen while a suspect answers questions about a crime, as well as a series of "comparison" questions that should not cause arousal (for example, "Is today Tuesday?"). The basic "theory" underlying the polygraph is that the act of lying creates physiological arousal. Specifically, the theory holds that lying causes a rise in blood pressure, an increase in skin moisture, and changes in heart rate and breathing patterns. If a suspect is lying, reactions to questions about the crime should be significantly stronger than reactions to the comparison questions.

The polygraph has remained controversial since it first appeared in the 1930s. Although some studies have demonstrated impressive rates of accuracy for detecting lies under highly controlled conditions, there is also a high rate of misclassifying truthful suspects as deceptive (National Research Council, 2003). In addition, people vary in their physiological reactions to lying. The polygraph cannot detect lies if the suspect does not react physiologically when lying. Alternatively, innocent people who fear that they will be falsely accused will react strongly to questions about whether they committed a crime. That reaction can cause innocent suspects to be classified as liars. Another problem concerns the use of countermeasures—self-stimulation tactics used to manipulate physiological arousal. For example, suspects may decrease their arousal by silently counting backwards from 100 by increments of seven while answering questions about the crime (Iacono, 2009). Some newer lie detection technologies focus on reactions such as pupil dilation or subtle heat changes in facial skin as indicators of deception. Like the polygraph, the theory underlying these methods is that lying will produce arousal and that this arousal will cause a nearly instantaneous physiological change.

Technologies used by cognitive neuroscientists have also been applied to the problem of lie detection. Two technologies—functional magnetic resonance imaging (fMRI) and the electroencephalogram (EEG)—are being used to look for evidence of lying in the brain. Functional magnetic resonance imaging (fMRI) produces an image showing blood flow to different areas of the brain while the participant is engaged in a task. Increased activity in an area of the brain requires more oxygen, which in turn is delivered by increased blood flow to the area. Functional magnetic resonance imaging (fMRI) enables researchers to see which regions of the brain are most active when people are lying (Langleben & Moriarty, 2012). Although some research suggests that the prefrontal cortex and the parietal cortex are more active when people are lying, this finding is not yet well established. One problem seems to be that there are significant individual differences in the brain areas activated during the act of lying.

The EEG monitors brain activity by means of electrodes placed on the scalp. Using these electrodes, readings are taken of electrical patterns in the brain that arise in response to an event or stimulus. Because the EEG is able to read neural impulses continuously in milliseconds, it allows researchers to pinpoint precisely *when* a change in brain activity occurs. Some research has found a significant change in brain waves after participants lie in response to a question. That change occurs between 250 and 600 milliseconds after the lie (Wolpe, Foster, & Langleben, 2010). However, as with fMRI, lie detection research using the EEG is still inconclusive.

Interrogation Tactics for Exposing Lies

Imagine that you are a criminal being questioned by the police. To lie convincingly, you must first construct a plausible false story about your activities around the time of the crime. Then, you must remember the details of your invented story, and carefully monitor yourself to make sure you don't slip up and contradict that story. You must also try to look like you are telling the truth by avoiding the kinds of behaviors (lack of eye contact, slow speech, fidgeting) that might arouse suspicions. Further, you must monitor the reactions of the police officers and continuously adapt your answers to their questions. Finally, throughout the interrogation, you must actively suppress the truth. All this deliberate mental effort is exhausting and difficult to sustain. In comparison, telling the truth is relatively effortless.

Researchers have developed interrogation strategies that exploit the already heavy cognitive load of liars. By increasing the mental exertion required to maintain a lie, these strategies may force suspects to make errors that expose the lie and reveal at least part of the truth. One such tactic is to require that suspects maintain eye contact with the interrogator while telling their stories. Another is to ask suspects to tell their stories in reverse. A third tactic is to ask unanticipated questions that force suspects to improvise their answers. Compared to truth-tellers, liars appear to have greater difficulty with such tasks because their cognitive resources are already depleted by the deliberate mental effort required to maintain their lies and manage their behavior. In several controlled studies, it was significantly easier for observers to spot liars who were subjected to such cognitive load increasing tactics (Vrij, Mann, & Leal, 2013). These strategies are beginning to be employed by actual interrogators.

Lying by Police in the Interrogation Room

The process of police interrogation is designed to induce a presumably guilty suspect to confess to a crime. In the United States, police interrogators are permitted to lie to suspects as a tactic for obtaining a confession. For example, an interrogator might tell a suspect that they have found his fingerprints at the crime scene when, in fact, there are no fingerprints. They may tell the suspect that an eyewitness has identified him as the perpetrator of the crime, even though there is no eyewitness. Police may falsely claim that they have video recordings, or shoe prints, or tire tracks, or GPS recordings that link the suspect to the crime. Sometimes, these tactics have convinced guilty suspects to confess to horrible crimes. Other times, however, these same tactics have convinced innocent people to confess to crimes they did not commit (Leo, Costanzo, & Shaked-Schroer, 2009).

Interrogators can also lie about the results of a polygraph exam. During an interrogation, a police officer may ask a suspect if he is willing to take a polygraph test. This is usually presented as "an opportunity to prove your innocence." If the suspect agrees to take the polygraph test, regardless of the actual results, the interrogators can tell the suspect that he failed. A "failure" on the polygraph gives interrogators considerable leverage over the suspect. The suspect must cope with the revelation that a seemingly scientific device has apparently identified him as a liar. For many suspects, continuing to deny involvement in a crime no longer seems like a viable option. Use of the polygraph during an interrogation usually entails three component lies: 1) that taking the polygraph test is an opportunity to prove one's innocence, 2) that the polygraph is an infallible lie detector, and 3) that the results of the polygraph exam prove unequivocally that the suspect is lying.

Conclusion

For centuries, people have searched for an infallible method of lie detection. Despite technological advances, no one has yet developed a reliable device for exposing lies. The underlying problem that limits technology-based lie detection is that there appears to be no "Pinocchio response"—no physiological reaction that is uniquely associated with lying. There is no distinctive shift in heart rate, blood pressure, skin temperature, or neural excitation that is exclusively triggered by deception. Although we have fairly precise measures of cognitive load and physiological arousal, changes in load and arousal can be caused by acts other than lying. Unless we eventually identify a signature pattern of physiological change that is unique to lying, we will have to rely on indirect measures.

For the foreseeable future, the legal system will rely on human observational powers to detect deception. Police officers will watch and listen to crime suspects and form judgments about whether those suspects are lying. Juries will watch and listen to witnesses and make inferences about whether those witnesses are being truthful. As noted by the U.S. Supreme

Court in a case that prohibited the use of polygraph evidence in some courts, "A fundamental premise of our criminal trial system is that the jury is the lie detector" (*U.S.* v. *Scheffer*, 1998, p. 1266). Psychological research can help interrogators and jurors understand the limits of lie detection and avoid the consequential error of falsely accusing or convicting an innocent suspect.

☐ Thinking Critically

1. One study described in this essay found that police detectives displayed a combination of high confidence and low accuracy in judging who is lying or "guilty." What might be the implications of this for the U.S. justice system, as well as for the people accused of committing crimes?

2. Why might an innocent person fail a lie detector test? Which social psychological concepts can explain why innocent suspects might confess to a crime they did not commit and why interrogators can be completely mistaken, yet confident in their assessment of guilt?

☐ Suggested Further Reading

Costanzo, M., & Krauss, D. (2012). *Forensic and legal psychology: Psychological science applied to law.* New York: Worth.

Leo, R. A. (2008). *Police interrogation and American justice.* Cambridge, MA: Harvard University Press.

☐ References

Bond, C. F., & DePaulo, B. M. (2006). Accuracy of deception judgments. *Personality and Social Psychology Review, 10,* 214–234.

Bond, C. F., & DePaulo, B. M. (2008). Individual differences in judging deception: Accuracy and bias. *Psychological Bulletin, 134,* 477–492.

Costanzo, M. (1992). Training students to decode verbal and nonverbal behavior: Effects on confidence and performance. *Journal of Educational Psychology, 84,* 303–313.

Costanzo, M.A., & Gerrity, E. (2009). The effects and effectiveness of using torture as an interrogation device: Using research to inform the policy debate. *Social Issues and Policy Review, 3,* 179–210.

Costanzo, M., & Leo, R. (2007). Research findings and expert testimony on police interrogations and confessions to crimes. In Costanzo, M., Krauss, D., & Pezdek, K. (Eds.). *Expert psychological testimony for the courts* (pp. 69–98). Mahwah, NJ: Erlbaum.

Iacono, W. G. (2009). Effective policing: Understanding how polygraph tests work and are used. *Criminal Justice and Behavior, 35,* 1295–1308.

Kassin, S. M., Meissner, C., & Norwick, R. J. (2005). I'd know a false confession if I saw one: A comparative study of college students and police investigators. *Law and Human Behavior, 29,* 211–228.

Langleben, D. D., & Moriarty, J. C. (2012). Using brain imaging for lie detection: Where science, law, and policy collide. *Psychology, Public Policy, and Law, 18,* 1–13.

Leo, R., Costanzo, M., & Shaked-Schroer, N. (2009). Psychological and cultural aspects of interrogation and false confessions: Using research to inform legal decision making. In

AFTERWORD

STEVEN PINKER

Steven Pinker is a Johnstone Family Professor in the Department of Psychology at Harvard University. He conducts research on language and cognition, writes for publications such as the *New York Times, Time,* and *The New Republic,* and is the author of eight books, including *The Language Instinct, How the Mind Works, Words and Rules, The Blank Slate, The Stuff of Thought,* and most recently, *The Better Angels of Our Nature: Why Violence Has Declined.*

The contributors to this volume have amply shown how academic psychology has helped us deal with many of the challenges facing us as individuals and as a society. In the courtroom and the classroom, the clinic and the legislature, the science of mind has provided insights that have reduced error, enhanced learning, and alleviated suffering.

But the efflorescence of psychology, I believe, deserves credit for far more than its numerous practical applications. It has changed our view of ourselves as a species, and accelerated the arc of human progress.

Human progress? News watchers, horrified by headlines of war, crime, and terrorism are apt to be incredulous at the very idea. But one of the things psychology tells us is that the news provides a distorted view of reality. The human mind tends to estimate the probability of an event from the ease with which it can recall examples, and scenes of bloodshed and mayhem, more available than ever, get burned into our memories and convince us we're living in increasingly depraved times. But the data (summarized in my book *The Better Angels of Our Nature: Why Violence Has Declined*) say otherwise. Wars have become less frequent and deadly. Less and less of the world's population lives under tyranny. Rates of violent crime, child abuse, capital punishment, and racial hatred have all plummeted. And all this quantitative progress accompanies the qualitative abolition of barbaric institutionalized practices that were a part of the human condition for millennia, such as human sacrifice, chattel slavery, debtor's prisons, pogroms, lynching, torture and mutilation as routine forms of criminal punishment, and the execution of heretics and infidels. We may be living in the most peaceful time in our species' existence.

Many historical forces have contributed to these happy developments, including democratic government, efficient trade, and robust institutions, but I believe that among the most powerful is the ascendance of a new view of ourselves. Fifty years ago, the critic Philip Rieff announced that the twentieth century was the era of "Psychological Man." This conception of who we are, he suggested, was the latest in a historical series that began with Political Man in Classical times, giving way to Religious Man in the Christian Middle Ages, and then to Economic Man in the Enlightenment. Now, rather than understanding ourselves in terms of our place in the social order, our relationship with God, or our rational pursuit of self-interest, we look to Freud's theory of psychoanalysis and its conception of a complex psyche balancing its instinctual origins with the demands of civilization.

Rieff erred in designating psychoanalysis as the official theory of Psychological Human (as we might call it today). But he was prescient in noting that we increasingly understand ourselves in terms of the inner workings of our minds, their origin in the natural world, and their interplay with the contents of culture and civilization. Today, political ideology, religious sentiment, and economic behavior—to take just the three spheres of life that defined the earlier stages of our self-concept—are themselves being studied in the psychology laboratory as manifestations of human nature. Also under the microscope are morality, aesthetics, reasoning, language, social relationships, and the other human obsessions.

More than Rieff could have predicted, the later decades of the twentieth century, and early decades of the twenty-first, have become the age of psychology. Academic research has increasingly become a part of the conventional wisdom, including dominance hierarchies, minimal groups, heuristics and biases, the Milgram and Asch experiments, and the theory of cognitive dissonance. And it's more than scientific psychology that has filtered into public awareness; it's a general habit of seeing human affairs through a psychological lens. We have seen the growth of a species-wide self-consciousness, in which we increasingly see our affairs from two vantage points: from inside our skulls, where the things we experience just *are,* and from a scientist's-eye view, where the things we experience consist of patterns of activity in an evolved brain, with all its illusions and fallacies.

Neither academic psychology nor conventional wisdom is anywhere close to a complete understanding of what makes us tick. But a little psychology can go a long way. A small number of quirks in our cognitive and emotional makeup give rise to a substantial proportion of avoidable human suffering. And a shared inkling of these quirks has made some dents in the toll of human-caused misery and has the potential to chip away at much more.

For example, humans tend to be overconfident in their prospects for success, so that when they fight each other, the outcome is likely to be bloodier than any of them thought. People strive for dominance for themselves and their groups; when contests of dominance are joined, they are unlikely to sort the parties by merit and are likely to be a net loss for everyone. People seek revenge by an accounting that exaggerates their innocence and their adversary's malice; when two sides seek perfect justice, they condemn themselves and their heirs to strife. And people are vulnerable to conformity effects that allow toxic beliefs to sweep through a closed society and bring it under the spell of a collective delusion.

A bit more than a century ago the world sleepwalked into a great war fueled by tribalism, revenge, dominance, overconfidence, and collective delusions, followed by an even more horrific rematch two decades later. Despite comparable provocations and grievances, for almost three generations, we've managed to avoid a similar disaster. It's not far-fetched to suppose that some of the credit for our good fortune should go to the dawning of the modern age of psychology.

D. Krauss & J. Lieberman (Eds.), *Psychological expertise in court: Psychology in the court-room* (Vol. 2, pp. 25–56). London: Ashgate.

Leo, R. A. (2008). *Police interrogation and American justice.* Cambridge, MA: Harvard University Press.

National Research Council. (2003). *The polygraph and lie detection.* Washington, DC: The National Academies Press.

United States v. Scheffer, 118 S. Ct. 1261 (1998).

Vrij, A., Mann, S., Kristen, S., & Fisher, R. P. (2007). Cues to deception and ability to detect lies as a function of police interview styles. *Law and Human Behavior, 31,* 499–518.

Vrij, A., Mann, S., & Leal, S. (2013). Deception traits in psychological interviewing. *Journal of Police and Criminal Psychology.* doi:10.1007/s11896-013-9125-y

Wolpe, P. R., Foster, K. R., & Langleben, D. D. (2010). Emerging neurotechnologies for lie-detection: Promises and perils. *American Journal of Bioethics, 10,* 40–48.